Adventures in the Book Pages

In Memoriam

Thomas Joseph Short

1926–2015

Adventures in the Book Pages

Essays and Reviews

Edward Short

GRACEWING

First published in England in 2015

by

Gracewing
2 Southern Avenue
Leominster
Herefordshire HR6 0QF
United Kingdom

www.gracewing.co.uk

No part of this publication may be reproduced, stored in a retrieval system, or transmitted in any form or by any means, electronic, mechanical, photocopying, recording or otherwise, without the written permission of the publisher.

The right of Edward Martin Octavius Short to be identified as the author of this work has been asserted in accordance with the Copyright, Designs and Patents Act 1988.

© 2015 Edward Martin Octavius Short

ISBN 978 085244 868 7

Cover design by Bernardita Peña Hurtado
based on a concept by Gabriela Calogero

Typeset by Word and Page, Chester, UK

CONTENTS

Preface	vii
Winston Churchill and the Old Cause	1
Immortal Blather	12
God and Man at Hippo	18
Charles Arnold-Baker: Anglo-Prussian Self-Portrait	23
Gladstone in His Books	28
Newman and the Idea of Sanctity	35
The Great Temple	49
G. K. Chesterton and the Appeal of Reality	53
W. H. Auden: The Figure in the Carpet Slippers	60
Rare Ben Jonson	64
Pockets of Prayer: The Catholic Tradition in English Poetry	71
A Memoir for the Commodore	87
Edward Burne-Jones: No Votary of the Actual	91
John Tenniel: Down the Rabbit-Hole	96
Becoming T. S. Eliot	101
Michael Burleigh: Brave Old Worlds	107
More Cautionary Horror Shows	114
The Catholic Novels of Graham Greene	118
Bad Ideas: The Prophetic R. G. Collingwood	128
The Queen Mother: Royal Charmer	134
Waugh Fathers and Sons: Underhill Revisited	141
In Agincourt Field	146
Richard Swinburne: An Oxonian Father Brown	152
The Unusual Maritains	158
The Guv'nor and the Wench	168
Leonardo and the Catholic Faith	175
New Irish Sweepstakes	179
Henry Mayhew and the Poor Mouth	184
Thackeray in Harvard Yard	190
No Flies on Ian Ker	197
Shakespeare and the Dangers of Thinking Too Much	201
All the King's Imperial Men	205
Hopkins in His Letters: "The Importance of Being Earnest"	212
Geoffrey Hill: The Light of Appraisal	217
Andrew Mellon: The Imperative to Acquire	223

McKim, Mead, and White and American Beauty 227
John Sloan and the Art of Painting in New York 233
Faith and Failure in Graham Greene 238
The Ampthill Succession. 245
Whigs and Namierites: The History of English History 249
Unsquashable: Churchill the Author 256
Andrew Roberts and the Vital Impulses of Victory 262
A. W. Pugin: "Like Arthur Come to Life Again" 267
Life of Bertie 273
London Lives 279
Dear Dirty Historical Dublin 284
The Quick and Piercing Word 291
Guinness Backstage 296
John Osborne: Mum's the Word 301
The National Gallery at War: A Defiant Outpost of Culture 306
Honest Chronicler: A. J. Liebling 311
The Ghost of George Lansbury 318
Samuel Johnson: "True, Evident and Actual Wisdom" 322
Dr. Johnson at 300 326
Painted Faces: Renaissance Portraiture 334
Henry's Way 339
Penelope's Odyssey 343
No Holiday for the Huguenots 349
G. K. Chesterton: Anti-Modernist 355
Foxhunting at Bay 358
Fascinating Rhythm: A Rave for Wilfrid Sheed 363
Organ Grinders: The Italian Front in the Great War 369
The Glory of the War Poets 375
The Angry Governess: Ruskin on Venice 382
William Trevor: Keeping Faith 387
The "Buried Life" of T. S. Eliot 391
Reclaiming the Age of Chivalry 396
Samuel Johnson and the Idiom of Words 401
A Bright New Look at Edith Sitwell 412
What Newman Would Have Made of Vatican II 418
Newman's University Redux 426
Index 433

Preface

The reviews and essays gathered together in *Adventures in the Book Pages* originally appeared in *The Weekly Standard*, *Books & Culture*, *City Journal*, *The New Criterion*, *First Things*, *Crisis* and *Catholic World Report*. I am thankful to the editors of each of these papers, including Philip Terzian, Roger Kimball, John Wilson, Paul Beston, Margaret Cabaniss and Carl Olson. I should also like to express my special gratitude to Tom Longford of Gracewing, who has given me so much good counsel and unflagging support. I should also like to thank Lucy Zepeda, who painstakingly helped prepare the various pieces for publication, and Gabriela Calogero, who kept a lovely, patient smile on her face while designing and redesigning the cover. Others to whom I am thankful for various kindnesses that have made these pieces possible include Brother Brian Grenier, Heinz and Stella Becker, Monica Manwaring, Caroline Van Horn, James and Virginia McGlone, Heather Cole, Constance Clare Short, Cecilia Hernandez, Francis Phillips, Julieta Schiffino, William Saunders, Andrew Roberts, Humfrey Butters, Richard Greene, Douglas Lane Patey, Andrew Jackson O'Shaughnessy, Jack and Nuala Scarisbrick, Michael Alexander, Tracey Rowland, Robert Crotty, Esq., Father Carleton Jones, OP, and Jo Anne and Eugene Sylva.

Lastly, I should like to thank my wife Karina and my daughter Sophia for making my real life adventures such a blessed joy.

Edward Short
7 March 2015
The Feast of Saints Perpetua and Felicity
Astoria, New York

Winston Churchill and the Old Cause

Forty years ago, on 25 January 1965, at the age of 91, Winston Churchill died at his home in Kensington. At his state funeral, one of the grandest ever mounted, three-hundred thousand people passed by his bier in Westminster Hall. For many, like Clement Attlee, he was simply "the greatest citizen of the world of our time". Harold MacMillan spoke for most of his political colleagues when he said, "Our finest hour and our greatest moment came from our work with him". Isaiah Berlin spoke for many more when he described him as "a man larger than life, composed of bigger and simpler elements than ordinary men ... superhumanly bold, strong and imaginative ... the saviour of his country".

Part and parcel of the heroic stature of the man was the range of his pursuits. As an impecunious aristocrat, he had to earn his living by his pen and by the time he was in his twenties he was one of the highest paid writers in Britain – though ducal extravagance always kept his finances precarious. After entering Parliament, he took to heart Samuel Johnson's dictum that "a decent provision for the poor is the true test of civilization" by providing unemployment insurance to working men. When Asquith made him First Sea Lord, the navy took all his attention: Lloyd George complained that he could not get his friend to debate politics because Churchill would "only talk of boilers". As Secretary of State for the Colonies, he helped reapportion the former territories of the Ottoman Empire, which included mapping out the political boundaries of Iraq. Then he took up munitions, then painting, then bricklaying. When Baldwin made him Chancellor of the Exchequer he even immersed himself in what Chesterton called "the horrible mysticism of money" only to admit later that "the biggest blunder in his life" had been returning Britain to the gold standard. This cursory list does not include what Lord Ismay, his chief of staff, called his "encyclopaedic" knowledge of military history or his "unrivalled" grasp of strategy. Or the years he spent working to rid the world of totalitarian evil.

Considering his truly catholic interests, it is remarkable that the matter on which he should have given least thought was religion. Yet his indifference was rooted in his upbringing. Neither his father, Lord Randolph, a brilliant, reckless, unbiddable man, whose political failure and early death haunted his son, nor his mother, Jenny Jerome, an American heiress, had any faith of their own to instill in their son. Although Lord Randolph would toy with the idea of becoming the mouthpiece of Ulster Protestantism – he coined the slogan, "Ulster will fight, and Ulster will be right" – his view of religion remained resolutely superficial. Religion could only be a tool of political expedience, or a nuisance. As his son would later write, describing the prevailing view: "Too much religion of any kind ... was a bad thing. Among natives especially, fanaticism was highly dangerous and roused them to murder, mutiny or rebellion."

In *A History of the English-Speaking Peoples* (1956), Churchill makes glancing references to Roman Catholicism but always with a decidedly whiggish dismissiveness. Of course, he is never positively abusive but, then, as a good whig, he believed that one should show a certain modicum of courtesy to one's defeated opponents. Then, again, if he was not altogether enamoured of English Protestantism, he could see its political point. Writing of the run-up to the English Civil War, he observes how "The Commons showed themselves to be in a most aggressive mood, and worked themselves into passion by long debates upon the indulgence and laxity with which the laws against Popery were enforced. This brought the great majority of them together; and the zealots, who, however intolerant, were ardent to purify what they deemed a corrupt Church, joined with the patriots who were laying the foundation of English freedom." Not all of Churchill's multi-volume history was written by Churchill himself – elsewhere in this collection, I write of a very poor book about the assiduous author in Churchill, who collaborated with so many good historians on his own various histories – but here the old Churchillian tang is unmistakable. "Just as the Moslem, defending his native soil, fortifies himself with the Koran, just as the rhinoceros trusts to his horn or the tiger his claws, so these harassed Parliamentarians found in the religious prejudices of England a bond of union and eventually a means of war."

Winston's own religion, such as it was, was formed by reading

Winwood Reade's *The Martyrdom of Man* (1872), one of the first general histories in English, when he was a 21-year-old subaltern in Bangalore. Among the book's many admirers was H. G. Wells, who based his own *Outline of History* (1920) on its exuberant anti-Christianity. Here is a representative passage:

> At the time of the Romans and the Greeks the Christian faith was the highest to which the common people could attain ... But now knowledge, freedom, and prosperity are covering the earth; for three centuries past, human virtue has been steadily increasing, and mankind is prepared to receive a higher faith. But in order to build we must destroy. Not only the Syrian superstition must be attacked, but also the belief in a personal God, which engenders a slavish and oriental condition of the mind; and the belief in a posthumous reward which engenders a selfish and solitary condition of the heart ... a season of mental anguish is at hand ... The soul must be sacrificed; the hope in immortality must die. A sweet and charming illusion must be taken from the human race, as youth and beauty vanish never to return.

Sandhurst might have given Churchill an excellent grounding in tactics, drill, gymnastics, and riding, but it passed over even the rudiments of what the ineffable Lloyd George once called "the old cause that saved our fathers". After finishing the book, Churchill revealed how persuasive he found Reade's impious ramblings. "One of these days," he wrote his mother, "the cold bright light of science and reason will shine through the cathedral windows and we shall go out into the fields to seek God for ourselves. The great laws of Nature will be understood – our destiny and our past will be clear. We shall then be able to dispense with the religious toys that have agreeably fostered the development of mankind."

This belief in progress, formed by his reading of the Whig historians Hallam and Macaulay, which he never abandoned, even in the trenches of France, became characteristic, as did an attitude towards Christianity that often amounted to little more than benign condescension. In a letter to his cousin Ivor Guest, written when he was 24, he wrote: "I deprecate all Romish practices and prefer those of Protestantism, because I believe that the Reformed Church is less deeply sunk in the mire of dogma than the Oriental Establishment".

The aristocrat in Churchill was particularly patronizing about the faith of the working classes: "I can see a poor parish – working men living their lives in ugly white-washed factories, toiling day after day amid scenes and surroundings destitute of the element of beauty. I can sympathize with them for their aching longing for something not infected by the general squalor and something to gratify their love of the mystic, something a little nearer to the 'all-beautiful' – and I find it hard to rob their lives of this one ennobling aspiration – even though it finds expression in the burning of incense, the wearing of certain robes and other superstitious practices". This echoes the decidedly unChurchillian Walter Pater, who once wrote that "the religious, the Catholic ideal is the only mode of poetry realizable by the poor".

Churchill got at the heart of what he found irksome about religion when he wrote that

> people who think much of the next world rarely prosper in this: that men must use their minds and not kill their doubts by sensuous pleasures: that superstitious faith in nations rarely promotes their industry, that, in a phrase, Catholicism – all religion if you like, but particularly Catholicism – is a delicious narcotic. It may soothe our pains and chase our worries, but it checks our growth and saps our strength. And since the improvement of the British breed is my political aim in life, I would not permit too great indulgence if I could prevent it without assailing another great principle – Liberty.

One might say that these were the attitudes of youth and unrepresentative of the mature man. Yet in his autobiography, *My Early Life: A Roving Commission* (1930), written when he was 56, Churchill still regarded Reade's book as "a concise and well-written universal history of mankind", proving that "we simply go out like candles". He admitted that this was a "depressing conclusion", but reading Gibbon, "who evidently held the same view", confirmed him of its truth. Later, "frequent contact with danger" impelled him "to ask for special protection" from enemy fire or for lesser things, and when he found that "throughout my life, I got what I wanted", he "adopted … a system of believing whatever I wanted to believe". With his fellow officers in Bangalore, he recalled, he found himself subscribing to what he called "The Religion of Healthy Mindedness".

In other words, "if you tried your best to live an honorable life and did your duty and were faithful to friends and not unkind to the weak and poor, it did not matter what you believed or disbelieved ... All would come out right." Nominal Christianity has never been more succinctly defined.

Belief in this philanthropic religion never stopped Churchill from affecting a certain heroic nihilism. When his wife Clementine lost her mother in 1925, Churchill offered this chilly condolence: "An old and failing life, going out on the tide after the allotted span has been spent and after most joys have faded is not a cause for human pity. It is only a part of the immense tragedy of our existence here below against which both our hope and faith have rebelled. It is only what we all expect and await." In 1938, writing of the death of his ancestor, John Churchill, the first Duke of Marlborough, Churchill borrowed the cadences of Gibbon to reiterate this puerile view of created life: "The span of mortals is short, the end universal; and the tinge of melancholy which accompanies decline and retirement is in itself an anodyne. It is foolish to waste lamentation upon the closing phase of human life. Noble spirits yield themselves willingly to the successively falling shades which carry them to a better world or oblivion."

Once Churchill put away "the religious toys" that had "agreeably fostered the development of mankind", he was open to alternatives. In 1937 in a letter to his wife, he wrote:

> The most remarkable thing happened on Saturday last. I was sitting at lunch, drinking my port, smoking my cigar. I found myself thinking, quite subconsciously, about the sheep Friendly and how I would like to give him some bread. But I knew he was too far away, right on the opposite side of the valley beyond the Gainsborough Road ... I looked up and down the opposite hill Friendly was marching. At first he walked and then he trotted and finally he cantered, until he came to the little gate on the middle dam ... It was an amazing case of thought transference and this most intelligent animal realized my intention to give him bread. Needless to say I gathered up whatever bread there was on the table and hastened down to the lake where I rewarded him for his occult intelligence.

Clemmie replied from Davos, "What you tell me about Friendly is extraordinary. You must show him at the circus at Olympia next year as your occult sheep."

If Churchill found it difficult to believe in religion as a spiritual reality, he enjoyed making fun of it. In February 1945 he invited King Ibn Saud of Saudi Arabia to dinner in the desert. The King's emissary told Churchill that the King would be honored to attend but could permit no smoking or drinking. Churchill replied that it was he who was giving the dinner, and if the King's religion forbade such things, my religion prescribed as an absolute sacred rite smoking cigars and drinking alcohol before, after, and if need be during all meals and the intervals between them". In his six-volume history of the Second World War, Churchill recalled an unexploded bomb detachment consisting of "the Earl of Suffolk, his lady private secretary, and his rather aged *chauffeur*. They called themselves 'the Holy Trinity'. Their prowess and continued existence got around among all who knew. Thirty-four unexploded bombs did they tackle with urbane and smiling efficiency. But the thirty-fifth claimed its forfeit. Up went the Earl of Suffolk in his Holy Trinity. But we may be sure that, as for Mr. Valiant-for-truth, 'all the trumpets sounded for them on the other side.'"

Churchill's flippant attitude toward religion was common in a society where religious philistinism was *de rigueur*. "We have the highest authority for believing that the meek shall inherit the earth", Churchill's boon companion, F. E. Smith, later Lord Birkenhead, wrote in an essay on Lord Curzon, the Viceroy of India, "though I have never found any particular corroboration of this aphorism in the record of Somerset House." One has to remember that in the years leading up to Churchill's arrival at 10 Downing Street the most celebrated cleric in England was not Ronald Knox or David Knowles but Harold Davidson, the Rector of Stiffkey, who met his untimely end, after a lifetime chasing girls, in a lion's cage at Skegness. It was not a devout age.

Considering his prejudices against the Faith, which were the traditional prejudices of the post-Reformation English, equating Rome with superstition, backwardness, and the ungovernable Irish, it is interesting that Churchill should have been as fascinated as he was by the historical character of the Church. His physician Lord Moran recalls him reciting on three separate occasions (by heart) the famous passage from Macaulay's review of Ranke's *History of the Popes*, in which the Whig historian descanted on the staying power of the Church:

> She saw the commencement of all the governments and of all the ecclesiastical establishments that now exist in the world; and we feel no assurance that she is not destined to see the end of them all. She was great and respected before the Saxon had set foot on Britain, before the Frank had passed the Rhine, when Grecian eloquence still flourished at Antioch, when idols were still worshipped in the temple of Mecca. And she may still exist in undiminished vigour when some traveler from New Zealand shall, in the midst of a vast solitude, take his stand on a broken arch of London Bridge to sketch the ruins of St. Paul's.

"I had a feeling", Moran concluded, "that he wanted desperately to believe in something, but from what he said he did not find it easy". Churchill had the same ambivalent feelings toward war. While attending German army maneuvers in 1909, he wrote his wife: "Much as war attracts me and fascinates my mind with its tremendous situations – I feel more deeply every year – and can measure the feeling here in the midst of arms – what vile and wicked folly and barbarism it is." Later, he would regret allowing Sir Arthur Harris to raze Dresden and in his memoirs never mentioned the retaliatory raids that killed tens of thousands of civilians.

Such compunction shows that Churchill was not without natural virtue. All who worked with him confirmed that his good points were very good indeed. For Sir Ian Jacob, Military Assistant Secretary to the War Cabinet in the crucial years 1939 to 1945, he "had tremendous fibre and toughness... He more than anyone could 'meet with triumph and disaster, and treat those two imposters just the same." For Jock Colville, his private secretary from 1941 to 1955, "his charm, his energy, the simplicity of his purpose, his unfailing sense of fun and his complete absence of personal vanity – so rare in successful men – were the Secret Weapons which outmatched any that Hitler could produce". More important, despite his often bullying manner, what struck Colville was his "humanity and sympathy for those in distress which were the basis of his character I never knew him to be spiteful. He once said to me, with reference to a disgraceful act which was alleged in Whitehall: "If there is one thing I abhor it is a manhunt."

This sympathy for people in distress grew out of his unhappiness as a child. Rebuffed by extraordinarily self-absorbed parents, Churchill found his own distress relieved by Mrs. Everest, his beloved nanny, whom he nicknamed "Woom" and even took once to Harrow, to the scandalized disgust of his more conventional contemporaries. When Churchill learned that she was to be discharged after twenty years of service, he wrote his mother pleading for her retention. When she was dying in 1897, Churchill, by then a Sandhurst cadet, rushed to her side, and afterwards arranged for her funeral and gravestone.

Many more examples of his fellow feeling could be cited. After being held captive by the Boers and making a characteristically dashing escape, he devoted much of his political capital to alleviating the lot of prisoners. In 1941, he even arranged for Oswald and Diana Mosley to share the same prison digs, thus making Oswald the first male prisoner ever enrolled in the records of Holloway. (They were interned under Regulation 18B, along with 1,769 other British subjects sympathetic to Hitler and Mussolini.) He felt profound empathy for his unfortunate father, who, for all his brilliance and mercurial charm, had deeply wounded his son. Dining once with his own son Randolph, Churchill remarked, "We have this evening had a longer period of continuous conversation together than the total which I ever had with my father in the whole course of his life". Shane Leslie thought Churchill's two-volume life of Lord Randolph "perhaps the greatest filial tribute in the English language ... Few sons have done more for their fathers." Attlee recalled "the tears coming down [Churchill's] cheeks one day before the war in the House of Commons, when he was telling me what was being done to the Jews in Germany".

When all England reviled Neville Chamberlain, after the policy of appeasement came to smash, Churchill alone showed him kindness and respect. In 1940, in Church House, to which the Members of Parliament had moved to evade the German bombers, Churchill bid his old opponent farewell in one of his most moving speeches.

> It is not given to human beings, happily for them, for otherwise life would be intolerable, to foresee or predict to any large extent the unfolding of events ... History with its

flickering lamp stumbles along the trail of the past, trying to reconstruct its scenes, to revive its echoes, and kindle with pale gleams the passion of former days. What is the worth of all this? The only guide to a man is his conscience; the only shield to his memory is the rectitude and sincerity of his actions...

It fell to Neville Chamberlain in one of the supreme crises of the world to be contradicted by events, to be disappointed in his hopes, and to be deceived and cheated by a wicked man. But what were these hopes in which he was disappointed? What were these wishes in which he was frustrated? What was that faith that was abused? They were surely among the most noble and benevolent instincts of the human heart – the love of peace, the toil for peace, the strife for peace, even at great peril and certainly to the utter disdain of popularity...

Lord Chandos, President of the Board of Trade during the Second World War, once said of Churchill that "perhaps not enough has been made of his magnanimity. He saw man as a noble, not as a mean creature. The only people he never forgave were those who, in words he so often used, 'fell beneath the level of events.'" But this was not true: Churchill forgave Chamberlain and Baldwin readily enough and certainly neither of them rose to the level of events. No, Churchill was magnanimous, period.

In *The Tablet*, the English historian John Ramsden claimed that "what Churchill believed in was himself... He was burdened with an almost megalomaniacal self-belief". This ignores the humility of the man. About the impact of his oratorical skills, he once turned to an aide in fallen France and said, "If words counted, we should win this war". When his butler Sawyer brought him the news that the Japanese had attacked Pearl Harbor, Churchill exclaimed: "So we had won after all! Once again in our long Island history we should emerge, however mauled and mutilated, safe and victorious. We should not be wiped out." He made no mention of his oratory in that calculus. When Lord Boothby, who had been Churchill's private secretary until 1929, asked him in 1951 what he thought his legacy would be, Churchill replied: "Historians are apt to judge war ministries less by the victories achieved under their direction than by the political results which flowed from them. Judged by that standard, I am not sure I shall be held to have done very well." There was nothing megalomaniacal about that. Nor about this – a letter he wrote his darling Clementine from the trenches in 1916: "Sometimes I think I would not mind stopping living very much – I am so devoured by egoism that I would like to have another soul in another world and meet you in another setting and pay you all the love and honour of the great romances..." Fortunately, before he finally did go, Clementine was sensible enough to fetch a priest.

Churchill had many of the virtues of the natural man. He lacked the cardinal virtues, in the sense in which Saint Augustine understood them, when he wrote (to quote from the admirable new Catechism):

> To live well is nothing other than to love God with all one's heart, with all one's soul and with all one's efforts; from this it comes about that love is kept whole and uncorrupted (through temperance). No misfortune can disturb it (and this is fortitude). It obeys only [God] (and this is justice), and is careful in discerning things, so as not to be surprised by deceit or trickery (and this is prudence.)

To judge Churchill, as Evelyn Waugh did when he heard of his death, as "always in the wrong, always surrounded by crooks, a most unsuccessful father – simply a 'Radio Personality' who had outlived his prime" is surely harsh, though one can understand why Waugh should refuse to join his contemporaries in treating a flawed man as though he had been infallible. After Churchill's field marshal, Viscount Alanbrooke published his highly critical diaries, Clementine said to Lord Moran, "You know, Charles, I am not really angry with Alanbrooke. We must get used to criticism of Winston. I realize the poor darling cannot be a demi-god forever."

In his "finest hour" speech of 18 June 1940, Churchill famously said that the Battle of France was over and the Battle of Britain had begun and "upon this battle depends the survival of Christian civilization". Churchill helped that civilization survive by reacquainting the Allies with the power of evil and rousing them to take up arms to combat it. What he could not have foreseen is that the Christian civilization he successfully defended against Hitler should now be even more radically threatened by a European political class intent on denying the reality of Hilaire Belloc's great truism, that "Europe is the Faith, and the Faith is Europe". Churchill's historical mind would have marveled at the irony of that. As far back as 1946, at Zurich University, he had urged Europeans "to build a kind of United States of Europe". In the spectacle of contemporary Europe unifying only to repudiate its Christian heritage, he would have seen a defeatism far more debilitating than any that gripped the proponents of appeasement. And implications for Europe's ability to eradicate the evil of terrorist Islam that are not reassuring. One can scarcely eradicate what one refuses to acknowledge.

Mary Soames, the youngest of the Churchill children, told her father in 1951 that "it is hardly in the nature of things that your descendants should inherit your genius – but I earnestly hope they may share in some way the qualities of your heart". For Catholics, Churchill exemplifies more than a brave heart. He is a reminder of the insufficiency of natural virtue. That a man with so many gifts – with so much courage, magnanimity, loyalty, wit, inventiveness, foresight – should have ended his days convinced, as he told his good friend Violet Bonham-Carter, that "death meant extinction" and that "eternity ... was a nightmare possibility" was tragic proof of that insufficiency. The virtues of the natural man, even the most extraordinary natural man, are poor things without sanctifying grace.

Immortal Blather

The Complete Novels, Flann O'Brien. Everyman. 785 pages.

FLANN O'BRIEN was one of the funniest writers who ever put pen to paper. Yes, he set the English novel ablaze with experimental fireworks that still dazzle. He was a brilliant linguist, who wrote Irish and Latin with witty fluency. He was a gifted playwright, who, if the Abbey and the Gate had been more receptive, might have gone on to rival O'Casey and Shaw. He was a legendary drinker whose great dictum – "a pint of plain is your only man" – will forever solace the drinking classes. He saw the reality of hell with the sensual vividness of Bruegel and Bosch. He was an inspired satirist who subjected the pretensions and idiocies of his Irish compatriots to daily mockery in an incomparable *Irish Times* column. He was an outspoken critic of the bogus Joyce industry. Yet more than anything else he was sublimely funny.

The splendid new Everyman's Library edition of the complete novels should gain many new readers for the work of an author who is still not as well-known as he deserves to be. Born in Strabane, County Tyrone, in 1911, the fifth of twelve children, Brian O'Nolan studied English, Irish, and German at University College Dublin before joining the Irish Civil service in 1935 where he was private secretary to successive Ministers for Local Government until 1953. In 1940, under the pseudonym Myles na Gopaleen, he began his famous satirical column for the *Irish Times* called "Cruiskeen Lawn", which, translated back from the Irish, means "the little brimming jug". Under the pseudonym Flann O'Brien, he wrote five novels: *At-Swim-Two-Birds* (1939), which Graham Greene persuaded Longman to publish; *The Third Policeman* (1940), which Longman rejected (it was published posthumously in 1967); *The Poor Mouth* (1941), which was originally written in Irish as *An Béal Bocht*; *The Hard Life* (1961); and *The Dalkey Archive* (1964). He died in 1966.

O'Brien is often paired with James Joyce. Both were good at using Dublin topography to comic effect, both looked askance at the pretensions of Irish nationalism (Joyce insisted on keeping his British passport, not only after the founding of the Irish Free State in 1922 but after the founding of Eire in 1937), both were masters of English prose, both were given to bold experimentation, both had an uneasy relationship with Irish Catholicism (Joyce broke with the Church altogether, while O'Brien remained a faithful critic), both shared a fondness for the sort of elaborate leg-pull perfected by Swift and Sterne in the eighteenth century. Yet what they were supremely good at was capturing the music of Dubliners talking. When a character in Joyce's short story "Ivy Day in the Committee Room" recommends that the Irish welcome a visit from Edward VII, another objects.

> "Why should we welcome the King of England? Didn't Parnell himself..."
>
> "Parnell", said Henchy, "is dead. Now, here's the way I look at it. Here's this chap come to the throne after his old mother keeping him out of it till the man was grey. He's a man of the world, and he means well by us. He's a jolly fine decent fellow, if you ask me, and no damn nonsense about him. He just says to himself, 'The old one never went to see these wild Irish. By Christ, I'll go myself and see what they're like.' And are we going to insult the man when he comes over here on a friendly visit?" ...
>
> "But after all," said Mr. Lyons argumentatively, "King Edward's life, you know, is not the very..."
>
> "Let bygones be bygones," said Mr. Henchy.

The Irish might have turned on Parnell after they discovered his affair with Kitty O'Shea, but they were willing enough to welcome the adulterous Edward VII once it became clear that his visit would "mean an influx of money into this country". For Joyce, the Irish might have been always ready to exchange principle for pelf – betrayal was in their subjugated genes – but for O'Brien, the Irish were not so easily pegged and to understand them you had to listen to their blather.

In *At-Swim-Two-Birds*, O'Brien's masterpiece, blather reigns supreme. One can hear it in the "voice-play" of Byrne and Kerrigan, friends of the book's student narrator who is writing the book about the book he is writing about an author who is also writing a book:

> "You're a terrible man for the blankets," said Kerrigan.
>
> "I'm not ashamed to admit that I love my bed," said Byrne.
>
> "She was my first friend, my foster-mother, my dearest

comforter.... Her warmth kept me alive when my mother bore me. She still nurtures me, yielding without stint the parturition of her cozy womb. She will nurse me gently in my last hour and faithfully hold my cold body when I am dead. She will look bereaved when I am gone."

Joyce makes a similar observation in *Finnegans Wake*: "the nice little smellar squalls in his crydle what the dirty old bigger'll be squealing through his coughin". The Irishman's attachment to his bed is driven by more than crapulence: It is an attachment to history, to matriarchy, to death itself. Byrne reaffirms the ancestral necrophilia.

In another passage, aggrieved characters of the author Dermot Trellis speculate on how to speed their tyrannical employer to an early grave. "Steam rollers are expensive machines...", remarked Shanahan, "What about a needle in the knee?" "A cut of a razor behind the knee," said Lamont. This leads to a consideration of the nature of torture, which the more literary victims of the IRA might have recalled with wry appreciation.

> The refinements of physical agony... are limited by an ingenious arrangement of the cerebral mechanism and the sensory nerves... Reason will not permit of the apprehension of sensations of reckless or prodigal intensity. Give me an agony within reason, says Reason, and I will take it, analyze it, and cause the issue of vocal admission that it has been duly received... But go beyond the statutory limit, says Reason, and I won't be there at all. I'll put out the light and pull down the blinds. I will close the shop...

Here O'Brien's blather reveals a fascination with savagery that gives this 1939 novel an oddly prophetic quality. Soon after its publication, Europe would devote itself to "the refinements of physical agony" as never before.

Then of course there is the Jumping Irishman. "Go where you like in the wide world, you will always find that the Irishman is looked up to for his jumping."

> Right enough, Said Furriskey, the name of Ireland is honored for that.
> Go to Russia, said Shanahan, go to China, go to France. Everywhere and all the time it's hats off and gra-ma-cree to the Jumping Irishman...

Readers intrigued by what could justify this boast will have to buy the Everyman edition to find out for themselves. Paraphrasing Flann O'Brien is not advisable – though requiring creative writing students to produce a Cliffs Notes version of *At-Swim-Two-Birds* might be good sadistic fun.

The first chapter introduces William Tracy, an author of cowboy books, all set in the Ringsend district of Dublin. Tracy is the first man in Europe to exhibit twenty-nine lions in a cage at the same time. Shorty Andrews and Slug Willard, two of his more popular characters, are described cantering up Mountjoy Square with their cowboy hats tilted back and their gun-butts swinging at their holsters. When not rounding up steers, these colorful cowpunchers gather in their Dublin bunkhouse where they smoke cigarettes and drink porter... Then there is a character called the Pooka MacPhellimey, described by O'Brien as "a member of the devil class".

O'Brien's second masterpiece, *The Third Policeman*, is only slightly less unparaphrasable, including as it does a detective story, a portrait of law enforcement in rural Ireland, a touching tale of frustrated love between a man and his bicycle, and the animadversions of one De Selby, a visionary polymath, who, among many other distinctions, designs a number of alternatives to Dublin's tumbledown tenements. One design

> had the conventional slated roof but no walls save one, which was to be erected in the quarter of the prevailing wind; around the other sides were the inevitable tarpaulins loosely wound on rollers suspended from the gutters of the roof, the whole structure being surrounded by a diminutive moat or pit bearing some resemblance to military latrines. In the light of present-day theories of housing and hygiene, there can be no doubt that de Selby was much mistaken in these ideas but in his own remote day more than one sick person lost his life in an ill-advised quest for health in these fantastic dwellings.

The other three novels included here are not as funny as the first two, though they have their moments. In *The Dalkey Archive*, James Joyce repents of his apostasy by mending the undergarments of Jesuits. O'Brien describes the darling of the academy only seeing the light after "the lonely exertion of keeping pace with a contrived reputation

... finally put the delicate poise of his head out of balance". *The Hard Life* is the weakest of the novels, a laborious satire which shows that clerical stupidity is no funnier in fiction than in life.

A Poor Mouth is in a class by itself. A parody of Gaelic reminiscences like Tomas Ó Criomhthain's *The Islandman*, the book mocks the sentimental caricatures of the *Gaeltacht* that became popular in the wake of Douglas Hyde's Gaelic League. In Corkadoragha, O'Brien's Gaelic inferno, there is nothing noble about the Gaelic speakers of the impoverished countryside, whose "likes would never be there again". Stripped of the varnish of nationalist myth, they are a sadly indigent lot and an unanswerable indictment of De Valera's rural theocracy. "In one way or another", the hapless narrator reports, "life was passing us by and we were suffering misery, sometimes having a potato and at other times nothing in our mouths but sweet words of Gaelic." Here is the poor mouth's one unvarying theme. If O'Brien's preoccupation with hell took a memorably lunatic turn in *The Third Policeman*, it becomes penitential in the rain-sodden wastes of Corkadoragha. Yet, now that the parvenus of the Celtic Tiger find themselves in an even more accelerated hell, they might begin to look back on this more primitive variety with a kind of nostalgia.

After Longman rejected *The Third Policeman*, O'Brien abandoned novel writing and devoted himself to his column in *The Irish Times*, which might have been a setback for comic fiction but proved the beginning of the funniest newspaper column of all time. Admirers of the work of Flann O'Brien can only hope that Knopf Everyman gathers together the rich hoard of non-fictional writings that this brilliant man left behind in a second omnibus edition, which, I hope, for I do hope, does not omit this bleak little gem.

> I met a poor man who was a stranger to these parts who asked me to direct him somewhere ... Then he pointed to a big building and said what's that. I said that's the Bank of Ireland. He said what do they be doing in there. Well, I said, banks lend money, you know. He looked wistfully at the Old House and said I wonder would they lend me ten bob. Why not try I said. Begor I think I will, he answered, a yellowish suffusion of worthless diluted blood mounting through his second-hand face, a symbol that the last thing to die in each

of us is hope. Grey carrion soul-mincing hope, the one quality above all others that makes the human creature ridiculous and pathetic.

God and Man at Hippo

Augustine of Hippo: A Life, Henry Chadwick. Oxford University Press. 168 pages.

No WRITER excelled at that exacting form, the short biography better than Henry Chadwick (1920–2008), the former Master of Peterhouse, Cambridge, and historian of the early Church. In *Augustine of Hippo*, posthumously prepared for print by his devoted wife, he returned to the greatest of the early Church Fathers to write a biography that is a delight from start to finish and a marvel of scholarly distillation.

St. Augustine is a figure about whom we know a good deal. Born at Tagaste in 354 in what is now eastern Algeria of a pagan father and Christian mother, he studied rhetoric at Carthage with an eye to becoming a lawyer but instead became a teacher, or what he called a "salesman of words in the market of rhetoric". Following ancient custom, he parted from the Carthaginian concubine with whom he had a son, once a suitable fiancé was found, though the parting distressed him keenly and he converted before he could marry the fiancé. A restless student of philosophy, Augustine embraced, in turn, Manichaeism, scepticism, and the Neo-Platonism of Plotinus before he found in Christianity the "rule of faith" he craved. Meeting and befriending Ambrose, bishop of Milan, changed his life forever. Although initially drawn to the style of Ambrose's preaching, Augustine soon found that what most moved him was its content – especially its elucidation of the Bible.

His mother Monica, who prayed for his conversion for years, naturally rejoiced in his change of heart, though Augustine only converted after a fierce interior struggle. Indeed, in the *Confessions*, he describes his "agony of hesitation" with great vividness. Longing to enter into what he called his "pact and covenant with God", and yet unready to forswear the guiles of concupiscence, he sat down in a Milan garden "deeply disturbed in spirit". To convert, he came to see, "one does not use ships or chariots or feet", but the will. Fittingly for this most literary of saints, it was a passage from Saint Paul that finally decided him: "Put on the Lord Jesus Christ and make no provision for the flesh in its lusts." He finally converted in 386.

After returning to Africa and setting up a quasi-monastic community, Augustine was ordained priest in 391. Four years later he became bishop of Hippo, and for the next 34 years, while ministering to his often unruly parishioners, he wrote a series of books that still deeply affect the life of the Christian Church, addressing as they do hermeneutics, the sacraments, dogma, history, grace, education, free will, original sin, and sex. Augustine died in 430, when the Vandals were at the gates of Hippo.

The hagiographer David Hugh Farmer estimated that his many writings, including the *Confessions* and the *City of God*, "have probably proved more influential in the history of thought than any Christian writer since St. Paul". Aquinas may have had Aristotle but Augustine had Augustine.

Chadwick shows how St. Augustine's thought, like that of Cardinal Newman, grew directly out of his relations with friends, family, colleagues, and parishioners. In this regard, although an ascetic – he left behind no will because he owned no possessions – he never entirely shunned the world. Indeed, one major theme of Chadwick's book is how this subtle, highly educated, discriminating man came to recognize how ordinary people often apprehend truths that the educated disdain or deny.

Monica was the great exemplar of unschooled insight. Of the first community Augustine set up in 386 in a villa 20 miles south of Como, Chadwick writes: "It would be idle to pretend that the intellectual equipment of the miscellaneous company ... [was] the sharpest steel." Yet since Monica was in tow, Augustine urged the community to learn from her wisdom.

Similarly, Chadwick shows how his episcopal duties forced Augustine to rethink the life of the mind. "How could his monastic vocation be reconciled with countless administrative cares sure to distract him both from and in his prayers?" For Chadwick, Augustine "was still in the process of discovering that ordinary churches are not places where half-educated fools imagine they worship God while the wise men are in a country villa studying oriental mysticism and Plotinus".

Mixing with men from all stations, "from dukes to dustmen", as Chadwick puts it, familiarized Augustine with the realities of human nature, which, in turn, informed his theology. If one of Augustine's most contested contributions to Christian orthodoxy was the doctrine of original sin, it was his encounters with unregenerate human nature, including his own, that convinced him of man's abiding need for sacramental grace to overcome that nature.

For Augustine, our propensity to sin bespeaks a deep-seated iniquity in human nature, to deny which flouts experience. "In Africa you may have to go far to find even one church where no one has been discovered in crime and where no clergy have been degraded." Augustine attacked the British monk Pelagius because, in denying original sin, he underestimated this ineradicable defect in our nature.

Nevertheless, Augustine appreciated that often it is our sinful nature that leads us to faith and, therefore, "one should not be put off by hypocrites, who are to be found in every profession". And, in any case, the hypocrite may truly wish to put hypocrisy behind him, a truth to which Augustine gives perceptive expression: "A convert will find many good Christians in the Church if he sets out to become one himself."

Then, again, in his African parish, Augustine often witnessed those who came to scoff and stayed to pray. He himself, he says, initially accounted the Bible "unworthy in comparison with the dignity of Cicero". It would take time for the fastidious rhetorician in him to discern the riches of scripture, especially since, as Chadwick notes, "the old Latin version of the Bible had none of the noble classical prose, of say, the King James Version or Luther's German Bible".

Eventually, Augustine recognized that while Ciceronian eloquence might be persuasive, the parish priest should stick to the Bible for the form of his preaching. At the same time, as Chadwick notes, Augustine was adamant that though "oratory is morally neither good nor bad, it is damnable when used to persuade people to accept error", a judgment which President Obama, with his deep interest in oratory, may find instructive.

Chadwick also nicely encapsulates Augustine's view of the state, which he set out in the *City of God*.

> Persecutions had discouraged the early Christians from looking to the state for any moral benefit other than the suppression of wickedness... Man's longing is for an ordered society of fellowship and love. This is something the state cannot

create or maintain. Man accepts the authority of positive law because order is preferable to anarchy and chaos; but in laws man seeks some vestiges of a higher justice.

Augustine was not overly sanguine about the prospects of the Christian empire either because, as he said, "the Emperor has become a Christian – the devil has not".

In his foreword, Peter Brown, the author of the definitive life of Augustine, praises Chadwick for his readiness to take issue with aspects of Augustine's thinking of which he disapproves, particularly his linking of sexuality with original sin. As Brown points out, since Chadwick's book was composed, an unpublished letter has come to light in which Augustine stresses that he "would be angrier by far with the one who praises me and takes what I have written as Gospel truth than the one who criticizes me unfairly".

However, whether Augustine would have been impressed with Chadwick's criticism is questionable. According to Chadwick, "it would be asking a lot to expect the man whose conversion to Christianity focused on a renunciation of sex to see it . . . as a natural gift of the good Creator to be used wholly innocently in accord with his commands". But Augustine always denied that his own personal experience informed his estimate of sexuality. For Augustine, "the transmission of Adam's sin and guilt to his posterity is a proposition without which the great mass of human suffering becomes an indictment of the Creator". This may be unsparing, but it is not incoherent, which is more than can be said for Chadwick's reading. "Twentieth-century man," he says, "more aware of his intimate affinity with the animal kingdom, regards sex as good and natural, but can easily make his exalted estimate of sex the concomitant of a low estimate of marriage". Is it really plausible that "twentieth-century man" had an "exalted estimate of sex" because of his "intimate affinity with the animal kingdom"?

This puzzling proposition notwithstanding, Chadwick's biography is a rewarding read. It certainly confirms Augustine's own sense of the wonder of conversion. In one passage from his writings, Augustine noted how "the daily miracles of creation are as great as those of the incarnate Lord", and to illustrate his point, as Chadwick says, he pointed to those "miracles of inward moral conversion", which "are greater than the material miracles once done by Christ himself", since "now the Lord opens not blind eyes but blind hearts". Only someone convinced equally of original sin and God's love could see the miraculous in quite those terms.

Anglo-Prussian Self-Portrait

For He is an Englishman: Memoirs of a Prussian Nobleman, Charles Arnold-Baker. Jeremy Mills. 408 pages.

To recommend the memoirs of an editor of a book of reference might seem odd special pleading, but then the *Companion to British History* (1996) is no ordinary reference book. When first reviewed, it was hailed as a work of heroic scholarship comparable to Johnson's *Dictionary*. And Charles Arnold-Baker was certainly no ordinary editor. Although a professor of law and architecture at London's City University, he was primarily a barrister, and his understanding of English history was refreshingly free of academic bias.

That is not to say that he did not have biases of his own, but they were certainly not those of the left liberals who dominate most history departments in England and America. "I see no reason to belittle the achievements of the British nations", he wrote in the preface to his *Companion*. "They have borne more responsibility for the conduct of human affairs than any nation since the Romans. There have naturally been terrible, disastrous, foolish or ill-natured episodes, but those who have not been involved in vast operations are ... in a weaker position to criticize than those who have." That this unfashionable good sense should have come from a Prussian aristocrat makes Arnold-Baker all the more interesting. Certainly, in the memoir, those familiar with the *Companion* will recognize the author's trademark ebullience. They will also enjoy his trenchant asides on military, diplomatic, social, and intellectual history. And for those unfamiliar with the *Companion*, the memoir will serve as the perfect introduction to that earlier book's massive, compendious learning.

The life of Charles Arnold-Baker (1916–2009) reads like one of Sybille Bedford's novels. He was born Wolfgang Charles Werner von Blumenthal in Berlin, the second son of Professor Baron Albrecht Werner von Blumenthal (1889–1945) of Pomerania and his English wife Alice Wilhelmine, *née* Hainsworth (1883–1978), the daughter of a Yorkshire industrialist. He spent his childhood in Prussia among his father's aristocratic family and was later profoundly affected by his parents' divorce. In fact, it is clear from these judicious pages that it was weighing his parents' conflicting loyalties against their mutual betrayals that turned him into an historian.

The divorce also exacerbated his rocky relationship with his mother, a possessive, implacable, mischievous woman, about whom he is amusingly unsparing. As for his father, by 1932, he had no doubts as to what the Nazis had up their sleeves and removed his two sons to England, where they changed their names and became naturalized British subjects. Arnold-Baker was the name of the author's stepfather, an estate agent whom his mother married after her divorce. This change of name and indeed of country could not have been easy for von Blumenthal senior, who, as the author relates, was "proud of his country and its people and achievements. Hegel, Goethe, Savigny, Mommsen were emblazoned on the breast of his eagle, as well as *Gott mitt Uns*".

After graduating from Winchester, Arnold-Baker went up to Magdalen, where his tutors were A. J. P. Taylor and C. S. Lewis. His assessment of the former is understandably harsh:

> Taylor, I thought, and think, was, for all his brilliance as a broadcaster and learning as a writer, something of a charlatan. His tutorials degenerated into Marxist and Slav propaganda, and when he tried to argue with me, a von Blumenthal [all of whose 53 properties were confiscated by the Soviets], that Russian policy, whether Czarist or Communist, had never been aggressive, I could only laugh behind my hand.

He found Lewis more sympathetic. "Nothing submerged that buoyant intelligence", he recalls. "His Christianity had something to do with this: a religious person, knowing his own insignificance, can be genial. An atheist sneers."

When war broke out, the author joined the Royal East Kent Regiment, otherwise known as the Buffs, and led one of the two platoons that guarded Churchill at Chartwell. About the indomitable war leader, Arnold-Baker writes: "Even in his convalescent state he drank more than I could safely manage at a third of his age. A bottle of brandy appeared at every dinner. We and the other officers drank about half of it ... and he invariably drank the rest." Nevertheless, in the Churchillian *modus operandi*, conviviality never compromised duty. "Once he cross-examined us about our needs", Arnold-Baker recalls, "and we told him about our shortage of up-to-date equipment. We were re-armed in 24 hours."

In 1943, Arnold-Baker married Edith May, née Woods, whom he had met at Oxford and with whom he had two children. They were happily married for over sixty years.

A deathbed convert to Rome, the author shared Graham Greene's fascination with the mundanity of evil. About a Nazi interrogation fort in Belgium, for example, he was moved to write, "The machinery of murder and cruelty is sordid and simple. Cells had been built of cheap naked brick on a concrete floor with internal windows covered with barbed wire. A kitchen table was used to strap a man down for interrogation; a single wooden joist across a corner to hang him. The place was at once horrible and dull." Later, he was happy to see it razed, though he was happier still to see these words scrawled on one of the bricks: *Marie, mère des pauvres, aide nos*.

In 1943, Arnold-Baker joined MI6, where he encountered the then unexposed Kim Philby, whom he recalls as "nasty and intellectually arrogant". That Philby managed to deceive the world about Guernica (against which, in fact, there was no aerial bombardment) becomes, in the author's telling, a case study not only in Marxist mendacity but Western gullibility. Indeed, the German archives reveal how puzzled the Germans were by reports of this fictitious bombing, which, in any case, from their standpoint, would have been "militarily pointless".

Nevertheless, later he would see the effects of real bombing when he visited his birthplace in 1945: "Imagine standing on the steps of Saint Paul's in London and having an unobstructed view of Earl's Court. Berlin was a rubble heap the size of Birmingham."

Arnold-Baker also took part in the liberation of Belgium, where he helped uncover the Nazis' network of local spies in Antwerp, mostly by befriending the town's omniscient courtesans, who presided over the cafes. In the same year, during the liberation of Norway, he captured the complete Gestapo archive and arrested the Deputy Commandant of Auschwitz, "a little runt of a man", as he recalls, "whom we naturally put into the custody of a Jewish guard, with strict instructions not to damage him, of course".

On whether the German citizenry were culpable for the atrocities of the Nazis, the author is clear-sighted:

> [The Germans] had adopted an abomination which promised them benefits in return for the destruction of law, democracy and certain scapegoats. These benefits went far beyond the tearing up of the Treaty of Versailles ... They would re-establish the frontiers (roughly speaking – what's a few million Slavs between friends?) of the ancient Reich – meaning something golden, glorious, and predatory. The German word *Krieg* (war) is connected with *kriegen* meaning to "get or take", and *Reich* (according to the dictionary "empire") means adjectively "rich". The Nazis appealed to the myth of the tribal horde with its roistering chieftains ready to fill your hat with gold ...

To those who argue that the Nazis were too brutal to be resisted, the author counters that they were resisted. "I knew Elizabeth von Thadden. She ran a girls' school and taught them to be truthful and upright and to look facts in the face. She was hanged on a tree in her own playing field." And thus his conclusion is ineluctable: The Germans "mostly helped themselves to the loot without many second thoughts ..."

After the war, Arnold Baker became a barrister, practicing in the Admiralty Division. Lawyers will delight in his observations about the pecking order that obtained in the Inner Temple.

> A clerk was paid a scale-based commission on his barrister's fees by the solicitors. Thus he had a personal interest to press his most successful and therefore most expensive barrister, to the disadvantage of the others, and as the latter were not allowed to practice without him, he could demand, ahead of his fees, a small non-returnable salary, which relieved him of the need to do anything much for the newly called. Thus the successful were chronically overworked, which under graduated taxation was decreasingly rewarded, while newcomers were underworked and sometimes starved. Most clerks became much richer than most barristers. One came to the Temple daily in a chauffeured Daimler. This imbalance still exists. In truth a clerk employed his barrister not the other way round.

Before commencing work on the *Companion*, Arnold-Baker turned his versatile genius to local council administration and the evolving constitution, on both of which he wrote groundbreaking books. The memoir also contains a fascinating chapter on the hurdles he scaled to write and publish the *Companion*, which is properly condemnatory of the stupidity and incompetence rampant in the publishing trade, though in the eventual critical and commercial success of the work that he and his son published on their own his good judgment was entirely vindicated.

The book shows again and again how it was the Prussian in Arnold-Baker that made him such a proud Englishman. Speaking of a holiday he took with his father in the mid-1930s, after he had changed his citizenship, he remarks: "In contrast with our present third-rate condition Britain [then] was deeply respected. A British passport was rarely inspected: so potent it was." And one emblem of this was the buying power of the pound. "We stayed a night at the Truffe Noire at Brive-la-Gaillarde," he recalls. "We had three bedrooms, a splendid four course dinner with two sorts of wine, brandies and coffee afterwards and breakfast next day. The *total* triple bill was just £5."

Then, after describing the pageantry and precision of the Aldershot Tattoo, which in its prime featured 5,000 troops and commanded an audience of 20,000, he observes, "As military and patriotic shows, ministering to a sense of national self-respect without militarization, I think that the tattoos were a true form of Art. They cost the nation nothing, for the troops were there anyway, and as a form of training in organization and staff work, they were valuable exercises in their own right. It is high time that they were revived." Whether Cameron's Britain will ever heed this advice is dubious. Still, one does not have to be English or Prussian to agree with Arnold-Baker when he says, with a nod to the multiculturalists who now have jolly old England by the throat, "I am hostile to those who despise patriotism. You might as well despise your own family or your elephant."

Gladstone in His Books

The Mind of Gladstone: Religion, Homer, and Politics, David Bebbington. Oxford University Press. 352 pages.

In his first book, *The State in Its Relations with the Church* (1838), written when he was still the conservative MP for Newark, Gladstone argued that the English state was morally obliged to uphold Anglicanism because it was "that form of belief which contains the largest portion of the elements of truth with the smallest admixture of error". This was an especially quixotic contention at a time when the liberal Whigs had effectively appropriated the Established Church to foil their Tory opponents, who were the traditional advocates of the prerogatives of the Church. Nevertheless, Gladstone was genuinely solicitous about the spiritual well-being of his compatriots and always insisted that politics serve religion. Writing to his father when he was 24, he defended the dignity of ministerial office on the grounds that "nothing could compete with the grandeur of its end or of its means, the restoration of man to that image of his Maker which is now throughout the world so lamentably defaced". Macaulay reviewed Gladstone's theoretical paean to the Established Church in the quintessentially liberal *Edinburgh Review* and saw only an apology for "roasting dissenters at slow fires".

> If the propagation of religious truth be a principal end of government... if it be the duty of a government to employ for that end its constitutional power... if the constitutional power of government extends... to the making of laws for burning of heretics... if burning be... in most cases, a most effectual mode of suppressing opinions; why should we not burn?

After this merciless *reductio ad absurdum*, Macaulay relented and expressed the hope that young Gladstone would "not suffer political avocations so entirely to engross him, as to leave him no leisure for literature and philosophy". He needn't have bothered. Gladstone sat in the House of Commons for over sixty years and led four governments as prime minister, but he always found "leisure for literature and philosophy". James Joyce no doubt had this aspect of the man in mind when he referred to him as "like a portly butler who has gone to night school". Gladstone wrote over thirty books and scores of articles. In *The Mind of Gladstone: Religion, Homer, and Politics*, David Bebbington delves into these neglected materials "to uncover the structure and development" of Gladstone's ideas. The result is a lively, deeply researched book that should coax readers to look again at that most peculiar concoction, Gladstonian liberalism. Earlier Gladstone scholars from John Morley to Colin Matthew chose to ignore these materials to concentrate on the political career. Bebbington shows that the statesman's political interests were "intertwined" with his religious and intellectual interests and cannot be understood apart from them.

Saint Augustine, one of Gladstone's heroes, once said that "no one should give up entirely his delight in learning, for the sweetness he once knew may be lost and the burden he bears overwhelm him". Gladstone's voluminous diaries prove that no burden – whether it was the threat of insurrection in Ireland or the menace of the Mahdi in Egypt or the debacle of Majuba Hill in South Africa – ever kept him from gratifying his "delight in learning". Entry after entry records the inveteracy with which this indefatigable statesman devoured books. Whether his reading enabled him to bear his political burdens with any more fortitude is doubtful: He complained ceaselessly about what he considered the slavery of public life. Reading certainly did not enable him to conduct his foreign policy with any more skill or success. One frequently hears complaints of the philistinism of politicians. Gladstone's career illustrates how philistinism, far from hampering, might actually discipline a statesman. No one can look dispassionately at Gladstone's career without agreeing with Walter Bagehot that it is not the intellectual who makes the best statesman, but the capable man of business. For Bagehot, the man who most fit this pragmatic bill was Sir Robert Peel, who passed Catholic Emancipation into law, repealed the protectionist Corn Laws, and gave the English their first metropolitan police force. "In common life", Bagehot argued, "we continually see some men as it were scarcely separable from their pursuits ... It is so with Sir Robert Peel. So long as constitutional statesmanship is what it is now, so long as its function is the recording of views of a confused nation, so long as success in it is confined to minds plastic, changeful, administrative, – we must hope for no better man. You have excluded the profound thinker; you must be content with what you can obtain – the business gentleman." A notable exception was the Marquess of Salisbury, the conservative prime minister, about whom Andrew Roberts has written so memorably, who demonstrated not only exceptional perspicacity – he wrote brilliant political journalism for *The Saturday Review* – but consistently sound political judgment, which Gladstone so glaringly lacked.

David Bebbington, Professor of History at the University of Stirling and an authority on nineteenth-century British evangelicalism would doubtless disagree. His Gladstone is not only a profound thinker but a prophetic politician. Bebbington defends these highly arguable claims by pointing out that Gladstone's thinking influenced the contemporary communitarian thinking of Alasdair MacIntyre and Charles Taylor and that his insistence on the community of nations inspired the opponents of Stalin and Hitler. Woodrow Wilson, who had a photograph of the great man hanging over his desk when he was hatching the Fourteen Points, was also a fan. (Teddy Roosevelt spoke for critics of both Gladstone and Wilson when he said "a milk-and-water righteousness unbacked by force is ... as wicked as and even more mischievous than force divorced from righteousness".) Bebbington might have also cited the historian N. G. L. Hammond, who heaped extravagant praise on Gladstone in his *Gladstone and the Irish Nation* (1938), observing of Gladstone's readiness to champion Irish home rule when it was neither popular nor profitable:

> In a world where armed strength was becoming more and more the undisputed master, a great statesman was asking one of the leading peoples to make its undoubted power obey the unarmed voice of justice. It is difficult to believe that Europe would not have had a nobler history if there had been a Gladstone in each of the great States moving so steadily towards war.

The idea of a Europe full of Gladstones is rather dizzying. In any case, it is questionable whether Gladstone would have been effective against Hitler, given his well-known aversion to force, which needlessly cost Gordon his life at Khartoum.

The most balanced chapter of the book reexamines Gladstone's highly eccentric brand of liberalism, to which he converted in 1850 after going to Naples and witnessing how the Neapolitan government was persecuting the liberal minister Carlo Poerio and his followers for their support of the constitution of 1848. Gladstone attended Poerio's trial and was present when the government sentenced him to twenty-four years' hard labor in chains. He even managed to gain admittance to the dungeon where Poerio and thousands of other hapless political prisoners were being left to languish. There Gladstone discovered a truth about European conservatism that he never forgot. As he wrote to Lord Aberdeen, the Foreign Secretary, "It is the wholesale persecution of virtue ... It is the awful profanation of public religion ... It is the perfect prostitution of the judicial office ... It is the savage and cowardly system of moral as well as physical torture ... This is the negation of God erected into a system of government." After this revelation, Gladstonian liberalism was born. What it was exactly is not easy to say. The historian John Vincent says it was "an intelligent way of making the best of a weak international position". Where Disraeli might have sought to create the illusion of state strength, Gladstone worked to create the illusion of state morality. G. M. Young says it consisted of "a horror of all coercive powers, great or small – Empires, Papacies, Parliaments, Sultans, Colonial Offices, Trade Unions – which do not rest their authority on consent, habitual or expressed ..." For Colin Matthew, the editor of Gladstone's diaries, it was "fiscal probity". Bebbington sees it as having been less liberal than communitarian, embodying Gladstone's conviction that "sectional selfishness, at whatever level, must give way to the common good". Whatever it was, it had nothing to do with our own liberalism. In a speech he gave in 1877 he confirmed one of his most fundamental political convictions:

> The best thing a government can do for the people is to help them to help themselves – that is, to remove the obstacles which are in the way of their so helping themselves. I have no faith in any system of Government which strikes at the root of human freedom; and if any Government pretends that it teaches men how to live, that it will undertake the finding for them of what as citizens and fathers of families they ought to find for themselves, the Government, be its intentions

good or bad, is not conferring a benefit, but inflicting an injury on the people.

As Bebbington remarks, "so much for the nanny state". Gladstone was equally illiberal – in our own terms – when it came to the study of the past. The seminaries of self-loathing and grievance into which our liberal elites have turned universities in both America and Great Britain would have appalled Gladstone. In 1885 he put up the money to replace Edinburgh's market cross and in an eloquent speech reaffirmed his Burkean commitment to the past:

> It is in my judgment a great misfortune to any country when it finds itself or thinks itself under the necessity of breaking the ancient traditions. It is a degradation to men to be reduced to the life of the present; and never will he cast forth his hopes, and his views, and his efforts towards the future with due effect and energy, unless at the same time he prizes and holds fondly clasped to his heart the recollections of the past.

Readers of John Henry Newman will be interested to see what Bebbington makes of Newman's influence on his subject. Bebbington is right that Gladstone agreed with Newman that Evangelicals laid too much stress on self-contemplation. What G. M. Young called "the intense introversion of Evangelicalism" was something to which Gladstone was prone all his life. His diary exhibits the anguish this caused him. When he read Newman recommending that we "shun the contemplation of our own feelings, emotions, frame and state of mind" and concentrate instead on Our Lord, he must have felt as though his own predicament had been starkly exposed. Then, too, Gladstone's experience of the rise of unbelief could only have verified the accuracy of Newman's claim that self-contemplation imparted principles that would "destroy all positive doctrine, all ordinances, all good works... foster pride, invite hypocrisy, discourage the weak, and deceive most fatally, while they profess to be the especial antidotes to self-deception". Where Gladstone differed with Newman was in seeing self-deception not in Anglo-Catholicism, which Newman came to see as a "mere theory and illusion, a paper theology that facts contradict" but in Roman Catholicism, about which Gladstone gave out that "no one can become her convert without renouncing his moral and mental freedom". Bebbington is wrong to suggest that by embracing Newman's critique of Evangelicalism, Gladstone was embracing Tractarianism. In his conclusion, Bebbington admits as much himself when he says that Gladstone, after his conversion to liberalism, turned away from Tractarianism, which after all, had been responsible not only for his two best friends, James Hope-Scott and Henry Manning, but also for his sister, Helen, converting to Roman Catholicism. Worst of all, from Gladstone's standpoint, was the effect that Tractarianism had on Newman, from whose desertion, Disraeli rightly predicted, the English Church would never recover.

It was to distance himself from Tractarianism that Gladstone adopted the positions of Broad Churchmanship. Later, it is true, he embraced what Bebbington refers to as "the liberal Catholicism of Charles Gore and his *Lux Mundi* circle that blended high ecclesiastical claims with wide intellectual and social sympathies", but this was something rather different from Tractarianism. And, incidentally, Gore was not a liberal Catholic: he was a liberal High Church Anglican. (Bebbington, like the Reformation historian Diarmaid MacCulloch, plays fast and loose with such terms.) For Bebbington, this later affiliation aligns Gladstone with the future because, as he says, these were the ideas that would "dominate the Church of England into the middle years of the twentieth century" – which is a comical *non-sequitur*. So many of the ideas held by the Church of England "in the middle years of the twentieth century" have since been blithely abandoned.

In refuting the mandarin agnosticism of the biologist T. H. Huxley and the jurist James Fitzjames Stephen, who spoke so frequently against revealed religion at meetings of the Metaphysical Society, Gladstone had recourse to Saint Augustine's famous dictum: *securus judicat orbis terrarum* – "the whole world judges rightly". For Gladstone, Bebbington observes: "Lawyers possessed no monopoly of reasoning skills; nor did the agnostics have a privileged avenue to truth. As in the national debate over the Eastern Question that was raging at the time, the mass of the people rather than the knot of so-called specialists seemed to Gladstone to have right on their side. The general consent of civilized humanity was preferable to the sectional opinion of an intellectual aristocracy". As this shows, Bebbington can be a judicious commentator. Certainly he is right to recognize that in Gladstone's greatest debate, the debate over the Vatican Decrees, "there can be little doubt that Newman showed Gladstone's fears about the loyalties of the Catholic community to be alarmist fantasies".

Despite its inconsistencies, Bebbington's book is worth reading. Hitherto, Perry Butler's monograph, *Gladstone: Church, State and Tractarianism: A Study of His Religious Ideas and Attitudes* (1982) was the only useful study in the field. Now, no one can delve into any matters related to Gladstone without consulting Bebbington, who has provided not only an astute analysis of the religious underpinnings of Gladstonian liberalism but an excellent account of Gladstone's combative response to the rise of unbelief.

On this topic, Richard Shannon, one of Gladstone's more recent biographers, recounts an amusing exchange between Gladstone and Mrs. Humphry Ward regarding her novel *Robert Elsmere* (1886), the hero of which jettisons his faith to pursue philanthropy. Mrs. Humphry Ward asked the veteran bibliophile if he had not read "the new lines of criticism", to which Gladstone fired back: "I don't believe in any new systems ... I cling to the old ... I believe in the degeneracy of man, in the Fall, – in *sin* –in the entirety and virulence of sin, and sin is the great fact of the world."

Here the Grand Old Man was only speaking good sense, though the long-suffering mother of the incorrigible Arnold Ward hardly needed lecturing on the virulence of sin. What was it that Shakespeare once said? "Good wombs have borne bad sons".

Newman and the Idea of Sanctity

When we speak of a saint, we usually have in mind someone of extraordinary holiness, someone of heroic virtue, someone animated by God's love and dedicated to His service. Then, again, we think of someone whose devotion to God is so extraordinary that he commands the veneration of the faithful. And yet when we think of actual saints, we begin to see the inadequacy of such general terms. Although they share a common love of the Creator and a common love of His creatures, the saints are so different, so unique. To name saints dear to the subject of this essay – Saint Paul, Saint Chrysostom, Saint Athanasius, Saint Ambrose, Saint Gregory the First, Saint Leo the Great, Saint Charles Borromeo, Saint Philip Neri – is to be reminded of just how profoundly different the saints are. As Chesterton once observed, "it is a real case against conventional hagiography that it sometimes tends to make all saints seem to be the same. Whereas in fact no men are more different than saints; not even murderers". Our general definitions of sanctity must, therefore, always be a kind of broad-brush shorthand, even if the personal force of sanctity is unmistakable.

In a recent piece in the *Catholic Herald* about Father Dominic Barberi, the Passionist who received Newman into the Church, the author noted:

> Dominic's encounter with Newman at Littlemore in October 1845 may perhaps be only a small part of his story, but it is important nevertheless. This is because Newman himself tells us that he entered the Catholic Church precisely at that moment because of the supernatural qualities he recognised instantly in the Italian missionary. "When his form came into sight, I was moved to the depths in the strangest way", Newman wrote years later. "His very look had about it something holy."

Before meeting Blessed Dominic, Newman might have been intellectually convinced that the Church of Rome was the "one true fold of the Redeemer", but in the presence of Dominic's sanctity he recognized that his heart had come to the same conviction. Then, again, when Dominic wrote that the most formidable obstacles to the true faith in England were "the extreme ignorance and indeed indifference" of the English people in religious matters, he supplied Newman with a good deal of the mission that would animate so much of his future Catholic work, so much of which centered on the fundamental need for sanctity. In this essay, I shall endeavor to capture something of the specific sanctity that can be found in the life and works of Blessed John Henry Newman which sets him apart from other saints and yet makes him so entirely at home in the Communion of Saints.

The first thing that we should bear in mind about Newman when it comes to his sanctity, is that there was nothing sanctimonious about it. In 1850, when a woman wrote to tell him how she and a friend thought him a saint, Newman replied with characteristically witty self-deprecation.

> I return you Miss Moore's letter. You must undeceive her about me, though I suppose she uses words in a general sense. She called Newman a saint. I have nothing of a Saint about me as every one knows, and it is a severe (and salutary) mortification to be thought next door to one. I may have a high view of many things, but it is the consequence of education and of a peculiar cast of intellect – but this is very different from *being* what I admire. I have no tendency to be a saint – it is a sad thing to say. Saints are not literary men, they do not love the classics, they do not write Tales. I may be well enough in my way, but it is not the "high line". People ought to feel this, most people do. But those who are at a distance have fee-fa-fum notions about one. It is enough for me to black the saints' shoes – if St. Philip uses blacking, in heaven.

This confirms something Chesterton once said, in that glorious book of his on Saint Thomas, "The holy man conceals his holiness; that is the one invariable rule".

What gives Newman's sanctity its abiding appeal is that it is rooted in his recognition that sanctity is not something with which most of us are comfortable. Some of this insight came from his own experience. Both his brothers became apostates: one renouncing Christianity for the utopian socialism of Robert Owen and the other leaving Christianity altogether for Unitarianism. Indeed, Frank Newman even went so far as to advocate euthanasia in the pages of the *Spectator*, as you will see in my own latest book, *Newman and his Family*. Then, again, Newman could see from growing up in the Church of England that many English Christians were only nominally Christian: They professed what they scarcely knew how to practice. The Oxford Movement can be seen as an attempt on the part of Newman and his friends to recover the reality of sanctity, not only for that strenuous thing called Anglican theology but for the religious life of individual Anglicans as a whole. Those familiar with that Movement will recall the mockery that greeted the fasts of Newman's friend Richard Hurrell Froude, which he recounted meticulously in diaries published after his early death. Froude's English contemporaries thought fasting ridiculous. They thought self-denial an affront to the dignity of the natural man. In response to Froude's diary entries recounting how he "looked with greediness to see if there was goose on the table for dinner" and how he "meant to have kept a fast and did abstain from dinner, but at tea eat buttered toast", Sir James Fitzjames Stephen, the judge and reviewer, who was also Leslie Stephen's brother and Virginia Woolf's uncle, observed how:

> Luther and Zwingli, Cranmer and Latimer, may still rest in their honoured graves. "Take courage, brother Ridley, we shall light up such a flame in England as shall not soon be put out!" is a prophecy which will not be defeated by the successors of the Oxonian divines ... so long as they shall be able to record, and to publish, contrite reminiscences of a desire for roasted goose, and of an undue indulgence in buttered toast.

Even for Froude sanctity was a novel, strange, foreign thing, though it was also a very attractive thing, especially in an England where, as Stephens shows, the very notion of self-denial had become risible. Newman proved his own sanctity by describing the barriers to sanctity that prevented his contemporaries from emulating the saints and making God's love the center of their lives. In exposing these barriers, Newman showed his contemporaries how they could be overcome. In his sermon, "The Weapons of Saints",

Newman sought to drive home to his Oxford audience just how spiritually revolutionary Christianity was. Before one can grasp what sanctity is, Newman contends, one has to understand the source of sanctity, and here he explicates those unforgettably ringing words from St. Matthew: "Many that are first shall be last, and the last shall be first."

> These words are fulfilled under the Gospel in many ways. Our Saviour in one place applies them to the rejection of the Jews and the calling of the Gentiles; but in the context, in which they stand as I have cited them, they seem to have a further meaning, and to embody a great principle, which we all indeed acknowledge, but are deficient in mastering. Under the dispensation of the Spirit all things were to become new and to be reversed. Strength, numbers, wealth, philosophy, eloquence, craft, experience of life, knowledge of human nature, these are the means by which worldly men have ever gained the world. But in that kingdom which Christ has set up, all is contrariwise. "The weapons of our warfare are not carnal, but mighty through God to the pulling down of strongholds." What was before in honour, has been dishonoured; what before was in dishonour, has come to honour; what before was successful, fails; what before failed, succeeds. What before was great, has become little; what before was little, has become great. Weakness has conquered strength, for the hidden strength of God "is made perfect in weakness". Death has conquered life, for in that death is a more glorious resurrection. Spirit has conquered flesh; for that spirit is an inspiration from above. A new kingdom has been established, not merely different from all kingdoms before it, but contrary to them; a paradox in the eyes of man – the visible rule of the invisible Saviour.

Having reaffirmed the Faith in these clarion terms, Newman could begin to encourage his auditors to see sanctity in less abstract terms. "Now let us apply this great truth to ourselves," he exhorted his listeners:

> for be it ever recollected, *we* are the sons of God, *we* are the soldiers of Christ. The kingdom is within us, and among us, and around us. We are apt to speak of it as a matter of history;

we speak of it as at a distance; but really we are a part of it, or ought to be; and, as we wish to be a living portion of it, which is our only hope of salvation, we must learn what its characters are in order to imitate them.

Newman wrote that in 1837, but it could describe his entire apostolate. In showing the many reasons why men decide against following the saints and making the devout life their own, Newman exhibited something of that psychological acuity which distinguishes so much of his spiritual counsel. In his sermon "Religion a Weariness to the Natural Man" he shows how the world itself disposes us to disparage religion in favor of its own appointments.

> The transactions of worldly business, speculations in trade, ambitious hopes, the pursuit of knowledge, the public occurrences of the day, these find a way directly to the heart; they rouse, they influence. It is superfluous to go about to prove this innate power over us of things of time and sense, to make us think and act. The name of religion, on the other hand, is weak and impotent; it contains no spell to kindle the feelings of man, to make the heart beat with anxiety, and to produce activity and perseverance.

Many have sought deep philosophical reasons for why men will not or cannot believe, but here Newman persuasively shows how much mere worldliness separates creatures from their Creator.

Then, again, Newman gave the devil his due by never underestimating the pride of the natural man. Indeed, he sees "the natural contrariety between man and his Maker" as

> still more strikingly shown by the confession of men of the world who have given some thought to the subject, and have viewed society with somewhat of a philosophical spirit. Such men treat the demands of religion with disrespect and negligence, on the ground of their being unnatural. They say, "It is natural for men to love the world for its own sake; to be engrossed in its pursuits, and to set their hearts on the rewards of industry, on the comforts, luxuries, and pleasures of this life. Man would not be man if he could be made otherwise; he would not be what he was evidently intended for by his Maker."

Keith Thomas, the Fellow of All Souls College, Oxford, who wrote the highly influential history, *Religion and the Decline of Magic* (1971), is something of a tout for the native atheism of the natural man, of which Newman spoke frequently with clairvoyant incisiveness. In his latest book, *The Ends of Life: Roads to Fulfilment in Modern England* (2009), which garnered extravagant praise, Thomas writes of how the goal of his seventeenth- and eighteenth-century English subjects was "subjective happiness". He cites Thomas Hobbes, who, as he says, "observed that what pleased one man displeased another and that total satisfaction was unobtainable, life being a matter of desire succeeding desire, ceasing only in death ..." He also cites John Locke, who thought it was idle to prescribe to others to seek "riches, or bodily delights, or virtue, or contemplation", because, again, every man was different with different desires. For Locke: the mind has a different relish as well as the palate; and you will as fruitlessly endeavor to delight all men with riches or glory (which yet some men put their happiness in) as you would to satisfy all men's hunger with cheese or lobsters, which, though very agreeable and delicious fare to some, are to others extremely nauseous and offensive. Here, where the end of life has been reduced to a question of man's hunger for lobster or cheese, the metaphysical, let alone the theological, hardly registers. One may marvel at the amount of scholarly research Thomas has undertaken to recreate his scrimmage of appetite, but one cannot deny its stubborn reality.

It is helpful to keep Thomas's evocation of the worldliness of post-Reformation England in mind when one reads Newman, because it is against this worldliness that he is always making his appeal for sanctity. For example, he writes:

> Many, indeed, of those unhappy men who have denied the Christian faith, treat the religious principle altogether as a mere unnatural, eccentric state of mind, a peculiar untoward condition of the affections to which weakness will reduce a man, whether it has been brought on by anxiety, oppressive sorrow, bodily disease, excess of imagination or the like, and temporary or permanent according to the circumstances of the disposing cause; a state to which we all are liable, as we are liable to any other mental injury, but unmanly and unworthy of our dignity as rational beings.

Here, also, is a good example of that barristerial skill which enabled Newman to identify and frame the arguments of opponents better than the opponents themselves.

Now, from our own twenty-first century standpoint, we might be inclined to imagine the nineteenth-century audience to which Newman directed his sermons more religious than the men of our time. But, in fact, Newman's contemporaries, like ours, were often bitterly opposed to anything that required them to take the obligations of religion seriously. And Newman's account of why this should be the case is as compelling to us as it must have been to his own contemporaries. "Truly it is a weariness to the natural man to serve God humbly and in obscurity", he reminded his readers in one of his sermons.

> It is very wearisome, and very monotonous, to go on day after day watching all we do and think, detecting our secret failings, denying ourselves, creating within us, under God's grace, those parts of the Christian character in which we are deficient; wearisome to learn modesty, love of insignificance, willingness to be thought little of, backwardness to clear ourselves when slandered, and readiness to confess when we are wrong; to learn to have no cares for this world, neither to hope nor to fear, but to be resigned and contented!

Having imparted these uncomfortable truths, Newman poses an even more unpleasant question: "Can we doubt that man's will runs contrary to God's will – that the view which the inspired word takes of our present life, and of our destiny, does not satisfy us, as it rightly ought to do? that Christ hath no form nor comeliness in our eyes; and though we see Him, we see no desirable beauty in Him?" Here is the natural man's view of things, stripped of all pretence and dissimulation, and for Newman there is a reason why it should be so unrelievedly bleak. "The nature of man is flesh," Newman says, "and that which is born of the flesh is flesh, and ever must so remain; it never can discern, love, accept, the holy doctrines of the Gospel. It will occupy itself in various ways, it will take interest in things of sense and time, but it can never be religious. It is at enmity with God."

Many of those who heard Newman preach his sermons at the Church of Saint Mary the Virgin in Oxford left accounts of how moving they were, but, here, where he does not mince his words, we can also appreciate how truly terrifying they could be.

> If our hearts are by nature set on the world for its own sake, and the world is one day to pass away, what are they to be set on, what to delight in, then? Say, how will the soul feel when, stripped of its present attire, which the world bestows, it stands naked and shuddering before the pure, tranquil, and severe majesty of the Lord its God, its most merciful, yet dishonoured Maker and Saviour? What are to be the pleasures of the soul in another life? Can they be the same as they are here? They cannot; Scripture tells us they cannot; the world passeth away – now what is there left to love and enjoy through a long eternity? What a dark, forlorn, miserable eternity that will be!

The moral Newman draws from these observations could not be more uncompromising. Nevertheless, his very disavowal of compromise reminds us that the appeal of sanctity is of a very serious urgency. Newman ends the sermon:

> It is then plain enough though Scripture said not a word on the subject, that if we would be happy in the world to come, we must make us new hearts, and begin to love the things we naturally do not love. Viewing it as a practical point, the end of the whole matter is this, we must be changed; for we cannot, we cannot expect the system of the universe to come over to us; the inhabitants of heaven, the numberless creations of Angels, the glorious company of the Apostles, the goodly fellowship of the Prophets, the noble army of Martyrs, the holy Church universal, the Will and Attributes of God, these are fixed. We must go over to them. In our Saviour's own authoritative words: "Verily, verily, except a man be born again, he cannot see the kingdom of God." ... It is not His loss that we love Him not, it is our loss. He is All-blessed whatever becomes of us. He is not less blessed because we are far from Him. It is we who are not blessed, except as we approach Him, except as we are like Him, except as we love Him. Woe unto us, if in the day in which He comes from Heaven we see nothing desirable or gracious in His wounds; but instead, have made for ourselves an ideal blessedness, different from that which will be manifested to us in Him.

> Woe unto us, if we have made pride, or selfishness, or the carnal mind, our standard of perfection and truth; if our eyes have grown dim, and our hearts gross, as regards the true light of men, and the glory of the Eternal Father. May He Himself save us from our self-delusions, whatever they are, and enable us to give up this world, that we may gain the next; – and to rejoice in Him, who had no home of His own, no place to lay His head, who was poor and lowly, and despised and rejected, and tormented and slain!

Here, again, Chesterton supplies a useful gloss. In the Father Brown stories, that sage detective has occasion to observe how "no man's really any good till he knows how bad he is, or might be ... till he's squeezed out of his soul the last drop of the oil of the Pharisees".

If the passion and pride of the natural man are barriers to sanctity, so too can be his intelligence, the very thing that should lead him to grasp the intellectual force of the Faith. In his sermon, "Truth Hidden When Not Sought After", Newman anticipated the fervor of those evangelical atheists of our own day who seek to disabuse us of what they consider the illusions of faith. And here again, Newman characteristically attends to the true attitudes of men, not what we might like those attitudes to be. "Let us honestly confess what is certain," he urges his listeners, "that not the ignorant, or weakminded, or dull, or enthusiastic, or extravagant only turn their ears from the Truth ... but also men of powerful minds, keen perceptions, extended views, ample and various knowledge." In his Oxford University sermons, Newman spoke brilliantly of how right reason cooperates with and supports faith; but he was also aware of how errant reason disables faith by insisting that intellect alone can verify the objects of faith. For Newman:

> the Christian revelation addresses itself to our hearts, to our love of truth and goodness, our fear of sinning, and our desire to gain God's favour; and quickness, sagacity, depth of thought, strength of mind, power of comprehension, perception of the beautiful, power of language, and the like, though they are excellent gifts, are clearly quite of a different kind from these spiritual excellences – a man may have the one without having the other. *This*, then, is the plain reason why able, or again why learned men are so often defective

> Christians, because there is no necessary connexion between faith and ability; because faith is one thing and ability is another; because ability of mind is a *gift*, and faith is a *grace*.

Then, again, in the highly intelligent and the dull alike, Newman recognized that there could be a tendency to spiritual sloth, a lazy indifference to the obligations of faith.

> Nothing is more common than to think that we shall gain religious knowledge as a thing of course, without express trouble on our part. Though there is no art or business of this world which is learned without time and exertion, yet it is commonly conceived that the knowledge of God and our duty will come as if by accident or by a natural process. Men go by their feelings and likings; they take up what is popular, or what comes first to hand. They think it much if they now and then have serious thoughts, if they now and then open the Bible; and their minds recur with satisfaction to such seasons, as if they had done some very great thing, never remembering that to seek and gain religious truth is a long and systematic work. And others think that education will do every thing for them, and that if they learn to read, and use religious words, they understand religion itself.

For Newman, nothing could be further from the truth. In one of his greatest sermons, "Unreal Words", preached in 1839, when he had first come to see the fundamental illegitimacy of the National Church, he warned his contemporaries against confusing not only profession with practise but profession with faith. To gain the faith, he insisted, we must do more than merely profess, we must embody the faith.

In a sermon that Newman wrote as a Catholic, aptly entitled "Nature and Grace", he called attention to another barrier to sanctity and that is the tendency on the part of Catholics to blend in, assimilate, and exchange their Catholic identity for a false accord with their non-Catholic neighbors. Speaking to his parishioners at the Birmingham Oratory, Newman called attention to how chummy they tended to be with those non-Catholic neighbors who, although contemptuous of the doctrines of the faith of Rome, were prepared to advance the political interests of Catholics for their own political gain. In this chumminess, Newman saw a distinct danger.

I do not mean to say that you are not bound to cultivate peace with all men, and to do them all the offices of charity in your power. Of course you are, and if they respect, esteem, and love you, it redounds to your praise and will gain you a reward; but I mean more than this; I mean they do *not* respect you, but they like you, because they think of you as of themselves, they see no difference between themselves and you. This is the very reason why they so often take your part, and assert or defend your political rights. Here again, there is a sense, of course, in which our civil rights may be advocated by Protestants without any reflection on us, and with honour to them. We are like others in this, that we are men; that we are members of the same state with them, subjects, contented subjects, of the same Sovereign, that we have a dependence on them, and have them dependent on us; that, like them, we feel pain when ill-used, and are grateful when well-treated. We need not be ashamed of a fellowship like this, and those who recognise it in us are generous in doing so. But we have much cause to be ashamed, and much cause to be anxious what God thinks of us, if we gain their support by giving them a false impression in our persons of what the Catholic Church is and what Catholics are bound to be, what bound to believe, and to do; and is not this the case often, my brethren, that the world takes up your interests, because you share its sins?

Here, faced as we are, with forces within our own country working aggressively to foist a Common Core curriculum on our Catholic elementary schools that would effectively uncatholicize those schools or, worse, healthcare mandates that have been expressly designed to coerce us into conniving in contraception, abortion, and sterilization, we can see the point of Newman's warning.

Here we can also see an illustration of Newman's conviction that there are only two ultimate alternatives open to men, Catholicism or atheism. In a letter to his good friend Rowland Blennerhassett, he wrote of how, as he said:

> I am very much grieved, but not surprised, at what you tell me about the rising talent of Oxford. In my own conviction, there is no medium *logically* between Catholicism and Atheism, and it is a matter of chance how far an inquirer, who

> does not go in the right direction, will go in the wrong. He goes a certain way – gets tired, or frightened – and stops – or the duties of life stop his inquiries – or secular motives come in, and he catches at some half reasons or other, and makes up a case for remaining at the point where he is. Or the influence of good men hinder his proceeding – Most men then settle down into something or other, as life goes on, short of the two extremes – still, as a matter of logic, the choice lies, I think, between those two.

How arresting that insight is: "the influence of good men hinder his proceeding". Some might find that an insupportable paradox, but Newman, who knew the ways of the world, knew how goodness can often miscarry in the world.

If Newman uncovered the many obstacles that can dissuade us from living the devout life, he was also full of sound advice as to how we should set about scaling those obstacles. And what is most encouraging about him is that he appreciates that embracing sanctity is not some grandiose or complicated undertaking, but, instead, a quotidian discipline. One thinks of those famous lines from "Lead, Kindly Light" –

> Lead, Kindly Light, amidst the encircling gloom,
>   Lead Thou me on!
> The night is dark, and I am far from home,
>   Lead Thou me on!
> Keep Thou my feet; I do not ask to see
> The distant scene – one step enough for me.

In his *Meditations and Devotions*, Newman even gives his readers a sort of road map to sanctity, and it is anything but labyrinthine. "He, then, is perfect", he says:

> who does the work of the day perfectly, and we need not go beyond this to seek for perfection. You need not go out of the *round* of the day. I insist on this because I think it will simplify our views, and fix our exertions on a definite aim. If you ask me what you are to do in order to be perfect, I say, first –
>
> Do not lie in bed beyond the due time of rising;
> give your first thoughts to God;

> make a good visit to the Blessed Sacrament;
> say the Angelus devoutly;
> eat and drink to God's glory;
> say the Rosary well;
> be recollected; keep out bad thoughts;
> make your evening meditation well;
> examine yourself daily;
> go to bed in good time, and you are already perfect.

Yet on this "short road to perfection", as he called it, Newman realized that we naturally need encouragement, a model, if you will. And for Newman no one is better for this purpose than Our Lady. In another Catholic sermon entitled "The Glories of Mary for the Sake of her Son", Newman explains how Mary is a pattern of our faith, a guide to the devout life, precisely because she is a remedy for the sins of Adam and Eve. Thus, in one of the most moving passages in all of his sermons, Newman speaks of how "kings of the earth, when they have sons born to them... honour the day, or the place, or the heralds of the auspicious event, with some corresponding mark of favour". And he insists that "the coming of Emmanuel" did not "innovate on the world's established custom".

> It was a season of grace and prodigy, and these were to be exhibited in a special manner in the person of His Mother. The course of ages was to be reversed; the tradition of evil was to be broken; a gate of light was to be opened amid the darkness, for the coming of the Just; – a Virgin conceived and bore Him. It was fitting, for His honour and glory, that she, who was the instrument of His bodily presence, should first be a miracle of His grace; it was fitting that she should triumph, where Eve had failed, and should "bruise the serpent's head" by the spotlessness of her sanctity. In some respects, indeed, the curse was not reversed; Mary came into a fallen world, and resigned herself to its laws; she, as also the Son she bore, was exposed to pain of soul and body, she was subjected to death; but she was not put under the power of sin. As grace was infused into Adam from the first moment of his creation, so that he never had experience of his natural poverty, till sin reduced him to it; so was grace given from the first in still ampler measure to Mary, and she

> never incurred, in fact, Adam's deprivation. She began where others end, whether in knowledge or in love. She was from the first clothed in sanctity, destined for perseverance, luminous and glorious in God's sight, and incessantly employed in meritorious acts, which continued till her last breath. Hers was emphatically "the path of the just, which, as the shining light, goeth forward and increaseth even to the perfect day"; and sinlessness in thought, word, and deed, in small things as well as great, in venial matters as well as grievous, is surely but the natural and obvious sequel of such a beginning. If Adam might have kept himself from sin in his first state, much more shall we expect immaculate perfection in Mary.

Much is made of the beauty of Newman's prose style but here is a good example of how it is the beauty of the content that makes possible the beauty of the style. For another example of this we can go to the conclusion of this wonderful sermon, where Newman leaves off writing prose altogether and instead takes up the language of prayer, the same language that we must employ to emulate the essence of Newman's sanctity.

> Such art thou, Holy Mother, in the creed and in the worship of the Church, the defence of many truths, the grace and smiling light of every devotion. In thee, O Mary, is fulfilled, as we can bear it, an original purpose of the Most High. He once had meant to come on earth in heavenly glory, but we sinned; and then He could not safely visit us, except with a shrouded radiance and a bedimmed Majesty, for He was God. So He came Himself in weakness, not in power; and He sent thee, a creature, in His stead, with a creature's comeliness and lustre suited to our state. And now thy very face and form, dear Mother, speak to us of the Eternal; not like earthly beauty, dangerous to look upon, but like the morning star, which is thy emblem, bright and musical, breathing purity, telling of heaven, and infusing peace. O harbinger of day! O hope of the pilgrim! lead us still as thou hast led; in the dark night, across the bleak wilderness, guide us on to our Lord Jesus, guide us home.

The Great Temple

Basilica: The Splendour and the Scandal: Building St. Peter's, R. A. Scotti. Viking. 299 pages.

Recently, in a special history issue of *The Times Literary Supplement*, various historians noted the resurgence of popular history. Tourism, television and mass education have played some part in this, but not as much, I would argue, as the unreliability of most academic history. One can see this most strikingly in art history. The anti-Catholic bias that the Swiss historian Jacob Burckhardt (1818–97) introduced into the study of Catholic art has proven stubbornly tenacious. Yet to behold St. Peter's is to see how profoundly false such bias is. No one can take in that incomparable pile and maintain that it was built by architects who were only humoring the faith of their patrons. All the successive architects of the basilica – Michelangelo, Bramante, Raphael, Giacomo della Porta, Bernini – were devout Catholics, and in their collective work, as R. A. Scotti affirms in her exuberant popular history, they "incised a symbol of the transcendent Christ". That symbol is not about neo-Platonism or humanist skepticism but about the Church on earth: the living Faith. By putting this essential truth at the very heart of her book Scotti restores balance to a subject that is often replete with learned distortion.

The history of the building of St. Peter's is involved. Constantine built Old St. Peter's in 342 on the site of the martyrdom of St. Peter near Nero's hippodrome below the Vatican Hill. In 1505 Pope Julius II undertook the rebuilding of the basilica and named Bramante his chief architect. After Julius's death in 1513 and Bramante's in 1514, Pope Leo X appointed Peruzzi and Raphael as joint chief architects. In 1520, Raphael died after proposing a Latin-cross plan for the basilica, which Michelangelo's Greek-cross plan, modified by Maderno in 1603 with the addition of a long nave, finally supplanted. In 1527, the Holy Roman Emperor Charles V and his Lutheran troops sacked Rome and, true to the sanctimonious barbarism of Luther, torched all the books in the Stanze. In the 1530s, Antonio de Sangallo the

Younger restored the building. In 1547, Pope Paul III appointed the 71-year-old Michelangelo as chief architect, who contributed the outer walls, the attic storey, and the massive drum. Between 1585 and 1590, the dome was designed and executed by Michelangelo's pupil, Giacomo della Porta – whom Scotti calls "the unsung hero" of the basilica. From 1607 to 1612 Borromini built the benediction loggia over the narthex, or the porch in front of the church. The church's magnificent baldacchino was designed by Bernini in 1624, as was the dazzling piazza between 1656 and 1667.

Scotti is the ideal armchair guide. Speaking of Bernini, who labored on the basilica for fifty-one years, she says: "In his final years, he never climbed a scaffold without an apprentice beside him for fear that he would become so absorbed in his construction that he might lose his footing and fall." Artists were not the only ones dedicated to the building. Of Pope Sixtus V, she writes: "He may have been history's first modern manager, because his only motivation was a desire to get the job done." Since the job in this case included completing the Gregorian chapel, transferring Cleopatra's Needle from the south side of the basilica to the center of St. Peter's Square, and raising the glorious dome of St. Peter's, the efficiency of Sixtus can hardly be exaggerated, especially if one considers that his pontificate spanned only five years.

Apropos the eventual design of the basilica, Scotti makes a sound point when she says:

> Few buildings have less of Alberti's *concinnitas* than the basilica of St. Peter. Through the years, architects and pontiffs followed one another in rapid and sometimes wanton succession... The perfectly proportioned Renaissance architecture, each part in exact geometric ratio to the other and to the whole, seems too tidy for such a sprawling, messy, overreaching institution as the Church of Rome. The baroque is its truer reflection.

Why? "The static perfection of the Renaissance was the art of the elite", she says. "The hot, intense Baroque was art to move the masses. It was popular art in the truest sense – cinematic special effects without a camera lens." Here she echoes another popular historian, Kenneth Clark, who broke with ingrained British prejudice when he remarked that "the great achievement of the Catholic Church lay in harmonizing, humanizing, civilizing the deepest impulses of ordinary, ignorant people". Thus, in his popular series, *Civilization* (1969), Clark showed how the Faith was the great mainstay of Western culture. Now that that culture is imperiled by barbarians outside and inside the gates, it is more crucial than ever to understand how the Faith can indeed harmonize, humanize, and civilize.

Some of Scotti's best passages pertain to the patron popes who commissioned the building of the basilica. About Julius II, she writes:

> Like the Medici in the previous century, he was a one-man MoMA, underwriting the best contemporary artists. With charm, threats, bribes, and flattery, he wheedled work from them that they had never shown themselves capable of before. The art that he commissioned became the masterpieces of Western civilization.

About Clement VII who presided over the papacy during the sack of Rome, she writes: "With the possible exception of Hamlet, no figure real or imagined has been a more infamous vacillator than this second Medici pope." And yet this same irresolute man commissioned Michelangelo to paint "The Last Judgment". Urban VIII was the polar opposite of indecisive: he never wavered in his support of Bernini, the devout Neapolitan whom he would commission to give St. Peter's its final Baroque splendor. And yet about this learned, charming, capable pope, Scotti writes:

> He is not remembered as the humanist scholar who consecrated St. Peter's Basilica, gave Bernini to Rome, or encouraged Galileo. Instead, he is dismissed as the narrow, close-minded pope who censured the scientist. In the annals of history, a very human story of friends turning against each other has been retold as the quintessential clash of faith and reason, religion and science.

With her brisk, lively account, Scotti joins the distinguished band of amateur historians from Vasari to Henry James who have given eloquent testimony to the power of Catholic art. Indeed, James was memorably brilliant in his own recollections of how the great basilica affected him. In *Italian Hours* (1909), he wrote:

> A good Catholic, I suppose, is the same Catholic anywhere before the grandest as well as the humblest altars; but to a visitor not formally enrolled St. Peter's speaks less of aspiration than of full and convenient assurance. The soul infinitely expands there ... When you are weary of the swarming democracy of your fellow-tourists, of the unremunerative aspects of human nature on Corso and Pincio, of the oppressively frequent combination of coronets on carriage panels and stupid faces in carriages, of addled brains and lacquered boots, of ruin and dirt and decay ... of the myriad tokens of a halting civilization, the image of the great temple depresses the balance of your doubts, seems to rise above even the highest tide of vulgarity and makes you still believe in the heroic will and the heroic act. It's a relief, in other words, to feel that there's nothing but a cab-fare between your pessimism and one of the greatest of human achievements.

It is a tribute to Scotti's incisiveness that she succeeds so admirably in disentangling that achievement's tangled history. *Basilica* is popular history that will stay popular long after many academic titles are forgotten.

G. K. CHESTERTON
AND THE APPEAL OF REALITY

Chesterton: A Biography, Ian Ker. Oxford University Press. 747 pages.

MANY WILL KNOW IAN KER as the author of the definitive life of John Henry Newman. Now he has focused his biographical and critical skills on G. K. Chesterton (1874–1936), the great journalist, critic, poet, novelist, and biographer, and the result is a marvelously discriminating portrait that does welcome justice to the full richness of Chesterton's hitherto undervalued work.

In his biography of Newman, Ker encapsulated his subject's quest for reality by translating Newman's motto, *Ex umbria et imaginibus in veritatem*: "Out of unreality into Reality". In this new biography, Ker persuasively argues that Chesterton was Newman's successor precisely because he shared the nineteenth-century convert's passion for reality, a quality which Hilaire Belloc also discerned in his friend. "Truth had for him", Belloc recalled, "the immediate attraction of an appetite. He was hungry for reality. But what is much more, he could not conceive of himself except as satisfying that hunger ... it was not possible for him to hold anything worth holding that was not connected with the truth as a whole."

Thus, Chesterton was a servant of truth, as well as a champion of reality, and it is these qualities together that make him so salutary a figure for our own age, which not only refuses to acknowledge objective truth but embraces unreality with frenetic abandon. The entertainer in Chesterton might have been intent on making his readers laugh, but he also extolled what many in his time and our own wish to see diminished, including the Christian tradition, the sanctity of life, the dignity of the family, and personal liberty, and it is refreshing to see these vital aspects of the man given their prophetic due.

With the same critical distillation that distinguished his life of

Newman, Ker has sifted through Chesterton's massive output to identify several major themes, which, taken together, demonstrate the unity and depth of his thought. In his introduction, Ker writes:

> Chesterton's philosophy of wonder ... is well known, but I have highlighted the complementary principle of limitation that informs all his thinking about art, literature, politics, and religion. Linked, too, to his philosophy of wonder is his concept of the role of the imagination in enabling us to see the familiar afresh, as it were for the first time.

Of course, laughter and paradox were the means with which Chesterton mapped out his "philosophy of wonder", and he was never more profound than when making his readers laugh. Thus, in *Where All Roads Lead* (1922), Chesterton called attention to a fact that Richard Dawkins and his friends have overlooked: "If there were no God, there would be no atheists." Then, again, in his novel, *Manalive* (1915), he offered this useful distinction: "As for science and religion, the known and admitted facts are few and plain enough. All that the parsons say is unproved. All that the doctors say is disproved." And there is this *aperçu* from one of his pieces in *The Illustrated London News* (1925):

> When we look at [a man] for the very first time, in the full and frank use of our commonsense, we never *do* look at him as an animal ... If somebody said, "There is another animal in the garden", and you found it was the Vicar, you would be surprised.

Unlike other commentators, who insist on seeing Chesterton the thinker as somehow separate from Chesterton the funny man, Ker appreciates how the two were fused. For Chesterton, our misconceptions, our lies, our manifold allegiances to unreality cry out for exposure, and it was his abiding sense of *caritas*, no less than his keen sense of humor that impelled him to use paradox to show his readers the comic discrepancies between truth and falsehood. Every reader will have his favorite Chestertonian sallies. One of mine is from his introduction to *David Copperfield*:

> The wise old fairy tales never were so silly as to say that the prince and the princess lived peacefully ever afterwards. The

> fairy tales said that the prince and princess lived happily ever afterwards; and so they did. They lived happily, although it is very likely that from time to time they threw the furniture at each other. Most marriages, I think, are happy marriages; but there is no such thing as a contented marriage. The whole pleasure of marriage is that it is a perpetual crisis.

Marriage meant a good deal to Chesterton, and it is another merit of Ker's life that he shows how it at once saved and renewed his wayward hero. But to appreciate this fully, one needs to know something of Chesterton's life.

Born on Campden Hill in 1874, Chesterton was educated at Saint Paul's School and the Slade School. His father was the head of a firm of estate agents and his mother, Marie Louise Grosjean, was of Franco-Scottish ancestry. Her Aberdeen forbears, the Keiths, gave Gilbert his middle name. A dilatory learner, Chesterton never shone in his studies, though he excelled at comic drawing. It was after becoming a publisher's reader that he took up journalism and for the rest of his life he would see himself as a journalist, who only wrote novels and plays, poetry and biographies as a sideline.

This insistence on Chesterton's part that he was only a journalist has always led some to conclude that he was shallow. Yet, in a piece on Ferdinand Foch, which would have amused his mother, he gave the lie to such unjust denigration.

> There was a great deal about Foch that was intensely and peculiarly French. Nobody but a Frenchman would have launched that direct and yet dazzling epigram in the midst of the Battle of the Marne: "My right gives way; my left retreats; situation excellent; I attack." Where that phrase was so typically French is that it has three separate meanings, and they are all true. A superficial person will take it as a fine piece of faronade, a romantic defiance and refusal to accept defeat. A more sagacious person will see that it is a piece of irony almost worthy of Voltaire ... The most sagacious person will observe that it was also a piece of cold, hard, scientific fact. It really was true that the Germans pursuing the Allied retreat on one side created the strain and the weak point at which Foch suddenly struck. That is the French genius; to say things that only look witty and are also wise. That is the

achievement of all French literature and philosophy; it is the supreme and splendid triumph of looking shallow, and being deep.

Given his marked differences with the Modernists, it is ironic that Chesterton should have grown up in Bedford Park, London's first garden suburb, where W. B. Yeats also grew up. Chesterton and Yeats make for a lively contrast. Both inspired rhetoricians, they could not have taken more different roads philosophically. In 1922, Chesterton converted to Rome, what he called the "rock of reality", while Yeats left the Protestant agnosticism bequeathed him by his father to convert to the table tapping and hocus-pocus of Madame Blavatsky. Chesterton and Yeats also differed in their view of the common man. Yeats, the last hurrah of the Anglo-Irish ascendancy that had produced Swift and Burke, always took a very seigniorial line with his Catholic countrymen, speaking of them by turns as having been "born in the peasant's cot / where men may forgive if the belly gain", "fumbling in a greasy till", "adding the halfpence to the pence / and prayer to shivering prayer", and, most abusively, as "base born products of base beds". Chesterton, by contrast, exulted in the common man. Indeed, as Yeats's friend Ezra Pound once observed, "Chesterton *is* the mob".

On this theme, which runs throughout Chesterton's work, Ker is wonderfully revelatory. As he points out, "aversion to the masses, Chesterton dares to suggest, is really aversion to their energy. The misanthropes pretend that they despise humanity for its weakness. As a matter of fact, they hate it for its strength." For Chesterton, only the humble can appreciate the "colossal vision" of "things as they are". The intellectuals who looked down on the common man – especially such progressives as Carlyle, Shaw, and Nietzsche – were heretics in his eyes precisely because they discounted the good sense of the common man.

The amount of lasting work that Chesterton produced despite his delight in the bonhomie of Fleet Street, where he wrote for the liberal papers *The Speaker* and *The Daily News*, was impressive. One can point to his novels, *The Napoleon of Notting Hill* (1904) and *The Man Who Was Thursday* (1908); to his great Father Brown stories; to his critical studies of Robert Browning and Charles Dickens; and to his wonderfully witty essays, his "tremendous trifles", in which he managed to pack such a wealth of insight.

Chesterton's marriage to Frances Alice Blogg in 1901 transformed his life. In 1909, Frances had the good sense to remove her husband to Beaconsfield, far away from the beckoning public houses of Fleet Street. She also moved him towards the Catholic faith. A devout Anglo-Catholic, Frances tutored her husband in many aspects of Christian orthodoxy in which his upbringing had left him ignorant. Without her benign influence, it is fair to say, Chesterton might never have managed his greatest works, including his works of apologetics, *Orthodoxy* (1908) and *The Everlasting Man* (1922), and his brilliant biographies, *St. Francis of Assisi* (1922) and *St. Thomas Aquinas* (1933), the last of which Etienne Gilson considered the best book ever written about Aquinas.

Frances's eminently sensible voice complements Chesterton's own throughout the book. Asked during the couple's hectic American lecture tour what her plans were for the future, she replied that she was "organizing a campaign for the emancipation of the wives of famous men". Ker also includes the voices of many other contemporaries. When the Chestertons met Ezra Pound in Rapallo, and he told them that his neighbor Max Beerbohm was backing a financial scheme of his to save the world, Beerbohm bemusedly responded to Chesterton's secretary: "Am I? One has only to smile, look pleasant and avoid an argument to be accused of something one knows nothing about." Shaw, Belloc, and Wells also figure prominently in the festivities.

Ker is excellent on Chesterton the critic, showing how trenchant he was not only on his beloved Dickens but on the Victorians as a whole. In *The Victorian Age in Literature* (1913) Chesterton described how the English might have resisted the French Revolution but underwent a revolution of their own when the rich used their game laws and enclosures to turn England into a land not of common landowners but landlords, who then set about making the rationalism of Bentham, Mill, Darwin, and Huxley the new national faith. And in response to these depredations, Chesterton saw a series of spirited counterattacks, launched not only by the Romantic poets but by Cobbett, Carlyle, Newman, Dickens, Ruskin, Arnold, and the Pre-Raphaelites. The Victorian middle classes accepted the revolution of their oligarchs to avoid a more drastic democratic revolution, but, as Chesterton recognized, this only emboldened the "enemies of the Victorian compromise" to intensify their own counter revolutions. That Chesterton mounted these barricades himself only reinforces Ker's point that he belongs in the company of Newman and the other Victorian sages.

Ker highlights the magnanimity of Chesterton. Again, like Newman, he looked for what was good in those he criticized, even those, like Matthew Arnold, who disparaged his religious convictions. In his biography of the painter G. F. Watts, for example, he has occasion to praise Watts's great portrait of Arnold, about which he says:

> The portrait-painter of Matthew Arnold obviously ought not to understand him, since he did not understand himself. And the bewilderment which the artist felt for those few hours, reproduced in a perfect, almost an immortal picture, the bewilderment which the sitter felt from the cradle to the grave.

Most critics would have left matters at that, but how typical of Chesterton to add that "the bewilderment of Matthew Arnold was more noble and faithful than most men's certainty".

In drawing his own portrait of Chesterton, Ker exercises an artful self-effacement which lets the inimitable wit and wisdom of his subject take center stage. In this, he embraces something of his subject's own respect for limitation. As a narrator, Ker reminds one of James Joyce's artist, "within or beyond or above his handiwork, invisible, refined out of existence ... paring his fingernails". Rather than interjecting his own views into those of Chesterton, or, worse, paraphrasing him, Ker allows his eloquent subject to speak for himself. And as a result the book is not only laugh-aloud funny but full of surprise and charm and profound good sense.

There are some genuinely good books on Chesterton. Maisie Ward, who knew the great man, wrote a superb biography in 1944. William Oddie recently wrote a groundbreaking study of Chesterton's early life. D. J. Conlon edited two volumes of criticism on Chesterton by the likes of T. S. Eliot, Auden, V. S. Pritchett, John Gross, Kingsley Amis, P. J. Kavanagh, and Wilfrid Sheed. But the need for a proper critical biography has long been acknowledged and it is this which Ker has splendidly supplied. Now, and for the foreseeable future, for any true understanding of the scope of Chesterton's achievement, one which captures not only the sage but the good, gentle, generous man, Ker's biography will be indispensable.

The Figure in the Carpet Slippers

Auden and Christianity, Arthur Kirsch. Yale University Press. 240 pages.

"The port from which I set out", Henry James told a friend when he was 57, "was, I think, the *essential loneliness* of my life – and it seems to be the port... to which my course again finally directs itself". Auden might have said the same. His brother John confirms this: "Seen unawares in an armchair, *The Times* crossword on his knee, a vodka martini by his side and cigarette-ends covering large dishes, there was an isolation and sadness which arose from his uprooted and solitary existence." In his long introspective poem "New Year Letter", written after he had settled in America in 1939, Auden wrote that "aloneness is man's real condition". Yet unlike James, Auden understood aloneness in Christian terms. As he jotted down in a notebook, "in every man there is a loneliness, an inner chamber of peculiar life into which God only can enter". For Auden, learning to hear what God had to say in that chamber was the essence of prayer. In a haiku written towards the end of his life he wrote: "He has never seen God / but once or twice he believes / he has heard Him."

Auden has never wanted for critical attention. Edward Mendelson, Anthony Hecht, and John Fuller have all written full-dress commentaries. Randall Jarrell and Philip Larkin praised his versatility, while deploring what they saw as the deterioration in his later works. He has also been the subject of biographies by Humphrey Carpenter and John Davenport-Hines. And the object of affectionate raillery: George Orwell called him "the high-water mark of Socialist literature, a sort of gutless Kipling" and Seamus Heaney said he resembled in his later years "an ample, flopping, ambulatory volume of the *Oxford English Dictionary* in carpet slippers". Evelyn Waugh was the wittiest of his critics. In a review in 1939, he observed, "At certain seasons, the critics seem to set out piously to find a reincarnation of Shelley ... A year or two ago they ... exhibited Mr. Auden. It is unfair to transfer to him the reproach that properly belongs to them. His work is awkward and dull, but it is no fault of his that he has become a public bore."

Nearly thirty years later, Auden would review *A Little Learning* (1964) and compliment Waugh on his "lucidity and elegance of verbal expression". He forgave those who trespassed against him.

None of Auden's critics have hitherto delineated the unifying Christian pattern in his work. In *Auden and Christianity*, Arthur Kirsch brilliantly supplies this omission. The book is a model of judicious, civilized criticism, which deserves a wide readership. Those already familiar with Auden will have their fondness for "Horae Canonicae" and "For the Time Being" renewed and those unfamiliar with him will find the perfect introduction to a man who was not only an accomplished poet but a crack critic.

Throughout the 1930s it was Auden's ambition to find a form "that's large enough to swim in / And talk on any subject that I choose / From natural scenery to men and women / Myself, the arts, the European news". No sooner had he found this form than the pilgrim in him became restive. He no longer aspired to become what he called "a patriot of the Now". As Europe resumed the war it had left unfinished in the trenches, Auden's faith in Marxism lapsed. His interest in politics and psychology gave way to absorption in the springs of love. "The first criterion of success in any human activity, the necessary preliminary", he wrote, "whether to scientific discovery or to artistic vision is intensity of attention, or, less pompously, love". This exposed the futility of:

> Ashamed civilians come to grief
> In brotherhoods without belief,
> Whose good intentions cannot cure
> The actual evils they endure ...

Still, he never underestimated the allure of hopelessness. "Good Friday", he once said, "is easy to accept: what scandalizes us is Easter. Modern man finds a happy ending, a final victory of Love over the Prince of this World very hard to swallow." In this, modern man was like Ahab, unwilling to relinquish his identifying despair.

As Prof. Kirsch shows, in a lively discussion of his subject's criticism, when Auden looked at the approved sages of the 1930s – Blake, Lawrence, Freud, Marx – he began to see only Christian heretics in disguise and found himself returning willy-nilly to the High Anglicanism of his childhood. Confronted with Hitler's rejection of Christianity, he realized he had a choice to make. "Unless one was prepared to take a relativist view that all values are a matter of personal taste, one could hardly avoid asking the question: 'If, as I am convinced, the Nazis are wrong and we are right, what is it that validates our values and invalidates theirs?'" (The recrudescence of anti-Christian Islam has yet to inspire contemporary Europe with any comparable clarity of mind.) Then, in 1937, Auden traveled to Barcelona to cover the Spanish Civil War and was surprised to find how much shut churches offended him.

Reading Charles Williams's *The Descent of the Dove* (1939), an inquiry into history and the Holy Ghost, Auden discovered the work of Kierkegaard, which convinced him of the role the individual must play in holy history. As he wrote in a later essay, "the liturgy uses *we* for the general confession because each of us is in part responsible for the sins of our neighbor but in the creed it says *credo*, not *credamus* – nobody can put the responsibility for his faith upon others". This responsibility first presented itself to Auden one summer night in 1933, when he was sitting on a lawn with some friends and felt for the first time what it means to love one's neighbor as oneself. "I felt their existence as themselves to be of infinite value and rejoiced in it."

Auden's homosexuality also returned him to his faith. He was never comfortable with what might be called the Fire Island side of his being and craved sacramental forgiveness for what he recognized was sinful behavior. Curiously enough, he was a great advocate of marriage. In one of his essays, he remarked: "Like everything which is not the involuntary result of fleeting emotion but the creation of time and will, any marriage, happy or unhappy, is more interesting and significant than any romance, however passionate." In one review, he even declared that "to be a good husband and father is a larger achievement than becoming the greatest artist or scientist on earth".

Auden's Christian faith tempered his understanding of art. Doubtless with Yeats in mind, he once said that "our hearts as well as our intellects are corrupted when we use words for purposes to which the judgment true or false is irrelevant". In *The Sea and the Mirror*

(1944), Auden's commentary in verse and prose on Shakespeare's *The Tempest,* he set out "to show in a work of art the limitations of art". He succeeded in giving bravura expression to his abiding conviction that art is essentially frivolous and can never be a proper substitute for religion. In the long prose section of the poem, Auden has Caliban drive this point home in a parody of Henry James's late style, which is itself a criticism of James's settled conviction that "Art makes life, makes interest, makes importance".

> The dedicated dramatist in representing to you your condition of estrangement from the truth, is doomed to fail the more he succeeds, for the more truthfully he paints the condition, the less clearly can he indicate the truth from which it is estranged ... and ultimately, what other ... justification has he, what else exactly is the artistic gift ... if not to make you unforgettably conscious of the ungarnished offended gap between what you so questionably are and what you are commanded without any question to become.

Apropos this pivotal theme of becoming, Prof. Kirsch quotes a review in which Auden, echoing the Saint Augustine of the *Confessions*, reminded his readers that "Christianity is a way, not a state, and a Christian is never something one is, only something one can pray to become".

In his introduction, Prof. Kirsch speculates that "Auden might have been wary of any academic study of his faith ... especially one written from the point of view of an agnostic non-Christian". On this score, he is dead wrong. Auden would have rejoiced in this sympathetic, tactful, and altogether radiant study.

Rare Ben Jonson

Ben Jonson: A Life, Ian Donaldson. Oxford University Press. 533 pages.

On the cover of Ian Donaldson's new biography of Ben Jonson (1572–1637), there is a portrait of the poet and dramatist by the Flemish painter Blyenberch showing him regarding the viewer with amused intentness, as if poised to make some choice rejoinder. Here is the man of the theatre, the bon vivant, the exuberant conversationalist whose table talk William Drummond recorded with such zest. Here is also the controversialist, who delighted in taking courtiers to task as much as fellow wits, and paid for his barbs by being sent to prison again and again for sedition and disorderliness. Indeed, after killing a man in a sword fight, he was even locked up for manslaughter. But there is another portrait in this generously illustrated book, an engraving by Robert Vaughan showing Jonson looking disconsolate and world-weary. Here we see more of the private Jonson, the scholar, the convert, the affectionate father, the disappointed husband, the meditative, vulnerable, rueful man whose lyrics, epitaphs, odes, and epistles place him among our finest poets. In this magisterial biography, Donaldson does justice to all aspects of this fascinating figure.

Irrepressible talent is the hallmark of Jonson's tumultuous life. Born in London in 1572, he was the son of a poor clergyman, probably from Carlisle, who died before Jonson was born, after losing his estate in the reign of Mary Tudor. When Jonson was still a "little child in long coats", his mother remarried a bricklayer. At Westminster School, he studied under the famous headmaster William Camden, who gave him not only his lifelong love of Terence, Plautus, Horace, and Virgil but his passion for long-distance walking. To the man who helped him find his poetical feet Jonson was always deeply grateful, hailing him in one poem as "Camden! most reverend head, to whom I owe / All that I am in arts, all that I know . . ."

Westminster was renowned for its poets: George Herbert, Henry King, Abraham Cowley, and John Dryden all studied with Camden, who set his charges to write out their verses in prose before casting them in metre, which would become Jonson's *modus operandi*. (Yeats, too, would follow Jonson in this.) It is also from Camden that Jonson learned another useful lesson: "ready writing makes not good writing".

After returning from St. John's College, Cambridge, where he could not afford the fees, Jonson had no alternative but to enter the bricklaying trade, to which he was forced to return even after he had found success on the stage. Indeed, he could often be heard on building sites regaling his fellow laborers with swathes of Homer. However, in the 1590s he left the trade to become a soldier in the Low Countries. As he later liked to remind Drummond, he "had in the face of both camps killed an enemy and taken *optima spolia* from him".

Once returned to civilian life, Jonson "betook himself to his wonted studies", as he told Drummond, though the wolves were always at the door. Early and late, poverty was one of his great themes. In "Epistle Mendicant", addressed to the Lord Treasurer, he describes himself as a besieged city awaiting royal rescue.

> Disease, the enemy, and his engineers
> Want, with the rest of his concealed compeers,
> Have cast a trench about me, now, five years;
>
> And made those strong approaches, by faussebraies,
> Redoubts, half-moons, horn-works, and such close ways,
> The muse not peeps out one of hundred days;
>
> But lies blocked up, and straitened, narrowed in,
> Fixed to the bed and boards, unlike to win
> Health, or scarce breath, as she hath never been,
>
> Unless some saving honour of the crown
> Dare think it, to relieve, no less renown
> A bed-rid wit than a besiegèd town.

In his commonplace book, *Discoveries*, Jonson went further and insisted that "no great work, or worthy of praise, nor memory, but came out of poor cradles. It was the ancient poverty that founded Commonwealths, built Cities, invented Arts; made wholesome Laws; armed men against vices; rewarded them with their own virtues; and preserved the honour, and state of Nations, till they betrayed themselves to Riches".

Jonson vividly captured the betrayal of his own generation in this regard in his "Epistle to Elizabeth, Countess of Rutland", in which he speaks of the power of money at court:

> while it gains the voice
> Of some grand peer, whose air doth make rejoice
> The fool that gave it; who will want, and weep,
> When his proud patron's favours are asleep;
> While thus it buys great grace, and hunts poor fame;
> Runs between man and man; 'tween dame and dame;
> Solders cracked friendship; makes love last a day;
> Or perhaps less: whilst gold bears all this sway
> I that have none (to send you) send you verse.

In the autumn of 1592, Jonson entered the theatre where he would write *Every Man in His Humour* (1598), *Every Man out of His Humour* (1599), *Sejanus* (1603), *Volpone* (1606), *The Alchemist* (1610), *The Devil is an Ass* (1616), and *Staple of News* (1626), among others which have not survived. The last listed here is a satire on the first stirrings of what would become journalism, which Jonson assessed with prescient wit, speaking of it as "the House of Fame":

> Where both the curious and the negligent,
> The scrupulous and careless, wild and staid,
> The idle and laborious: all do meet
> To taste the *cornupcopiae* of her rumours
> Which she, the mother of sport, pleaseth to scatter
> Among the vulgar. Baits, sir, for the people!
> And they will bite likes fishes.

As a result of his lost play, *The Isle of Dogs* (1597), Jonson was imprisoned and nearly sent to the gallows. In prison, he converted to Catholicism after meeting with a Jesuit confrere of Robert Persons, SJ, who headed up the Jesuit mission in England during the Elizabethan Terror. In 1611, after twelve years as a papist, Jonson rejoined the Church of England, though Drummond characterized his friend as "for any religion, as being versed in both". He also described him as "oppressed with fantasy", which doubtless deepened his faith.

In 1594, Jonson married Anne Lewis, whom he described to Drummond with acerb succinctness as "a shrew yet honest". In 1603, Jonson lost his son Benjamin, which inspired some of his most moving lines:

"Rest in soft peace, and, asked, say here doth lie / Ben Jonson his best piece of poetry." In 1633, when his good friend and patroness Venetia Digby was found dead of a cerebral hemorrhage, Jonson confessed, "Twere time that I died too now that she is dead / Who was my muse, and life of all I said". Here is the fusing of thought and feeling that T. S. Eliot believed fled English poetry after the seventeenth century.

No other English poet mines classical models as sedulously or as inventively as Jonson. Tradition, for so learned a talent, was never a set of oppressive precedents but a summons to rethink the present in terms of the past and vice versa. This was the aspect of Jonson that made him so congenial not only to Eliot but Joyce, who read Jonson very closely. The author of *Ulysses* (1922), after all, used classical scaffolding to rear his vision of Edwardian Dublin in much the same way that Jonson used such scaffolding to rear his vision of Jacobean London, especially in *Sejanus*.

Eliot saw this even before Joyce set to work when he observed how "in order to enjoy [Jonson] at all, we must get to the centre of his work ... and see him unbiased by time, as a contemporary. And to see him as a contemporary does not so much require the power of putting ourselves into seventeenth-century London as it requires the power of setting Jonson in our London" – or our Washington, as the case may be. Certainly, when we read *Volpone*, it is not difficult to see the playwright as a very trenchant contemporary, especially when he has his venal merchant Corvino exclaim, "Honour? tut, a breath / There's no such thing in nature; a mere term / Invented to awe fools ..."

Donaldson's commentary on the poetry is judicious and illuminating, though in seeing Calvinism in one of Jonson's greatest poems, "To Heaven", he misses the mark widely. Nevertheless, he is revelatory on the court masques that Jonson wrote in tandem with the inspired architect and costume designer Inigo Jones (1573–1652). When Jonson learned that King James I believed passionately in witches and sorcerers, he gave them center stage in *The Masque of Queens* (1609), though later in *The Devil is an Ass* he complimented his monarch for growing skeptical of those whom he had formerly referred to as "detestable slaves of the Devil". For the court entertainer in Jonson, the customer was always right.

Apropos Jonson's career as a whole, Swinburne was full of admiration: "There is something heroic and magnificent in his lifelong dedication of all his gifts and all his powers to the service of the art he had elected as the business of all his life and the aim of all his aspiration." Proof of this is in the work itself. However, despite its range and power, it has not always been given the due it deserves.

Indeed, if after the death of Shakespeare, whom Jonson confessed to admiring "this side idolatry", there was no poet in England who enjoyed greater esteem than Jonson, after his own death in 1637 his reputation began to decline. The eighteenth century found Jonson a sort of bungling Waller and the nineteenth only read him to compare him unfavorably with Shakespeare. It was not until Yeats, Pound, and Eliot paid him mind that he and his work began to receive renewed critical attention. Hugh Kenner added to this belated acclaim when he wrote of how Jonson "attached himself to a company of actors, began writing plays, got into trouble more than once with the law, even carried to his grave the hangman's brand on his thumb; but never amid the twistings and turnings of a merely picturesque existence lost sight of his self-imposed obligation to reform the English stage according to the best models, and simultaneously to establish in his own person, the dignity of the profession of letters". The new seven-volume edition of Jonson's works that Cambridge University is publishing will give that dignity a proper showcase.

In June of 1618, at the peak of his success, Jonson set out on a "foot voyage" from London to Scotland on the Great North Road, arriving in Edinburgh in late August. He intended to fashion a great travelogue out of these heroic peregrinations, but his draft was lost when his house burned down in 1623. Nevertheless, it was in Scotland that he met the bibliophile Drummond, who left behind the fullest record of Jonson's life, even though Donaldson believes Drummond may have skewered the record. In this sense the Scottish Drummond was not unlike the Scottish Boswell in coloring his subject's prejudices to suit his own. For example, Jonson's great regard for Shakespeare was not one Drummond shared. After all, as Donaldson points out, when Jonson wrote of Shakespeare that "he was not of an age, but for all time", he was not reaffirming "an uncontested truth" but venturing "a bold prediction". Drummond may have attributed to Jonson so many slighting references to Shakespeare to try to qualify a prediction that he found over the top.

Rare Ben Jonson

From Donaldson's scrupulous labors, Jonson emerges as witty and urbane, gregarious, combative, sworn to eternal truth without ever being unmindful of the feverish fashions of his age, humorously self-effacing and yet coolly proud. Both of the latter qualities are evident in a poem Jonson wrote on writer's block, brought on by a few too many glasses of wine, which he addressed to one of his friends:

> Would God, my Burges, I could think
> Thoughts worthy of this gift, your ink,
> Then would I promise here to give
> Verse, that should thee, and me outlive,
> But since the wine hath steeped my brain,
> I can only the paper stain;
> Yet with a dye, that fears no moth,
> But scarlet-like outlasts the cloth.

Jonson's poetry teems with his inimitable personality. When he lost his books and papers in the fire that burned down his house, for example, he dashed off "An Execration upon Vulcan", a *jeu d'esprit* which reveals the great charm of the man. It also reveals how wit was a virtue for Jonson in a way that it never was for Donne. Here, Vulcan is personified as a sort of unmannerly arsonist and chided for overdoing matters:

> Thou mightst have yet enjoyed thy cruelty
> With some more thrift, and more variety:
> Thou mightst have had me perish, piece by piece,
> To light tobacco, or save roasted geese.
> Singe capons, or poor pigs, dropping their eyes;
> Condemned me to the ovens with the pies;
> And so, have kept me dying a whole age,
> Not ravished all hence in a minute's rage.

Then, he speaks of the volumes he would have offered Vulcan in exchange for his own, had they come to some agreement beforehand.

> The whole sum
> Of errant knighthood, with the dames, and dwarfs;
> The charmèd boats, and the enchanted Wharfs,
> The Tristrams, Lancelots, Turpins, and the Peers,
> All the mad Rolands, and sweet Oliveers...
> These, hadst thou pleased either to dine or sup

Had made a meal for Vulcan to lick up.
But in my desk, what was there to excite
So ravenous, and vast an appetite?
I dare not say a body, but some parts
There were of search and mastery of the arts.

Here is the colloquial élan that can be found throughout Jonson's poetry, which anticipates, by over a century, Wordsworth's insistence that poets write in the "real language of men".

Although King James I made Jonson King's Poet in 1616, he was not overly impressed by the honor, referring to the laureateship as "a kind of Christmas engine: one that is used, at least once a year, for a trifling instrument of wit". That he also declined a knighthood impressed Robert Graves, who commended the great poet for referring to titles as "birdlime for fools" and poetry as "the Queen of Arts, which has her original in Heaven". Ian Donaldson has written a splendid life of this extraordinary man, which all claimants to the "tribe of Ben" will savor and prize.

Pockets of Prayer:
The Catholic Tradition
in English Poetry

GEORGE ORWELL once gave it as his opinion that "Orthodox Catholicism seems to have a crushing effect upon certain literary forms, especially the novel", which prompted him to ask: "During a period of three hundred years, how many people have been at once good novelists and good Catholics?" Flannery O'Connor might have been answering Orwell directly when she said, "I have found that people outside the Church like to suppose that the Church acts as a restraint on the creativity of the Catholic writer and that she keeps him from reaching his full development". But she was quite adamant that if Catholics had made a poor showing in certain arts, this was attributable to the failure of individual Catholics, not the Faith.

> There is no reason why fixed dogma should fix anything that the writer sees in the world. On the contrary, dogma is an instrument for penetrating reality. Christian dogma is about the only thing left in the world that surely guards and respects mystery. The fiction writer is an observer, first, last, and always, but he cannot be an adequate observer unless he is free from uncertainty about what he sees.

Indeed, she went further: "The Catholic sacramental view of life is one that sustains and supports at every turn the vision that the storyteller must have if he is going to write fiction of any depth." The novels of James Joyce ultimately disappoint precisely because they repudiate this "Catholic sacramental view of life". *Ulysses* (1922) is one of the most stupefying exhibitions of virtuosity in the language, and yet how redolent it is of a man who would write of anything other than what Newman called "the one thing needful" – the true spirit of love, "the love of God, and of man for His sake". Stanislaus Joyce told his brother apropos his oddly sterile book: "To me you seem to have escaped from the toils of the priest ... only to fall under the oppression of a monstrous vision of life itself. Where so much has been recorded, I object to what has been omitted. There is no serenity or happiness anywhere in the whole book."

Stanislaus was even more opposed to Catholic teaching than his brother, but he recognized, despite himself, the price apostasy exacts. Most critics claim that Joyce only became an artist by rejecting the Roman Church, as though apostasy were somehow the handmaiden of art. O'Connor explodes this fallacy. The Church, "far from restricting the Catholic writer, generally provides him with more advantages than he is willing or able to turn to account, and usually his sorry productions are a result, not of restrictions that the Church has imposed, but of restrictions that he has failed to impose on himself". It is not necessary to belabor how applicable that last stricture is to the author who spent years amplifying the riddles of *Finnegans Wake*.

Many of the same objections made about the Catholic novel have been made about Catholic poetry. Gerard Manley Hopkins (1844–89) is often trotted out as an example of the gifted artist hobbled by a repressive faith. "It is doubtful", claims one of his biographers Norman White, "if he ever achieved complete coherence – he seems always afraid of his unconquered demons, and took strong measures to keep them down". Here, White regards the Faith to which Hopkins converted as a kind of voluntary straitjacket. Of course, the Faith did try Hopkins – it tries souls to remake them – but that it barred him from becoming a freer, happier, better poet is not tenable. Hopkins joined the Roman Church in emulation of the heroic example of Newman. Even Yeats recognized that "the Catholic Church created a system only possible for saints, hence its prolonged power. Its definition of the good was narrow, but it did not set out to make shopkeepers". The Ignatian discipline of the Society of Jesus gave Hopkins all the spiritual grist that his poetic mill could require. He would have understood what Maritain meant when he said that "Christianity does not make art *easy*. It deprives it of many facile means ... to raise its level". As he wrote in his journal, "there's none but truth can stead you. Christ is truth". Elsewhere he insisted that "this life though it is hard is God's will for me". In his poem on Saint Alphonsus Rodriguez he described how:

> Honour is flashed off exploit, so we say;
> And those strokes once that gashed flesh or galled shield
> Should tongue that time now, trumpet now that field,
> And on the fighter, forge his glorious day.

This was one type of heroism. Yet Hopkins knew that his own heroism would be quite different. Strokes that gash flesh or gall shield make visible war.

> But be the war within, the brand we wield
> Unseen, the heroic breast not outward-steeled,
> Earth hears no hurtle then from fiercest fray.

This interior war has never had a better chronicler than Hopkins. He knew its battles like he knew the back of his hand. He also knew that its unheralded trials offered his art rare advantages, opportunities for innovation that he was never reluctant to turn to account. After all the boldly innovative poetry of the Modernists and their successors, the reports that Hopkins sent back from the dark night of the soul still astonish.

> I wake and feel the fell of dark, not day.
> What hours, O what black hours we have spent
> This night! What sights you, heart, saw; ways you went!
> And more must, in yet longer light's delay.

Good as they are, his last sonnets were aberrations. Hopkins died, after all, when he was 45 and not of despair but of bad Irish drains. If one looks at his work as a whole one sees that praise is at its heart. Glorying in the wonders of God, he knew that despair is transient, "the Resurrection, a heart's clarion!" This is why he cried:

> Away grief's gasping, joyless days, dejection.
> Across my foundering deck shone
> A beacon, an eternal beam. Flesh fade, and mortal trash
> Fall to the residuary worm; world's wildfire, leave but ash:
>
> In a flash, at a trumpet crash,
> I am all at once what Christ is, since he was what I am, and
> This Jack, joke, poor potsherd, patch, matchwood, immortal diamond
> Is immortal diamond.

Hopkins is a good starting point for any consideration of Catholic English poetry because he is emblematic of a tradition that survived by going against the grain. Of course, after the Reformation, virtually all English poetry became Protestant, with a religious poetry that eventually reflected the full spectrum of Protestant faith from George Herbert to Milton to W. H. Auden. Catholic poets only survived within this Protestant domain as an eccentric minority, though one which acted as a continual reminder not only of what English poetry had lost but what it might still reclaim. Catholic poetry before the Reformation paid special homage to Our Lady. Here is Chaucer:

> Lady! thy bountee, thy magnificence,
> Thy vertu, and thy grete humilitee
> Ther may no tonge express in no science;
> For som-tyme, lady, er men praye to thee,
> Thou goost biforn of thy benignitee,
> And getest us the light, thurgh thy preyere,
> To gyden us unto thy sone so dere.

Anonymous lyrics of the fifteenth century confirm the devotion the faithful felt for the Queen of Heaven. They also exhibit a tender kinship with her, proof that her mediatorial role between the Creator and His creatures was one to which the pre-Reformation English warmly responded.

> Mother and maiden
> Was never none but she;
> Well may such a lady
> Goddes mother be

Hopkins would revive this Marian tradition in a poem that recalls Ruskin's *The Queen of the Air* (1869), a collection of essays on Greek mythology. In "The Blessed Virgin Compared to the Air We Breathe" (1883), Hopkins made Mary Queen of the Air:

> Be thou then, O thou dear
> Mother, my atmosphere;
> My happier world, wherein
> To wend and meet no sin;
> Above me, round me lie
> Fronting my forward eye

> With sweet and scarless sky;
> Stir in my ears, speak there
> Of God's love, O live air
> Of patience, penance, prayer:
> Worldmothering air, air wild,
> Wound with thee, in thee isled,
> Fold him, fast fold thy child.

The Jesuit Robert Southwell (1561–95) testified to the reality of the Faith at a time of persecution.

> O dying soules, beholde your living spring:
> O dasled eyes, behold your sonne of grace:
> Dull eares, attend what word this word doth bring:
> Up heavie hartes: with joye your joye embrace.
> From death, from darke, from deafenesse, from dispaires:
> This life, this light, this word, this joy repaires.

Southwell paid dearly for his own testament to the Faith. The domestic chaplain to the Countess of Arundel, he was abducted on his way to Mass in 1592, and hanged, drawn, and quartered after being tortured for three years. (In 1970 Pope Paul VI canonized him as one of the Forty Martyrs of England and Wales.) Many verses chronicle this time of torment. One anonymous poet laments:

> The time hath been we had one faith,
> And strode aright one ancient path,
> The time is now that each man may
> See new religions coined each day.
> Sweet Jesu, with thy mother mild,
> Sweet Virgin, mother with thy child,
> Angels and saints of each degree,
> Redress our country's misery.

Yet not all the Catholic poetry that endured the Elizabethan persecution was cut out of Southwell's heroic cloth. The poetry of John Donne (1572–1631) records a tragic turning away from the Faith. Born into a devoutly Catholic family, Donne was related to Saint Thomas More on his mother's side. His uncle, Jasper Heywood was head of the Jesuit mission in England. At the age of 11, after being educated at home by Catholic tutors, he entered what is now Hertford College, preferred by recusants because it had no chapel. He also spent some time studying at Cambridge and then visited Italy and Spain, where, as Sir Herbert Grierson dryly remarked, "he saw perhaps other sides of life ... than that of the Seminaries". In 1593, when his brother was imprisoned for concealing a Catholic priest, Donne renounced his Catholic faith. After secretly marrying the niece of his patron, he was briefly imprisoned himself, which barred him from receiving any civil posts. For the next 14 years he lived on handouts from friends and relations. His decision to take holy orders in the Established church was made more for financial than spiritual reasons. In later years he wrote a number of prose works attacking the Faith.

Speaking of the appeal of suicide, Donne wrote:

> I have often such a sickly inclination; and whether it be because I had my first breeding and conversation with men of a suppressed and afflicted religion, accustomed to the despite of death and hungry of an imagined martyrdom ... or because my conscience assures me that no rebellious grudging at God's gift, nor other sinful concurrence accompanies these thoughts in me, or that a brave scorn or that a faint cowardliness beget it, whensoever any affliction assails me methinks I have the keys of my prison in my own hand, and no remedy presents itself so soon to my heart as mine own sword.

One does not have to be an armchair psychologist to suspect that this account was evasive and that the real cause for these self-destructive tendencies was guilt over his renunciation of the Faith. Donne might have been licentious but he was not unconscionable. Certainly, his divine poems show the terrible fear he felt as death closed in – they all but totter under what he calls his "low devout melancholy". "Death Be Not Proud" was not so much a resolution of these fears as a whistling in the dark.

Apropos his love lyrics, Dryden famously complained that Donne "perplexes the minds of the fair sex with nice speculations of philosophy, when he should engage their hearts and entertain them with the softness of love". If one compares Donne's involved conceits to Shakespeare's "Love's feeling is more soft and sensible / Than are the tender horns of cockled snails", one can see Dryden's point. There is precious little of the "softness of love" in "The Canonization".

> We can die by it, if not live by love
> And if unfit for tombs or hearse
> Our legend be, it will be fit for verse;
> And if no piece of chronicle we prove,
> We'll build in sonnets pretty rooms;
> As well a well-wrought urn becomes
> The greatest ashes, as half-acre tombs
> And by these hymns all shall approve
> Us canonized for love ...

This is elephantine foolery. C. S. Lewis was right to note the joylessness in Donne's love poetry, despite its manic badinage. "The effect of all these poems is somehow serious", Lewis observed. "Seldom profound in thought, not always passionate in feeling, they are none the less the very opposite of gay. It is as though Donne performed in deepest depression those gymnastics which are usually a sign of intellectual high spirits." Even in his religious poetry he could not resist clowning and clowning of a peculiarly dreary sort. Addressing God, the Father, in one of his last poems, he asks:

> Wilt thou forgive that sin where I begun
> Which was my sin, though it were done before?
> Wilt thou forgive that sin, through which I run
> And do run still: though still I deplore?
> When thou hast done, thou hast not done,
> For I have more ...

In Richard Crashaw (1613–49) we have a Catholic convert expressing his faith in ways that George Herbert and the other devotional poets of the seventeenth century would have found *outré*. Since the time of John Foxe and his *Book of Martyrs* (1554), detailing the persecution of Protestants during Queen Mary's reign, the English had been drilled in the enormities of hagiolatry. Crashaw's devotion to Saint Teresa confirmed their prejudices. Chaucer could borrow from the French, and Spenser from the Italians, but Crashaw was never forgiven for borrowing from the Spanish. In the squarely Protestant canon of English poetry he gets only a very grudging nod. Yet to Catholics he must always appeal as an impassioned original, a holy exile.

O thou undaunted daughter of desires!
By all thy dower of lights and fires;
By all the eagle in thee, all the dove;
By all thy lives and deaths of love;
By thy large draughts of intellectual day,
And by thy thirsts of love more large than they;
By all thy brim-fill'd bowls of fierce desire,
By thy last morning's draught of liquid fire;
By the full kingdom of that final kiss
That seiz'd thy parting soul, and seal'd thee his;
By all the heav'ns thou hast in him,
Fair sister of the Seraphim!
By all of him we have in thee;
Leave nothing of myself in me.
Let me so read thy life, that I
Unto all life of mine may die.

The art historian Kenneth Clark doubtless had Crashaw in mind when he described how the Counter-Reformation parried Luther and his cohorts:

> The leaders of the Catholic Restoration had made the inspired decision not to go half-way to meet Protestantism in any of its objections, but rather to glory in those very doctrines that the Protestants had most forcibly ... repudiated. Luther had repudiated the authority of the Pope: very well, no pains must be spared in making a giant assertion that St. Peter, the first Bishop of Rome, had been divinely appointed as Christ's Vicar on earth. Ever since Erasmus, intelligent men in the north had spoken scornfully of relics: very well, their importance must be magnified, so that the four piers of St. Peter's itself are gigantic reliquaries ... The veneration of relics was connected with the cult of the saints, and this had been equally condemned by the reformers. Very well, the saints should be made more insistently real to the imagination and in particular their sufferings and their ecstasties should be vividly recorded.

Another good Catholic poet of this period was William Habington (1605–54). Born in Hindlip, Worcestershire, of an Old Catholic family, he was educated at Saint Omer and Paris. His father, Thomas, was imprisoned and his uncle Edward executed for conspiring in the Babington plot to kill Queen Elizabeth and free Mary. Hindlip had long been the meeting place for Jesuits in the Midlands. Habington had access to the court of Charles I and Queen Henrietta and his poetry exhibits a kind of courtly Catholicism.

> When I survey the bright
> Celestial sphere;
> So rich with jewels hung that Night
> Doth like an Ethiop bride appear:
>
> My soul her wings doth spread
> And heavenward flies,
> The Almighty's mysteries to read
> In the large volume of the skies...

Regarding Charles I and the Old Catholics, the Whig historian George Trevelyan recounted how "in 1642 a quarter of a century had passed away since the legal penalties and fines had been regularly inflicted on the recusants, and it was for this reason that they were both willing and able to save Charles from financial ruin". Protestants were right to fear Catholic wealth. "The Earl of Worcester, reputed the greatest monied man in England, had an annual rental of €24,000. He gave it almost wholesale to the King." Still, many Old Catholics must have found Habington baffling. As David Matthew pointed out in his history of English Catholicism, "Ethiop brides were the very last thing in which Catholic gentlemen could be expected to display an interest and one can almost see them returning to the fireside seat and the ale".

Nevertheless, Habington saw something in the offing that most of his compatriots missed. In the same poem (*Nox nocti indicat Scientiam*), he wrote:

> For the bright firmament
> Shoots forth no flame
> So silent but is eloquent
> In speaking the Creator's name...
>
> It tells the Conqueror
> That far-stretched power,
> Which his proud dangers traffic for,
> Is but the triumph of an hour...

> Thus those celestial fires,
> Though seeming mute,
> The fallacy of our desires
> And all the pride of life confute:
>
> For they have watched since first
> The world had birth:
> And found sin in itself accurst,
> And nothing permanent on Earth.

After abandoning their traditional faith, the English gave their hearts to the nation state and then to empire. Habington saw this coming with prophetic clarity. Two centuries later, in 1850, John Henry Newman would detail the consequences of England's apostasy:

> A thousand years had well-nigh rolled, and this great people grew tired of the heavenly stranger who sojourned among them. They had had enough of blessings and absolutions, enough of the intercession of saints, enough of the grace of the sacraments, enough of the prospect of the next life. They thought it best to secure this life in the first place, because they were in possession of it, and then to go on to the next, if time and means allowed.... Anyhow, they would pursue a temporal end, and they would account any one their enemy who stood in the way of their pursuing it. It was a madness; but madmen are strong, and madmen are clever; so with the sword and the halter, and by mutilation and fine and imprisonment, they cut off, or frightened away from the land, as Israel did in the time of old, the ministers of the Most High, and their ministrations... And as for the remnant of His servants whom they left, they drove them into corners and holes of the earth, and there they bade them die out ... And so they turned to enjoy this world, and to gain for themselves a name among men, and it was given unto them according to their wish. They preferred the heathen virtues of their original nature, to the robe of grace which God had given them: they fell back, with closed affections, and haughty reserve, and dreariness within, upon their worldly integrity, honour, energy, prudence, and perseverance; they made the most of the natural man, and they "received their reward". Forthwith they began to rise to a station higher than the heathen Roman, and have, in three

centuries, attained a wider range of sovereignty; and now they look down in contempt on what they were, and upon the Religion which reclaimed them from paganism.

After Crashaw, Catholic poetry languished. John Dryden, it is true, converted. But it was not until the nineteenth century that Catholic poetry regained its vigor. Newman, Hopkins, Coventry Patmore, and Francis Thompson all renewed the Catholic tradition, which, like the Catholic Church, showed remarkable resilience. Newman famously celebrated what he called the Second Spring in 1850, when the territorial hierarchy was restored in England by Pius IX.

> No one could have prophesied its fall, but still less would any one have ventured to prophesy its rise again. The fall was wonderful; still after all it was in the order of nature;–all things come to naught: its rise again would be a different sort of wonder, for it is in the order of grace, –and who can hope for miracles, and such a miracle as this!

Nevertheless, when Francis Thompson (1859–1907) began "The Kingdom of God" with the exultant lines:

> O world invisible, we view thee
> O world intangible, we touch thee,
> O world unknowable, we know thee,
> Inapprehensible, we clutch thee!

he was reaffirming a faith that was virtually unknown in the poorer districts of nineteenth-century London. In the course of the interviews he conducted for *London Labour and the London Poor* (1851), Henry Mayhew found that "not three in one hundred costermongers had ever been in the interior of a church, or any place of worship, or knew what was meant by Christianity". For Thompson to envision Jacob's Ladder "Pitched betwixt Heaven and Charing Cross" was to envision something miraculous indeed. But Catholic poetry, so humdrum in many ways, battens on the miraculous.

In the twentieth century Hilaire Belloc (1870–1953) and G. K. Chesterton (1874–1936) renewed Catholic poetry again. Belloc exemplified perhaps the greatest of all the contributions made by Catholic poets to English poetry by keeping alive the poetry of prayer. Here are lines from a poem called "The Prophet Lost in the Hills at Evening":

> Strong God which made the topmost stars
> To circulate and keep their course,
> Remember me; whom all the bars
> Of sense and dreadful fate enforce...
>
> The long descent of wasted days,
> To these last have led me down;
> Remember that I filled with praise
> The meaningless and doubtful ways
> That lead to an eternal town.
>
> I challenged and I kept the Faith,
> The bleeding path I trod;
> It darkens. Stand about my wraith,
> And harbour me – almighty God.

In that penultimate line one can hear an echo of Landor's famous boast: "I warmed both hands before the fire of Life / It sinks, and I am ready to depart" but one which entirely eschews Landor's costume stoicism. The note of wholehearted prayer that Belloc and many other Catholic poets sound is echoed by the Anglican poet Geoffrey Hill, whom many consider the best of living poets:

> What is there in my heart that you should sue
> so fiercely for its love? What kind of care
> brings you as though a stranger to my door
> through the long night and in the icy dew
>
> seeking the heart that will not harbour you
> that keeps itself religiously secure?
> At this dark solstice filled with frost and fire
> your passion's ancient wounds must bleed anew...

Chesterton is a far better poet than is usually acknowledged. The Modernist poets may have been more fashionable but none of them wrote anything as memorable as "The Rolling English Road". That Chesterton is also funny does not endear him to the solemn. But then no one ever exposed the pretensions of the solemn more brilliantly than G.K.C.

> The sages have a hundred maps to give
> That trace their crawling cosmos like a tree,
> They rattle reason out through many a sieve

> That stores the sand and lets the gold go free:
> And all these things are less than dust to me
> Because my name is Lazarus and I live.

The Welsh poet David Jones (1895–1974), whose experiences in the trenches first opened his eyes to the Faith, wrote at length about the sign-making, sacramental nature of poetry. He would have approved of Chesterton's "The Song against Grocers":

> God made the wicked Grocer
> For a mystery and a sign,
> That men might shun the awful shops
> And go to inns to dine;
> Where the bacon's on the rafter
> And the wine is in the wood,
> And God that made good laughter
> Has seen that they are good.

Jones is worth reading on how the Faith relates to poetry. In a piece called "Religion and the Muses" (1941), he says:

> The Church, strictly speaking, does not create an art-form; she has used and given significance, or a new twist to, this or that cultural expression ... She can be either inimical to a particular creativity, or be an inspiration and patroness of its efflorescence. It depends on circumstances ... As, in marriage, she is witness to a sacrament but cannot bestow it, still less determine in whom or where true love shall operate – so, in the arts, she can encourage and bless, or not bless and neglect, but she cannot dispose in whom or where a new creativeness shall surprise the world and invigorate the generations.

This tallies with what Maritain called for in the Christian poet: "Let's make no mistake about it: what is required is the very actuality of love, contemplation in charity. Christian work would have the artist, as man, a saint. It would have him possessed by love. Let him then make what he wishes."

In his brilliant book, *Medievalism: The Middle Ages in Modern England*, Michael Alexander shows how Jones's long poem *In Parenthesis* (1937), in refusing to see the Great War as pointless, took inspiration from the Church.

Though the point may not have been evident to those who fell, their sacrifice is presented as not without meaning. The kind of heroism implied is not especially valorous, more a question of putting up with things – Milton's "the better part of patience and heroic martyrdom", where "martyr" means "witness". The cause is obscure, the motive is a sense of duty rather than the need to resist Prussian militarism; and the kind of Christianity implied is of the most inclusive sort. Jones's notion of the Catholic Church was that it included "many chaps who did not know that they were in it".... The broken texture of *In Parenthesis*, its relapse into prose, is related to the intense strain of finding any formal analogy in human and sacred history to the dire actuality of a subject matter which did not easily yield sense, still less grandeur. Yet the soldiers of the First World War were not the first soldiers, or men or women, to feel themselves godforsaken. On the cross, Jesus himself repeated the opening of Palm 22, traditionally attributed to King David, of a thousand years earlier: "My God, my God, why hast thou forsaken me?"

Elizabeth Jennings (1926–2001) decided to become a poet at 13 after reading Chesterton's "Lepanto". When Robert Conquest included her work in an anthology of young British poets, which included Philip Larkin, Donald Davie, Thom Gunn, and Kingsley Amis, the group was hastily dubbed "The Movement", though its members had little in common. One wit remarked that Jennings, the only Catholic and the only female, fit into the group "like a schoolmistress" thrown together "with a bunch of drunken marines". In our current critical ethos, which still looks for spiritual sustenance to such muddled poets as Yeats and Wallace Stevens, the Catholic lucidity of Jennings is tonic. Few Catholic poets of any era have taken up the theme of Good Friday with this compelling immediacy:

> We nailed the hands long ago,
> Wove the thorns, took up the scourge and shouted
> For excitement's sake, we stood at the dusty edge
> Of the pebbled path and watched the extreme of pain.
> But one or two prayed, one or two
> Were silent, shocked, stood back
> And remembered remnants of words, a new vision.

> The cross is up with its crying victim, the clouds
> Cover the sun, we learn a new way to lose
> What we did not know we had
> Until this bleak and sacrificial day,
> Until we turned from our bad
> Past and knelt and cried out our dismay,
> The dice still clicking, the voices dying away.

Siegfried Sassoon (1886–1967) saw his indifference to religion shattered in the trenches, though he did not enter the Church formally until he was in his seventies. After reading Newman's work, he wrote: "I wonder what effect it would have made if someone had given it to me ten years ago. Everything I needed is there, waiting for me! All clear as daylight. And simple as falling off a log – just unconditional surrender." In "A Prayer in Old Age", Sassoon exhibited something of the same wholehearted sincerity that I have tried to identify as characteristic of other Catholic poets.

> Bring no expectance of a heaven unearned
> No hunger for beatitude to be
> Until the lesson of my life is learned
> Through what Thou didst for me.
>
> Bring no assurance of redeemed rest
> No intimation of awarded grace
> Only contrition, cleavingly confessed
> To Thy forgiving face.
>
> I ask one world of everlasting loss
> In all I am, that other world to win.
> My nothingness must kneel below Thy Cross.
> There let new life begin.

What can one say in conclusion about the Catholic tradition in English poetry? Newman was careful to stress what he considered a fundamental feature of all literature:

> Man's work will savour of man; in his elements and powers excellent and admirable, but prone to disorder and excess, to error and to sin. Such too will be his literature; it will have the beauty and the fierceness, the sweetness and the rankness, of the natural man ...

What gives Catholic poets their power is their understanding of this natural man, not only his flaws but his craving for God. Hopkins described the natural man as "so haggard at the heart, so care-coiled, so fagged, so fashed, so cogged, so cumbered", as to be consumed with that craving. This is why he and so many other Catholic poets fill their poems with prayer.

> God, lover of souls, swaying considerate scales,
> Complete thy creature dear O where it fails,
> Being mighty a master, being a father and fond.

A Memoir for the Commodore

Dead End Gene Pool: A Memoir, Wendy Burden. Gotham Books. 280 pages.

WENDY BURDEN'S *Dead End Gene Pool* is many books rolled into one. A fascinating autobiography about what it was like growing up the great-great-great-great granddaughter of Cornelius Vanderbilt, the railroad tycoon whose fortune left the Burden family one of the richest in New York, it is also a family memoir that merits a place beside the equally brilliant memoirs of Alexander Waugh and Lorna Sage. Then, again, it is an unforgettable portrait of a daughter and mother, which, in its lacerating comedy, resembles Mary Karr's reminiscential effusions. It is also a social history that revisits Fifth Avenue in the fifties, sixties, and seventies, as well as Desert Island in Maine and the Jupiter Island Club in Florida. And, lastly, it is something of a detective story, with a denouement that is as sad as it is insoluble.

Sadness suffuses the book, which makes the author's wonderful jokes all the more welcome. Her father committed suicide when she was six and she spent most of her childhood shuttling back and forth between her mother's houses – first in Georgetown and then in London – and her grandparents' opulent homes in Manhattan and Maine. Burden's descriptions of her grandparents and their twenty-odd servants are priceless, as are those of her uncles and her lubricious stepfather, whom she appropriately dubs "Adolf".

Then, there is her inimitable mother. After the loss of her husband, Leslie (née Hamilton) takes to the role of merry widow with unseemly celerity and becomes *persona non grata* among her dead husband's family. Consequently, Wendy and her brothers are brought up by their grandparents – or, more accurately, by their servants, for whose kindness, loyalty and indefatigable energy the author has great affectionate respect. For her mother, she can feel only exasperation and a sort of involuntary love, after years of being passed over for boyfriends and booze.

Indeed, the stride in which the author takes the heartbreaks of her life is admirable. There are no recriminations here or exhibitionistic self-pity. Readers expecting to encounter a poor little rich girl will come away disappointed. Even when her family is at its lowest ebb – and the ebbs here can be very low indeed – Burden is always ready to confound sorrow with witty laughter.

In one passage, for example, she recalls paying a visit to her grandfather, William A. M. Burden II, the erstwhile president of the Modern Museum of Art, in his palatial apartment on Fifth Avenue, when he had begun to sink into his unenviable dotage:

> As my grandfather's drinking worsened, his brain rewarded him by undergoing a series of strokes that deprived him of his two favorite diversions: speech and taste.
>
> He continued to consume food and wine as if his senses were unaltered, but dining with him was a different experience. One could now voice an opinion – on anything: thermonuclear war, the amount of coke being done in the Studio 54 bathroom, genital mutilation, mixed marriages, civil libertarianism, Super Tampax versus Regular. The only word he could get out was a relatively harmless "phooey". Except one time, when we were discussing my cousin Connie's upcoming nuptials to a man named Rosengarten, and he began to splutter and thrash around in his wheelchair, and finally managed to choke out, "J . . . J . . . J . . . JEW! JEW! JEW-WWWW!!!" He continued to call the word out throughout the rest of the meal, and was put to bed still repeating it. Luckily, by the next morning he was back to good old "phooey".

In Burden's unforgettable grandfather, the WASP distaste for Jews is combined with the WASP fondness for tippling. Of course, American literature is full of drunks: Edgar Allen Poe, Hemingway, Thurber, Fitzgerald, Lardner, Faulkner, Cheever – the list goes on and on, Yet in all the annals of literary dipsomania there are few passages funnier than this: "It's amazing how resourceful an addict can be. In the midst of this self-medicated madness, my grandfather invented and patented the Tippler's Bathroom. Fed up with broken bones and telltale bruises, he designed a john that was entirely padded . . . You could bounce around dead drunk in the shower and never hurt yourself". Reading this, no one will be surprised that the author spent a fair amount of her literary apprenticeship working with the American humorist P. J. O'Rourke, another social critic alive to the contributions drink has made to fortifying the nation's culture.

But it was a mark of her grandfather's selfishness that he did not share his brilliant invention with his wife, Florence (née Partridge) who, as Burden recalls, "bravely and consistently wore the black and blue (and green and yellow) badge of Dubonnet and withstood all four of her slippery, sharp-angled bathrooms like the Christian she was". That the Fifth Avenue apartment was designed by Philip Johnson in the modern minimalist style only added to the hazardous angularity of the place. Indeed, for Burden, for all the falls her poor grandmother sustained, "she might as well have just kept herself packed in ice", an observation which leads to an architectural aside that would have amused John Betjeman, whose own family owed their modest wealth to the patenting of a lockable drinks cabinet: "Modernism is such an inhospitable décor scheme for drinkers; there's a reason the classic English drawing room has remained soft and downy throughout the ages."

Clothes horses will savor the author's attention to sartorial details, not only the Best & Co. dresses that she wears as a child but the Charvet shirts and ties and John Lobb shoes that her grandfather sports. Speaking of her grandfather's manservant, Adolphe, Burden observes: "Impeccably turned out as he was – daytime black jacket, gray waistcoat, and pinstripe trousers; evening tailcoat with white gloves and wing collar – Adolphe ensured his master was too, whether in white tie with decorations for a dinner at the White House, a navy Huntsman business suit for the office, or spotless flannel tennis whites for the weekend court. Not a molecule or lint could be found on either man, and this was before the most important invention of the twentieth century: the rolling pet hair remover."

Food is another topic to which the book pays sumptuous attention. Burden's grandfather was a fan of such discriminating gourmands as A. J. Liebling and Elizabeth David and enjoyed entertaining on the grand scale. The author's recollections of the chef Arturo, the undisputed king of the servants, are some of the most vivid in the book. "For my grandmother, a Kon-Tiki enthusiast", she recalls, "he fashioned Tahitian cucumber outriggers with little oars of carrots, filling them with composed salads of lobster or crab or tiny diced vegetables, bound with copious amounts of mayonnaise", which the author nicely calls "French luncheon glue".

Burden's mother, on the other hand, who is obsessed with her weight and suntan, only turns to cooking when she has no alternative, and then with calamitous results. After describing the inedible messes her mother prepares, Burden styles the maternal cookery "Early New England Regional Cuisine as Interpreted by an Alcoholic with an Eating Disorder".

Together with the sadness, there is also something brave about this book. To understand this bravery, we have to appreciate why people write memoirs in the first place. In an essay entitled "On Suicide" H. L. Mencken once ventured the hypothesis that "men work simply in order to escape the depressing agony of contemplating life ... their work, like their play, is a mumbo-jumbo that serves them by permitting them to escape from reality". No one familiar with the solitary toil that writing requires can altogether discount this, and yet if there is one genre of writing about which none of the above applies it is the memoir. Someone writing about the Hundred Years War can lose himself in labyrinths of military, legal, economic, and social history. But to write a memoir is necessarily to embrace "the agony of contemplating life", and not just any life but one's own, with all its sins, illusions, pettiness and failure.

A pivotal passage in Burden's book occurs when she receives a handwritten note from her crapulous grandmother apologizing for her misbehavior when she had downed too much Dubonnet the night before. "My grandmother had been raised a Christian Scientist," she recalls. "It was ingrained in her to disregard in life whatever she found too distressing to handle ... Her note to me was a bombshell. I knew she had a problem, and I knew that she knew I knew, but to admit it was so bleakly out of character, I wanted to vaporize."

But she did not vaporize. Instead, she summoned the old WASP sense of duty and wrote this glorious memoir, which, in its way, is her own handwritten note not only to her mother and father, but to her grandparents and their servants, her uncles, her brothers, and even to the old Commodore himself. And its central message is the same that the author finds on one of the New Age websites that her dotty brother Edward visits: "Heal Your Life NOW by Healing Your Past Lives!"

Edward Burne-Jones: No Votary of the Actual

The Last Pre-Raphaelite: Edward Burne-Jones and the Victorian Imagination, Fiona McCarthy. Harvard University Press. 629 pages.

To account for the yearning for beauty that animates so much of Edward Burne-Jones's highly stylized art, the novelist Penelope Fitzgerald, who wrote a good biography of the artist in 1975, stressed the frightful squalor of his native Birmingham, which, as she says, was "neither policed nor lighted (except in winter) until 1839" and where "dozens of families clung together" in noisome courts and rookeries, "sharing one tap and one privy". Drunkenness was ubiquitous and, at night, as Carlyle recalled, "the whole region burned like a volcano, spilling fire from a thousand tubes of bricks". It was to escape this industrialized inferno that the framer's son who lost his mother when he was six days old became an artist, exchanging these Brummagem horrors for the knights and ladies of mediaeval romance. Blake famously believed that "if the fool would persist in his folly he would become wise". Persisting in his own dream-laden folly never made Burne-Jones wise – he was the first to admit his want of wisdom when it came to beautiful women – but it did turn him into a good artist, who knew that his own importunate imagination, not the world's appointments, must be the source of his deeply personal art. In her superb new biography, Fiona McCarthy, the author of the definitive life of William Morris, captures the richness of the artist and his epoch with enviable verve. No one interested in the English nineteenth century should pass it up.

Born in 1833, Burne-Jones set his heart from early youth on becoming an Anglican clergyman. He was fascinated by John Henry Newman, the star of the Oxford Movement, about whose influence he would say: "In an age of sofas and cushions, he taught me to be indifferent to comfort; and in an age of materialism, he taught me to venture all on the unseen." When the young acolyte went up to

Exeter College in 1853, "omniscient", as he said, "in all questions of ecclesiastical rights, state encroachments, church architecture and priestly vestments", he was disappointed to find that the spirit of Newman had been superseded by a liberalism that wanted nothing to do with the Anglo-Catholics and their via media. Disillusioned, Burne-Jones then met the single most important figure in his life, William Morris, who persuaded him to abandon theology for art.

McCarthy vividly recreates the great affection that Burne-Jones felt for this indefatigable craftsman, whose respect for the integrity of art left such an abiding influence on his Pre-Raphaelite associates and indeed his age as a whole. For Burne-Jones, Morris was "a rock of defence to us all, and a castle on top of it, and a banner on top of that". With "Topsy", as he nicknamed Morris, because of his unruly hair, he shared rooms in Red Lion Square, where the two ambitious artists set about embodying their vision of art not only in painting but in stained glass, tiles, mosaics, embroidery, tapestry, furniture, jewelry, and book illustration. They also made their great discovery of the three books that would have such an abiding influence on their later work: Ruskin's *Stones of Venice* (1851), Malory's *Morte d'Arthur* (1484), and Chaucer's *Canterbury Tales* (1478). Despite their later differences – Burne-Jones never shared his friend's fondness for Icelandic legend or Socialist rabble-rousing – the two were inspired collaborators. Together with Rossetti, the poet painter and another key influence on Burne-Jones, they remade the very conception of art among the philistine English, a conception which stressed not only the beauty but the utility of art.

Sojourns to Florence, Siena, Rome, and Venice, paid for by the princely largesse of John Ruskin, may have opened Burne-Jones's eyes to the extent of that philistinism but they did not supply the underlying catalyst of his art, which, as his son Philip recognized, was much more contemporary.

> With all his passionate devotion to the past . . . he was surely at heart a Modern of the Moderns. Deep, undoubtedly, was the influence which Italian art exercised over him, but . . . it was in reality with eyes immeasurably different from those of a Florentine in the days of Botticelli that he regarded the ancient world or sought to interpret its legacies. The sadness of expression in his faces . . . is due, I take it, partly to a certain

Celtic melancholy ... and partly to the unconscious reflection of the troubled and transitional age in which he lived; an age, it must be remembered, which bore the brunt of the first onslaught of a new and strange materialism upon old and established faiths, leaving its children lonely and wistful at the parting of the ways.

Besides Morris, the other key figure in Burne-Jones's life was his wife Georgie, about whom McCarthy is particularly insightful, especially about her close bond to Morris, who had his own reasons for regretting a spouse's infidelity. McCarthy also extols Georgie's two-volume life of the artist for its well-researched acuity. Indeed, in calling attention to one of its most moving revelations – "I think I should be a better companion to him if he came back", Georgie confesses at the end of the book – McCarthy calls attention to one of her own greatest virtues as a biographer: her unflagging, discriminating sympathy.

This great virtue notwithstanding, McCarthy is not always at her best when she discusses the works themselves. On the fascinating *Perseus* series that Burne-Jones painted for Arthur Balfour, for example, of which Wyndham Lewis thought so highly, she can only say that the theme "gripped his imagination". Then, again, what might be called the *Guardian* element in McCarthy gets the better of her when she suggests that the real value of the paintings lies in their being "a critique of contemporary society in all its moral crassness and its lack of responsibility for the environment". Burne-Jones, in other words, is worth looking at because he is green. Readers looking for a more critical consideration of the work may wish to dip into the catalogue for the Metropolitan Museum's centennial exhibition, *Edward Burne-Jones: Victorian Artist-Dreamer* (1998) edited by Stephen Wildman and John Christian, which includes good commentary on *Chant d'Amour* (1865), *The Annunciation* (1876–9), *The Beguiling of Merlin* (1872–7), *Laus Veneris* 1873–5), and *Briar Rose* (1894). Another good book on Burnes-Jones's work is Allen Staley's *The New Painting of the 1860s*, from Yale, which shows how the artist's innovative work in watercolor paved the way for the later oil paintings of the 1870s, 1880s and 1890s. These were the works that made him such a fixture of the Grosvenor Gallery and the New Gallery when they were challenging the hegemony of the Royal

Academy. Some thoughtful defense of Burne-Jones as a painter is still in order when the old estimate of *King Cophetua and the Beggar Maid* (1883) by R. H. Wilenski still hovers about his reputation. Looking at the painting, the popular critic could only see "the silliest possible still-life record of two models posing in fancy dress on a heap of Wardour Street bric-a-brac". McCarthy hardly mounts the case for the defense effectively when she invokes the admiration felt for the artist by the likes of Pierre Cardin, Andrew Lloyd Webber, and Jimmy Page.

Still, and this is a testimony to her considerable biographical skills, as well as to the exuberance of her subject, that she has nothing bright to say about the art does not take away from her portrait of the artist. Throughout the book, McCarthy turns to brilliant account a striking discovery made by Graham Robertson, a family friend of the painter, who recalled seeing the great man as a boy. "He might have been a priest newly stepped down from the altar, the thunder of great litanies still in his ears, a mystic with spirit but half recalled from the threshold of another and fairer world; but as one gazed in reverence the hieratic calm of the face would be broken by a smile so mischievous, so quaintly malign, as to unfrock the priest at once and transform the mage into the conjurer at a children's party." This is the man behind the artist that McCarthy presents with such marvelous fidelity by capturing his abounding charm, his chivalric kindness, his wonderful sense of the ridiculous, and his horror of anyone and everything that smacked of the bumptious.

In her deeply researched life, McCarthy shows us the fastidious aesthete who was driven nearly out of his wits by Mrs. Wilkinson, the bossy charwoman who insisted on mopping his studio when he was trying to work; the would-be lothario who could never find the courage to run off with his enrapturing Greek mistress, Maria Zambaco; the brilliant letter-writer who once told his nephew Rudyard Kipling, apropos his brother-in-law Edward Poynter, the Royal Academician who could not get enough honors: "The Lord has hit Uncle Edward hard for his knighthood. He is an ex-officio member of about every utterly uninteresting society in England and spends his evenings eating with bores."

The raconteur in Burne-Jones sheds a good deal of light on the artist in him, an aspect of the man which Robertson noticed when he remarked, "wonderfully quick as he was to observe and note passing events of a sad or comic or quaint character, all such material as would be useful to the novelist or the poet, he saw nothing from the pictorial point of view". Another painter under whom Robertson studied "would come in from a walk full of almost inarticulate delight at the memory of black winter trees fringing the jade-green Serpentine, or of a couple of open oysters lying on a bit of blue paper or of a flower girl's basket of primroses seen through grey mist on a rainy morning. Burne-Jones would have woven a romance or told an amusing tale about the flower girl, but would not have noticed the primroses; the combination of the silvery oysters and the blue paper would not for a moment have struck him as beautiful; he had not the painter's eye." Precisely, but it is his uncanny sense of narrative that gives so many of his paintings their distinct allure, especially when the narrative is so suspended as to capture something of the profound mysteriousness of recollected time. *The Mill* (1870–82) exemplifies this: no dance ever led its viewers a more mystifying dance than this Pre-Raphaelite meditation on the dancers of Lorenzetti and Botticelli.

Henry James once said that the artist was no "votary of the actual". This is true but at the same time he did give actuality to an art that is too often confused with escapism. When he contended that what he meant by a picture was "a beautiful, romantic dream of something that never was, never will be – in a light better than any light that ever shone – in a land no one can define or remember, only desire", he was calling attention to an extraordinarily real yearning without which art is impossible. Moreover, this shows how the man who began his days desiring to be a priest never entirely abandoned that unworldly calling.

When Burne-Jones's own story ended at the age of 64 in 1898, Kipling commended the family funeral at Rottingdean, outside Brighton, for including "no mobbing", "no jabber", and "no idiotic condolences"; he also left behind this memorable diary entry about the last of the Pre-Raphaelites: "His work was the least part of him. It is him that one wants – the size and the strength and the power and the jests and the God given sympathy of the man." These are the things that Fiona McCarthy captures with such admirable art in her wonderfully unputdownable biography.

John Tenniel: Down the Rabbit-Hole

Artist of Wonderland. The Life, Political Cartoons, and Illustrations of Tenniel, Frankie Morris. University of Virginia Press. 406 pages.

In her introduction to *Artist of Wonderland: The Life, Political Cartoons and Illustrations of Tenniel*, Frankie Morris recounts that it was in "the land of counterpane" that she was introduced to the drawings of Sir John Tenniel (1820–1914). During a long childhood illness she had been given the Alice books as a gift from her school and she recalls that "the strangeness of those books was like a private place to which I returned again and again to imbibe its odd flavor". *Strangeness* nicely captures the elusive essence of Wonderland. If Tenniel had been set to illustrate Dickens or Surtees or Thackeray or Trollope, he might have produced illustrations of a high order – his *Punch* cartoons prove how adaptable, professional, ready to please he was – but he would never have got hold of the peculiar strangeness that we see displayed in the Alice books, a strangeness that allowed him to forsake the expectations of his *Punch* readers and go instead down the rabbit-hole of his imagination.

Virginia Woolf said that since childhood somehow survived intact in Lewis Carroll, "he could do what no one else has ever been able to do – he could return to that world; he could recreate it, so that we become children again". But surely Carroll could never have recreated that world entire without Tenniel's wonderful drawings. To read Woolf's description of that world is to be reminded of a collaboration unparalleled in literature.

> "Down, down, down, would the fall *never* come to an end?" Down, down, down we fall into that terrifying, wildly inconsequent, yet perfectly logical world where time races, stands still; where space stretches, then contracts. It is the world of sleep; it is also the world of dreams. Without any conscious

effort dreams come; the white rabbit, the walrus, and the carpenter, one after another, turning and changing one into the other ... It is for this reason that the two Alice books are not books for children; they are the only books in which we become children. President Wilson, Queen Victoria, *The Times* leader writer, the late Lord Salisbury – it does not matter how old, how important, or how insignificant you are, you become a child again. To become a child is to be very literal; to find everything so strange that nothing is surprising; to be heartless, to be ruthless, yet to be so passionate that a snub or a shadow drapes the world in gloom. It is to be Alice in Wonderland.

If as readers we tend to find book illustration disappointing, it is because the illustrations in our heads always seem better than those on the page. How frequently do we glance over at the Phiz illustrations in Dickens and think, "Well done, amusing; but nothing at all like the people I had in mind". This never happens with Tenniel. We never think, "Well, that is how Tenniel sees Wonderland. Fine in its way but I see it differently". No, Tenniel's Wonderland *is* Wonderland and yet how incomparably strange it is!

The man who achieved this feat was born in Marylebone, London on 24 March 1820. The son of a dancing-master and Scottish-born beauty, Tenniel had what Morris describes as a classic London childhood, one which witnessed "milk women making their rounds with pails suspended from the wooden yokes across their shoulders, crossing sweepers, dustmen with leather flaps at the back of their caps, the barrel-organ man, the muffin man, the peep show man, the Punch-and-Judy man, and the man wheeling a 'happy family' cage of small animals" – all familiar to readers of Mayhew's *London Labour and the London Poor* (1851–62). Mayhew, incidentally, was one of the founders of *Punch*.

The influence that London had on Tenniel is reminiscent of the influence that it had on Turner, about which Ruskin wrote so eloquently. "No Venetian ever draws anything foul; but Turner devoted picture after picture to the illustration of effects of dinginess, smoke, soot, dust, and dusty texture; old sides of boats, weedy roadside vegetation, dung-hills, straw-yards, and all the soilings and strains of every common labour."

Tenniel, too, could make himself at home in the squalor of London. And, yet, like Turner, most of his best work – certainly his illustrations for the Alice books – can be seen as an attempt to escape what Ruskin called "multitudinous, marred humanity".

Tenniel was educated at a private school in Kensington and once a schoolboy, "would have advanced to trousers, perhaps buttoned to the close-fitting jacket of a shell or skeleton suit such as he gave Tweedledum and Tweedledee". Subsequently in Fitzroy Square he studied antiquities and the nude and then anatomy and the Elgin marbles at the British Museum. He was a lifelong fan of the theatre and drew pencil studies from performances of Shakespeare plays. Later he immersed himself in the study of costume and armor, which he would put to good use in the Alice books. In 1845, he won a contest to depict Dryden's "St. Cecilia" in the House of Lords and went off to Munich for a year to learn fresco technique. For four years Tenniel toiled amidst the sewer gases of the Thames. Yet when the fresco was finished it only confirmed his "irrepressible tendency to see the absurdities that might accompany lofty aspirations". In 1895, the fresco had become so blistered that it was mercifully covered over.

A quiet, modest, popular man, Tenniel joined *Punch* in 1850. One of his earliest and best cartoons, which unfortunately Morris does not include in her book, is of Lord John Russell as Jack the Giant-Killer advancing to attack Cardinal Wiseman during the period known as Papal Aggression (1850–1), which aptly captures the paranoia that greeted the reestablishment of the Catholic hierarchy in England. *Punch* was robustly anti-Catholic. Indeed, Tenniel was only engaged after the Catholic Richard "Dicky" Doyle resigned in protest over the paper's anti-papal pronouncements. Ruskin was memorably witty about the paper's editorial slant: "You must be clear about Punch's politics. He is a polite whig, with a sentimental respect for the Crown, and a practical respect for property. He steadily flatters Lord Palmerston, from his heart adores Mr. Gladstone, steadily but not virulently caricatures Mr. Disraeli, violently and virulently castigates assault on property of any kind, and holds up for the general idea of perfection, to be aimed at by the children of Heaven and earth, the British Hunting Squire, the British Colonel and the British sailor."

"Pater" Evans, the paper's editor-in-chief, would rightly claim that "sociability is the seat of the success of *Punch*". Elaborate dinners were routinely held at the paper's offices in Bouverie Street, as well as at the Song and Supper Rooms on the Piazza at Covent Garden. There were also outings each year to Richmond, Hampton Court, Greenwich, Dulwich, and, of course, the Derby at Epsom Downs. No doubt these festivities were in Tenniel's mind when he illustrated the tea-party of the March Hare and the Hatter in *Alice's Adventures in Wonderland* (1865) and the banquet at the end of *Through the Looking Glass* (1872). In later life, Charles Dodgson (a.k.a. Lewis Carroll) gratified his fondness for banquets by taking charge of the Senior Common Room at Christ Church, in the cellars of which he was careful to lay down stores of excellent port.

In his political cartoons, Tenniel was at his best portraying Disraeli, whom he depicted by turns as "Great Wizard", "Great Medicine Man", "Asian Mystery", "showman", "acrobat", "conjurer", "trickster", "farceur", "Sphinx" – all suitable roles for the man who managed to humbug both Bismarck and Queen Victoria.

When Tenniel resigned his position at the paper in 1901 – after producing a staggering two thousand cartoons – a dinner was held in his honor at the Hôtel Métropole with Prime Minister Balfour presiding over a gathering that included notables from every walk of life. When the toast was made, Tenniel, who had begun to go blind, broke down. By his death in 1914, he was stone blind, a sad end to the life of a man whom Balfour accurately called a "great artist and a great gentleman".

Morris's book is a series of essays, including biographical sketches as well as pieces on the political cartoons and different aspects of the Alice books. The biographical and Alice sections are the best.

Morris makes a valiant attempt to find bright things to say about the political cartoons but, perhaps inevitably, they disappoint. The entry for Tenniel in the old *Dictionary of National Biography* recalled that "through fifty years it was his mission to shoot at folly, to strike at fraud and corruption, to touch with delicate though firm hand the political problems of the hour. This task he accomplished with unfailing fancy and with a delightful humor which never degenerated into coarseness nor was lacking in dignity. Tenniel was never carried away by private feeling. His aim was to treat all public men with equality and fairness, and to be severe without being vindictive. Thus, he was always careful to make the politician, not the man, appear ridiculous, and the laugh raised is almost invariably good-natured." Here, in a nutshell, is why Tenniel disappoints as a cartoonist: he was too nice. Compare him to James Gillray (1757–1815), the scourge of Napoleon, George III, Burke, and Charles James Fox, and one sees at once how very vital nastiness is to good political caricature. Tenniel was too much the Victorian gentleman to be nasty and his cartoons suffered accordingly.

But this did not affect the immortal illustrations of the Alice books, where Tenniel's otherworldly geniality was a decided asset. For fans of those illustrations, Frankie Morris's handsome, well-researched, well-illustrated book can be highly recommended.

Becoming T. S. Eliot

The Letters of T. S. Eliot, Volume 1: 1889–1922, Volume 2: 1923–5, edited by Valerie Eliot and Hugh Haughton. Yale University Press. 871 and 878 pages.

In 1909 Henry James took thousands of letters that he had received over the years into his garden at Lamb House in Rye and committed them to a great bonfire. In his last years, what time he could spare from refining his ever more rarefied fiction he devoted to confounding his biographers. Indeed, he instructed his nephew that since his "sole wish" was "to frustrate as utterly as possible the post-mortem exploiter", he was insistent that his will include "a curse no less explicit than Shakespeare's own on any such as try to move my bones". T. S. Eliot also spent a good deal of time trying to thwart his biographers, stipulating in his will that no biography should be written until 50 years after his death. But as these two volumes of letters show, his epistolary candor was always at odds with his yearning for concealment, which now seems, in retrospect, to have been the unavailing protest of a profoundly confessional man.

In these adroitly annotated volumes, the poet's conquest of literary London is brought brilliantly to life. Here we see Eliot assuming the mantle of that great tradition of poet critics that had ruled English literature from Dryden to Arnold. We see him pushing the Georgian bookmen from their stools and touting the work of his friends, Ezra Pound, Wyndham Lewis, and James Joyce. We also see him making alliances with Richard Aldington, John Middleton Murray, and Herbert Read, all in an attempt to introduce rigorous new critical standards, a campaign which often leaves him throwing up his hands. As he remarks to one correspondent, "there are so very few people who will take the trouble to write well". Some sins can be laid at Eliot's door, but not that one.

The letters also take up his harrowing marriage to Vivien Haigh-Wood and his always arduous spiritual progress, which eventually leaves him on Margate sands connecting nothing with nothing. Here, the despair that underlies so much of Eliot's early verse is ubiquitous. Correspondent after correspondent is regaled with his fiscal woes, physical woes, marital woes, editorial woes, social woes, familial woes. Then, again, his distress can have an oddly literary quality. Vivien once remarked how "poetry and literature are the only things Tom cares for or has the faintest interest in". In a letter to Murray, written in 1925, it is as if he can only approach the ruin of his marriage by resorting to literature.

> In the last ten years – gradually, but deliberately – I have made myself into a *machine*. I have done it deliberately – in order to endure, in order not to feel – *but it has killed V* … I have deliberately killed my senses – I have deliberately died – in order to go on with the outward form of living – This I did in 1915. What will happen if I live again? "I am I" but with what feelings, what results to others – Have I the right to be I – But the dilemma – to kill another person by being dead, or to kill them by being alive? … Does it happen that two persons' lives are absolutely hostile? Is it true that sometimes one can only live by another's dying?

In this one passage, he invokes Coleridge's Ancient Mariner, Shakespeare's *Richard III*, Dostoyevsky's Raskolnikov, and Henry James's *The Sacred Fount*, the inspiration for which was the novelist's fascination with the beautiful Minny Temple, who died at the age of 24 and became the prototype for Isabel Archer and Milly Theale. As James told his brother, what he sought to capture in the novel was "the gradual change and reversal of our relations: I lowly crawling from weakness and isolation and suffering into strength and health and hope: she sinking out of brightness and youth into decline and death".

The parallels to Eliot's marriage are striking. When Eliot first met Vivien in a dance hall, she was bright and unconventional and promised to rescue him from the dreary academic career that might otherwise have been his fate at Harvard. More than anyone, Vivien encouraged the poet in him. "I do think he is made to be a great writer", she confides in one correspondent. Eliot, in turn, plundered Vivien's insights and battened on her maladies. When Vivien claimed, for example, "As to Tom's *mind*, I am his mind", she was not entirely exaggerating, at least for the period covered in these letters. And yet no sooner did they marry (months after meeting) than Vivien began her long descent into madness, while Eliot went from strength to strength as a poet and critic. In one letter he boasts, "I really think that I have far more *influence* on English letters than any other American has ever had, unless it be Henry James". Thus, the vampirism of James's novel reappears in Eliot's marriage with eerie fidelity.

At the same time, apropos Eliot's complex, tragic marriage, it is surprising to see the editors citing Carole Seymour-Jones's entirely unreliable *Painted Shadow: The Life of Vivienne Eliot* (2001), which Ann Pasternak Slater demolished in *Areté*. Despite the guilt Eliot felt over the collapse of his marriage, he was a dutiful husband. Certainly, there are no grounds for blaming him for Vivien's travails. Lyndall Gordon's excellent entry on Vivien in the new Oxford DNB, which incorporates Pasternak Slater's insights, albeit without acknowledgment, supplies a far more credible account.

Behind all of the letters looms the Great War. "Everything looks more black and dismal than ever", Eliot writes in March of 1918. "The whole world simply lives day to day", an observation that oddly recalls something once said by Jules Laforgue, whose poetry had such an indelible influence on Eliot: "Ah, what a day-to-day business life is!" For Eliot and his generation, however, the quotidian had become lacerating. "We feel sometimes as if we were going to pieces", Eliot writes his mother, "and just being patched up from time to time". Still, the suffering of civilians was nothing compared to that of combatants. Vivien's brother, Maurice, a lieutenant in the Manchester Regiment, whom Eliot found "very aristocratic and very simple too", briefed his brother-in-law on the horrors of the trenches, painting

> a picture of a leprous earth, scattered with the swollen and blackening corpses of hundreds of young men ... Swarms of flies and bluebottles clustering on the pits of offal. Wounded men lying in the shell holes among the decaying corpses; helpless under the scorching sun and bitter nights, under repeated shelling. Men with bowels dropping out, lungs shot away, with blinded, smashed faces, or limbs blown into space. Men screaming and jibbering. Wounded men hanging in agony on the barbed wire ...

After sharing these images with Eliot, Maurice admitted how "these are only words, and probably only convey a fraction of their meaning to their hearers". Of course, Eliot would spend most of his life immersed in what he called "the intolerable wrestle with words and meanings", though the evils of the First World War gave this "wrestle" an entirely new consequence, one with which we struggle still.

The letters chronicle the formative years of the *Criterion*, the magazine with which Eliot put his highly cosmopolitan stamp on the criticism of his age. In one letter, he describes his exemplary vision for the magazine:

> I wish, certainly, to get as homogenous a group as possible: but I find that homogeneity is in the end indefinable... I do not expect everyone to subscribe to all the articles of my own faith, or to read Arnold, Newman, Bradley, or Maurras with my eyes. It seems to me that at the present we need more dogma, and that one ought to have as precise and clear a creed as possible... but a creed is always in one sense smaller than the man, and in another sense larger; one's formulations never fully explain one... I do not, for myself, bother about the apparent inconsistency... between my prose and my verse. Why then should I bother about particular differences of formulations between myself and those whom I should like to find working with me?

The *Criterion* letters show what unrelenting demands the review placed on its unsalaried editor, though the biographical index here furnishes too scanty a profile on Lady Rothemere, without whose largesse the magazine would never have been launched.

Several letters take up the theme of *aboulie* ("want of will"), a major preoccupation of Eliot's poetry from paltering Prufrock onwards. In one letter, the ruthlessly practical Eliot observes how "there can be no contemplative or easy chair aesthetics... only the aesthetics of the person who is about to do something". This might serve as an epigraph for Eliot's handling of the related themes of atonement and conversion. The theme also appears in the family letters, for failure of will was wired into the very DNA of the Eliot family. "It is almost impossible", Eliot says at one point, "for any of our family to make up their minds". Their letters related to travel, for example, are of a Byzantine indecisiveness. In one letter, the poet nicely describes the Eliot penchant for putting on "climbing irons to mount a molehill".

Proof of the strength of Eliot's own will can be seen in the success he made of his position at Lloyd's Bank, where he handled all of the firm's foreign correspondence in an underground office in

Henrietta Street. "Within a foot of our heads when we stood", the critic I. A. Richards recalled, "were the thick, green glass squares of the pavement on which hammered all but incessantly the heels of the passers-by". Before leaving the bank, Eliot was making £500 pounds per annum, a good salary in mid 1920s London. Nevertheless, it is startling to see how much Eliot connived in Pound's *bel esprit* scheme, which sought to free him from the bank by enabling him to live off the bounty of his friends. If there was a capable businessman in Eliot, there was also something of a chancer.

The acid pen of Viriginia Woolf serves as a kind of mocking chorus throughout these pages. In one aside, for example, she astutely observes of Eliot, "I suspect him of a concealed vanity & even anxiety about this" and in another she describes Mrs. Eliot as "so scented, so powdered, so egotistic, so morbid, so weakly" that it almost makes her want to "vomit". Caritas was not one of Virginia's strong suits.

Yet, unlike Seymour-Jones, Woolf had no illusions about the unbearable burden that the increasingly insane Vivien placed on Eliot, exclaiming in one journal entry, "But oh Vivienne! Was there ever such torture since life began! to bear her on one's shoulders, biting, wriggling, raving, scratching, unwholesome, powdered, insane, yet sane to the point of insanity ... This bag of ferrets is what Tom wears round his neck."

That Woolf, the darling of the feminists, should confute the feminism that instigated Seymour-Jones's assault on Eliot is an amusing irony.

Henry Ware Eliot, the poet's brother brings welcome comic relief to a series of letters that can be unremittingly grim. In one letter of 1925, for example, this wonderfully good-hearted, generous man holds forth on the subject of marriage, at exactly the point at which Eliot's own marriage is in tatters.

> Good God, how does anyone get married? I would not accept a job as a traffic manager or shipping clerk because I know nothing about it, and yet here is a job which every man accepts apparently on the blithe assumption that knowledge of the business is innate in him. Should I take a course in obstetrics, infant feeding and household management? On top of my present duties [Henry worked in printing, publishing and advertising], and the necessity of making a change

in my whole mode of life, I cannot casually pick up these things. I have often puzzled over the marriage relationship, which seemed to me the most incongruous, impossible, and inconsistent thing ever conceived. One has to translate an iridescent fantasy into the hardest and ugliest of facts.

Of course, Henry's brother found his marriage to Vivien equally appalling, though his matrimonial troubles led to musings of a more meditative cast:

> The awful daring of a moment's surrender
> Which an age of prudence can never retract
> By this, and this only, we have existed
> Which is not to be found in our obituaries
> Or in memories draped by the beneficient spider
> Or under seals broken by the lean solicitor
> In our empty rooms.

When Eliot looked back on *The Waste Land* from the perspective of his later, happier years, he dismissed it as "a grouse against life". In many letters here, the poet's grousing is fierce. After his father dies, he writes, "I feel that both he and mother in spite of their affection were lonely people, and that he was the more lonely of the two – he hardly knew himself ... in my experience everyone except the fools seem ... warped or stunted". In quite a few of the letters, Eliot himself appears "warped and stunted". He is arrogant, pompous, and inveterately thin-skinned – indeed, at times, he reminds one of Gilbert Osmond, the supercilious aesthete in James's *Portrait of a Lady* who subordinates everything, except his vanity, to his dedication to art.

Yet if these pages reveal the flawed man of talent in Eliot, they also reveal the emerging moralist, who does not flinch from confronting either his flaws or his demons, which he wrote so much of his finest work, including "Ash Wednesday" and *Four Quartets*, to drive out. The man who emulated Dante by setting out "to purify the dialect of the tribe" never forgot that this would require purifying himself.

BRAVE OLD WORLDS

Earthly Powers: The Clash of Religion and Politics in Europe from the French Revolution to the Great War, Michael Burleigh. Harper Collins. 530 pages.

IN HIS GREAT HISTORY OF THE RUSSIAN REVOLUTION, *A People's Tragedy* (1996), Orlando Figes quotes Trotsky on what might be called the first principles of social engineering:

> What is man? He is by no means a finished or harmonious being. No, he is still a highly awkward creature. Man, as animal, has not evolved by plan but spontaneously, and has accumulated many contradictions. The question of how to educate and regulate, how to improve and complete the physical and spiritual construction of man, is a colossal problem which can only be conceived on the basis of Socialism. We can construct a railway across the Sahara, we can build the Eiffel Tower and talk directly with New York, but we surely cannot improve man. No, we can! To produce a new, "improved version" of man – that is the future task of Communism. . . .

Like Marx, Trotsky might have dismissed religion as the "opiate of the people" but he recognized that if communism was to supplant religion it would willy-nilly have to preoccupy itself with the "spiritual construction of man". It would have to usurp, not merely repudiate, religion. Like so many before and after him, Trotsky found that undermining religion necessarily required travestying it.

In *Earthy Powers*, Michael Burleigh shows how Marxism and other surrogate religions from the French Revolution to the Great War reaffirmed not the senescence but the indispensability of religion. Francesco Crispi, the anti-clerical statesman who helped unify Italy, spoke for many founders of these new faiths when he said: "In man religiosity is something innate, organic like sexuality, property, and the family ... No system will succeed in suppressing religiosity in the myriad forms in which this instinct manifests itself. It is the task of politicians to direct it towards good, and the maximum benefit of society." How nineteenth-century politicians – together with reformers, revolutionaries, and counter-revolutionaries – ushered in a period in which the maximum misery of society was achieved is one of Burleigh's overriding themes.

Most historians of nineteenth-century Europe give religion only a marginal role in a drama driven by science and secularization. Burleigh shows religion to have been the unacknowledged fulcrum of the period. He quotes Tocqueville on the French Revolution to make his point: "Because the Revolution seemed to be striving for the regeneration of the human race even more than for the reform of France, it lit a passion which the most violent political revolutions have never before been able to produce ... Thus, in the end, it took on the appearance of a religious revolution which so astonished contemporaries. Or rather it itself became a new kind of religion, an incomplete religion, it is true, without God ... and without life after death, but one which nevertheless like Islam, flooded the earth with its soldiers, apostles, and martyrs".

No one can read Burleigh's boldly original history without being uncomfortably reminded that Europe now confronts Islam not with its old Christian confidence but with the false secular faith that it first began cobbling together out of the philosophical wreckage of the French Revolution. "From wrong to wrong the exasperated spirit proceeds", T. S. Eliot wrote in "Little Gidding" (1942). While the soldiers, apostles, and martyrs of Islam loom ever more menacingly, the exasperated spirit of Europe turns against itself in self-loathing and defeatism. How the once faithful, the once ingenious Europeans came to this pretty pass is an involved story, but Burleigh tells it with brio and point. For anyone interested in the past, present, or future of Europe, *Earthy Powers* should be required reading.

Apropos communism, Burleigh shows how many of the key terms of the Marxist lexicon parodied the Judeo-Christian tradition: consciousness (soul), comrades (faithful), capitalist (sinner), counter-revolutionary (devil), proletariat (chosen people), and classless society (paradise). Moreover, far from breaking any new philosophical ground, Marxism "combined the assurance that everything was operating according to the dispositions of secularized versions of higher powers with Gnostic sectarian belief that the messianic elect that had grasped these laws was morally entitled to destroy existing society ... in order to achieve earthly paradise. Communists took it upon themselves to realize heaven on earth through transforming violence ..."

Of course, it was only in the twentieth century and after 100 million people had been murdered that the followers of Marx achieved his Gnostic dystopia. But Burleigh shows how its roots lay in the "conspiracy of equals" that Gracchus Babeuf launched in 1798 against the Directory. "The perpetual cause of the enslavement of peoples is nothing but inequality," Babeuf declared, "and as long as it exists the assertion of national rights will be illusory as far as the masses are concerned."

This was what led Marx to imagine that religion was "the illusory sun turning around man as long as he does not yet turn around himself". Yet his deification of man, as Burleigh shows, substituted humanity for the Christian God in an oddly ahistorical eschatology. If the proletariat was at once the beginning and the end of history, how was it that they had only emerged in the mid nineteenth century and then only as 5 per cent of the total population? Here Burleigh demonstrates a common feature of the many surrogate religions that sprang up in the wake of the Jacobins' appropriation of religion in the French Revolution: their incoherence.

The first new faith he looks at is nationalism. The French historian Jules Michelet hailed his native land in terms that still find echoes in European football stadiums: "It is from you that I shall ask for help, my noble country, you must take the place of the God who escapes us that you may fill within us the immeasurable abyss which extinct Christianity has left there." The Italian nationalist Garibaldi drew up his own ten commandments, the seventh of which was "thou shalt not steal, other than Saint Peter's pence in order to use it for the redemption of Rome and Venice". The German philosopher Fichte described how churches could accommodate the new nationalist faith: "On Sunday morning ... when all parishioners have arrived, the church doors are thrown open and amid soft music the congregation enters ... When all are seated the great curtains at the altar are drawn aside, revealing the cannon, muskets, and other weapons which constitute the parish armoury. For every German youth from his twentieth birthday to his death is a soldier. Then there appears the justice of the peace, who unfurls the flag ..." As this shows, besides being wonderfully informative, Burleigh has a delightful sense of the ridiculous.

When Cardinal Manning denounced what he called the "deification of the civil power" few could have guessed the lengths to which the Germans would go to accomplish it. Nevertheless, once the Great War broke out, the dark side of nationalism had become undeniable. When the German philosopher Ernst Troeltsch exhorted his countrymen to remember that "the German faith is a faith in the inner moral and spiritual content of Germanness, the faith of the Germans in themselves, in their future, in their world mission", the madness was already stirring that would lead to the German death camps. (A historian trained in German history, Burleigh is also the author of a brilliant history of the Third Reich.)

Anyone who had to slog through Auguste Comte at university will particularly enjoy Burleigh's witty demolition of that unbalanced fellow's most celebrated brainchild, positivism. Comte may have tried to reconcile progress and order – the great intellectual idols of the period – but when it came to the spiritual content of his thinking, British skeptics were not far wrong in characterizing his positivism as "Catholicism without Christianity". In all events, in Comte's ideal world, as Burleigh observes, "the middle class would disappear, leaving 120 million proletarians ruled by two thousand patrician bankers" – which would not be everyone's idea of the earthly paradise. Somehow it seems only fitting that Comte's greatest disciple should have been the impossibly lecherous Freddy Ayer.

Next, Burleigh takes up Charles Fourier and Saint-Simon and their respective brands of utopian socialism. The store clerk Fourier drew on the ideas of Rousseau and Sade to propose a new world order made up of *phalansteries* or communes dedicated to harmony and self-fulfillment, where religion would be superfluous. In this heaven on earth, the elderly would be provided with compliant young sexual companionsM those prone, like Nero, to mass-murder would be employed as butchers; and armies would be engaged in endless games of chess. The environment was another of Fourier's concerns. Long before Al Gore, he insisted that the climate be monitored. His other pet schemes called for diverting rivers, melting glaciers, reforesting mountains, making polar icecaps habitable, and draining the world's seas of salt in order to refill them with lemonade.

According to Saint-Simon, whom Burleigh calls the "guru of all future technocratic solutions to social problems", religion was "the collection of applications of general science by means of which enlightened men rule the ignorant ... I believe in the necessity of a religion for the maintenance of the social order". For Burleigh, "that was the beginning of the Orwellian double morality whereby the enlightened elite espoused one code of values while force-feeding the donkeys with another".

Much the same criticism could be lodged against the late nineteenth-century advocates of Ultramontanism, who imagined that the only defense against liberalism within and outside the Church was a despotic papacy. On this defining issue of the end of his period, Burleigh might have drawn on the debate between Gladstone and Newman over the Vatican Decrees, in which Newman exposed the willful distortions of liberal enemies of the papacy and extolled the freedom of the Catholic conscience.

In the later chapters of his book, Burleigh cites three instances in which the Church and the Catholic faithful displayed admirable moral leadership – leadership which he believes both must exhibit again at a time when Islamic terrorism and moral relativism radically threaten the West.

When the papacy came under fierce attack during the pontificate of Pius IX (1846–78), Pius responded by issuing a comprehensive condemnation of contemporary errors in his 1864 Syllabus, the last of which was that the pope should reconcile himself with progress, liberalism, and modern civilization. "What is not often stressed is that in article 39 the pope denounced the doctrine that 'the State, as being the origin and source of all rights, is endowed with a certain right not circumscribed by any limits'. The Moloch-like expansion of the modern state into areas where it had hitherto acknowledged limits was one of the most important aspects of these nineteenth century conflicts, and Catholics were not slow to draw attention to this as they sought to limit state authority ... In the eyes of many ... an authoritarian pope became the ultimate defender of liberty against states that liberals were pushing in a highly illiberal direction."

The Catholic historian Christopher Dawson would echo this concern with the ramifying encroachments of state power when he observed in *Religion and the Modern State* (1935) that "the statesman of the past would no more have dared meddle [with the legion areas of existence with which present statesmen concern themselves] than with the course of the seasons or the movements of the stars".

The second instance was the stand the German Catholic Centre party made against Bismarck and his anti-Catholic *Kulturkampf* legislation. In response to these depredations, Burleigh observes, "Catholic Germany (and Catholic Poland) mounted an impressive counter-campaign of civil disobedience and passive resistance" ...

> During the Kulturkampf, the [Catholic] Centre Party's vote doubled, and their representation in the Reichstag rose from sixty-three seats in 1871 to ninety-three by 1877. Capable Centre Party leaders ... used their parliamentary platform to inveigh against the anti-Catholic legislation, despite the efforts of the President of the Reichstag to ignore their presence whenever they rose to speak. Despite being slight and virtually blind, Windthorst routinely got the better of Bismarck in debate, where the latter seemed blustering, bullying and tetchy. Centre Party leaders repeatedly exposed the hypocrisy of their liberal opponents by championing the freedoms that the latter preferred to overlook. They were also steadfast in opposing Bismarck's draconian Anti-Socialist Law, seeing parallels between their own fate and attempts to stigmatize an entire class. Although secular liberal Jews were enthusiastic supporters of the Kulturkampf, the Centre Party leadership resisted attempts by individual Protestant and Catholic anti-Semitic demagogues to lure them on board platforms allegedly based on supra-confessional, or just "Christian", values that thinly camouflaged anti-Semitism.

In his final chapter, Burleigh cites the peace proposals that Benedict XV broached during the Great War to resolve what he regarded as "a terrible manifestation of nationalism, the collective suicide of a great Christian civilization" at a time when most Protestant clergymen in Germany and England were content to treat the conflict as a kind of jingoistic holy war. It was only in 1917 after the debacle of Caporetto, when 200,000 Italians were killed and 400,000 deserted, that the Italians were prepared to heed his proposals. Burleigh also cites the successful humanitarian efforts that Benedict oversaw, which resulted in 26,000 wounded prisoners of war being dispatched to Swiss sanatoria. If the Church had sometimes played its political cards poorly in the world that succeeded the contagion of the French Revolution, it showed a certain level-headed responsibility at the end of the period, when the game got very rough indeed. Burleigh should be applauded for urging that the Church play a similarly responsible role today.

On why so many of the surrogate religions hatched to replace the Church came to grief, Talleyrand was perhaps most instructive. When a projector buttonholed the great survivor and asked him how to ensure longevity for some new religion, Talleyrand replied: "I would recommend you to be crucified and rise again the third day."

More Cautionary Horror Shows

Sacred Causes: The Clash of Religion and Politics from the Great War to the War on Terror, Michael Burleigh. HarperCollins. 557 pages.

With the release of *Sacred Causes*, Michael Burleigh completes his two-volume history of the political religions of the nineteenth and twentieth centuries. Together with *Earthly Powers*, published last year, this second volume constitutes an indispensable study of the horrors men get up to when they put themselves at the center of their own God-defying religions. Winston Churchill was certainly not the most religious of men but even he recognized that those "non-God religions, Nazism and Communism ... are as alike as two peas. Tweedledum and Tweedledee were violently contrasted compared with them. You leave out God and you substitute the devil".

Showing how the totalitarian regimes of Italy, Spain, Germany, and Russia as well as the terrorist organizations of Sinn Fein and Al Qaeda used religion to advance their political ends, Burleigh conducts his reader through an infernal labyrinth of violence and megalomania, the principles of which the Russian philosopher Semyon Frank presciently outlined before the October Revolution of 1917: "The great love of mankind of the future gives birth to a great hatred for people; the passion for organizing an earthly paradise becomes a passion for destruction." In these man-made religions, Frank perceived, the revolutionary is a nihilistic monk, who "shuns reality, avoids the world, and lives outside genuine, historical, everyday life, in a world of phantoms, daydreams and pious faith ... The content of the faith is an idolatry founded on religious unbelief, of earthly material contentment ... A handful of monks, alien to and contemptuous of the world, declare war on the world ... to gratify its earthly material needs." This is the essential pathology that animates all of Burleigh's political religions.

If the despots in Burleigh's period were busy appropriating religion, what were religious proper doing? During and after the Great War, Burleigh shows, Benedict XV marshaled Vatican resources to alleviate the suffering of prisoners of war. The Opera dei Prigionieri dealt with 600,000 pieces of correspondence inquiring after captives. By January 1917, the Vatican had taken custody of 26,000 sick prisoners of war and arranged for them to recuperate in Swiss sanatoria. All told, the Vatican spent 82 million lire on humanitarian relief. By 1922, this largesse had so depleted Vatican coffers that they dwindled to the USD equivalent of $19,000. Only the generosity of North American Catholics staved off papal bankruptcy in the 1920s.

Burleigh also details the opposition that Pius XI and Pius XII voiced to the dictators. As Pius XI wrote, the totalitarian claim that the individual owed the state total allegiance, whether in the domestic or the spiritual realm, was "a manifest absurdity in the theoretical order, and would be a monstrosity were its realization to be attempted in practice". The libels that the KGB cooked up to discredit these two admirable popes in the eyes of their Eastern European satellites gained new life in the books of John Cornwell, but Burleigh refutes them with the help of the pioneering research of David Dalin, Rudolf Morsey, and Konrad Repgen.

Few would disagree with Burleigh that Hitler's "sallies into theological matters" were tantamount to "the musings of a saloon-bar bore". Yet the Fuhrer was shrewd enough to recognize that "the Catholic Church has but one desire, and that is to see us destroyed". Hitler no doubt gathered this from many brave Catholic clerics, including the archbishop of Mainz, who defied the Nazi storm troopers by reaffirming that "the Christian moral law is universal and valid for all times and races, so there is a gross error in requiring that the Christian faith be suited to the moral sentiments of the Germanic race" – a stricture reminiscent of Frank Borkenau's observation that National Socialism was a kind of pinchbeck Judaism, with Hitler as Abraham and the Aryan Germans as the Chosen People.

Hitler would also have seen the Church's opposition to National Socialism in the encyclical that Pacelli composed for Pius XI, *Mit Brennender Sorge* (1937), which, as Burleigh shows, was "an immensely astute critique of everything that Nazism stood for", anticipating "virtually all the themes that scholars of Nazism, especially in continental Europe, are currently pursuing". Pacelli had no illusions about the Nazis or their spiritual pretensions. "Whoever does not wish to be a Christian", he wrote, "ought at least to renounce the desire to enrich the vocabulary of unbelief with the heritage of Christian ideas".

Even before he became pope, Pacelli's opposition to Hitler was well-known. After a three-hour meeting with Pacelli in Berlin in 1937, the US Consul Alfred W. Klieforth reported that Pacelli "opposed unilaterally every compromise with National Socialism. He regarded Hitler not only as an untrustworthy scoundrel but a fundamentally wicked person. He did not believe Hitler capable of moderation, in spite of appearances, and he fully supported the German bishops in their anti-Nazi stand." Once pope, Pacelli even acted as an intermediary for a plot to remove Hitler, planned by German generals, including Ludwig Beck, which, however, Lord Halifax failed to exploit.

Burleigh shows that Pius XII was right to eschew outright condemnation of Hitler's persecution of the Jews, which would only have increased the deportations. Rather than confront Hitler directly, and risk reprisals against Catholics and Jews, Pius chose a more oblique approach, which freed him to continue to save lives behind the scenes. At his insistence, Church-owned buildings throughout Western and Eastern Europe hid thousands of Jews who would otherwise have been sent to the death camps. Armchair moralists who enjoy the benefit of sixty years' hindsight should take into consideration something Pius's colleague Cardinal Faulhaber once said: "With the Concordat we were hanged; without the Concordat, we were hanged, drawn and quartered." In that impossible situation, Pius worked wonders.

The British chief rabbi, Hertz, acknowledged this when he told Cardinal Hinsley, "Jews throughout the world will revere the Pope's noble memory as a feared champion of righteousness against the powers of irreligion, racialism and inhumanity". Rome's chief rabbi Israel Zolli also acknowledged this when he took the baptismal name of Eugenio before converting to Christianity in February 1945. Even Albert Einstein recognized that "only the Church stood squarely across the path of Hitler's campaign for suppressing the truth. I had never any special interest in the Church before, but now I feel a great admiration because the Church alone has had the courage and persistence to stand for intellectual truth and moral freedom. I am forced thus to confess, that what I once despised, I now praise unreservedly." That stand was only made possible by Pius XII's adroit diplomacy.

So why do so many still contend that Pius was "Hitler's Pope"? Burleigh does not mince his words: "Making use of the Holocaust... against the Church, simply because one does not like its policies on abortion, contraception, homosexual priests or the Middle East is as obscene as any attempt to exploit the deaths of six million European Jews for political purposes." What Burleigh omits to mention is that those who call for the so-called "rights" of abortion, contraception, euthanasia, and homosexuality are themselves adherents of a new *Ersatzreligion* that is as opposed to the Roman Catholic Faith as any of the other gimcrack faiths that made the nineteenth and twentieth centuries such cautionary horror shows.

Michael Burleigh is a brilliant historian whose history of the clash between religion and politics should not be missed. All people of good faith will find his analysis of the tragic past instructive and welcome his encouraging conclusion, namely that "clearly identifying a problem takes one halfway to its resolution".

The Catholic Novels of Graham Greene

In a review of the final volume of Norman Sherry's biography of Graham Greene, the English journalist and biographer of Carlyle and Enoch Powell, Simon Heffer, baulked at the attention Sherry gives to Greene's Catholic faith, arguing that for non-Catholics it is "simply irrelevant" or, worse, "an exposition of hypocrisy". For Heffer, if one takes into account the novelist's chronic adultery, his inveterate absence from the communion rail, and his own admission that he was what he called a "Catholic agnostic", Greene's religion was "a pose ... which he turned into a series of money-making opportunities".

To suggest that Greene can be read without reference to his Catholic faith is like suggesting that Surtees can be read without reference to fox hunting. To suggest that his faith was bogus, or assumed to sell books, is simply false. His faith was central to his being both as a man and as an author. That he failed to adhere to certain Church teachings does not invalidate his recognition of the binding truth of those teachings. Or brand him a hypocrite. He saw his failings only too clearly and never tried to appear better than he was. If anything, like Swift, he delighted in appearing worse than he was. In all events, in failing the Faith, he blamed himself, not the Faith. In "A Visit to Morin", one of his later short stories, a lapsed Catholic novelist declares: "I can tell myself now that my lack of belief is a final proof that the Church is right and the faith is true. I had cut myself off for twenty years from grace and my belief withered as the priests said it would. I don't believe in God and His Son and His angels and His saints, but I know the reason why I don't believe and the reason is – the Church is true and what she taught me is true. For twenty years I have been without the sacraments and I can see the effect. The wafer must be more than wafer." This is hardly the writing of someone whose faith was factitious. As Samuel Johnson once observed "he that is most deficient in the duties of life, makes some atonement for his faults, if he warns others against his own failings, and hinders, by the salubrity of his admonitions, the contagion of his example".

One measure of the boldness of Greene's achievement is the persistence with which readers continue to misread him. The knuckle-rapping from the English reviewer recalls George Orwell's famous review of *The Heart of the Matter* (1948). There Orwell upbraided Greene for perpetuating "the idea, ... floating around since Baudelaire, that there is something rather *distingué* in being damned; Hell is a sort of high-class night club, entry to which is reserved for Catholics only, since the others, the non-Catholics are too ignorant to be held guilty..."

That Catholics have been given the means of recognizing sin more accurately than non-Catholics and are therefore more damnable is a teaching that atheist socialists should find consoling. But Orwell was implacable. His objections to Scobie, the hero of *The Heart of the Matter*, were of a piece with his objections to Christianity: he thought both absurd and inhumane. He took particular exception to Greene quoting Charles Péguy for the book's epigram – *Le pécheur est au coeur meme de chrétienté* – on the grounds that "all such sayings contain, or can be made to contain, the fairly sinister suggestion that ordinary human decency is of no value". But it was precisely to examine the limits of "ordinary human decency", when bound by pity and pride, that Greene wrote *The Heart of the Matter*. In another piece, Orwell declared: "I do not want the belief in life after death to return, and in any case it is not likely to return ... Reared for thousands of years on the notion that the individual survives, man has got to get used to the notion that the individual perishes. He is not likely to salvage civilization unless he can evolve a system of good and evil which is independent of heaven and hell." This is comical stuff coming from someone who objected to the allowances the Church makes for invincible ignorance. Orwell complained that Greene assumed that "no one outside the Catholic Church has the most elementary knowledge of Christian doctrine". The problem was that Greene assumed altogether too much knowledge. When it came to matters of the Faith, Orwell was rather like Pinkie's girlfriend in *Brighton Rock* (1938), about whose unfamiliarity with evil Greene says, "It was as if she were in a strange country: the typical Englishwoman abroad, she hadn't even got a guide book".

Before considering how his faith informs his novels, it might be useful to look at how it developed. Greene's conversion was haphazard. In 1925, at the age of 21, while working in Nottingham as a sub-editor of *The Times*, he sought instruction to please his Catholic fiancée, Vivien Dayrell-Browning. As he told an interviewer later in life, "I slipped a note into a collection box in the cathedral ... I wanted to understand what she believed in ... I had no thought of becoming a convert". Then he met Father Trollope, who was a convert himself. Before entering the Church and becoming a priest, he had been on the London stage for ten years, playing villains. In his autobiography, *A Sort of Life* (1971), Greene described his stage-struck, convert catechist as "a very tall and very fat man with big smooth jowls which looked as though they had never seen a razor ... he resembled a character in one of those nineteenth-century paintings to be seen in the wrong side of Piccadilly – monks and cardinals enjoying their Friday abstinence by dismembering enormous lobsters and pouring great goblets of wine". Catechist and catechumen debated points of theology while traveling by tram. Greene tried parrying Trollope's doctrinal thrusts with the arguments of atheism. In *Brighton Rock*, Greene's first Catholic novel, there is an exchange that one can readily imagine Greene having with Trollope. "I don't believe in what my eyes don't see", one character says. To which, Pinkie, the hell-haunted gang leader responds, "They don't see much then". When Greene eventually recognized the reality of the Faith, he made his general confession with "somber apprehension". He was surprised by the depth of his conversion. "Suppose I discovered in myself what Father Trollope had once discovered, the desire to become a priest ... At that moment it seemed by no means impossible." Later, in Mexico in 1938, when the socialists had outlawed the Church, he felt his faith deepen when he saw what he described in *The Power and the Glory* (1940) as "an odd grove of crosses" standing up "blackly against the sky ... some as high as twenty feet, some not much more than eight" – palpable proof of the "dark and magical heart of the faith". And its resilience.

Years later, when he felt his faith wavering, he described the counsels of the lapsed with sad precision: "we ... become hardened to the formulas of confession and skeptical about ourselves: we ... only half intend to keep the promises we make, until continual failure or the circumstances of our private life, finally make it impossible to make any promises at all and many of us abandon Confession and Communion to join the Foreign Legion of the Church and fight for a city of which we are no longer full citizens". For all its jauntiness, this is a tragic admission. Intellectual pride had convinced him that impenitence was the price of integrity: a mad conviction that someone of Greene's moral intelligence should have been smart enough to discredit. But alas we all do silly things. The circumstances of his private life that kept Greene away from the communion rail were a series of long-term adulterous affairs. At first with Dorothy Glover, an intellectual bohemian with whom he shared a passion for Victorian detective fiction; then with Catherine Walston, a theology-besotted beauty who was as rich as she was sexually insatiable; and finally with Yvonne Cloetta, a married Breton woman, whom Selina Hastings, Evelyn Waugh's biographer, described as "a brightly coloured Barbie doll ... a glamorous bourgeoisie ... smart, sexy, practical and tough". He also invested a fair amount of time and money in the society of prostitutes. The remarkable thing is not only that he remained married to his long-suffering wife Vivien but that he remained on friendly terms with both her and his other lady friends. Clearly, Greene was something of a card – a *pistolero*, to use a word he uses to good effect in *The Power and the Glory* – but an unusually charming one. Evelyn Waugh, to name just one longtime friend, delighted in him, seeing in his subversiveness and dry, mocking wit a mirror image of his own anarchic genius.

Here, it might be useful to address Greene's anti-Americanism. Such prejudice has become so conventional in academic circles that it is easy to forget just how unconventional Greene's own variety was. Yes, in interviews and letters to the editor he found fault with America's policies in Vietnam and Central America. He baited Hollywood in 1936 by accusing Shirley Temple of being a "complete totsy". He declared that if he had his choice between living in America or Soviet Russia he would opt for the latter. And he probably would have agreed with Waugh that "*of course* the Americans are cowards. They are almost all the descendants of wretches who deserted their legitimate monarchs for fear of military service". But, really, a good deal of this was teasing, of a piece with his spreading the story that he spent his adolescence playing Russian roulette. His other motivations were hardly more sinister. Greene badmouthed America, in part, to curry favor with Moscow so he could spy on fellow travelers for British intelligence. And, in part, to retaliate against the State Department for refusing him a visa in the 1950s on the grounds that he had briefly been a member of the Communist party as an undergraduate at Oxford. Whatever his real feelings about America, it has to be remembered that the great love of his life, Lady Walston, was born and bred in Rye, New York.

In his brilliant book on the four last things, *Life Everlasting* (1952), the French Thomist Reginald Garrigou-Lagrange remarks that "the mysteries of iniquity and wickedness, and their consequences, are more obscure than the mysteries of grace. They are obscure not only to us, but even in themselves". In *Brighton Rock*, a book of breathtaking originality, about the writing of which Greene once said "I have never again felt so much the victim of my own inventions", he revealed the heart of that mystery with stunning vividness. V. S. Pritchett rightly observed that Greene's greatest achievement was to revive the sense of evil in the English novel, from which it had been absent since the death of Henry James. "His religion", he says, "has the egocentricity, the scruple, the Puritanism and aggression present in English nonconformity, though it finds more savour in failure than success". The Brighton in which the book is set is a tawdry, seaside inferno, where the only character aware of the stakes of good and evil is Pinkie, a nail-biting young thug who declares that "when they christened me, the holy water didn't take. I never howled the devil out". The extraordinary thing about this most relentlessly nasty book is how exhilarating it is. It has the propulsive drive and wild exultant energy of early rock and roll. And although no good Catholic novel should read like a theological tract, it is remarkable that a book whose hero has his heart set on damnation should ultimately reaffirm the power of grace. The book proves with a vengeance Garrigou-Lagrange's point that: "Darkness and evil show in their manner the value of eternal light, of the sanctity that cannot be lost". Or as Lacordaire put it, "a soul, the most precious work of the Creator, will live on forever. You can soil that soul, but you cannot destroy it. God, whose justice you have challenged, turns even lost souls into images of His law, heralds of His justice".

"Nobody here could ever talk about a heaven on earth", observes the narrator in *The Heart of the Matter* (1948). "Heaven remained rigidly in its proper place on the other side of death; on this side flourished the injustice, the cruelties, the meanness that elsewhere people so cleverly hushed up. Here you could love human beings nearly as God loved them, knowing the worst." In Greeneland, the worst is inescapable. Boredom and deceit and loneliness abound and what virtue there is – like Scobie's honesty – is poised to miscarry. The only thing that redeems many of the characters is their sense of their own unworthiness. There are no plaster saints in Greene's universe. The special attention that Pope Benedict XVI accords the Eucharist makes one doubly admire the humility and the awe with which Greene's characters approach the body and the blood of Our Lord. Neither for Scobie nor the whiskey priest is the focal point of the Mass what Scobie's lover calls "hooey". The words of the Latin liturgy haunt both of them: *Domine, non sum dignus ... Domine, non sum dignus ... Domine, non sum dignus.* Scobie's prayer is the prayer of nearly all of Greene's wayward Catholics: "O God, I have deserted you. Do not you desert me."

In *The End of the Affair* (1951) Greene ransacked the details of his affair with Catherine Walston to create a vision of love and hate that transforms the tradition of the novel of adultery, uncovering possibilities in the genre that never occurred to Tolstoy or Flaubert. Aside from its theological interest, the story has the simplicity of melodrama. (Greene was an avid student of Henry James's moral melodramas.) As Evelyn Waugh pointed out in a review, it is a sort of Catholic *Brief Encounter*. An adulterous affair ends – or perhaps one should rather say begins – when the heroine, Helen, vows to God during a bombing raid to cut off her illicit relations if He spares Maurice, her lover. Maurice is spared and Helen makes good her promise. When she dies shortly thereafter, reconciled to the Church and to God, Maurice is left to ponder the nature of his lover's devout departure. For him, God has absconded with his one irreplaceable lover, and he spends the rest of the book protesting the fact in a rage of jealousy and hate.

The funny bits of the novel are some of the funniest Greene ever wrote. Despite his preoccupation with sin and damnation, or perhaps because of it, Greene was a superb comedian.

> "You'd be surprised," Miss Smythe said. "People are longing for a message of hope."
>
> "Hope?"
>
> "Yes, hope," Smythe said. "Can't you see what hope there'd be, if everybody in the world knew that there was nothing else than what we have here? No future compensation, rewards, punishments." His face had a crazy nobility... "Then we'd begin to make this world like heaven."
>
> "There's a terrible lot to be explained first," I said.
>
> "Can I show you my library?
>
> "It's the best rationalist library in South London," Miss Smythe explained.

In another memorable exchange, Maurice is speaking with his lover's husband, Bendrix, and the topic of the Real Presence comes up. Bendrix says, "In the Mass they still believe in transubstantiation". To which Maurice responds, "Materialism isn't only an attitude for the poor... Some of the finest brains have been materialist, Pascal, Newman. So subtle in some directions: so crudely superstitious in others. One day we may know why: it may be a glandular deficiency." For all its jokes, there is a serious side to the book. The blasphemies heaped on God by Maurice are the blasphemies of impenitence. Garrigou-Lagrange describes this rebellious state with chilling lucidity:

> the soul has a horror of God, an aversion which comes from unrepented sin which still holds it captive. Continuing to judge according to its unregulated inclination, it has not only lost charity, but it has acquired a hatred of God. Thus it is lacerated by an interior contradiction. It is carried towards the source of its natural life, but it detests the just judge, and expresses its rage by blasphemy.

There is no better gloss on the God-hating hero of *The End of the Affair*.

In 1949, Evelyn Waugh wrote to his good friend Nancy Mitford, "I had an excruciating weekend in a convent in Surrey conducting a 'Catholic Booklovers Week-end'... The sorts of questions are, of course, 'Why does Mr. Greene have such a nasty mind?'" Greene's nasty-mindedness was deliberate. He used nastiness not to gratify prurience or remonstrate with the ill-behaved or exhibit the pathologies of vice but to appeal to his readers' sense of goodness. In *The Power and The Glory*, which is probably his best book, the whiskey priest is thrown in jail for being caught with a bottle of brandy. There, in a crowded cell, he encounters a fellow prisoner who "had the tiresome intense note of a pious woman". The priest surmises that the woman has been locked up "for having a holy picture in her house". The novel is set in Mexico in the late 1930s when the Marxists were persecuting the Church. Such women "were extraordinarily foolish over pictures. He had always been worried by the fate of pious women: as much as politicians, they fed on illusion: he was frightened for them. They came to death so often in a state of invincible complacency, full of uncharity. It was one's duty, if one could, to rob them of their sentimental notions of what was good." When the woman objects to some prisoners copulating in a corner of the cell, the priest turns to her and says: "Saints talk about the beauty of suffering. Well, we are not saints, you and I. Suffering to us is just ugly. Stench and crowding and pain. *That* is beautiful in that corner – to them. It needs a lot of learning to see things with a saint's eye." The woman is shocked. "I can see you're a bad priest", she says. "You sympathize with these animals". The priest does sympathize with the animals, as did Greene, who proved his sympathy by disabusing his readers of "sentimental notions of what was good". His nasty-mindedness was salutary.

John Henry Newman, whom Greene read closely, always insisted that Catholic literature should not be confused with theology. Otherwise, the "literary layman" might very well "wince at the idea, and shrink from the proposal, of taking part in ... the formation of a Catholic literature, under the apprehension that in some way or another he will be entangling himself in a semi-clerical occupation". Greene sought to obviate this confusion by reminding readers that he was a novelist who simply happened to be a Catholic. But to no avail: all his life he was obliged to defend himself against criticisms from Catholics who charged that his novels *were* theology and bad theology at that. If the criticisms of his co-religionists were muddled, those of secular critics were worse. In his biography of Greene published in 1994, Michael Shelden accused his subject of being homicidal, sadomasochistic, homosexual, anti-Semitic, misogynistic, and treasonous. And anti-Mexican. But he was particularly venomous about Greene's faith, which he contrived to see as the faith of a double agent. According to Shelden, the "Catholic Church [for Greene] was an enormous edifice that could sustain heavy assaults without collapsing. He could subject it to one indignity after another, turning its good points into bad ones, making its God a devil, and Lucifer a saint. He could ridicule its priests and parody its rituals. Best of all it was possible to do this from within, to pose as a friend in the day and to chip away at the foundations at night. And in the end the Church would have to forgive him, because that is what religion is all about." A propos *The End of the Affair*, a book which he misreads ludicrously, he says, "No major novelist has shown as much ingenuity in abusing the God of Christianity. It is a dubious distinction, but one that Greene fully deserves." Shelden is a highly regarded literary biographer, with acclaimed biographies of George Orwell and Cyril Connolly to his credit. But his ignorance of the Faith disables him from saying anything accurate about Greene's art, or anything just about his life.

Some of the best insights into Greene's Catholic art can be gleaned from his critical writings. Like T. S. Eliot, he wrote a fair amount of what Eliot called "workshop criticism", in which he examined the work of others with an eye to refining and developing his own work. Thus, about G. K. Chesterton he says, "Much of the difficulty of theology arises from the efforts of men who are not primarily writers to distinguish a quite simple idea with the utmost accuracy. [Chesterton] restated the original thought with the freshness, simplicity, and excitement of discovery. In fact, it was discovery: he unearthed the defined from beneath the definitions ..." This is precisely what Greene does when he gives dramatic life to such theological concepts as damnation or blasphemy, goodness or pride. In a brilliant series of pieces on Frederick Rolfe, the mandarin novelist and priest manqué, Greene notes in passing that "the greatest saints have been men with more than a normal capacity for evil, and the most vicious men have sometimes narrowly evaded sanctity" – an observation that distills the essence of *The Power and the Glory*. As the narrator says of the whiskey priest, after he has been condemned to death, "He felt like someone who has missed happiness by seconds at an appointed place. He knew now that at the end there was only one thing that counted – to be a saint." In an essay on Somerset Maugham, Greene said, "Rob human beings of their heavenly and their infernal importance, and you rob your characters of their individuality". Greene may have agreed with Mr. Smith in *The Heart of the Matter* that people are longing for a message of hope but he would never have agreed with him, or George Orwell, that that message was possible without reference to "their heavenly and their infernal importance".

Greene's Catholic novels are his best because they reaffirm the basis of hope, which is truth. Not the truth as it appears to Scobie, when he claims: "The truth ... has never been of any real value to any human being – it is a symbol for mathematicians and philosophers to pursue." But the truth of the saints, who understand, like Saint Francis de Sales, that "let us go where we will, be where we will, we shall always be where God is".

Bad Ideas: The Prophetic R. G. Collingwood

History Man: The Life of R. G. Collingwood, Fred Inglis. Princeton University Press. 385 pages.

"One day when I was eight years old curiosity moved me to take down a little black book lettered on its spine "Kant's Theory of Ethics", the philosopher R. G. Collingwood recalled in *An Autobiography* (1939), "and as I began reading it ... I was attacked by a strange succession of emotions. First came an intense excitement. I felt that things of the highest importance were being said about matters of the utmost urgency: things which at all costs I must understand. Then, with a wave of indignation, came the discovery that I could not understand them ... Then third and last, came the strangest emotion of all. I felt that the contents of this book, although I could not understand it, were somehow my business." Other English boys might have dreamed of being cricketers or engine-drivers but Collingwood wanted to do something different. "There came upon me by degrees ... a sense of being burdened with a task whose nature I could not define except by saying, 'I must think'".

Thinking was indeed the governing passion of Collingwood's life and in *History Man: The Life of R. G. Collingwood*, Fred Inglis of the University of Sheffield takes up that passion with something of his subject's irrepressible brio.

Robin George Collingwood (1889–1943) was born at Cartmel Fell, Lancashire, the only son of the four children of W. G. Collingwood and his wife Edith Mary, the daughter of Thomas Isaac, a corn merchant. His delight in the life of the mind came from his father, a painter, archeologist, and writer, who later became John Ruskin's secretary and biographer. After being educated at home, where his father taught him Greek and Latin and included him in archeological digs in the Lake District, Collingwood, thanks to a rich patron, entered Rugby.

There, his precocity set him apart. "The boys were nothing if not teachable", he recalled. "They soon saw that any exhibition of interest in their studies was a sure way to get themselves disliked, not by their contemporaries, but by the masters; and they were not long in acquiring that pose of boredom towards learning and everything connected with it which is notoriously part of the English public school man's character."

If Collingwood took learning seriously, he had interests outside his academic work. He was an accomplished pianist and took a lifelong interest in art, about which he wrote with discriminating panache. A fan of Agatha Christie and Dorothy Sayers, he also had a wonderful sense of fun, which often enlivened his otherwise abstruse philosophical musings. It certainly gave his prose a playful elegance. "Going up to Oxford", he wrote in his autobiography, "was like being let out of prison. In those days ... a candidate for honours was expected to read Homer, Virgil, Demosthenes, and the speeches of Cicero more or less entire ... This was not only leading a horse to water, but ... leaving him there. The happy beast could swill and booze on Homer until the world contained no Homer that he had not read."

At University College, he also made time for "many long walks in the country, many idle afternoons on the river, many evenings spent playing and hearing music, many nights talking until dawn". After obtaining a first in classical moderations in 1910, he turned to Greats, in which he duly received another first. In 1912, he was elected to a fellowship and tutorship in philosophy at Pembroke.

During the First World War, Collingwood worked with the intelligence department of the Admiralty, after which he taught philosophy at Pembroke and Lincoln. In 1918, he married and had two children. In 1927, he became university lecturer in philosophy and Roman history. In 1941, his wife dissolved their marriage and in the same year, he married one of his former students, with whom he had one daughter. He died in 1843 of pneumonia.

Throughout his career, Collingwood set himself one goal: "to bring about a rapprochement between philosophy and history", which would culminate in his best book, the posthumous *The Idea of History* (1946). Although the thesis of the book is not entirely persuasive – all history is *not* the history of thought – its insights into the way history animates philosophy are still compelling. Other notable works of his include *An Essay on Philosophical Method* (1933) and *The Principles of Art* (1938).

Better than most historians, Collingwood recognized how "we all approach history infected with tendentiousness". Accordingly, he was convinced that "our actual historical labour must consist largely in overcoming it and ... endeavouring to bring ourselves to a frame of mind which takes no sides and rejoices in nothing but the truth". For Collingwood, to give way to tendentiousness meant "ceasing to be an historian and becoming a barrister; a good and useful member of society, in his right place, but guilty of an indictable fraud" if one claimed to be an historian. Of the tendentiousness that first arose in the histories of the early twentieth century Collinwood was profoundly prescient.

> It is said, and widely believed, that history has hitherto been written by capitalists, and from a capitalist point of view. It is time, therefore, to take it out of their hands and write it deliberately from a proletarian point of view, to construct a history of the world in order to show the proletariat as the permanently oppressed hero and the capitalist as the permanent villain and tyrant of the human drama. This proposal, however strange it may seem in an Oxford lecture-room [Collinwood was writing in 1926] is today a matter of practical politics; numerous people are acting on it, and are manufacturing the literature which it demands. The result is a type of history somewhat recalling the anti-religious histories of the eighteenth-century – a history inspired by hatred and endeavoring to justify itself by, most anachronistically, projecting the object of that hatred, by an obsession that partakes of the nature of madness, into the whole course of human development.

The acuity of Collingwood's work came at a cost. Unremitting writing, lecturing, and tutoring left him frazzled, and before he was out of his forties he had had two strokes. It was to help him recuperate that an inspired doctor ordered him to take a six-month cruise to Java, during which Collingwood wrote his sprightly autobiography. If not his best book, it is certainly his most enjoyable.

The rise of the dictators in the 1930s confirmed Collingwood's belief in the power of history to animate and rouse moral action.

At the end of his autobiography Collingwood made a pledge that few intellectuals of the time could echo: "I know now that Fascism means the end of clear thinking and the triumph of irrationalism. I know that all my life I have been engaged unawares in a political struggle, fighting against these things in the dark. Henceforth I shall fight in the daylight."

That philosophy could learn from history was not an approved conviction in the philosophical circles of Oxbridge between the wars. If Collingwood was convinced that "we might be standing on the threshold of an age in which history would be as important for the world as natural science had been between 1600 and 1900", Bertrand Russell distrusted history, seeing it merely as Gibbon's "register of the crimes, follies and misfortunes of mankind". Indeed, in *Principles of Social Reconstruction* (1916) he repudiated history, arguing that a new civilization needed to be built to replace the one that was being obliterated in the trenches. Collingwood disagreed: "Destroy history, and you destroy the nourishment on which philosophy feeds; foster and develop a sound historical consciousness, and you have under your hand all ... that philosophy needs."

The First World War proved Collingwood's point. After the war, he looked back on "the characteristic theory of the state which we have learnt to call Prussianism" and saw a theory which "starts from the undoubted fact that the individual man is by himself powerless for good or evil, that as he owes his literal, physical life to a social fact – the union of his father and his mother – so he owes his economic, political, and spiritual life to the society into which he is born". From this, it followed that "all originative and creative power is vested in the state, and that the state is, therefore, so to speak, God". In our own time, we have seen this conception gain new ground, though its import remains the same. It is still a conception that imagines the state "as responsible to nothing higher than itself ... [with] no responsibilities, no duties, no obligations, no responsibilities to anyone except itself" – a bureaucracy, in fine, intent on perpetuating its own parasitical interests. And Collingwood had no hesitation in concluding that if "In framing this conception, [the Prussian state] was attempting to conceive the state in the likeness of God", though "it succeeded in creating a state that was rather an incarnation of the devil".

Here is a reading of the philosophical genesis of the Great War that one will not find in Liddel Hart or Evelyn Waugh's *bête noir*, C. R. M. F. Cruttwell. But it is a reading that offers a powerful corrective to our own growing statism. When Pope Benedict XVI visited England to beatify John Henry Newman, he warned his hosts (on the anniversary of the Battle of Britain) that it was precisely this deification of the state that had led to the horrors of Nazism in the Second World War and might lead to more ghastly mischief in the future.

Since Prof. Inglis was not given access to Collingwood's personal papers, *History Man* is more a commentary than a biography. Nevertheless, while he is good on Collingwood's feel for the richness of history, he overlooks his greatest accomplishment, which was to show how bad ideas wreak havoc beyond the academy. In this, Collingwood paved the way for one of our own most caustic historians, Theodore Dalrymple, who observes in *Life at the Bottom: the Worldview that Makes the Underclass* (2001), his collection of essays about his experiences as a doctor in an English slum hospital and prison, how irresponsibility, bred of fashionable notions of determinism now defines the underclass.

> Here the whole gamut of human folly, wickedness, and misery may be perused at leisure … abortions by abdominal kung fu; children who have children, in numbers unknown before the advent of chemical contraception and sex education; women abandoned by the father of their child a month before or a month after delivery; insensate jealousy, the reverse coin of general promiscuity, that results in the most hideous oppression and violence; serial stepfatherhood that leads to sexual and physical abuse of children on a mass scale; and every kind of loosening of the distinction between the sexually permissible and the impermissible.

In this lamentable catalogue Collingwood would have seen the harvest of what he called "the modern pretense that psychology can deal with what once were called the problems of logic and ethics". For Collingwood, such pretense required "the systematic abolition of all those distinctions, which, being valid for reason and will but not for sensation and appetite, constitute the special subject-matter of logic and ethics: distinctions like that between truth and error, knowledge and ignorance, science and sophistry, right and wrong, good and bad, expedient and inexpedient". And since these distinctions "form the armature of every science", psychology "regarded as the science of the mind, is not a science. It is what 'phrenology' was in the nineteenth century, and astrology and alchemy were in the Middle Ages and the sixteenth century: the fashionable scientific fraud of the age."

The incoherence that now characterizes our own culture is the result of that fraud, and no one foresaw its vicious reign more clearly than R. G. Collingwood.

Royal Charmer

The Queen Mother: The Official Biography, William Shawcross. Alfred A. Knopf. 1,096 pages.

In Evelyn Waugh's *Brideshead Revisited*, Anthony Blanche warns the hero Charles Ryder against what he calls "simple, creamy English charm". Indeed, Anthony is convinced that "Charm is the great English blight. It does not exist outside these damp islands. It spots and kills anything it touches. It kills love, it kills art."

One wonders whom Waugh's character had in mind when he articulated this odd stricture, because England's most charming artists – one thinks of Jane Austen or Edward Elgar or Thomas Lawrence – tend to be her most accomplished artists, charm and artistry going hand in hand. In any case, in his admirable new biography, William Shawcross shows that when it came to Queen Elizabeth (1900–2002), the beloved consort of King George VI and mother of Queen Elizabeth II, her charm was profoundly life-affirming. When Hitler called Queen Elizabeth "the most dangerous woman in Europe" he was paying tribute to the strength of that charm. Ryder's epicene friend had something more superficial in mind. With incisiveness and verve, Shawcross chronicles how Queen Elizabeth's Edwardian upbringing formed not only her strong, resilient, dutiful character but her abounding sense of fun. He has drawn on an immense array of sources to fashion a narrative that has all the grace, good sense, and vitality of his subject.

Elizabeth Angela Marguerite Bowes-Lyon, the ninth of the Earl of Strathmore's ten children, was born on 4 August 1900 at the family home of St. Paul's Walden Bury, near Hitchen, Hertfordshire, though the failure of her father Lord Glamis to register a birth certificate within the required forty-two days of her birth gave rise to speculation that she might more likely have been born in a horse-drawn ambulance in Mayfair.

The Bowes were a raffish lot: spendthrift, hard-drinking, and mad about sport. One of her eighteenth-century ancestors, known as

Stony Bowes, was described by a contemporary as "surely the lowest cad in history ... He was the type of seedy, gentlemanly bounder ... He was cunning, ruthless, sadistic, with rat-like cleverness and a specious Irish charm. He was a fortune hunter of the worst type." Doubtless it was this *louche* ancestry that gave Elizabeth so much of her delight in the turf, strong drink, and the society of courtiers.

Her father, Lord Glamis, later 14th Earl of Strathmore, was educated at Eton and served in the Life Guards. A philoprogenitive, gentle, unassertive man, he was particularly fond of Elizabeth, who reciprocated by "looking round to see if he wants anything – and lighting his cigarettes". Her devout mother Cecilia Cavendish Bentinck was the great-granddaughter of the third Duke of Portland, who was twice prime minister in George III's reign. After her clergyman father died when she was 3, Cecilia lived with her mother in Florence and the Italian Riviera. Some of Elizabeth's fondest childhood memories were of days spent with her mother and aunts in various Italian villas.

When home, Elizabeth resided in the family's Queen Anne house, the rose brick walls of which were covered with magnolia and honeysuckle, or the fifteenth-century Glamis Castle in Scotland, near Dundee. Local tradition held that the imposing, turreted, ghost-laden castle was the inspiration for Shakespeare's Macbeth. Elizabeth never forgot her grandparents celebrating their golden wedding anniversary there in 1903 when they invited 571 children from the surrounding neighborhood for fireworks, tea, sports, and a conjuring show. Later she bought and restored Barrogill Castle in Caithness, which she called what it had originally been called, the Castle of Mey.

Like most young ladies of her class, Elizabeth was educated at home by a succession of governesses who taught her piano, dancing, drawing, gymnastics, history, geography, mathematics, science, French, and German. When not putting her governesses through their paces, she formed her lifelong love of horses. It was also as a girl that she acquired her voracious appetite. Years later, when recovering from a bout of flu in Buckingham Palace, she wrote Princess Elizabeth, "I am ... still a little achy, and still living on tea! I hope by tomorrow that I shall be eating Irish stew, steak & kidney pudding, haricot mutton, roast beef, boiled beef, sausages & mutton pies, not to mention roast chicken, fried chicken, boiled chicken, scrambled chicken, scrunched up chicken, good chicken, nasty chicken, fat chicken, thin chicken, *any* sort of chicken".

During her childhood, Elizabeth formed an inseparable bond with her shy brother David, later the godfather of Princess Margaret, who confided to her sister after the loss of George VI, that it had been he who had encouraged the stammering Duke of York to pursue her before they married. In a letter divulging his long-kept secret, David explained that he was only breaking his silence "because in Your Majesty's terrible loneliness I believe that it may bring one tiny grain of comfort".

Another David, Lord David Cecil, the biographer of Lord Melbourne, who was so instrumental in the education of Queen Victoria, recalled Elizabeth as a child: "I turned and looked and was aware of a small, charming rosy face around which twined and strayed rings and tendrils of silken hair, and a pair of dewy grey eyes ... From that moment my small damp hand clutched at hers and I never left her side ... Forgotten were all the pretenders to my heart. Here was the true heroine." Cecil would be the first of Elizabeth's many literary friends, who would later include the Sitwells, John Betjeman, Noel Coward, and Ted Hughes.

On 4 August 1914, when the First World War broke out, Elizabeth was 14. As she lay in bed that night, jubilant crowds moved their way up the Mall towards Buckingham Palace. "The streets were full of people shouting, roaring, yelling their heads off," she recalled, "little thinking what was going to happen." After war was declared, Lord Glamis converted the Castle into an army hospital and the Edwardian idyll that had been Elizabeth's childhood came to an abrupt end.

In 1916, three months after the battle of the Somme began, Glamis Castle caught fire and it was only Elizabeth's aplomb that saved it from burning down, with all its treasures. News of her heroic fire-fighting made her the toast of Highland society. Afterwards, she helped tend to the convalescing soldiers, even writing them a poem about a shell-shocked sergeant, which had them in stitches. "Isn't it sad, in so young a lad / Such lunacy to see / For he drank his cup and saucer / And forgot about his tea!"

It was during these unforgettable war years that Elizabeth acquired her lifelong respect for soldiers. Later, before the Second World War, she was visiting the Black Watch at their barracks in Perth and noticed her nephew John Elphinstone among the officers. "It gave me such a shock to see John in his Black Watch uniform," she confided to Queen Mary, "He suddenly looked exactly like my brother Fergus who was killed at Loos, & in the same regiment. It was uncanny in a way, & desperately sad to feel that all that ghastly waste was starting again at the bidding of a lunatic."

Shawcross nicely sums up the impact of the First World War on Elizabeth: "She had acquired, through her experience of the suffering of family, friends and soldiers from all over the world, an understanding of pain, and of the difficulties of others, which served her and her country well in the years to come." If, towards the end of her life, she was often called "the last of the Edwardians", she was always careful to remind her countrymen that there were aspects of the Edwardian legacy that were worth preserving.

Elizabeth's marriage to George V's diffident second son, Prince Albert, proved deeply happy. Unsure at first whether she could adapt to her new role as Duchess of York, she eventually succeeded simply by making the role her own. When a friend asked her how he should address her, she replied: "I really don't know! It might be anything – you might try 'All Hail Duchess', that is an Alice in Wonderland sort of Duchess, or just 'Greetings' or 'What Ho, Duchess' or 'Say, Dutch' – in fact you can please yourself, as it will certainly please me".

Reading this, one can see why so many fell in love with Elizabeth. As one admirer told a former biographer: "Her charm was indescribable ... She was also very kind and compassionate. And she could be very funny – which was rare in those circles. She was a wag." Before accepting Prince Albert's third proposal, she received two from other beaux. Even George V, a morbidly implacable man, had to admit that "Bertie is a lucky fellow".

If her marriage was unexpected, her husband's accession to the throne was even more so. In this, Queen Elizabeth could not have been more different from Queen Mary, whose marriage to George V was carefully plotted. No one, least of all Elizabeth herself, planned to make Elizabeth Bowes-Lyon Queen of England. Edward VIII thrust the throne on her and her husband after Stanley Baldwin insisted that he either dump Wallace Simpson or abdicate. When he chose to abdicate, Elizabeth's life was changed forever. Shawcross vividly recreates the day-to-day drama of the abdication crisis.

No sooner had George VI ascended the throne than war broke out. When he and his Queen Consort visited the bomb-battered streets of London, there was nothing perfunctory about their empathy. "I'm glad we've been bombed," the Queen assured a London bobby after Buckingham Palace had been hit. "It makes me feel I can look the East End in the face." The quote has been quoted a million times in a million places and still it gets to the very heart of what makes a good queen tick.

Throughout the war, George VI and his Queen Consort rallied the home front by visiting towns and cities bombed by the Luftwaffe – including Plymouth, Bristol, Cardiff, Coventry, and Liverpool – and refusing to leave London. They also lifted morale by refusing to have the princesses removed to Canada. When England stood alone against the full fury of the German bombers, Queen Elizabeth responded to a letter of sympathy from Eleanor Roosevelt with a letter of her own.

> Sometimes one's heart seems near breaking under the stress of so much sorrow and anxiety. When we think of our gallant young men being sacrificed to the terrible machine that Germany has created I think that anger perhaps predominates, but when we think of their valour, their determination and their great *grand* spirit, pride and joy are uppermost. We are prepared to sacrifice everything in the fight to save freedom, and the curious thing is, that already many false values are going, and life is becoming simpler and greater every day.

When it came to bringing up her two daughters, Elizabeth considered their spiritual education paramount, and, as Shawcross notes, "here her mother's influence ran deep. She brought up her own children in the Christian principles she had learned; her letters to her daughters remind them to be kind, to be thoughtful to others, and to keep their temper and their word." She was also keen on showing consideration to the sensitivities of children, "something she felt her husband's upbringing had lacked". In one note, she urged her husband, "Remember how your father, by shouting at you, & making you feel uncomfortable lost all your real affection".

Elizabeth assumed her regal role with ready poise. As she wrote to Queen Mary, "I have great faith in Bertie – he sees very straight, & if this terrible responsibility comes to him he will face it bravely".

George VI proved an exemplary king, at a time when Great Britain's very survival hung in the balance. Much of the credit for his success was due to his good, brave, loving wife.

When George VI died at fifty-six from lung cancer after years of heavy smoking, she wrote her brother David: "Things can never be the same again without his energy & fun & goodness & kindness. He really was the kindest and most selfless person I have ever known." After Edith Sitwell sent her some poems by George Herbert, she wrote back: "how small and selfish is sorrow. But it bangs one about until one is senseless, and I can never thank you enough for giving me such a delicious book wherein I found so much beauty and hope."

Once her daughter ascended the throne in 1953, Queen Elizabeth played her new role of Queen Mother with zest. It was Churchill who convinced her that she must continue to play a national, indeed an international role. (From Balmoral, she wrote Lord Salisbury of their mutual friend: "He is truly a remarkable man, & with great delicacy of feeling.") In addition to becoming a symbol of enduring tradition, she became a perennial favorite of the Commonwealth, especially in Canada, where she made 13 visits. Like Churchill, she was an unrepentant imperialist and watched with deep dismay as Robert Mugabe and his jackals ruined Rhodesia. At home, she was never convinced of the benefits of socialism. "I am extremely Anti-Labour," she told one friend. As Shawcross rightly points out, "It was an intuitive antipathy, a sense ... that socialism sought to drag everything down into uniform and unimaginative drabness and political humbug."

That she regularly overdrew her account at Coutts was proof of more than her extravagance; she was unstintingly generous to those in straits. When her dear friend D'Arcy Osborne became hard up in old age, Queen Elizabeth wrote him from Clarence House: "D'Arcy, one or two of our old & loving friends have sent a small sum to your banking account in Rome, in case it might come in handy some time." To which the old man replied: "Dear Ma'am, How KIND!" Her munificence would allow him to take taxis and give him "the invaluable benefit of peace of mind and freedom from fussing over small and ignoble matters". What greater gift could any queen bestow?

Shawcross quotes Princess Alice, Countess of Athlone on the "arduous profession" of royals. "Their daily tasks, for months ahead, are prescribed and set out in a diary of engagements from which only illness can excuse them. None but those trained from youth to such an ordeal can sustain it with amiability and composure. The royal motto 'ich dien' is no empty phrase. It means what it says – I serve." Queen Elizabeth served with unflagging diligence but she also rewarded herself with many private visits to France and Italy, during which, as Shawcross notes, "little changed from year to year. She moved in an exquisitely geared time machine, cocooned against the harsher realities of the modern world. Her traveling companions remained constant and vigilant; on each occasion she was generously and charmingly entertained by members of the local nobility or even royalty; and each year she saw beautiful churches, castles, palaces, houses, museums, monuments, gardens and landscapes in two countries which she had loved since she was young." Doubtless such getaways confirmed her defiant insouciance. "The world staggers on from crisis to crisis," she assured one old friend in 1961, "but I have a feeling that human beings are beginning to become accustomed to these rather bogus upheavals, & take them more philosophically than the slightly hysterical reporters and newscasters!" Whether she would regard the upheavals that currently menace the world as altogether bogus is an interesting question.

In a long and yet never tedious book, Shawcross emulates something of his subject's reserve, which is refreshing in a biographer. For example, he says nothing of the more lurid aspects of the Windsors, so beloved of the tabloids, only remarking how: "There were some in the Royal Household who wished Queen Elizabeth would give [the Prince of Wales] robust advice. But that was not her style. She never liked to acknowledge, let alone confront, disagreeableness within the family. It was a characteristic which had earned her the nickname 'imperial ostrich'". Here, again, she proved the quintessential Edwardian.

After they attended a gala together at the Royal Opera House, the Duchess of Devonshire observed of Queen Elizabeth: "One forgets between seeing her what a star she is & what incredible and wicked charm she has got." William Shawcross captures that charm in all its life-affirming effervescence.

Waugh Fathers and Sons: Underhill Revisited

Fathers and Sons: The Autobiography of a Family, Alexander Waugh. Doubleday. 521 pages.

In *Fathers and Sons*, Evelyn Waugh's grandson Alexander revisits some fascinating family history. Here is the story of four generations of Waughs told with wit and *brio*. Evelyn Waugh has been fortunate in his biographers – Frances Donaldson, Selina Hastings, and Douglas Lane Patey all wrote brilliantly about him – but *Fathers and Sons* reveals aspects of the novelist's poisonous relationship with his father, Arthur, that have never been given adequate attention. Anyone interested in the Waugh family or family history per se will find it an absorbing read.

The book opens with a portrait of Arthur's father, Alexander, otherwise known as "the Brute", an award-winning doctor who delighted in shooting and fishing. With his booming voice, Dundreary whiskers, and mad, piercing eyes, he terrified family and associates alike. He took particular pleasure in flogging his dogs. Perhaps unsurprisingly, none of his three daughters ever married. When the word "sadist" was first explained to Arthur, he is reported to have thought a minute and said, "Ah that is what my father must have been".

Although "the Brute" congratulated Arthur on winning the Newdigate Prize for his epic poem about Gordon of Khartoum, he died before he could see his son's later attainments as publisher, poet, biographer, and critic. The only interests father and son shared were amateur theatricals and cricket.

The theatrical interest would become a Waugh family staple. Arthur regularly recited passages from Dickens, Shakespeare, and the great Victorian poets to both his sons at Underhill, the family home in Hampstead. Evelyn endowed most of his books with the pace, economy, and seamlessness of good theatre. He might also have been a first-rate theatre critic, as a review he wrote of a 1955 production of *Titus Andronicus* demonstrates. Here is his description of Vivien Leigh as Lavinia:

> When she was dragged off to her horrible fate she ventured a tiny impudent, barely perceptible roll of the eyes, as who should say: "My word! What next!" She established complete confidence between the audience and the production. "We aren't trying to take you in," she seemed to say. "You're too clever, and we are too clever. Just enjoy yourself." It was the grain of salt which gave savour to the whole rich stew.

Evelyn also enjoyed playing theatrical roles himself, the most memorable being the one described in *The Ordeal of Gilbert Pinfold* (1957): "a combination of eccentric don and testy colonel" which he acted relentlessly in his later years. Like Pinfold, he "offered the world a front of pomposity mitigated by indiscretion that was as hard, bright and antiquated as a cuirass".

Cricket played an immense part in Arthur's family life. "With a thorough knowledge of the Bible, Shakespeare and *Wisden's Cricketing Almanac*", he would tell his sons, "you cannot go far wrong". In 1893 Arthur married, and five years later had his first son, Alec, whom he always referred to as "the son of my soul", not least for his cricketing prowess at Arthur's own school, Sherborne.

Arthur's love for his first-born son was all-consuming. When Alec was boarding at Sherborne, Arthur wrote him daily and awaited his responses "in the palpitating manner of a teenage paramour". Something was not right in this picture. "I think Arthur may have suffered from the same syndrome that is claimed of the pop star Michael Jackson," Alexander observes. "Those who are brutalized by their fathers often find themselves unable to grow up: They are consumed with a need to relive their childhood over and over again to get it right." Alec was the golden boy he had never been able to be himself.

Where did this leave Evelyn? Alexander puts matters succinctly: "Alec and Arthur were a two-man gang from which Evelyn was excluded." The second son, whose difficult birth had come five and a half years after Alec's, was never shown the attention he craved. Both parents had wanted a girl and let Evelyn know it. He was not the golden boy and, as Alexander shows, the resentment this caused stayed with him for the rest of his life.

Meanwhile, all was not well at Sherborne: Alec was discovered *in flagrante delicto* and stripped of all his schoolboy honors. He wrote his first novel, *The Loom of Youth* (1917) to expose the homoeroticism rife at public schools. A *success de scandale*, the book won him praise from the likes of J. C. Squire and Arnold Bennett. Then Alec went off to war and witnessed the horrors of Passchendaele from an abandoned German pillbox. However, when he returned home, it was his experiences in French brothels that he was eager to share with his wide-eyed brother.

Alexander calls Alec an "erotomaniac". Evelyn and his friends called him "the bald-headed lecher". Although married twice, he never put down roots and was happiest trotting the globe in search of exotic conquests. Tahiti was his favorite destination. "Polynesians, as hula dancers," he discovered, "acquire an astonishing mobility between the knees and navel".

While Alec was already setting himself up as a successful novelist, Evelyn floundered. He did poorly at Oxford. He took teaching jobs from which he was ignominiously sacked. He even enrolled in a course for carpenters. But mostly he drank. When he did finally put pen to paper, settling scores with his father became paramount. In *Rossetti* (1928), his first book, he was careful to differentiate his own from his father's brand of biography, which he claimed only produced "catafalques heaped with the wreaths of august mourners, their limbs embalmed, robed, uniformed and emblazoned ... their faces serenely composed and cleansed of all stains of humanity".

In *Decline and Fall* (1928), Evelyn's first novel, Arthur is mocked in the character of Prendergast, a sentimental glutton, whose death, as Alexander points out, "must have been especially galling to Arthur: his head is sawn off by a madman who wants to be a carpenter".

In 1930, Evelyn had Arthur's shortcomings in mind when he wrote a piece called "What I Think of My Elders":

> I admire their lack of scruple. It takes a great deal to rouse them, but when some feature of their comfort is really threatened they will suddenly plunge into conflict with every artifice their long lives have taught them. I admire their lack of ambition. I admire the resolution with which they hold to their own opinions; their indifference to the traps and pitfalls of logical proof. I admire their sense of humour, those

curious jokes which seem to gain lustre and pungency with each repetition.

When Evelyn's story "The Man Who Liked Dickens" (1933) appeared, the mere title must have made the old man shudder. "What new onslaught – what new patricidal biffing am I in for now?" (Alexander provides inspired interior monologue.)

Everyone in literary London knew that Arthur loved Dickens. He was president of the Dickens Fellowship. He lectured on Dickens. For over thirty years, as managing director of Chapman and Hall, he published Dickens. The actress Ellen Terry called him "Mr. Pickwick". Evelyn took his father's harmless delight in the novelist and turned it into a comic nightmare in which a shipwrecked explorer falls into the clutches of a lunatic half-caste who insists on having his captive guest read the works of Dickens over and over again. Later Waugh would make the story the gruesome finale of *A Handful of Dust* (1934).

When Arthur took revenge by writing his second son out of his autobiography, Evelyn retaliated with incendiary ruthlessness. Arthur's diary for 29 January 1935 records: "Woke at 4am to a strong smell of burning. On opening the bookroom found the room ablaze." Evelyn recounted the episode two years later in a piece he wrote for *Pall Mall Magazine*:

> My father is a literary critic and publisher. I think he can claim to have more books dedicated to him than any living man. They used to stand together on his shelves, among hundreds of inscribed copies from almost every English writer of eminence, until on one of my rather rare recent visits to my home, I inadvertently set the house on fire, destroying the carefully garnered fruits of a lifetime of literary friendships.

Evelyn's literary star rose with dazzling celerity. *Decline and Fall* (1928) and *Vile Bodies* (1930) sold more copies in a week than all Arthur's and Alec's books put together. His diaries document the gusto with which he enjoyed his success. Many writers can look back on robust drinking days but few persisted in them with Evelyn's bacchanal abandon. His heroic intake only decreased when he retired to country hotels to write his books or to faraway jungles to research his travelogues. But then his first wife, Evelyn Gardiner (a.k.a. She-Evelyn) left him for a man whom Evelyn nicely called a "ramshackle oaf", and his bright young world toppled around him. As he told one friend, "I did not know it was possible to be so miserable and live".

After converting to Rome in 1930, Evelyn spent the rest of his days trying to see himself and the world *sub specie aeternitatis*. Alexander suggests that the novelist's conversion was simply another outrage undertaken to disconcert his already reeling father; but this is obviously not true. Evelyn might have relished playacting but there was nothing make-believe about his Catholic faith. That Alexander does not grasp this elemental fact may also have something to do with his boorish swipes at Ronald Knox, of whom, of course, his grandfather was immensely fond.

Once his first marriage was annulled, Evelyn married Laura Herbert, an imperturbable nineteen-year-old who spent most of her married life doting on her beloved cows. Alexander implies that Laura and Evelyn disliked their six children. Evelyn, it is true, told Diana Cooper that "I can only regard children as defective adults". But the letters he wrote to his children when unhappy at school (especially to his son, Auberon) are models of parental affection and good sense.

Towards the end of his life, after he had survived the ordeal of bringing up Auberon, Evelyn mellowed. The hurt that Arthur had caused still rankled, but he could see it in a larger light. In his autobiography, he paid the memory of his father a fitting tribute. Speaking of Arthur's recitations in the bookroom at Underhill, Evelyn recalled:

> In these recitations of English prose and verse the incomparable variety of English vocabulary, the cadences and rhythms of the language, saturated my young mind, so that I never thought of English literature as a school subject, as matter for analysis and historical arrangement, but as a source of natural joy. It was a legacy that has not depreciated.

Fathers and Sons puts one in mind of something Sir Francis Bacon once said: "Use the memory of thy predecessors fairly, and tenderly; for if thou dost not, it is a debt will sure be paid, when thou art gone." On that score, Alexander Waugh has nothing to fear.

IN AGINCOURT FIELD

Agincourt: Henry V and the Battle that Made England, Juliet Barker. Little Brown. 445 pages.

HENRY V, THE LANCASTRIAN KING who at 28 led the English to victory at Agincourt (1415), the most celebrated battle of the Hundred Years War, has never been without his critics. William Hazlitt conceded that Shakespeare's Henry might be "an amiable monster" but the historical Henry "seemed to have no idea of any rule of right or wrong, but brute force, glossed over with a little religious hypocrisy". The Whig historian J. R. Green contrasted Henry with his predecessor Edward III, the victor of Crécy (1346), and Poitiers (1356), and argued that "Edward had been forced into the struggle against his will by the ceaseless attacks of France ... The war of Henry ... was ... a wanton aggression on the part of a nation tempted by the helplessness of its opponent". More recently, in *Shakespeare's Kings* (1999) John Julius Norwich charged that Henry's claim to the French throne "was without a shred of legal or moral justification" and that Agincourt "marked the climax of a military adventure of almost criminal foolhardiness and irresponsibility".

The Henry that Juliet Barker describes in her superb new history of Agincourt has more in common with the Henry of the chronicler Edward Hall, who spoke for all Tudor England when he wrote, "Henry was a king whose life was immaculate and his living without a spot ... This captain was a shepherd whom his flock loved and lovingly obeyed. He was merciful to offenders, charitable to the needy, indifferent to all men, faithful to his friends, and fierce to his enemies, toward God most devout, toward the world moderate, and to his realm a very father."

The skeptical reader will look askance at such praise but Barker's meticulously researched book substantiates many of its claims. Henry did take a fatherly interest in the well-being of his subjects. He inspired not only obedience but love. He was a genuinely devout Catholic. As E. F. Jacob maintained in *The Fifteenth Century* (1961) he "took the sacring of his coronation more seriously than his predecessors and ... for him the prestige and success of his country were connected with the moral and religious qualities of the monarchy". And if he could be ruthless in war, he was magnanimous in peace.

An expert on mediaeval English tournaments, who has also written good biographies of Wordsworth and the Brontës, Barker brings to her subject not only redoubtable scholarship but shrewd judgment of character. She also writes what Coleridge once called a "good nervous mother-English". Alfred Burne, Christopher Hibbert, and Anne Curry have all written good books on Agincourt, but Barker's is the best.

Several factors prompted Henry to invade France. He needed a successful invasion to justify his father's dethronement of Richard II, secure his own embattled rule, stop French pirates plundering English shipping, and satisfy English veterans itching to get their hands on the lucrative ransoms of war. Strategically, Henry sought a cross-Channel empire based at Calais to gain control of Normandy to the south, Picardy to the east, and Flanders to the west. This would give him not only mastery of the Seine, the Somme, the Straits of Dover, and the Channel but drive a wedge between his ancient enemies, France and Scotland. Then there was the vulnerability of France itself. With Charles VI mad, the Dauphin incompetent, and John the Fearless and the Burgundians waging civil war against Charles d'Orléans and the Armagnacs, the country was ripe for invasion.

Apropos the king's determination to invade, Jacob remarked that "the picture given in the *Gesta* [the *Gesta Henrici Quinti*, the most thorough eyewitness account of the events surrounding Agincourt] is of a profoundly orthodox king and there is little doubt that Henry was one of his own most voluble propagandists, unwearying in his belief in the justice of his claims and in God's favour". Lord Norwich thought those claims trumpery: Henry used the same argument that his great-grandfather, Edward III had used, that Edward's mother Isabella was the rightful heir to the childless Charles IV. The French countered by citing the Salic Law of Charlemagne which recognized male heirs only. Barker disputes this. "Nicely dressed up with an entirely spurious ancestry dating back to the eighth century, the new law ... made no mention of whether the right to succeed could be passed down through the female line. Edward III could therefore still legitimately claim to be the rightful heir." Moreover, for Barker, Henry's invasion was "not made out of egotism or the desire for personal aggrandizement, but rather because he wanted, and considered it his duty, to recover the 'just rights and inheritances' of the crown". The French historian Édouard Perroy epitomized the French attitude to all such English claims when he referred to the Hundred Years War as "essentially a feudal quarrel between a Gascon vassal and his French overlord".

Barker is good on the elaborate system of indenture that, at a time when there was no standing army, supplied the king with his troops. In the small retinues that wealthy men-at-arms formed to fight for the king one can see in embryo the discipline, cohesiveness, and *esprit de corp* that would later distinguish the regimental system.

Barker also shows how resourceful Henry was at raising funds for the expedition. No English king ever received more generous grants from Parliament. He even wrote his own begging letters, which were by turns wheedling and minatory. Most English merchants contributed handsomely, but foreigners doing business in England were not so forthcoming. In May 1415, as Barker relates, "ten partners in Italian merchant houses were summoned before the privy council and, when they refused to make loans totaling £2,000, were flung into the Fleet prison – a nicely sardonic touch, since this was the jail for debtors".

Once Henry began his investment of the French port town Harfleur, he met inspired resistance from Raoul de Gaucourt, who held out for five heroic weeks. Barker makes the point that "military historians, rightly, have an exhaustive interest in battle formations, positions and tactics but sometimes seem to forget that the chess pieces on the board are human beings, each with their own distinctive character and history, even if the future is not always theirs". Her fascinating portrait of Gaucourt and many other gallant Frenchmen proves her immunity from such unfeeling abstraction.

With the siege of Harfleur, Henry's fortunes plummeted. His men, gorging on shellfish and bad fruit, contracted dysentery. Two thousand had to be shipped back to England. On his punishing seventeen-day march to Calais, it rained incessantly. And when he finally met up with the French army it was at least four times the size of his own. On the eve of the battle, the French were so confident that they would win that they cast dice for Henry and his nobles.

Swayed by Shakespeare or Olivier's charming film, we tend to regard the martial pretensions of the French at Agincourt as derisory but Barker is surely right when she says that "the French were not vainglorious amateurs playing at war, as they are so often portrayed. They were hardened veterans who had spent their lives in arms: on crusade, fighting in Italy, Spain and Portugal and, most recently, in their own civil wars. They were as used to wearing their armour as their civilian clothes." It was not incompetence that defeated the French.

The battle of Agincourt took place in a funnel-shaped field between two woods on Saint Crispin's Day, 25 October 1415, with the French ranged in three columns at the wider and the English in one line at the narrower end. Since one of the axioms of mediaeval warfare was that when "foot soldiers march against their enemy face to face, those who march lose and those who remain standing still and holding firm win", both armies stood still for the first four hours of their encounter. Then Henry, knowing his men were dead-tired, famished, and unlikely to survive any longer standoff, gave the famous order, "Advance banner", at which his whole army knelt, made a cross on the ground, kissed it, and began their march forward. When his archers were approximately 250 yards from the first French column, they drove in the stakes that would wreak havoc with the retaliating French cavalry and opened fire. Barker's description of that first volley shows with what enviable panache she writes:

> Five thousand archers then raised their longbows and loosed a volley of arrows so dense, so fast and so furious that the sky literally darkened over as though a cloud had passed before the face of the sun. One can imagine how the English stood listening to the reverberations from the bow-strings and the whistling of the flights as they sped through the air, followed, after a few heart-stopping moments, by the thud of bodkin arrowheads striking through plate-metal armour and tearing into flesh, and the screams of the wounded and the dying.

When the first French attack failed to break the English line, many of the French either fell in hand-to-hand combat or were thrown back into their own advancing second column. Their difficulty was increased by the rain-soaked ground which gave them nearly as much trouble as the mud of Passchendaele gave the English in 1917. But what decisively worked against them was their very numerical superiority. As they advanced forward in the funnel-shaped field, they had less and less room for maneuver and became bunched together, which made them a perfect target for the stunning efficacy of the English pole-axe. Within half an hour, the first and second French columns had been so decimated that the dead towered over the living.

Then word reached Henry that the French were preparing a third assault. As it happened, this never materialized. Still, he had to be ready to repel it. And then he learned that his tents had been attacked. Rather than risk encirclement he ordered all but the most illustrious prisoners put to death. Fifteen hundred were killed outright.

Here was an order that flouted every convention of civilized warfare, but Henry's first responsibility was to the protection of his troops, and if he had spared the prisoners, he would have exposed his troops to annihilation and lost the battle. (Churchill's sinking of the French fleet after the fall of France in July 1940, which cost the lives of 1,500 French sailors but kept the fleet out of German hands was a similar act of necessary beastliness.)

Apropos the French attack on Henry's tents, Dover Wilson, the old Shakespeare editor, observed: "Fluellen's exclamation, "Tis expressly against the law of arms, 'tis as arrant a piece of knavery, mark you now, as can be offert!', is in accordance with much contemporary comment on the battle, which shows that the treacherous assault left a deep stain upon the chivalry of France." Barker confirms this, stressing that the French blamed their own marauders, not Henry, for the dispatch of their prisoners. G. M. Young neatly summed up matters when he said: "Henry V commanding his men to kill their prisoners was *improbus*. But he won Agincourt."

That win gave the English a sense of destiny that would stay with them for centuries. As Gerald Harriss points out in *Shaping the Nation* (2005), "Agincourt became the centerpiece of a carefully constructed myth: that God had deliberately stacked the odds against the English, reducing their numbers through sickness and their self-confidence by the long march, in order to demonstrate His support in their divinely ordained mission". Henry's own personal mission was to take him to Jerusalem where he would "repulse", as he put it, "the miscreants". But alas before he could go he died.

Barker dedicates her book to Maurice Keen, who taught her mediaeval history at Balliol. Keen, in turn, was taught by R. W. Southern, another brilliant mediaevalist. No doubt he is as proud of his pupil as Southern was of his. In her marvelous history of what the French still call *la malheureuse journée* she maintains a very high standard indeed.

An Oxonian Father Brown

Was Jesus God?, Richard Swinburne. Oxford University Press. 192 pages.

IN 1942, ROBERT LOWELL wrote his good friend, the storyteller Peter Taylor, "The Catholic Church almost always makes great pragmatical claims so that one might almost say that common sense is impossible without faith in Christ. However, neither books nor letters nor talk will convert you, but only prayers principally your own with God's grace. Read Hopkins's letters, he says this to Bridges who wrote that before joining any religion he would have to be intellectually convinced – a stubborn and typically late Victorian bit of irrationality." To a degree, Lowell was right: if we mean to be truly converted, we cannot expect reason to do the hard work of faith, nor neglect prayer. But he was wrong to slight the considerable role reason plays in faith. Etienne Gilson, the great Thomist, whose books were instrumental in converting Lowell (briefly) to Roman Catholicism, would certainly not have considered the later Victorians "irrational" for requiring to be "intellectually convinced" of the claims of Christianity, though he would have agreed with Hopkins that a more expedient way to foster faith in Christ is to give alms. Why? "It changes the whole man," Hopkins assured his skeptical friend, "not his mind only but the will and everything."

Since philosophers of religion can help form minds to appreciate the vitality of alms, as well as the claims of faith, it is heartening to encounter one who is at once skillful and devout. In *Was Jesus God?*, the former Nolloth Professor of the Philosophy of the Christian Religion at Oxford, Richard Swinburne adroitly marshals the evidences of natural theology to affirm the cogency of the Christian faith. A leading light in the philosophy of religion, he has also written an acclaimed trilogy defending Christianity, which includes *Faith and Reason* (2005). His latest book serves as a popular coda to that extended work and will be enjoyed by anyone interested in a field that has been reshaped by Swinburne and other clever logicians such as Brian Davies and Alvin Plantinga.

Swinburne begins his book by observing that "Different people have different reasons for believing that there is a God. Some people have deep private 'religious' experiences, as it seems to them of the presence of God. Others believe that there is a God on the basis of testimony; that is, because their parents or teachers or priests tell them there is a God, and they think their parents or teachers or whoever are knowledgeable and trustworthy." Apropos, religious experience, he says, "If we did not believe that what . . . we are experiencing (perceiving or feeling) is really there, when there are no good reasons for doubting that that thing is really there, we couldn't believe anything". As to testimony, "if we didn't believe what others told us, for example, about history or geography, until we had checked it for ourselves, we would have very few beliefs". It follows from this, Swinburne argues, that "most people need positive arguments in favour of the existence of God if they are to have good reason to believe that there is a God, but they also need grounds to believe that arguments against the existence of God do not work".

Here, he clearly has in mind the philosophers Daniel Dennett, A. C. Grayling, Michael Onfray, and Sam Harris, the biologist Richard Dawkins, and the journalist Christopher Hitchens, all of whom have recently attacked religion as irrational, barbarous, and evil. The purpose of Swinburne's newest book, however, is not so much to answer the objections of this newest batch of atheists – he is convinced that he sufficiently accomplished that in his earlier volume, *Is there a God?* (1996) – but to defend the doctrines encapsulated in the Nicene Creed (381), which he calls the "central doctrines of Christianity, common to virtually all Christians".

Roman Catholics might very well counter that the "central doctrines of Christianity" are only defined and embodied in the Roman Catholic faith. They will also balk at Swinburne's reference to what he calls "the Church", which he defines "as the Apostolic Church founded by Jesus". The logician in Swinburne must recognize that defending this Protestant fiction lands him on shaky ground. He makes his ground shakier still when he claims that "there is no need for me, when considering the truth of these doctrines, to face the difficult issue of what are the boundaries of the Church, that is, which one or more ecclesial bodies constitute it". Yet, in speaking of "the Church", there is a very clear logical sense in which one can only be referring to the Roman Catholic Church. It is entirely illogical to imagine that God would have founded more than one Ἁγίαν, Καθολικὴν καὶ Ἀποστολικὴν Ἐκκλησίαν. Nonetheless, even Catholics can benefit from Swinburne's witty defense of the Trinity, the Incarnation, the Atonement, the Resurrection, the Ascension, and the Four Last Things.

Apropos the Trinity, Swinburne follows Richard of Saint Victor in arguing that "The love of the Father for the Son must include a wish to cooperate with the Son in further total sharing with an equal; and hence the need for a third member of the Trinity, whom, following the tradition, we may call the Holy Spirit, whom they will love and by whom they will be loved". He follows Augustine in holding that "a solitary God would have been an ungenerous god and so no God". From this Swinburne concludes that "the Father and the Son would have been less than perfectly good unless they sought to spread their mutual love of cooperating in further sharing with an equal"; hence, the Holy Spirit. He might also have cited the insights of other Fathers. Irenaeus, for example, describes the different but related functions of the three persons thus: "The Spirit prepares man for the Son of God; the Son leads man to the Father; the Father gives man immortality." Gregory of Nyssa sums up how the three persons relate to one another with epigrammatical élan: "Nor must you be surprised, if, as if speaking in riddles, we produce the new and paradoxical conception of a united separation and a separated union."

Swinburne appeals to common sense to defend the reasonableness of the Virgin Birth. "Since [Jesus] had, to all appearances, normal human bodily characteristics, he presumably had a full set of chromosomes and so genes such as normal humans derive from two parents ... But it would not have taken a very large miracle for God to turn some of the material of Mary's egg into a second half-set of chromosomes, which, together with the normal half-set derived from Mary, would provide a full set." But what would be the point of Jesus having a human mother? Swinburne's explanation is rather muddled. "It would mean that Jesus came into existence as a human on earth partly by the normal process ... and partly as a result of a quite abnormal process. It would thus be a historical event symbolizing the doctrine of the Incarnation, that Jesus is partly of human origin and so has a human nature, and partly of divine origin and so has a divine nature." To say that Jesus was "partly human" and "partly divine" mutilates the mystery of Christ, who, as the Nicene Creed states, became fully human (ἐνανθρωπήσαντα) and was yet "true God of true God" (Θεὸν ἀληθινὸν ἐκ Θεοῦ ἀληθινοῦ).

That Swinburne should be so unclear about Christ's relation to Mary is attributable perhaps to his having been brought up in the Anglican tradition, which has always comparatively neglected Our Lady, even though there have always been exceptions, like Newman's dear friend, John Keble, whose poetry abounds with references to the Blessed Virgin. Newman himself, of course, even as an Anglican, recognized that "Mary is our pattern of faith, both in the reception and in the study of Divine Truth. She does not think it enough to accept, she dwells upon it; not enough to possess, she uses it; not enough to assent, she develops it; not enough to submit the Reason, she reasons upon it; not indeed reasoning first, and believing afterwards, with Zacharias, yet first believing without reasoning, next from love and reverence, reasoning after believing." Here are truths that not all philosophers of religion manage to keep in mind.

Swinburne shows his independence from so many of his philosophical fellows by refusing to downplay his differences with them. For example, he sensibly sees only unacceptable objections to the reasonableness of eternal damnation. God could, of course, endow the wicked after death with good desires, "but that would impose on them a character which they had persistently and knowingly chosen not to have ... But if he is to respect humans as people, if he gives them a choice of character, he must respect that choice and permit them permanently to reject him and all he stands for. Otherwise in creating humans God would be like a puppet master who ensures that in the end every human does what (God) wants, and has no ultimate freedom to determine the sort of person they are to be." Conversely, "if we come to have a good character God will give us the wonderful life of Heaven. Christianity thus offers us salvation from the guilt of the past and from wrongdoing in the present, in order to live a holy life for ever in the future. The Creed expresses this by its claim that God the Son became incarnate "for us humans and for our salvation".

In considering the question of whether Jesus is God, Swinburne sounds like a good detective – a sort of Oxonian Father Brown.

> It is not merely the case that Jesus is the only serious candidate in human history about whom we have evidence that he lived the right kind of life which ended with divine signature. Jesus was both the only prophet in human history about whose life there is good historical evidence of the first kind (evidence that he or she lived a perfect life with much suffering, claimed to be divine, claimed to be making atonement, gave plausible moral and theological teaching, and founded a Church to continue his work), and also the only prophet about whose life there is good historical evidence of the second kind (evidence that his or her life ended with a miracle recognizable as a divine signature). Not merely did Muhammad or the Buddha not give the right sort of teaching (they did not claim to be God Incarnate etc.), but their lives ended in altogether non-miraculous ways. And similarly for all other great prophets about whom we have evidence … This shows that the coincidence of the two sets of evidence about one prophet that his or her life exhibited both features would be very improbable in the normal course of things. It would be very improbable unless God arranged it. And … it would have been dishonest of God to arrange evidence of this kind unless that prophet was indeed God Incarnate. And in virtue of his perfect goodness God would not do that. Hence, the coincidence of the two kinds of evidence does not merely make it very probable that, if there is a God, he became incarnate in Jesus, but it makes it much more probable than it would be otherwise that there is a God.

Reading this, one can only imagine the howls of exasperation it would provoke from Richard Dawkins and his God-denying acolytes. But Swinburne has unpalatable things to say to those in his own camp as well. Having left the Anglican for the Eastern Orthodox Church, he will not endear himself to his current co-religionists with this.

> The observance of prayer, fasting, and almsgiving, with a proper attitude of humility before God and avoiding these as a means of acquiring a good reputation on earth, are also evident themes of Jesus's teaching. So too is honesty, and thus the avoidance of hypocrisy. It is, he taught, more important to show love to those in need than to conform to exact details of ritual.

Swinburne is not only insightful, he is encouraging, and that is not something one can say about many philosophers, living or dead. *Was Jesus God?* is an entertaining, bracing, compelling book, and welcome proof that not all of our academics have turned their backs on what Hopkins once called "the fine delight that fathers thought".

The Unusual Maritains

Jacques and Raïssa Maritain: Beggars for Heaven, Jean-Luc Barre, translated by Bernard E. Doering. University of Notre Dame Press. 496 pages.

THE OTHER EVENING I met a bright young woman at dinner who had studied philosophy at Stanford and when I told her I was reviewing a new biography on Jacques Maritain she said she had never heard of him. That one of the greatest Catholic philosophers of the twentieth century should now be unknown on the very campuses where, just a generation ago, he was universally read and admired – indeed taught – is profoundly disheartening. No other philosopher appeals to the natural idealism of youth like Maritain. The fact that he has been jettisoned from the curriculum to make room for the abject nominalism of Michel Foucault and his friends speaks volumes about the intellectual defeatism that holds sway over our academic elites. *Jacques and Raïssa Maritain: Beggars for Heaven* by the French journalist and historian Jean-Luc Barré should help revive interest in the work of a man who still rewards study.

While not definitive, the biography provides a fascinating portrait of a special marriage and shows how many disparate lives were enriched by the couple's passion for truth. Jean Cocteau, Allen Tate, Marc Chagall, Erik Satie, T. S. Eliot, Francois Mauriac, Georges Bernanos, Georges Rouault, and Charles Péguy were just a few of the many people lucky enough to move in the Maritains' enchanted circle. If Mr. Barre's book is not the critical biography for which one might have hoped, a biography of the caliber of Ian Ker's brilliant intellectual life of John Henry Newman or Peter Brown's critical life of Saint Augustine, it nonetheless shows the extent to which love – there is no other word for it – animated all his work. For anyone interested in the intellectual history of the twentieth century or philosophy, period, the book is a must.

Mr. Barre is particularly good at showing how indispensable Raïssa was to Maritain's moral and intellectual development. She introduced him to the work of Aquinas, helped him confront the anti-Semitism that still degrades French society, impressed upon him the need for a universalism that could combat atheist communism without neglecting Christian charity, and led him steadily onward in the life of contemplation. Without her, Maritain would never have written such compelling philosophy. As Maritain said himself, with a chivalry worthy of the troubadours, "If you want to know where I am, don't look for me where I am, look for me where I love and am loved, in the heart of my blessed Raïssa".

The book has serious omissions. It does not provide sufficient background on the Dreyfus Affair or *Action francaise* or the intellectual and moral malaise that led to the fall of France in 1940 or the relationship between the Catholic Church and Vichy. On these matters readers might wish to consult Theodore Zeldin's lively two-volume history of modern France in the Oxford History of Modern Europe series, Guy Chapman's account of the Dreyfus Affair, Alistair Horne's great trilogy on the Franco-Prussian conflict, and Robert Gildea's *Marianne in Chains: Daily Life in the Heart of France During the German Occupation* (2003).

Why the French have never had the distinguished biographical tradition that the English and the Americans have is a puzzle. Nevertheless, they have always been good at anatomizing marriage and Mr. Barre is no exception. About the Maritain marriage, he says that it "proceeded less from pure chance than from a kind of inspired confluence, brought on by a similar intellectual precocity, a similar demand for intellectual truth, a similar spiritual disquiet". He does full justice to *l'amour fou* – the mad, absolutely unconditional love that Jacques and Raïssa felt for one another. Before converting to Catholicism, they were so despondent that they seriously considered suicide. As Maritain would later recall, "This life that I did not choose, I no longer wanted to live in such darkness. This comedy had turned sinister." Two very different individuals, they were nonetheless "formed by the same desire for the absolute – an alliance against nothingness and the night, a fusion brought about by the most profound hope". After converting, they vowed that their marriage would be celibate. In lieu of children, Maritain later wrote, "it was a spiritual progeny that these spouses expected from God, and it was to this progeny that they gave themselves".

One need only read entries from their diaries to realize what an enormous sacrifice this must have entailed. In one entry, Maritain remarks: "Raïssa's eyes continue to be strangely inattentive, or rather inwardly attentive; a lovely gaze that rests on objects without penetrating them, and seems suspended. Her voice is clear and soft like that of a child, but it seems to have a kind of imperceptible hesitation, which makes one think of the instant of waiting in the flight of a bee, close up to a flower without resting on it." It is clear that the decision was not based on any disdain for nature. "In our journey toward the absolute", Maritain explained, "and in our desire to follow ... at least one of the counsels of the life of perfection, we wanted to leave the field completely open to our quest for contemplation and union with God."

Beaumarchais once said that of all serious things marriage is the most ludicrous. Maritain would have agreed. Yet the comedy he saw was divine comedy. As he observed in a wonderful book called *Reflections on America* (1959), "marriage is essentially spiritual in nature – a complete and irrevocable gift of one to another. Thus it is that marriage can be between man and woman a true community of love, built not on sand, but on rock, because it is built on genuinely human, not animal, and genuinely spiritual, genuinely *personal* love ... Then in a free and unceasing ebb and flow of emotion, feeling and thought, each one really participates, by virtue of love, in that personal life of the other which is, by nature, the other's incommunicable possession. And then each one may become a sort of guardian Angel for the other – prepared as guardian Angels have to be, to forgive a great deal ... Each one, in other words, may become really dedicated to the good and salvation of the other." No one will get this sort of thing from Michel Foucault.

Like Chagall, Raïssa Oumançoff never left behind the world of her childhood. Born at Rostov-on-Don in 1883, she spent her first ten years in a Chagallian world of rabbis, beggars, fiddlers, and harlequins. The assassination of Czar Alexander in 1873 gave that childhood a kind of prelapsarian perfection. The assassination led to reprisals against Russia's Jews that caused several hundred thousand of them to emigrate to America and Western Europe. What decided Raïssa's father to emigrate was the Czar's *ukase* stipulating that only a limited number of Jews would be considered for seats in the lycées and universities. This solicitude for her education caused Raïssa to remark that her parents "had understood, even before I could know it myself, that this was where I would find my life – the happiness of my life".

Before settling in Paris, the family stayed for a while with Raïssa's maternal grandfather in Marioupol on the Azov Sea. "Their hospitality was proverbial", Raïssa recalled. One of the great themes of Mr. Barre's book is how Jacques and Raïssa would offer similar hospitality in the households they set up in Versailles, Meudon, and Princeton, where their faith and their charity became "a little bridge thrown across the abyss". They formed a little community, a lay apostolate dedicated to sharing the life of faith. Later, when Maritain urged the Catholic laity to take a more active role in the Church, he was only preaching what he had always practiced.

Born in 1882, Maritain never got to know his father, a lawyer, whom Mr. Barre piquantly describes as part "skeptical aesthete" and part "sensual playboy". His only passion seems to have been shopping for antiques. The many spiritual mentors to whom Maritain would later apprentice himself, from Saint Thomas to Léon Bloy, Father Clérissac to Dom Delatte, were, to some degree, substitutes for his absent father. After a brief, unhappy marriage, his parents divorced. Geneviève Favre was one of the first divorcées in France, which only legalized divorce in 1885. In 1904, Paul Maritain took his own life, a fact which neither this nor any other biography properly addresses. In all events, Jacques experienced a childhood full of abrupt moves from ramshackle households where the only stability came from his schooling, first at the Lycée Henry IV and then at the Sorbonne, where he read Bergson and Spinoza. Certainly, the death of his father by his own hand must have exacerbated Maritain's sense of the desolating instability of the mundane.

It is amusing that his fiercely anti-clerical mother should have insisted on his being initially tutored by a liberal Protestant. Maritain would entirely repudiate this tuition in his first book, *Trois Reformateurs* (1925), in which he took Luther, Descartes, and Rousseau to task for alienating the modern self from God. Later, he would include Kant, Schopenhauer, and Bergson in his criticism of what he called "the abdication of the mind". At the same time, he would insist that it was the mission of Thomism "to reconnect with being, to make fruitful all our bonds with human experience". This confidence in the mind's ability to apprehend truth is what has made him a pariah in a post-modernist ethos where the very idea of truth is rejected out of hand, when it is not caricatured as the construct of oppression.

The seminal event in Maritain's development was his response to the Dreyfus Affair. In 1899, when Clemenceau called for the complete vindication of Dreyfus, Maritain rallied to his cause. To a friend he wrote that he was "ready to suffer anything – even the rude slamming of doors in my face – for the noble cause of the innocent and tortured prisoner". A good précis of the case of the Jewish army staff captain wrongly convicted of spying is provided by Zeldin:

> the case ... split the country in two. On the one hand, the Dreyfusards ... standing for justice and for the individual, demanding his acquittal whatever reasons of state or military prestige stood in the way ... Against them, the army, devoted to order, hierarchy, obedience, possessing a different set of values from the republicans, with Catholic officers perpetuating the ideals of the *ancien régime*. Against them were also the anti-Semites, who saw in the Dreyfus case an enormous Jewish conspiracy, backed by Protestants – for the Dreyfusards included a lot of both – undermining the integrity of the nation. The clergy took up this cry and the hierarchy refrained from condemning them ... The truth about this case has not been fully established ... Dreyfus was not guilty but it is not known who was ... It was difficult to be rational when all the facts were not known and nearly everybody knew only some of the facts ... It was thus a human, psychological failure ... The Dreyfusard intellectuals claimed that they were clarifying issues when they insisted that the French ... were inexorably divided by the Revolution, between those who accepted and those who rejected its principles. It may be claimed that they set France back thirty years by this, refusing to let it go forward to the solution of the problems of the day.

"It was through the Dreyfus Affair", Mr. Barré writes, "that Jacques Maritain would become conscious of ... his temporal mission ... of his particular responsibility to his century". It is true that the injustice Dreyfus suffered impressed on him the need for taking principled stands on public issues, but the inherent incoherence of French politics often involved him in positions that he would later regret, so much so that in 1935 in his *Lettre sur l'indépendance* he insisted that he was neither right nor left-wing. "On the temporal plane as on the spiritual ... it is to the same law of independence ... that Christians are dedicated. The liberty that they have to manifest at the greatest depth of the world is an incarnate liberty. At the heart of the suffering that all the earth is experiencing today, there is doubtless a divine necessity for breaking, not with the world, but with the old servitudes of this world – these are the hard demands of engaged liberty." It is precisely his "engaged liberty" that has made Maritain, in the words of the philosopher William Sweet, "too liberal for conservatives and too conservative for liberals". This spirit of independence came partly from his mother, who, when warned by her concierge, at the age of 84, that she was borrowing trouble by entertaining Jewish women in her apartment at the height of the deportations, responded: "Not to worry. This is where the stars meet."

The man who converted the Maritains was Léon Bloy, a proudly penurious novelist, whose career Barré describes in suitably melodramatic terms. "This humiliated Christian, beat down by crushing poverty and handed over to the sneers of the multitude was a man at war ... Bloy held on by his faith and survived because of it." His impact on the Maritains was instantaneous. "Instead of being a whitened sepulcher like the Pharisees of any and every age," Maritain recalled, "he was more like a charred and blackened cathedral. The whiteness was within, in the hidden heart of the tabernacle. Upon crossing the threshold of this house all values were shifted around ... We knew ... that there was only one sorrow, and that was not to be saints. When Maritain's mother got wind of his conversion, she regarded it as a "catastrophe". Her son had gone over to the enemy. Geneviève Favre was no St. Monica.

One of the great puzzles of Maritain's career is why he associated himself with *Action française*. Although supportive of the Church as an agent of order, this right-wing royalist movement was also determined to root out what it perceived to be the enemy from within, including Jews, Freemasons, Protestants, and *métèques*, or resident aliens. Curiously enough, it was Maritain's spiritual director, Father Clérissac who recommended that he join the movement, which Clérissac saw as a bulwark against the depredations of liberal democracy. In a letter of 1910 to another spiritual director, Dom Delatte, Maritain showed how much his Catholic mentors had soured him on the republican ideas that had inspired his youth: "We thank you for having pointed out so clearly to us the venom of liberalism and for having provided an irrefutable historical justification for disdain that every Catholic should feel instinctively... for all the diminutions, concessions and vilenesses of modern times."

Maritain only repudiated the movement after Pius XI condemned it in 1926. Why he continued marching under the *Action française* banner for seventeen years remains a mystery. Mr. Barre suggests that one reason might have been Maritain's desire to convert Charles Maurras, the movement's leader, who, by all accounts, was a confused, unsavory, brilliant man. To judge from the amount of time and effort that Maritain spent trying to convert Gide and Cocteau, this might well have been the case. In all events, it is not as though Maritain did not recognize or indeed understand anti-Semitism. In "The Mystery of Israel" (1939), a pivotal essay, he wrote: "It is difficult not to be struck by the extraordinary baseness ... of anti-Semitic propaganda ... To a mind sufficiently alert, this baseness itself seems disquieting: it must have a mystical meaning. Stupidity pushed too far impinges upon mystery and hides the demonic instinct of the shadow world of the irrational." It is dismaying that so few contemporary Europeans realize that it is precisely with this demonic shadow world that we are contending in resurgent Islam.

Despite his interest in the world around him, Maritain always recognized that his real role must be played out in his work. In 1925, he published his brilliantly provocative *Art et Scolastique*, which summoned artists to find "once more the spiritual conditions of *honest* work" – a revolutionary summons at a time when Tristan Tzara was launching the Dada movement. In 1927, he published his groundbreaking *Primaute du spiritual*, which gave eloquent expression to his vision of a renewed Thomistic universalism. "It is to a universal expansion of the intelligence that we are called by love," he wrote. "The time is now. The soul demands pure adherence to the absolutism of truth and charity." In 1934, he published *Humanisme integrale*, which, taking stock of "the liquidation of four centuries of classical culture", exhorted Christians to undertake "the most true and perfect heroism, the heroism of love", to "work toward the establishment of a new temporal order of the world". Here was a true Christian humanism. In 1932, he published what many consider his masterpiece, *Distinguer pour unir: ou Les Degrès du savoir*, which rejected the nominalism in Kantianism, idealism, pragmatism, and positivism, and asserted instead that the mind can know what really exists. In the different degrees of knowledge there is the science of the visible and measurable but also the science of revealed mysteries, or theological wisdom, which is known not only by reason but by faith as well. And then there is the highest of all knowledge which is mystical knowledge, acquired through the exercise of spiritual contemplation. In this, he was deeply influenced by the work of the Spanish mystic and poet Saint John of the Cross.

Mr. Barré is good on how the fall of France affected Maritain. No sooner had the Germans taken possession than the Gestapo went looking for Maritain. They requisitioned his Meudon villa, removed his books from the bookstores, and suspended his classes. Addressing Maritain as "My dear Teacher", de Gaulle urged him repeatedly to join his exiled government in London. Maritain wisely stayed put in New York. Most French intellectuals chose to collaborate. The French episcopate embraced Vichy wholeheartedly. "The Church always rendered unto Caesar what was Caesar's", Robert Gildea writes in his account, "The Vichy regime made it easy by reversing much of the anticlerical legislation that had been passed since 1870. Religious instruction could be given in state schools for the first time since 1882. State subsidies could be made to private Catholic schools for the first time since 1886." In return, all the Church had to do was keep mum about the deportations. It was particularly appalling for Maritain to see his old spiritual ally Reginald Garrigou-Lagrange doing the bidding of Vichy. Maritain spent much of his time in New York helping Jewish professors who had fled the Nazis find teaching positions with American colleges.

In *A travers le desastre*, one of the first great works of the Resistance, secretly distributed throughout France in 1942, Maritain boosted morale by instilling solidarity and calling a spade a spade: "The Vichy government is in fact prisoner of the enemy in a trap where it threw itself and all of France along with it." Well-meaning historians continue to see nuances in the occupation. Maritain saw only "abominable betrayals everywhere". He was particularly savage about how Pierre Laval and Maréchal Pétain had dishonored their country: "To betray her traditional laws of political hospitality, to accept for herself and for her own laws the bestial ignominy of Nazi racism, to hand over foreign Jews welcomed by her since 1935 as into a human and faithful land, to hand over even those who fought for her and in her army in the course of the present war, never in all history has such an infamy been imposed on France." How many Jews did the French hand over? Nobody knows. The fact that 75,000 French Jews died in the German camps can only give an approximate number.

After the war, Maritain served as De Gaulle's ambassador to the Vatican. Monsignor Ronald Knox, the Catholic convert, once advised that "he who travels in the the barque of Saint Peter had better not look too closely into the engine room". Maritain saw altogether too much of the engine room and concluded that "Catholics are not Catholicism. The mistakes, the clumsiness, the inefficiencies, the lack of concern of Catholics do not involve Catholicism itself. It is not the responsibility of Catholicism to furnish an alibi for the shortcomings of Catholics."

Maritain's reputation first began to wane with the rise of Jean-Paul Sartre and Albert Camus after the Second World War, when Existentialism first exposed the triviality at the heart of European philosophy. Whether the time is ripe for a Maritain revival is hard to tell. Even if he doesn't return to the classroom, readers interested in aesthetics, the philosophy of science, metaphysics, moral philosophy, political philosophy, and theology will always find in Maritain insights that are at once fresh and practical. Like John Henry Newman, he lays a great deal of emphasis on action. His is a philosophy for doing, not wool gathering. Rowan Williams, the Archbishop of Canterbury, hit the nail on the head when he recently said that Maritain's work was a "revolt against textbook scholasticism". Ralph McInerny engages in no special pleading when he says that Maritain was "a model of the intellectual life as lived by a Christian believer".

When Maritain returned to Paris after the Second World War and found that he was practically forgotten, he received a letter from his fellow Thomist, Étienne Gilson, who took the liberty of advising his old friend on what Samuel Johnson once referred to as "the justice of posterity". "Whether you realize it or not, you are great," Gilson told him,

> and this is something for which you will never be forgiven. You will have to pay for this, my good friend. This cannot be avoided ... I have had, and this was as much as thirty years ago, good friends who hated you (already!); one of them was a priest ... ; even today I have friends whom you don't even know and who don't like you very much at all ... ; I never could understand why ... I also have friends who adore you ... I am the ideal witness to assure you that your work is great, true, salutary, fruitful ... Only I know that such great works are not produced for a given time. There is no chronology for ideas. Go on with your work, which is irreplaceable, and don't worry about anything; the rest is of no account.

Judging from what Maritain once said about his own sense of his mission, it is probable that Gilson's advice did not go unheeded. "I feel like a man walking on a slippery slope", he admitted, "carrying a very heavy weight in his arms. He must beware of the slightest misstep. What can one do? When it is a question of God's grace, one can only close one's eyes and let it work."

The Guv'nor and the Wench

A Strange and Eventful History: The Dramatic Lives of Ellen Terry, Henry Irving, and Their Remarkable Families, Michael Holroyd. Farrar, Straus and Giroux. 620 pages.

For twenty-four years, Ellen Terry and Henry Irving conducted one of the most beloved partnerships that the theatre has ever known, though this was too long for Bernard Shaw, who was convinced that Terry had wasted her talents by working with an actor whom he charged had stultified the English stage. After all, Irving sentimentalized Shakespeare and preferred hoary melodramas to Ibsen. Fond as he was of "the originality and modernity" of Terry's talent, Shaw confessed "that it would have been better for us twenty five years ago to have tied [Irving] up in a sack with every existing copy of the works of Shakespeare, and dropped him into the crater of the nearest volcano".

In his wonderful biography of the Irving and Terry families, *A Strange and Eventful History*, Michael Holroyd shows that Shaw not only found the artist in Irving wanting: he also resented the man. Irving never mounted any of Shaw's plays and Shaw, despite reams of witty love letters, never budged Terry from her devotion to the aloof, imperious, driven man whom his colleagues called "the Guv'nor".

The groundwork for the Irving and Terry partnership was laid in 1871 when the then-manager of the Lyceum, Hezekiah Bateman, an American from Baltimore, hired Irving to play the lead beside his actress daughters, a last throw of the dice for a stage father on the brink of bankruptcy. It was only after Irving persuaded him to mount *The Bells*, which proved a huge success, that Bateman was saved from the bailiffs. In 1874, Irving followed this unexpected triumph with a production of *Hamlet* that secured his reputation as England's foremost actor. As *The Times* noted, Irving's Hamlet owed nothing to Macready or Kean. His Dane was "a prince and gentleman who failed to do the great things demanded of him, not so much from weakness of will as from excess of tenderness". In 1878, to crown his success, Irving took over the management of the Lyceum and hired

Terry as his leading lady, with whom he would work until 1902, mounting spectacularly truncated productions of *The Merchant of Venice, Romeo and Juliet, Much Ado about Nothing, Twelfth Night, Macbeth*, and *Cymbeline*, as well as such romantic melodramas as *Olivia* (based on Goldsmith's *The Vicar of Wakefield*) and *The Lady of Lyons*.

Irving chose Terry as his partner because he knew she was an actress of genius who would not require hand-holding. For her part, Terry admitted, "I might have deteriorated in partnership with a weaker man whose ends were less fine, whose motive was less pure. I had the taste and artistic knowledge that his upbringing had not developed in him." Irving would often consult her on matters of set design, as well as acting, and it was at the Lyceum during their long reign that house lights were first dimmed during performances.

From the start, Irving must have known that he had made a brilliant choice. "Miss Terry's performance", one contemporary critic noted, "takes high rank among contemporary efforts, in right of its poetic sensibility, its girlish grace, its simplicity, its subtlety, its exquisite elocution, and that surprising picturesqueness of aspect, pose and movement, which seems the peculiar and exclusive possession of the actress". These were qualities that critics and admirers noted again and again about the actress who became known as "the sweetheart of England". In 1906, to mark Terry's jubilee, Beerbohm Tree gave his own personal tribute:

> Stand here, dear sister-artist, England's pride,
> The Genius of her stage personified
> Queenlike, pathetic, tragic, tender, merry –
> O rare, O sweet, O wondrous Ellen Terry.

Throughout her jubilee, Terry proved the consummate trouper. Losing Irving a year before had put her in no mood for celebrations, but she refused to let her bereavement spoil the festivities. "So", as Holroyd relates, "she accepted the long affectionate applause of the audience and the wild demonstrations of the crowds outside as tributes to their partnership". Later, she recalled: "Many were anxious to show me honour because I had worked with Henry Irving for a quarter of a century. I represented a chapter in the history of the English theatre, of which they were proud." There was nothing in her memoirs, or, indeed, her life, to corroborate Shaw's claim that Irving had been "our national theatrical Minotaur", to which her talents had been sacrificed.

Irving and Terry were a study in contrast. Before appearing on the London stage, Irving, whose real name was John Brodribb, put in a punishing 700 performances in the provinces, where he was often hissed for his crab-like gait and odd verbal tics. He was the antithesis of an overnight success. After being entrusted by his parents to the charge of his mother's sister and her tempestuous husband, he was brought up in Cornwall, which, in the mid-nineteenth century, was a wild, half legendary place, only reachable by steamboat. The strict Methodist household shunned drink but not the theatre. Seeing itinerant players enacting blood-curdling melodramas in the Cornish hills inspired Irving to become a player himself. Reunited with his parents at the age of 9, he developed a severe speech-impediment, made only worse by his mother's insistence that he become a Methodist preacher. Overcoming his stammer left his pronunciation in tatters. Gordon Craig recalled the great actor's strange elocution: "For good Irving said god – sight was seyt – stood was stod – smote became smot – hand was often hond, or hend."

Irving's decision to go on the stage so scandalized his Methodist mother that she disowned him. Later, when Irving married Frances O'Callaghan, the daughter of an Irish surgeon-general in the India service, she, too, disapproved of his acting. Riding with her husband in a hansom cab one evening after his first great triumph in Hamlet, she demanded that he stop making a fool of himself and quit the stage. Irving calmly got out of the cab and never saw her again. For the sake of their two boys, however, and his own social standing, he never divorced her. Frances, for her part, never missed Irving's first nights, though she brought up her sons to regard their father as a bounder and always referred to his leading lady as "the wench".

Terry was born into a famous theatrical family and had her London debut at the age of 9 playing the boy Mamillius in Charles Keane's production of *The Winter's Tale*. By the time she was a teenager, she was an accomplished comedienne. Terry's voice was just as distinctive as Irving's, "that most sweet voice," as Holroyd describes it, "half-whisper and half sigh, which enchanted everyone: a soft, veiled, husky, intimate, thrilling sound, mysterious in its power." Irving was fond of saying that Terry was fatal to criticism because she turned her critics into lovers, but it was not only critics who fell in love with her. In 1864, when she was 16, the 47-year-old Pre-Raphaelite painter G. W. Watts became so infatuated with her that he married her. Browning, Tennyson, Disraeli, and Wilde all flocked to Little Holland House to visit with his charming child bride. Johnston Forbes Robertson, the most dashing of the actor managers, had a crush on Terry from the day he set eyes on her. Bram Stoker, Irving's major domo and the author of *Dracula* (which was based on Irving) recalled that Terry "moved through the theatre like embodied sunshine". Even Gladstone, who pinched some of his oratorical tricks from Irving, found Terry irresistible. But perhaps Terry's most prestigious conquest was Dr. Furnivall, the great textural scholar, who wrote the actress after seeing her in *The Merchant of Venice*, "a lady gracious and graceful, handsome, witty, loving and wise, you are his Portia to the life".

In 1868, after her marriage to Watts was dissolved, Edward Godwin, the architect and interior designer, whom Max Beerbohm called "the greatest aesthete of them all", fell in love with Terry while she was on tour in Bristol. Within months, they ran away together to Hertfordshire and had two children, Ted and Edy, both of whom later took the name Craig. Their strange and eventful histories dominate the second half of Holroyd's book, which some will find slow going: how the children of the famous come to grief does not always make for riveting reading. Still, Holroyd treats the children of Irving and Terry with admirable sympathy. Moreover, their failure casts an interesting light on the success of their parents. Terry, for one, never deceived herself on this score: "What fools we are in bringing up our children!"

Holroyd describes Godwin as "a man with a visionary future but no actual present", which could as equally describe his talented but undisciplined son. Terry's love for Godwin was not entirely reciprocated. As Holroyd observes, Godwin "filled her life but she did not quite fill his. He was a romantic, living off his nerves, seeing in her beauty an image of what he passionately desired, but never losing for long his mysterious discontent". In Holroyd's family portrait, it is not so much love as thwarted love that binds together the different family members. Most families suffer from this, but in the case of the Irving and Terry families it wrought havoc.

Irving was in many respects a cold, cruel, egomaniacal man who delighted in making others suffer the same denial of love that he had suffered at the hands of his mother. He took no interest in his sons when they were growing up and hardly noticed when Laurence, his younger son, tried to kill himself. In one letter, Harry, the older son, complained to his mother: "I wonder why Irving avoids writing to us ... Of course we have heard nothing from our affectionate father. It would be a good thing if we could make the old cab-horse take a little trouble." Such letters confirm that the dialogue in Ivy Compton-Burnett's novels was not fanciful: the Edwardians really did express themselves with acid felicity.

Irving also kept Terry at a distance. "He knew only one way out of his isolation," she observed, "and that was by turning it to some use, even to grim enjoyment on the stage". For her part, Terry loved Irving despite his personal limitations. As Holroyd remarks, she "loved his unpainted face, that splendid face he wished to hide".

Terry was drawn to Irving's isolation because it was so different from her own blithe gregariousness. Some, like Shaw, might have imagined that playing beside Irving diminished her, but in Holroyd's book she is always the star, the radiant center. In her memoirs, she recalls the first time she crossed the Atlantic: "the ship was laden with pig-iron and she rolled and rolled and rolled. But she could never roll too much for me! I have always been a splendid sailor, and I feel jolly at sea". Here was the jaunty heroine that so many of her contemporaries found so infectiously endearing.

Still, for all her ebullience, Terry was saddened by her son's fecklessness. "Talk – and not do," she wrote him in one gently remonstrating letter, "it's bad in a woman but terrible in a man." Much has been made of Craig's influence on film lighting and set design, but Holroyd also shows that he was a terrible pseud, whose delusions of grandeur made him partial to Mussolini and Hitler. "Gordon Craig has made himself the most famous producer in Europe", Shaw quipped, "by dint of never producing anything, while Edith Craig remains the most obscure by dint of producing everything". Edy's career both as a costumier and a director was more productive than her brother's, though her personal life was blighted by her mother's over-protectiveness. One revelation of Holroyd's book is that England's sweetheart was no model mother.

In 1905, after Irving died, Terry married an American actor thirty years her junior. Edy found the man's youth ludicrous: he was younger than she was. Craig welcomed him, convinced that he would shed ten years off his own life. "How wonderful", he wrote his mother after he learned of the nuptials. "We are a queer family." This was putting it mildly. Terry kept her relations with Irving impenetrably veiled, but her children opted for an almost exhibitionistic transparency. Craig would go on to have thirteen children with eight women and Edy established a lesbian colony in Kent that even Vita Sackville-West found *outré*.

That he should be the first actor in England to be knighted amused Irving. Max Beerbohm saw him on his way to the station for Windsor Castle. "His hat was tilted at more than his usual angle and his long cigar seemed longer than ever," Beerbohm recalled "and on his face was a look of such ruminant sly fun as I have never seen equaled. I had a moment's glimpse of him; but that was enough to show me the soul of a comedian reveling in the part he was about to play … I was sure that when he alighted on the platform of Paddington his bearing would be more than ever grave and stately with even the usual touch of bohemianism obliterated."

In his biographies of Lytton Strachey, Augustus John, and Shaw, Holroyd made a specialty of bohemianism. But what gives his latest book its distinction is its understanding of something far stranger than bohemia, and that is family, especially the failures of family. When it comes to this aspect of his subject, Holroyd writes with eloquence. Here he is on the solipsism that undermined Irving's marriage.

> Irving's instinct, so alert in theatrical affairs, was blind to the nuances of personal relationships. He simply did not know what Florence was thinking or feeling and could not pick up signs from how she looked or clues from her tone of voice. She was again pregnant, but her husband's time and energy were devoted to his work. The truth was inescapable: Irving loved the theatre far more than her, their son, and their unborn child. He placed a world of bright lights above the needs of his family. She had come to realize that there was something fundamentally wrong with him and, with surprise and consternation, Florence found that she could not change him, could not penetrate that solitude he carried

within himself or match his single passion for the stage. As she waited outside the Lyceum in her brougham after the first performance of *The Bells*, waited in mounting irritation for him to detach himself from the braying crowds within, and heard the chorus of fatuous adulation spilling out on to the streets, her anger rose. Tired almost beyond endurance, anxious to get home, convinced that her husband had forgotten her pregnancy, she was nevertheless obliged to go on to a celebratory supper and hear him praised by people who had no knowledge of the real Irving. No one else knew what he was like. The boredom, injustice and mockery of it were too much for her.

In passages like these Holroyd proves his mastery of biography anew by heeding what Henry James called "the ever-importunate murmur, 'Dramatize it, dramatize it!'" That James also happened to be Irving's most relentless critic, finding his productions blatant and crude, is another story.

Leonardo and the Catholic Faith

Leonardo da Vinci: Flights of the Mind, Charles Nicholl. The Viking Press. 623 pages.

THE ART OF LEONARDO DA VINCI is an art of mystery. No depiction of the adoration is as puzzling as Leonardo's. *The Virgin of the Rocks* bristles with questions about Revelation and human history. His portraits are some of the most inscrutable ever painted. Yet for centuries scholars have claimed that Leonardo was dismissive of the mysteries of the Catholic Faith.

This dubious tradition has a lively adherent in Charles Nicholl. In his new biography, he commends the autodidact in Leonardo for looking afresh at anatomy, hydraulics, aerodynamics, and many other fields but rejects the possibility that the artist may have reexamined his doubts about the Faith. Still, Nicholl's book is worth reading. Admirably researched and full of panache, it should spur readers to make their own judgments about his enigmatic subject.

Leonardo was born illegitimate in Vinci in 1452, the son of a notary and peasant girl. When his father refused to make a morganatic match, Leonardo was brought up by his mother and a stepfather, and never received the sense of belonging or the education he craved. His lifelong refusal to accept the received wisdom of the many arts and sciences he studied can be attributed to the prickly independence that this upbringing instilled in him.

Nicholl is particularly good at evoking the cities and towns where Leonardo's genius took shape. To this day, Vinci is a center of basket-weaving, the intricacies of which Leonardo reproduced in the elaborate braids and knots of his incomparable drawings. The countryside of Vinci was the model for the haunting landscapes in many of his paintings. It was also in Vinci that he became fascinated with flight, recording in his notebooks that "the first memory of my childhood ... [was] when I was in my cradle ... [and] a kite came to me, and opened my mouth with its tail, and struck me several times with its tail inside my lips". In this first indelible memory, Leonardo found the "flights of the mind" that would supply him with themes for a lifetime.

From Vinci, Leonardo went to Florence, "the preeminent city of craftsmanship", as Nicholl observes, "where there were more woodcarvers than butchers", which included not only 270 woolworker shops, 84 woodworker studios, and 83 silkworker shops but 108 churches, 50 piazzas, 33 banks, and 23 *palazzi*. It was also a center of fashion, abounding in weavers, dyers, tanners, and furriers, which turned the provincial Leonardo into a confirmed dandy.

In Florence, Leonardo worked as an apprentice under Andrea Verrocchio, painting that wonderfully translucent dog in Verrocchio's own *Tobias and the Angel*. He also had a hand in placing the orb and cross on Brunelleschi's Duomo, 350 feet above the ground, an experience that must have first opened his eyes to the possibilities of inspired engineering.

Verrocchio, Perugino, and Botticelli were key influences, although about the work of the last Leonardo noted: "I saw some days ago a picture of an angel making the Annunciation, who seemed to be chasing Our Lady out of the room . . . and Our Lady seemed as if she were going to throw herself in despair out the window." Leonardo was no more deferential about Michelangelo: "You should not make all your muscles of the body too conspicuous . . . otherwise you will produce a sack of walnuts rather than a human figure." Another influence was the architect, poet, painter, philosopher, and musician Leon Battista Alberti, the original *uomo universale*. The sense of mystery that animates Leonardo's work grew out of his delight in the *sacra rappresentazione*, the sacred plays in which, as the art historian Dale Kent points out, "the Word was made Flesh, incarnating the Christian mysteries only described in Scripture and the liturgy".

From Florence Leonardo went to Milan to work for Ludovico Sforza, offering his services not as a painter but a military engineer. At this fortress court, where military power counted for all, Leonardo worked for years on an equestrian statue to honor his patron's father only to see it rendered down into weaponry when Sforza was attacked by the French, an irony which was not lost on Leonardo, who came to recognize in war "the most brutal kind of madness there is". It was also in Milan that Leonardo developed his darker, more somber palette and *sfumato*, or smoky style – which Nicholl characterizes as "more than a depiction of light and shade ... it is a mood or atmosphere, an autumnal suffusion of transience and regret" altogether different "from the sharp-edged, sun lit aesthetic of his Florentine training".

If Leonardo was in some respects a disappointed man – scarred by his illegitimacy, unable often to finish his work, doubtful of his achievements – he never lost his sense of humor. Nicholl quotes the story Vasari tells of how the prior of the monastery in Milan kept pestering Leonardo to hurry up and finish *The Last Supper* and complained of Leonardo to the Duke. Leonardo explained that he was still searching for a face depraved enough to represent Judas, but that if he failed he could always use the prior's face.

After the fall of Sforza, Leonardo went to work for another strong man, Cesare Borgia, whose motto was *Aut Caesar aut nullus*. Nicholls paints a vivid picture of Leonardo and Machiavelli accompanying the tyrant on his murderous campaign through Perugia and Siena. While Machiavelli would mine his experiences for *The Prince* (1532), Leonardo retreated into his notebooks, making observations that Nicholl nicely describes as "tangential, serene, escapist: [Leonardo] is looking the other way".

Leonardo spent his last years in France, where, recalling the lion-house he had loved in Florence in his youth, he created a mechanical lion for François Premier, which advanced as if to attack, halted, opened its head, and revealed a bunch of lilies against a blue background.

Kenneth Clark observed that "Leonardo is the Hamlet of art history whom each one of us must recreate for himself". Nicholl's Leonardo is the conventional hero of science, a sort of Cartesian pantheist, hostile alike to authority and faith, who dies preoccupied with millenarian floods. But he also reveals a more vulnerable Leonardo, a man whose intellectual and artistic ambitions never healed the wounds of his illegitimacy. Nicholl sees "the old man with the toothless nutcracker profile", who appears so often in the artist's sketchbooks, as "a kind of cipher of Leonardo himself: the impotent, paltry, self-deluding figure who is the dark twin of the great Renaissance achiever".

On the question of Leonardo's faith, Vasari had no doubts whatever: "When Leonardo finally became old, he wished to be carefully informed about the Catholic faith and about the path of goodness and the holy Christian religion, and then, with much lamenting, having confessed and repented, he devoutly desired to take the most Holy Sacrament out of bed, even though he could not stand upon his feet and had to be supported by his friends and servants."

Nicholl says that Vasari invented this conversion. But did he? A year before his death, Leonardo joined the Confraternity of Saint John of the Florentines. Why? Perhaps the "disciple of experience", as Leonardo referred to himself, had finally experienced something beyond nature.

Leonardo may not have been conventionally devotional in his work but he was hardly dismissive of the Faith. The man who reintroduced the smile into Western art knew better than to succumb to the gloom of agnosticism.

New Irish Sweepstakes

Luck and the Irish: A Brief History of Change from 1970, R. F. Foster. Oxford University Press. 228 pages.

WHEN THE IRISH ABANDONED their Irish parliament in 1800 and accepted the Act of Union with Great Britain, in return for bribes that were extravagant even by the generous standards of Georgian venality (each parliamentarian received £7,000, or what today would be £364,197.63), a turning point was reached in Irish history that would profoundly affect the future course of the country. The Act of Union paved the way for systemic English misrule, famine, Fenianism, the unbridgeable divide between North and South, and the cult of sectarian violence that has only recently begun to recede. In *Luck and the Irish*, Roy Foster looks at another Irish turning point: the economic boom of the last twenty odd years, which has brought changes to Ireland's religious, political, and cultural life comparable to those wrought by the Union.

Professor of History at Hertford College, Oxford, and author of *Modern Ireland 1600–1972*, *Paddy and Mr. Punch*, and a magisterial two-volume biography of Yeats, Foster comes to his analysis with impressive credentials. Despite the fact that academic historians do not as a rule shine when tackling contemporary history – look at Linda Colley on Hillary Clinton or Niall Ferguson on what he insists on calling the American empire – Foster treats his vexed subject with judiciousness and panache. Readers interested in Ireland or economic, political, or social history will find *Luck and the Irish* an entertaining, provocative study.

An English equities trader christened the "Celtic Tiger" in 1994, to liken the surging Irish economy to the "East Asian Tigers" – South Korea, Singapore, Hong Kong, and Taiwan – during their period of rapid growth in the 1980s. The extent of the Irish boom was impressive. In the decade after 1995, Foster points out, Ireland's output increased by 350 percent, personal disposable income doubled, exports increased fivefold, trade surpluses mounted into the billions, employment skyrocketed, and the number of immigrants soared. At the beginning of the 1990s there were fewer than 50 immigrants applying for asylum; by 2001 the number had reached 11,000. By 2001, immigrants from Latvia, Lithuania, Poland, the Philippines, and Romania were pouring into the country and 36,000 work permits were issued. The boom they helped to sustain made many Irishmen rich as Croesus. Terence Brown vividly substantiates this in his recent survey, *Ireland: A Social and Cultural History 1923–2002*: in 1995, Irish consumers spent £23 billion on goods and services, in 1999, £34 billion, and in 2000 £40 billion. What caused this unprecedented prosperity?

Foster identifies two schools of thought regarding the Tiger's birth: one of "Boosters" and the other of "Begrudgers". The Irish historian Declan Kiberd, an outspoken Booster, claims that the Celtic Tiger sprang to life when the Irish rediscovered the ideals of the Gaelic revival of the late nineteenth and twentieth centuries and effectively combined "the sense of local pride with the idea of self help". For the Begrudgers, the boom was largely the result of American firms – among them Hewlett-Packard, Dell, and Intel – going into Cathleen Ni Houlihan's backyard and exploiting her talented labor for the gain of American stockholders.

There is more Irish blather than reliable analysis in these readings. Yes, Irish initiative and American firms contributed, but the factors that most drove the boom were low taxation, pro-business regulatory policies, and a tech-savvy young workforce. For many multinationals the decision to do business there was made easier still by generous incentives from the Industrial Development Authority. EU membership was also helpful, giving the country lucrative access to markets that it had previously only through the UK and pumping huge subsidies and investment capital into the Irish economy. In recent years, as economic growth has slowed, the Celtic Tiger has lost much of its ferocity. Rising wages and inflation, poor infrastructure, and the addition of new members to the EU since 2004 have all contributed to a blunting of Ireland's competitive edge. In addition, low fertility rates, which had initially buoyed the economy, may soon sink it as the population, a third of which is now aged 25–44, begins to grey. But this is a still unfolding story; what Foster concentrates on is how the boom has changed the character of Irish society.

One of the best chapters of the book examines the changes that have recently occurred in Ireland's religious life. Foster attributes the decline of the Irish Catholic Church to three factors. First, Irish feminism, largely imported from America and promulgated by Mary Robinson, the former President of Ireland, whose liberal stance on contraception, abortion, and divorce helped undermine the Church's teachings on these matters; second, the mishandling of the pedophile scandals within the Irish clergy, which inspired understandable contempt for a hierarchy more intent on protecting criminal priests than vulnerable children; and last, the new materialism now rampant in Ireland, which is rather similar to the old materialism described in Kate O'Brien's 1962 book *My Ireland*, from which Foster quotes:

> Dublin has picked the simplest rule – and made it absolute. You can be anything you like within her Four Hundred – but you must be a successful person. That is all. Successful in the plainest and commonest sense – that you make, and spend, a very great deal of hard cash in pursuit of whatever you do, and that your name is very often in the papers. That is the simple regulation which keeps the ruling class down to a very manageable, neat proportion in Dublin; it might also seem to threaten that class with monotony, but in practice this is not so – since where every kind of creature is eligible, from duke to disc jockey, variety and comedy are non-stop, and easily observed in any decently expensive public place.

Whether the majority in the Irish Republic will remain at odds with Catholicism remains to be seen. As unbridled materialism continues to coarsen Irish society, some may begin to question the benefits of secularism. Some may even see a certain prescience in the Irish hierarchy's pastoral letter of 1979, *Human Life is Sacred* in which the faithful were enjoined to repudiate the idolatry of self, in which "money, alcohol, drugs and sex are ... given a place and status ... not too different from the place occupied by the gods of money, wine and sex in pagan times". What is surprising is that, as the appeal of the Church of Rome has dwindled, the Church of Ireland, long considered moribund, has rebounded. The doctrinal elasticity of the Anglo-Irish faith perfectly suits the new liberal Irish middle classes. Daniel O'Connell, the architect of Catholic Emancipation – passed by the Peel government in 1829 – must be turning in his grave.

Foster is least persuasive about the boom's influence on Ireland's cultural life. It is true that in the past Ireland has produced an inordinate amount of first-rate literary talent. In the twentieth century alone, one can cite Elizabeth Bowen, Flann O'Brien, Molly Keane, and Lord Dunsany, author of the immortal "Jorkens" stories. But for Foster to tout the work of such pretentious mediocrities as Colm Toibin and John Banville as proof of the boom's cultural dividends shows a lamentable lapse of judgment and taste. His gushing over the likes of Bono, Shane McGowan, Bob Geldof, and the producers of *Riverdance* is similarly tell-tale. These are exemplars of cultural decadence, not vitality. Foster is on surer ground when he sticks to politics.

In those realms of dross, he can be wonderfully entertaining. Here he paints a portrait of the ineffable Charles Haughey, the Fianna Fail politico, who served three times as Taoiseach, from 1979 to 1992. "His model of grandeur", Foster writes,

> was an odd combination of Napoleonic enigma, Ascendancy hauteur, Gaelic chieftain and Tammany boss. Like his rival Garrett FitzGerald, Haughey had a certain cult of France; but, while FitzGerald's tastes had been formed by youthful holidays with French families and a keen appetite for philosophical discussions with Catholic intellectuals, Haughey's Francophilia involved lavish visits to Paris, hand-stitched shirts from the legendary Charvet *atelier*, a cellar of chateau-bottled claret and a running bill at Dublin's plutocratic French restaurant Le Coq Hardi.

He was also an embezzler, extortionist, and brazen tax evader, who held extravagant court over the seamier side of the boom. As Foster notes, Haughey entirely took to heart "the exhortation given by Guizot to the subjects of Louis-Philippe: "Enrichissez-vous!"

Who gained most from the boom? Members of the Dunne family, owners of the supermarket chain, who "might have stepped straight from Balzac", as Foster nicely describes them, were some of its most corrupt beneficiaries. By the 1990s they sold 48 percent of the food sold in Ireland. They were also grateful patrons of Haughey. In gratitude to his looking the other way at their fiscal irregularities, they paid him £1.3 million. On the morning of 19 February 1992, however, the free ride ended when Ben Dunne went berserk in a hotel in Orlando, Florida. "After an incident involving a bag of cocaine, call girls and a violent psychotic episode on a seventeenth-floor balcony," as Foster relates the story, "he was carried from the hotel hog-tied to a pole. (This is the point where the story of modern Ireland demands its Zola rather than its Balzac.)" The singer Bono was also in the hotel on that same morning, a coincidence which Foster notes with the avid interest of the most besotted teenybopper.

In his conclusion, Foster recalls the character of James Tyrone from Eugene O'Neill's *Long Day's Journey into Night*, played so memorably by Ralph Richardson in the Sidney Lumet film. Tyrone, based on O'Neill's father, wastes his theatrical talents playing the Count of Monte Cristo night after night until he can play nothing else. "O'Neill intended this syndrome to be emblematic of the Irish in general", Foster writes. "One of the profound changes of attitude experienced by the Irish in the late twentieth century was the realization that they could play more roles, and that history did not dictate a determinist and stereotypical fate." But is this true? Surely, over the centuries, the Irish have played an immense variety of roles. Think of Burke, Wellington, Parnell, Constance Gore-Booth (later Countess Markievicz), Lady Wilde ("Speranza"), William Russell, Shaw, and Yeats – to name only a few of Ireland's more mold-breaking sons and daughters. These were not people who felt constrained by any "stereotypical fate". No, the Irish have always been a resourceful people. They did not need the Celtic Tiger to bring out their native inventiveness.

A more interesting question is how the Irish will respond to the social chaos and overdevelopment that the boom has brought. Can those genies ever be returned to their bottles? And what of the Irish themselves? Will they become walking, talking parodies of Irishness, like those imitation Irish pubs that one sees throughout Europe? Or gradually lose their distinctness altogether as they succumb more and more to the one-size-fits-all popular culture that has leveled and degraded so many Western societies? "The options of Irishness at the end of the twentieth century reflect a great dislocation", Foster notes in the penultimate chapter. "Looking at the new motorway encircling Dublin, the cultural commentator Anne Marie Hourihane caustically pronounced: "History is finished here. Now we are going to live like everybody else." This might be the Celtic Tiger's most lasting legacy.

Henry Mayhew
and the Poor Mouth

London Labour and the London Poor, Henry Mayhew, edited by Robert Douglas-Fairhurst. Oxford University Press. 472 pages.

From 1849 to 1850, the author and journalist Henry Mayhew set about anatomizing the life of the London poor in a series of 82 articles in the *Morning Chronicle*, which would eventually lay the groundwork for the greatest study of the English poor ever written, the 4-volume *London Labour and the London Poor* (1851–65). In meeting with and interviewing hundreds of men, women, and children throughout the city and recording what Thackeray called their "wondrous and complicated misery", Mayhew's "earnest hope", as he said, was "to give the rich a more intimate knowledge of the sufferings, and the frequent heroism ... of the poor – that it may teach those ... to look with charity on the frailties of their less fortunate brethren". In this new abridgement, we can see that "earnest hope" in all its large-hearted fellow-feeling. In one section, Mayhew meets with an elderly female street seller, whom he hears has been tending to her sick husband for many years.

> The poor creatures lived in one of the close alleys at the east end of London. On inquiring at the house to which I had been directed, I was told I should find them in "the two-pair back". I mounted the stairs, and on opening the door of the apartment I was terrified with the misery before me. There, on a wretched bed, lay an aged man in almost the last extremity of life. At first I thought the poor old creature was really dead, but a tremble of the eyelids as I closed the door, as noiselessly as I could, told me that he breathed. His face was as yellow as clay, and it had more the cold damp look of a corpse than that of a living man. His cheeks were hollowed in with evident want, his temples sunk, and his nostrils pinched close. On the edge of the bed sat his heroic

wife, giving him drink with a spoon from a tea-cup. In one corner of the room stood the basket of tapes, cottons, combs, braces, nutmeg-graters, and shaving-glasses, with which she strove to keep her old dying husband from the workhouse.

Here was the sort of heroism that Mayhew had in mind. And yet, as Thackeray attested, the suffering that made it necessary "had been lying by your door and mine since we had a door of our own. We had but to go a hundred yards off and see for ourselves, but we never did". Why? Thackeray could not have been more categorical: "We are of the upper classes; we had ... no community with the poor."

Mayhew's claim to be regarded as one of Britain's best social historians has not always been granted. Too often he is treated as a sort of proto-sociologist, whose real aspiration was to write the sort of pseudo-scientific history that came into vogue in the late nineteenth century. It is true that the author of *London Labour* can be excessively fond of statistics, but he was first and foremost a reporter, who never let his regard for the quantifiable stand in the way of his deep sympathy for the poor. Then, again, Mayhew eschewed the jargon that makes so many social historians unreadable, a jargon which resembles the costermongers' slang. (Meeting the costermongers in their pubs, Mayhew noticed how "if any strangers are present, the conversation is still further clothed in slang, so as to be unintelligible even to the partially initiated. The evident puzzlement of any listener is of course gratifying to the costermonger's vanity, for he feels that he possesses a knowledge peculiarly his own.") Moreover, Mayhew was a truth teller. At a time when so many of his contemporaries were celebrating the Great Exhibition (1851), that paean to material progress, Mayhew was content to study the direst poverty imaginable in rookeries and alleyways where respectable Londoners seldom, if ever, ventured.

What gives *London Labour* so much of its ungainsayable life are the voices that rise from its pages, like inexpiable ghosts, as here, where the old lame woman tells Mayhew, "If God tikes him, I know he'll sleep in heaven. I know the life he's spent, and I am not afraid: but no one else shall take him from me – nothing shall part us but death in this world." Similarly, when Mayhew encounters an old strumpet in the Haymarket, nothing he says about her tragic life can match her own pungent account. "You folks as has honour, and character, and feelings, and such, can't understand how all that's been beaten out of people like me. I don't feel. *I'm used to it.*" Then, again, when he falls among the "duffers", or peddlers of pretended smuggled goods, an informant tells him how "it is really astonishing ... how these men ever succeed, for their look denotes cunning and imposition, and their proceedings have been so often exposed in the newspapers that numbers are alive to their tricks, and warn others when they perceive the "duffers" endeavoring to victimize them; but, as the thimble-men say, "There's a fool born every minute".

If Mayhew often describes his subjects with a novelist's eye for the defining detail, he could also write with the prescience of a prophet. In this portrait, he might almost be describing what we are in danger of becoming if we continue to allow our political class to swell the national debt.

> Foremost among beggars, by right of pretension to blighted prospects and correct penmanship, stands the Begging-Letter Writer. He is the connecting link between mendicity and the observance of external respectability. He affects white cravats, soft hands, and filbert nails. He oils his hair, cleans his boots, and wears a portentous stick-up collar. The light of other days of gentility and comfort casts a halo of "deportment" over his well-brushed, white-seamed coat, his carefully darned black-cloth gloves, and pudgy gaiters. He invariably carries an umbrella, and wears a hat with an enormous brim. His once raven hair is turning grey, and his well-shaved whiskerless cheeks are blue as with gunpowder tattoo. He uses the plainest and most respectable of cotton pocket handkerchiefs, and keeps his references as to character in the most irreproachable of shabby leather pocket-books. His mouth is heavy, his under-lip thick, sensual, and lowering, and his general expression of pious resignation contradicted by restless, bloodshot eyes, that flash from side to side, quick to perceive the approach of a compassionate-looking clergyman, a female devotee, or a keen-scented member of the Society for the Suppression of Mendicity.

This exhibits another characteristic of Mayhew's work: its droll humor. In this, *London Labour* is reminiscent of George Orwell's *The Road to Wigan Pier* (1937), which was ostensibly written to expose the evils of poverty but ended up celebrating the comedy of class. Mayhew's researches led him into similarly amusing byways. For example, apropos the "sham indecent literature" peddled by straw sellers in sealed packets in the Strand and Holborn, Mayhew commiserates with the elderly gentlemen who fork over for these packets only to find that they contain not French postcards but religious tracts. In another passage he describes overhearing a burglar refusing to break bread with a pickpocket. "No, no! I may be a thief, sir; but, thank God, at least I'm a respectable one."

Henry Mayhew (1812–87) could write with such sympathy about those trying to keep body and soul together because he had struggled to make a living himself. Born in London, he ran away from Westminster School at sixteen and soon afterwards began writing popular novels with his brother. Then, he turned his sights on the theatre with a farce called *The Wandering Minstrel* (1834), which had only a modest success. After editing a satirical paper called *Figaro*, he returned to novel writing. In 1841, he founded *Punch*, but was fired shortly thereafter. (John Tenniel, the *Punch* illustrator of *Through the Looking Glass* based his White Knight on Mayhew.) He also wrote travel pieces and books for children. Years of extravagance landed him in bankruptcy court in 1846 and wrecked his marriage. It was a sad irony that the man who spoke so glowingly of the blessings of home should have lost his own by incurring debts of over £2,000 for the redecoration and furnishing of his large house in Parson's Green. When the *Morning Chronicle* commissioned him to write a sketch on London, Mayhew submitted "A Visit to the Cholera Districts of Bermondsey" (1849), which became the genesis of *London Labour*. After this lone success, he failed to make a go of a railway magazine entitled *Iron Times* and died in 1887, not actually in Queer Street but close by – the *Oxford Dictionary of National Biography* states that he left behind £90 10s. 0d.

It was doubtless the newspaperman in Mayhew that was drawn to what he calls "the multifarious tribe of 'sturdy rogues'", or those who refused to work, not because of physical or mental unfitness but because they preferred thieving, swindling, and begging. In her brilliant book, *The Idea of Poverty: England in the Early Industrial Age* (1984), Gertrude Himmelfarb observed how "even the most compassionate reader might find himself more impressed by the ingenuity of these outcasts than their miseries". Mayhew was clearly fascinated by the layabouts and scoundrels he encountered – the ancestors of those whom Andrew Roberts recently dubbed "the non-working, anti-working, would-do-anything-sooner-than-work class" – but he also spoke with many who were clearly keen on working. The old lame woman who went mad rather than see her bed-ridden husband thrust on the parish is a good case in point. Indeed, the resourcefulness of London's poor is one of the book's great revelations. Mayhew presents not only fruit sellers, flower sellers, sandwich sellers, omnibus drivers, coffee-stall keepers, chimney sweeps, and dock workers, but sellers of nutmeg graters, dog collars, boot-laces, corn salve, firecrackers, and rat poison, not to mention rat killers, bone grubbers, rag-gatherers, and even sewer hunters He also came upon a number of people who made their living, however precariously, by buying such things as rags, glass, bones, umbrellas, parasols, metal, bottles, and dung. Then, again, some of his best chapters are on those who entertained London's poor, including the Punch-and-Judy men; ballad sellers; hurdy-gurdy players; snake, sword, and knife-swallowers; street clowns; strolling actors; and various street musicians, some of whom plied their trade with the help of dancing dogs.

W. H. Auden made a trenchant observation about the fate of this extraordinary industry that still obtains. "Even when I was a child," the poet recalled, "the streets were full of vendors, musicians, Punch-and-Judy men and such. Today they have vanished. In all modern societies, the public authorities, however at odds politically, are at one in their fear and hatred of private enterprise in the strict sense; that is to say, self-employment."

Of course, in our own time, we have seen this hatred of the State for private enterprise intensify into an ever more insatiate encroachment into nearly every aspect of our lives – our healthcare, our commerce, even our religion. The question of what ought to be the relationship between the State and the private citizenry also exercised the English, especially after they dissolved the monasteries in the sixteenth century, which deprived the poor of so much of the charitable foundations that had been set up to relieve their distress. When almshouses gave way to work houses, the seeds of the modern welfare state were sown, the tyrannical powers of which still ramify. Prof. Himmelfarb says that what the Victorians found most shocking about Mayhew's book was that it described a "street-folk [who] were literally regressive, a throwback to a pre-industrial, even pre-civilized state, a primitive 'tribe' surviving in the very heart of civilization". That may have been true but it was not the whole truth. What shocked them even more was that the book should reveal the humanity of the poor. For Mayhew, unaccommodated man was not a poor, bare, forked animal: he was a fellow creature. This is why, despite the appalling poverty it describes, *London Labour and the London Poor* manages to be such a life-affirming book. In this most "hands-on" of histories, Mayhew shows the poor to be real people with real troubles whose distress calls out for real alms, not the travesty of charity offered by the bureaucratic State and its parasitic ministers.

Thackeray in Harvard Yard

The Correspondence and Journals of the Thackeray Family, edited by John Aplin. Five Volumes, 2,000 pages. Pickering and Chatto.

The Inheritance of Genius. A Thackeray Family Biography 1798–1875, Memory and Legacy. A Thackeray Family Biography, 1876–1919, John Aplin. Both 320pp. Lutterworth.

The Adventures of Thackeray in His Way Through the World: His Fortunes and Misfortunes, His Friends and His Family, Heather Cole, Curator. Houghton Library, Harvard University.

In 1853, when William Makepeace Thackeray made his first lecture tour of America, Boston particularly pleased him because, as he said, its "vast amount of toryism and donnishness" reminded him of Edinburgh. Today, there may be precious little toryism or donnishness left in Boston but there remains a sturdy affection for Thackeray and one proof of this is the superb exhibition that Harvard's Houghton Library has mounted to commemorate the bicentenary of the great novelist's birth.

By assembling a catalogue full of the abiding appeal of Thackeray's life and work, Heather Cole, the curator of the exhibition, has nicely captured the witty charm and ebullience of her subject. Thus, she includes the famous bust of Thackeray as a boy, the portrait of him with his parents, sitting atop a pile of folios and gazing out at the viewer with preternatural zest, and his wonderfully funny *Punch* drawings. She also includes many of his letters to his female confidants, his exquisite sketches of his daughters, Annie and Minny, pages from his manuscripts, the bright yellow installments of *Vanity Fair* (1848), and a copy of *The Adventures of Philip* (1862), his penultimate novel, printed during the Civil War by a Confederate publisher, complete with advertisements for military merchandise. That a Confederate publisher should have printed the novel has a special aptness, for *Philip* is a paean to precisely the ideal of gentlemanliness that so many Confederate soldiers prized; it was, after all, what distinguished them from Yankees.

Thackeray has been blessed with exceptional biographers and critics. Although Gordon Ray wrote the definitive 2-volume biography over 50 years ago and produced a magnificent edition of the novelist's letters and private papers, D. J. Taylor and Peter Shillingsburg have written lively biographies since, and there is a wealth of good critical work on Thackeray from George Orwell, Geoffrey Tillotson and David Cecil to Joan Stevens, Ann Monsarrat and John Sutherland. To this illustrious body of work can now be added John Aplin's 5-volume edition of the Thackeray family letters and his 2-volume family biography, both of which constitute a major contribution to Thackeray scholarship, packed as they are with fresh material and incisive commentary.

No appreciation of Thackeray's genius is possible without some understanding of the flawed, good-hearted, supremely clubbable man himself. Thackeray was born in Calcutta in 1811, the son of Richmond Thackeray, an official in the East India Company and Anne Becher, the daughter of another Company official. He had an amusing augury of his future profession when his father unwittingly invited a handsome young Bengal Engineer to dinner, who had been in love with his wife before she went out to India. When Anne and the dashing Carmichael-Smyth finally met in private on that fatal night, they discovered their mutual misapprehensions: she had been told that he had died of fever and he that she no longer cared for him. After Richmond obligingly died in 1815, the reunited lovers married and settled in Paris. Thus, it was at home, not from novels, that Thackeray learned the rudiments of romance.

Educated at Charterhouse and Cambridge, where he left in 1830 without a degree, Thackeray entered the Middle Temple in 1831, but soon gave up law for journalism. In 1833, he bought *The National Standard*, where he was proprietor, contributor and illustrator. After the paper folded, he went to study art in Paris, where, at a masked ball, he met the adventuress on whom he would base his most brilliant heroine, Becky Sharp. On a later trip to the city, in a boarding house in the Faubourg-St-Honoré, he met a 17-year-old Irish girl from Cork named Isabella Shawe, with whom he fell in love at the proverbial first sight. In 1836, they were married in the British Embassy. Once settled in London, the couple went on to have three daughters, though the second, Jane, died at eight months. Included in the Houghton show is a droll drawing by Thackeray showing how he towered over his tiny wife.

After the birth of the third daughter, Minny, Isabella began to show signs of schizophrenia. At one point, she even tried to drown Annie. Afterwards, in 1840, while traveling by steamer from Cork to London, she jumped overboard and was only rescued after being 20 minutes in the sea. When no cure could be found, Thackeray arranged for her to live with a nurse in Camberwell, where she would outlive him by 30 years. Later, he characteristically told a friend, "Though my marriage was a wreck, I would do it over again, for behold love is the crown and completion of all earthly good".

To escape the guilt he felt over his wife's derangement and to pay off his abounding debts, Thackeray immersed himself in journalism. Before marrying, he had lost his fortune to an Indian bank failure. He was also an extravagant gambler. To keep the bailiffs at bay, he contributed regularly to *Punch*, *Fraser's Magazine*, the *Morning Chronicle*, the *New Monthly Magazine* and *The Times*. From this honorable scribbling he produced some of the funniest *jeux d'esprit* ever penned, including *The Memoirs of Mr. C. J. Yellowplush* (1837), *A Shabby Genteel Story* (1840), *The Great Hoggarty Diamond* (1841) and *The Book of Snobs* (1842). If Dickens was more inventive, Thackeray had a better sense of humor. When Henry James met him in Paris in 1857 he recalled the great man turning to his eight-year old sister Alice, who was dressed in the fashionable flounces of the day, and exclaiming: "Crinoline? – I was suspecting it! So young and so depraved!"

Vanity Fair (1848), the culmination of all that Thackeray had done as a comic journalist, is an unsparing portrait of the unregenerate world from a man who knew its follies and sorrows inside out. Nowhere else does one get a better sense of the fierce social insecurity that gripped early nineteenth-century England, or its ruthlessness. "In this vast town one has not the time to go and seek one's friends," the narrator observes; "if they drop out of the rank they disappear, and we march on without them. Who is ever missed in Vanity Fair?" The Victorians liked to imagine that Thackeray exposed their vices too unsparingly. Yet, he showed those culpable of folly an almost paternal indulgence. No other Victorian novelist, for example, would have shown the incorrigible Becky Sharp anything like the sympathy that Thackeray showed her.

At the same time, to a journalist who had taken exception to what he thought the satirical severity of *Vanity Fair*, Thackeray explained that the book's object was "to indicate, in cheerful terms, that we are for the most part an abominably foolish and selfish people 'desperately wicked' and all eager for vanities ... Good God don't I see (in that may-be cracked and warped looking glass in which I am always looking) my own weaknesses lusts follies shortcomings? ... We must lift up our voices about these and howl to a congregation of fools ... You have all of you taken my misanthropy to task – I wish I could myself: but take the world by a certain standard ... and who dares talk of having any virtue at all."

In the several novels that Thackeray wrote after *Vanity Fair* the English critic John Carey saw a "history of capitulation", in which the novelist succumbed to the very snobbery that he had written his earlier work to mock. "The novels after *Vanity Fair*", Carey argues, "are full of people not only of a higher class but nicer – noble fellows, angelic ladies. It is a condition of their insipidity".

This is not an altogether just assessment. Although *The Newcomes* (1855) and *The Virginians* (1859) may be dull reads, *Pendennis* (1850) and *Henry Esmond* (1852) are undeservedly neglected. Trollope thought the latter "the greatest novel in the language", citing "the excellence of its language", the "clear individuality of its characters", the faithfulness of its Queen Anne setting, and "its great pathos". If *Vanity Fair* is about what happens to people when they lose love, *Henry Esmond* is about what happens to them when they regain it, for as the Thackerayan narrator reminds his readers, "love *vincit omnia*; is immeasurably above all ambition, more precious than wealth, more noble than name. He knows not life who knows not that ..."

This may not be as entertaining as reading about how Becky and Rawdon contrive to live on nothing a year but it proves how deeply autobiographical Thackeray's fiction is, even his historical fiction.

Another late book worth reading is *The Roundabout Papers* (1864), which includes the immortal "Mississippi Bubble", in which Thackeray recalls going down the great river on a steamboat and meeting the Bearded Lady of Kentucky. "You would have fancied that, as after all we were only some half-dozen on board, she might have dispensed with her red handkerchief, and talked, and eaten her dinner in comfort: but in covering her chin there was a kind of modesty."

> That beard was her profession: that beard brought the public to see her: out of her business she wished to put that beard aside... as a barrister would wish to put off his wig. I know some who carry theirs into private life, and who mistake you and me for jury-boxes when they address us: but these are not your modest barristers, not your true gentlemen. Well, I own I respected the lady for the modesty with which, her public business over, she retired into private life. She respected her life, and her beard... All public men and women of good sense, I should think, have this modesty.

After Isabella went mad, Thackeray became infatuated with the literary hostess Jane Octavia Brookfield, the wife of one of his old Cambridge friends, with whom he entered into a strenuously chaste *ménage a trois*. "However much I may love her & bless her and admire her, I can't forgive her for doing her duty", he confessed, before putting a stop to what he called his "uncouth raptures". In all events, Thackeray was fortunate not to see the Brookfield–Thackeray triangle reproduced in Mrs. Brookfield's novels, *Only George* (1866) and *Not Too Late* (1868). On 23 December 1863 he returned home from dining, had a stroke and dropped dead.

Throughout his life, Thackeray was an ambivalent clubman, drawn to the confidential comfort of clubs but convinced that men without the civilizing society of women became boors. "The greatest good that comes to a man from woman's society", he once observed, "is that he has to think of somebody besides himself – somebody to whom he is bound to be constantly attentive and respectful". Here was a truth that only his treacherous egotism could teach him, and it made him not only a brilliant satirist but a grateful family man, and on the three women who meant most to him – his wife, his mother, and his daughter, Annie – Aplin's volumes are revelatory.

Apropos Isabella's mental illness, Aplin argues that most modern clinicians would probably diagnose it as "puerperal psychosis, affecting about one in a thousand women after childbirth with symptoms which may include depression, delusional behavior, hallucinations, and paranoia". At the same time, he shows that Isabella, towards the end of her life, enjoyed an unexpected serenity. Certainly, her delight in music never waned. Often Annie would visit her simply to hear her play Glück and Handel. "I was really *floored* one day with worry & nerves when I went to Mama's & lay on the sofa there while she played sweet hymn tunes & I felt like a child again & all unlocked & cried & cried." In those encounters, as Aplin observes, family tradition was renewed, for 50 years before it was Isabella's deep love of music that first endeared her to Thackeray.

Aplin also gives a more rounded portrait of Thackeray's mother, whom many have misrepresented as simply a zealot. By bringing her letters to light, Aplin reveals what an intelligent, witty, solicitous woman she was. He also shows how keenly perceptive she was about the deep love that Thackeray's daughters had for their father. When Thackeray remonstrated with her for trying, as he saw it, to instill them with her own passionate Calvinism, the old woman fired back: "I have one thing to say by which you may free yourself from any apprehension of yr children thinking, or believing otherwise than as you do; they have but one creed & that is 'Papa' ..."

The star of Aplin's volumes is Anne Thackeray Ritchie (1837–1919), whom her father once described as "a fat lump of pure gold, the kindest, dearest creature as well as a wag of the first water". After Thackeray's death, she married a handsome cousin seventeen years her junior and became the keeper of her father's flame, producing both the handsome Centenary Edition of his work and novels of her own. George Eliot once said that her fiction was the only modern fiction she cared to read. The historian James Bryce was taken with more than her novels. "Never have I known any one with quite the same charm, inexhaustible kindliness and sympathy with a freshness and genuinenss which made everyone feel wiser & better than themselves when they were in her company." This was an estimate of her character shared by many of those eminent Victorians with whom she was friendly, including Henry James, Leslie Stephen (who married her sister Minny), Robert Browning, Lord Tennyson, Charles Eliot Norton, Henry Cole (who mounted the Great Exhibition), the painters Sir John Millais and G. F. Watts, and the great "kitchen-table" novelist, Mrs. Oliphant, to whom Annie once wrote: "as I read your letter I somehow felt for the moment – blessed feeling – all one's life remains, things don't go, we fade, not they, it is all there".

Thanks to this wonderful correspondence, and Aplin's heroic labors, we can now share Annie's delight in this rich recollected past. For anyone interested in Thackeray or the social and literary history of the nineteenth-century, Aplin's combined volumes offer a treasure trove of new information. They also offer something else. When I was leaving the Thackeray exhibition at Harvard, Heather Cole turned to me and said that she had come to love Thackeray because he was so full of love himself – love and endless jokes. Well, John Aplin has done a fine job of showing how that love and wit bound together not only Thackeray's daughters and their families but a much larger extended family, the members of which will only grow with the publication of these marvelous books.

No Flies on Ian Ker

Mere Catholicism, Ian Ker. Crossroads. 224 pages.

Books of apologetics have always enjoyed a special place in the hearts of readers. Samuel Johnson recalled picking up William Law's *A Serious Call to a Devout and Holy Life* (1728) when he was an undergraduate at Pembroke, "expecting to find it a dull book ... and perhaps to laugh at it". But he found Law "quite an overmatch for me; and this was the first occasion of my thinking in earnest of religion". John Henry Newman said of Thomas Scott's autobiography, *The Force of Truth* (1779) and his famous commentary on the Bible (1788–92)

> I so admired and delighted in his writings, that, when I was an undergraduate, I thought of making a visit to his Parsonage, in order to see a man whom I so deeply revered ... It was he who first planted deep in my mind the fundamental truth of religion.

Indeed, Newman spoke of Scott in his *Apologia* (1864) as the writer "to whom (humanly speaking) I almost owe my soul". C. S. Lewis credited G. K. Chesterton with opening his eyes to Christianity when he was a young don at Magdalen. For years he had enjoyed reading Chesterton despite his faith; then he read *The Everlasting Man* (1925). and "for the first time" he "saw the whole Christian outline of history set out in a form that seemed ... to make sense".

With *Mere Christianity* (1950), a collection of radio broadcasts, Lewis wrote an extraordinarily popular book of apologetics. In *Mere Catholicism*, Father Ian Ker takes Lewis's book as a starting point for an overview of the Roman Faith. The author of several superb books on Newman as well as *The Catholic Revival in English Literature 1845–1961* (2003), Ker brings impressive credentials to his task. It is obvious that he has taken to heart Newman's great summons: "Know what you say you know". Yet unlike many academics, he writes with grace and lucidity. Cradle Catholics, Catholic converts, and would-be Catholics will find his book a lively, instructive, persuasive read.

Those familiar with Lewis's book will know that by remaining mum on so many doctrines vital to Christianity, *Mere Christianity* promised more than it delivered. No book could claim to be an essential guide to Christianity that ignored Our Lady or that only covered the Incarnation, the Atonement, and the Resurrection. Father Ker fills in Lewis's enormous gaps by sharing his often trenchant insights into the Church, the Holy Spirit, the Blessed Virgin, the saints, the sacraments, the Eucharist, penance, purgatory, baptism, marriage, and prayer.

He rightly explodes the idea that "there is a sort of fundamental Christian faith that is all that really counts and that anything else is more or less optional". Throughout he gives his readers the guidance they need to recognize the fullness and the coherence of the Faith, based as it is on the one, holy, catholic, and apostolic Church. Thus, "Christians who profess the creeds that go back to the earliest centuries are not expressing an aspiration or ideal about what the Church should be, but instead the indispensable marks or notes of the Church". Father Ker made this same point in refuting Owen Chadwick's claim that Newman was in search of an ideal church when he converted to Rome. No, Newman converted to the real Church.

Father Ker has gentle fun with the Protestant obsession with the Bible. "If one thinks that everything depends on the written Scriptures, it is hard not to convict Jesus of a certain willful negligence." Indeed, those Protestants who claim that their beliefs issue exclusively from the Bible "might reasonably have expected to find the central Protestant doctrine of justification by faith alone categorically and specifically stated by Jesus". But, alas, Jesus left no writings behind. As Father Ker points out, Jesus was a doer, not a writer.

> On one occasion, for example, He cured a blind man not by words but by spitting on the ground and making a paste with his spittle, which He applied to the man's eyes. This mysterious teacher and miracle-worker by no means relied only on words. There was a strange earthiness attached to much of what He did, which sits uncomfortably with any concept of a religion bound up exclusively with the written word of the Bible.

When it comes to parrying objections, which is at the heart of apologetics, Father Ker is in his element. "Unbelievers may be amazed at what Catholics believe", he writes.

> But what unbelievers so often don't appear to appreciate, is that believers are also amazed, not to say shocked, that there are people who can live their lives in a meaningful way and with a sense of moral responsibility, while at the same time refusing to accept that there is any reason to think that this world could have an ultimate cause or purpose, or that this life should have any lasting meaning or significance, or that we will have to render account for the manner in which we live it.

Father Ker recognizes that non-Catholics can often have an oddly ambivalent attitude to the Faith. Apropos the unfair criticism heaped on Pius XII, he reminds his readers that the secular world has always held Catholics to a high standard: "It doesn't expect secular humanists to risk their lives in defense of the weak and helpless, but it does rightly expect ... Catholics, to do so ... [which] is revealing. For it shows that it is appreciatively aware of the self-sacrificing heroism which Catholic Christianity exemplifies at its best."

Regarding abortion, euthanasia, and contraception, Father Ker addresses some of the most insistent objections currently raised against the Church:

> Catholic teaching on all these matters ... has become increasingly unfashionable and unpopular in Western secular society. But this teaching does not claim to be based on revelation, it claims to be based on reason, reason that can discover the moral law unaided by any Christian or any religious belief. Our human reason can work out what the body is designed to do, that it has been given genitals for intercourse between man and woman, an intercourse which naturally leads to new life; just as it can tell us that the human destroying of life must be an inhuman act, whether it is killing an unborn child or an elderly or very sick person. But reasoning is not an automatic process. Somebody has to do the reasoning and that is a human person, a person endowed with conscience but also a sinful person ... Reason, therefore, can go disastrously wrong, especially when it is unaided by

religious belief and a sense of being answerable to a Creator. But ultimately, the modern secular world's hostility to Catholicism is not a hostility to its revealed doctrines but a hostility to reason itself.

This is true. When positivists like Freddy Ayer and Bertrand Russell attacked the rational basis for belief they succeeded not in eradicating the religious impulse but in degrading reason. Their postmodernist successors have followed suit. Contempt for the moral law is a consequence of this degradation of reason.

In paying special attention to Our Lady, whom he recognizes as "the most important member of the Church", Father Ker affirms the vital role of reason in understanding and practicing the Faith. In this, he follows Newman, who called Mary "our pattern of Faith, both in the reception and in the study of Divine Truth ... [who] symbolizes to us, not only the faith of the unlearned, but of the doctors of the Church also, who have to investigate, and weigh, and define, as well as to profess the Gospel; to draw the line between truth and heresy; to anticipate or remedy the various aberrations of wrong reason; to combat pride and recklessness ... and thus to triumph over the sophist and the innovator".

Father Ian Ker has written a book that defends the Faith with admirable élan. *Mere Catholicism* is a model of apologetics that will command the field for years to come.

Shakespeare and the Dangers of Thinking Too Much

> *Yond Cassius has a lean and hungry look.*
> *He thinks too much: such men are dangerous.*
> William Shakespeare, *Julius Caesar*

Shakespeare the Thinker, A. D. Nuttall. Yale University Press. 428 pages.

No literary compositions take a critic's measure like the plays of Shakespeare. They may inspire the very best critics to outdo themselves: Samuel Johnson, Coleridge, Eliot, and Auden all wrote brilliantly about the playwright whom Ben Jonson called "the wonder of our stage". But the plays can be unmerciful to lesser lights. Look at the critical shipwreck to which they led Harold Bloom. Look at how they exposed the superficiality of Sir Frank Kermode. The young can write ineptly about Shakespeare and move on to other more suitable things; but when older critics write about him and fail, the failure is gross and final. The plays have taken the measure of these hapless critics and found them wanting.

A. D. Nuttall's *Shakespeare the Thinker* passes the exacting test of the plays with flying colors. The book not only crowns his earlier efforts but shows how his own thinking about Shakespeare has deepened over the years. Sadly, this generous, witty critic died unexpectedly in January, 2007, before this book went to press.

A fellow of New College, Oxford, Nuttall never repudiated the classical humanism he imbibed as a classics student at Merton in the mid 1950s. In one of his earlier books he wrote: "I remember a conversation with a friend in which he suggested that we should have our names inscribed ... high on some ancient building, together with the legend "We never believed in Theory". *Shakespeare the Thinker* engages the claims of many theorists but only to show that the key to good Shakespeare criticism is not theory, but insight.

Nuttall mines chronology to chart the development of Shakespeare's thinking. Thus, the poet's study of stoicism, first essayed in *Julius Caesar*, makes way for what Nuttall calls the "subjective nightmare" of *Hamlet*. When Brutus says: "Between the acting of a dreadful thing / And the first motion, all the interim is / Like a phantasma, or a hideous dream", he is thinking of Caesar but prefiguring the paralysis of the cerebral Prince. Hamlet looks at Horatio and sees someone "more an antique Roman than a Dane", who "is not passion's slave". But when Hamlet tries to emulate his friend's stoicism, a rather more complicated subjectivism results, in which, "There is nothing either good or bad, but thinking makes it so". Most commentators gloss over this as a stoic platitude, but Nuttall rightly recognizes it as the arrival of a demoralizing relativism.

On the vexed issue of Shakespeare's religious faith, Nuttall is admirably balanced. While unconvinced that Shakespeare's Catholicism was central to his thinking, Nuttall does recognize it as an abiding factor. Certainly, he rejects the view that Shakespeare was a nihilist. He shows the tragic world of *King Lear* underscoring, not obliterating, the differences between good and evil. The world that blinds Gloucester and kills Cordelia may be unjust but it is not meaningless.

One of the unifying themes of the book is how Shakespeare's "brilliant articulateness" colored his plays. Nuttall nicely describes what would be a most enviable predicament for most other writers when he says Shakespeare "is oppressed by his own verbal facility. Effortlessly he hits every nail on the head, finds the stirring image, lights upon the undermining parody, and, amid all this, hears in the distance a voice that says, 'Slow down'". Much of the innovation in Shakespeare's plays came from his having to find ways to challenge his prodigious technical mastery – a search which only ended with Prospero abjuring his author's "rough magic" in *The Tempest*.

It was precisely this facility that led him to take up the theme of rhetoric in *Julius Caesar* and *Coriolanus*. As Nuttall observes, Auden might have been right that "poetry makes nothing happen", but rhetoric does makes things happen and usually "on a frightening scale". Shakespeare is fascinated by the power of rhetoric not only to persuade people but to loosen their very hold on reality. Nuttall puts Shakespeare's interest in rhetoric in context when he says: "It remains a curious fact that in later ethical philosophy we shall see reason displaced as the proper director of moral action and feeling substituted – and this switch is first made in the handbooks of rhetoric." We are still contending with the consequences of that particular trend.

Verbal facility as something of a curse also appears in the comedies. Regarding the unrelenting banter of *Love's Labours Lost*, Nuttall observes: "If one is trapped in the convention of restless badinage so that one is never able to look steadily at anything, the appropriate reality will be perhaps the great negative fact of death; this alone can stop the witticisms." Hence, the Elizabethan use of "die" for "orgasm". John Donne, in his strenuously witty lyrics, also suffered from this "restless badinage", which made C. S. Lewis doubt whether Donne ever really understood human love as anything other than a kind of verbal athletics.

Then there are Beatrice and Benedick of *Much Ado About Nothing*, whose jousts of wit, Nuttall observes, "look at first like displays of festive freedom but at last compose a glittering cage in which it is impossible for either party to say, simply, 'I love you'". This is rather different from what Craig Raine in his recent study of Eliot called "the perverse platitude that language is always an obstacle to expression", which continues to enthrall the postmodernist academy. The very articulateness of Shakespeare's would-be lovers may frustrate their desires, but the plays do not support the notion that language per se necessitates their separation. On the contrary, as Nuttall affirms, the plays show how "words when they become transparent ... *can* engage reality". There is nothing determinist in Nuttall's Shakespeare.

Nuttall shows how feeling humanizes Shakespeare's thought. Although engaging enough about the various philosophical systems in which Shakespeare dabbled – Nominalism, Realism, Gnosticism – Nuttall is shrewdest when his analysis calls for psychological insight. For example, speaking of Othello, he says: "He does not really know Desdemona and marvels that she, so beautiful, could love one like him. So he turns, as Iago knew he would, to the familiar: to the genial male friend, the experienced solider, 'honest Iago'. There is something frightening about the strength of the love of a woman when it comes to one till then cocooned in comforting male solidarity. It is as if we had a Romeo who instinctively felt he could not be loved by Juliet, turned back to his old friend Mercutio – and found that Mercutio hated him." This is good old character analysis after the manner of

A. C. Bradley, and Nuttall, who is not afraid of singing Bradley's unfashionable praises, is superb at it.

Nuttall's close reading of *Richard II* is perhaps the best in the book. "Richard has grown up", he says about the man who goes to his death with newfound bravery. He has "matured to the point of full *anagnorisis*, in the sense in which that term applies to Sophocles' Oedipus, self-understanding. Perhaps the trauma of usurpation is itself enough to account for the change. But we do not see enough of the transition. The movement at the end is so profound that it engages the audience entirely. We have no mental leisure to wonder any more how such a thing could happen. Suddenly we love Richard. But I am not sure that we should." In revisiting this study of regal introspection, Nuttall sounds more an inspired stage director than a critic poring over the play in his library.

What sets Nuttall apart from many other critics is his readiness to question his own assumptions. This intellectual humility is a trait he shares with Shakespeare, who, for all his protean thinking, never lost sight of the larger scheme of things in which thought is merely a part. Apropos the great speech in *A Midsummer Night's Dream*, in which Bottom, scrambling Saint Paul, exclaims: "The eye of man hath not heard, the ear of man hath not seen, man's hand is not able to taste, his tongue to conceive, nor his heart to report, what my dream was", Nuttall proves his critical mettle. For Frank Kermode, this "fanatasticated" allusion was tossed out merely to divert an audience fond of Scripture. For Nuttall it is very much more: "At one level Bottom's hilarious confusion of ear and heart makes nonsense of the Pauline thesis; at another level it deepens it. Paul is striving to lead our minds to a place where the ordinary categories no longer apply. Bottom's wild synaesthesia enforces the idea of a reality beyond categories."

Shakespeare the Thinker is a gloriously good book which deserves to be read and reread by all who love the poet who remains "the wonder of our stage".

All the King's Imperial Men

The Men Who Lost America, Andrew Jackson O'Shaughnessy. Yale. 480 pages.

IN HIS GROUNDBREAKING HISTORY of the American War of Independence from the British standpoint, *The War for America* (1964), Piers Mackesy argued that "to understand the war, one must view it with sympathy for the Ministers in their difficulties, and not with the arrogant assumption that because they were defeated they were incompetent, and that all their actions proceeded from folly". Taking Mackesy's call for sympathetic balance as his starting point, Andrew Jackson O'Shaughnessy revisits the men who sought to recapture America and finds that there was a good deal to admire in their otherwise ill-starred endeavors. In his superb new study, *The Men Who Lost America*, he shows sympathy not only for the Mother Country's ministers but for her officers as well, who fought the war to keep her empire intact and yet ended by relinquishing the empire to maintain her parliamentary institutions. As the intellectual historian J. G. A. Pocock pointed out in *Virtue, Commerce, and History* (1985), "the loss of an empire was a high price to pay for institutional stability", but "the empire was surrendered, and the stability of institutions maintained".

In following the unfolding of this paradoxical outcome, O'Shaughnessy gives center stage to the biographical aspects of his subjects. In his well-researched and well-written pages, readers can see the personal strengths and foibles that animated his fascinating cast of characters, from George III, Lord North, Lord Germain, Lord Rodney and Lord Sandwich to the Howe brothers, John Burgoyne, Sir Henry Clinton, and Lord Cornwallis. He also shares with readers the relentless criticism heaped on Lord North's government by Edmund Burke, the Elder Pitt, John Wilkes and Charles James Fox. And since O'Shaughnessy also plunders the diaries and letters of such astute eyewitnesses as Horace Walpole, Edward Gibbon and Nathaniel Wraxall, his text is full of witty contemporary commentary.

One of the great strengths of the book is its biographical structure, which gives O'Shaughnessy's analysis of events a rich, layered, novel-like multiplicity of perspectives. It also enables his readers to appreciate the inherent difficulty of establishing any reliable historical interpretation from those often conflicting perspectives.

The central contention of the book is that we can only appreciate the character and scale of the American victory if we appreciate the skill and resourcefulness of the British conduct of the war, even though the tactical skills of Britain's gifted commanders were finally no match for the war's manifold logistical difficulties. Or the more fundamental difficulty of trying to win back the loyalty of those convinced, as Benjamin Franklin told Admiral Howe in July of 1776, that

> it is impossible we should think of Submission to a Government, that has with the most wanton barbarity and cruelty, burnt our defenceless Towns in the midst of winter, excited the Savages to massacre our Farmers, and our Slaves to murder their Masters, and is even now bringing foreign mercenaries to deluge our Settlements with Blood. These atrocious Injuries have extinguished every remaining Spark of Affection for that Parent Country we once held so dear.

Here Franklin exploded not only the myth that America was full of loyalists but the concomitant myth that if only Britain waged the war fiercely enough the colonists would be cowed into submission. King George III never left off believing that the colonists "will be lions, whilst we are lambs; but if we take the resolute part, they will undoubtedly prove very meek". Edmund Burke might insist that "magnanimity in politics is not seldom the truest wisdom; and a great empire and little minds go ill together". But for the king such magnanimity only emboldened the seditious minority to tyrannize over his loyal American subjects and he would not hear of it.

If resolve characterized George III, irresolution characterized his First Minister, Lord North, who was convinced that he was not the man to salvage an unwinnable war, even if it was crucial to Britain's imperial prestige. O'Shaughnessy's portrait of this ungainly, popeyed, ingenious figure is a model of evenhandedness. While he takes him to task for failing to unite the cabinet around an agreed policy, he extols his management of the huge war debt, which went from 127 million in 1775 to 232 million at war's end.

He also praises North's "unalterable suavity" in debate. As one can see from Hansard, his jousts with the opposition were marvelously deft. No less a critic than Gibbon considered him "a consummate master of debate, who could wield with equal dexterity the arms of reason and ridicule". Gibbon, in fact, would later credit the late eighteenth-century House of Commons, of which North was such a skillful member, with training him to become an historian by educating him in the arts of government.

The most ambivalent of King George's commanders were the Howe Brothers – Major General William Howe who had scaled the heights of Abraham and captured Quebec in 1759 and Lord Admiral Richard Howe who had fired the first shot of the Seven Years War from *HMS Dunkirk* and later became a pioneering expert on amphibious warfare, precisely the thing that might have saved Burgoyne and Cornwallis from their respective debâcles at Saratoga and Yorktown. Like Burke, the Howe brothers were convinced that the British in America were at war with their own principles. As Burke argued in his great speech, *On Conciliation with America* (1775), "Deny [the colonists] ... participation in freedom, and you break that sole bond, which originally made, and must preserve the unity of the empire". Yet, as Samuel Johnson argued in *Taxation No Tyranny* (1775) the colonists had the same *virtual* representation that all British subjects had.

For David Hume, such arguments were beside the point. "Arbitrary power can extend its oppressive Arm to the Antipodes", the Scottish savant wrote a friend in October of 1775, "but a limited Government can never long be upheld at a distance, even where no Disgusts have intervened..." Hume's recommendation had, therefore, a certain ineluctable logic. If the British insisted on war, they would have to be prepared to "annual all the Charters, abolish every democratical Power in every Colony; repeal the Habeas Corpus Act with regard to them; invest every Governor with full discretionary or arbitrary Powers; confiscate the Estates of all the Chief Planters; and hang three fourths of their clergy". The only problem with this course of action was that "to execute such Acts of destructive Violence twenty thousand Men will not be sufficient; nor thirty thousand ..." The only solution was to leave the colonies to govern themselves. "Let us therefore lay aside all Anger; shake hands, and part Friends", Hume concluded. "Or if we retain any anger, let it only be against ourselves for our past Folly; and against that wicked Madman, Pitt, who has reduced us to our present Condition".

Despite their reservations, the Howe Brothers arrived in New York full of high hopes, convinced that their chances of victory were hardly negligible. With 32,000 troops to Washington's 19,000, they certainly had numerical superiority. General Howe was initially successful in the Battle of Long Island in August of 1776 – which, many argue, gave the British their best chance to win the war with one knockout victory – but shortage of food and supplies prevented him from following up the victory. Howe also claimed that he held back to avoid estranging what he thought the loyalist majority in America. But it was not British might but British plunder that turned the Americans against the redcoats, which, even if necessitated by shortages, gravely undermined the professional standards of Howe and his colleagues. When Franklin upbraided the British for their "barbarity and cruelty", he was attacking those professional pretensions at their tenderest point.

This brings up an interesting irony. If there was one thing that united the commanders of the British Army, with all their differences, it was precisely their pride in their professionalism. Lifelong students of warfare, many went on to distinguished military careers after their defeat in America. In hindsight, however, their contempt for amateurism is surprising. After all, in nearly every field of endeavor, Georgian England teemed with brilliant amateurs. In *The Pleasures of Imagination* (1997), the historian John Brewer showed how Horace Walpole transformed the arts of England. Yet it was not until Britain's professional commanders met the Americans in the field that they began to appreciate how amateurs could revolutionize the waging of war. For John Burgoyne, the consummate professional, the colonists might be led by "profligate hypocrites" whose political views were animated by "sophistry and frenzy", but they exhibited "great ability" in the field, especially when they transformed their militiamen into marksmen whose accuracy was a continual bane to the more conventionally trained British. The amateur colonists also brought an extraordinary pertinacity to their war making, which was part and parcel of their devotion to liberty. As General Nathaniel Greene was fond of saying, "we fight, get beat, rise and fight again".

If the Howe brothers and John Burgoyne became increasingly skeptical about the prospects for victory, especially after Saratoga, Lord George Germain, who succeeded Lord Dartmouth as Colonial Secretary, was intent on winning the war before the French entered it by isolating revolutionary New England and moving the conflict south, where he expected large numbers of loyalists to help him secure and extend his victories. If the southern campaign failed, Germain feared, France might install Washington at the head of what would amount to a French dictatorship. In the event, Britain's imperial commitments in Canada, Ireland, and the British Caribbean prevented her from giving her commanders the troops and supplies they needed to repulse this decisive French factor. Moreover, as Washington recognized, naval superiority would prove the "pivot upon which everything turned". Had Lord Rodney prevented the comte de Grasse from controlling the Chesapeake, Cornwallis would never have been entrapped at Yorktown.

Apropos the elusive loyalists that were such a lynchpin of British strategy, O'Shaughnessy estimates that only 16 percent of the colonial population could be described as loyalist, hailing mostly from the Hudson Valley, southern Pennsylvania, New York, and the southern frontier between Georgia and Virginia. Still, they were a sizable contingent in an imperial war that often resembled a civil war. During hostilities, some 19,000 loyalists fought for the British. However, since the British Army never accorded loyalists equal status, their loyalty was always questionable, even if they were prepared to defy the retaliatory wrath of their rebel neighbors. They also resented Britain's enlisting native Indians and slaves and thought the Crown's soldiers irreligious. Even in the eighteenth century, the "Bible-faced Yankees" were never indifferent to religious faith.

Germain's southern policy was complicated by the appointment of Sir Henry Clinton as Howe's successor in New York. An overly cautious, querulous man, Clinton was convinced that he had been set up to take the blame for defeat in America after Howe and Burgoyne lost Saratoga. This obsessional defeatism was exacerbated by feelings of resentment towards Lord Cornwallis, who treated his colleague with seigniorial disdain. Still, O'Shaughnessy nicely captures the scale of Clinton's difficulties. "He was expected to conquer South Carolina, advance into the Hudson Valley and attack the coast of

New England all at the same time." To give Clinton his due, he managed a brilliant siege of Charleston, giving the British one of their greatest victories. After tallying the spoils, Clinton had captured the largest and most prosperous city in the South; seven generals; three battalions of artillery; four frigates; several armed boats; and 400 pieces of ordnance, not to mention 2,571 regular troops and 800 militia. And this against only 76 British killed and 179 wounded. Clinton would often lament in later life that if he had only resigned after Charleston, he would have been known as Britain's greatest commander in America. Instead, he sailed for New York and left Cornwallis in charge of a southern command that would culminate in Yorktown.

O'Shaughnessy's portrait of Charles, Earl Cornwallis is one of the best in the book. Here we see that prior to his defeat at Yorktown the ruthless general had an impressive victory at the Battle of Camden in which his opponent General Gates lost 1,000 men to Cornwallis's 68 killed and 256 wounded. Weeks before Yorktown Cornwallis was still the most feared of all Britain's commanders. Yet, as was so often the case, he could never keep what he conquered. So he marched his army from one conflict to the next, never securing any lasting advantage. Indeed, he even described himself in one letter as "quite tired of marching about the Country in Quest of Adventure". Then, too, he showed pathological contempt for his men, ordering them to divest themselves of their packs, which left them not only without food and tents but boots. That he meant to transform them into a light force to prevent General Greene from teaming up with the legendary Daniel Morgan hardly justified this futile sadism. Clinton rightly complained that by treating his men so harshly his colleague was behaving "like a barbaric Tartar". Horace Walpole was no less unsparing. Cornwall, he wrote, "has conquered his troops out of shoes and provisions and himself out of troops". In ten weeks Cornwallis lost 4,000 men. When it came to what the French called *la petite guerre,* or warfare by small skirmishes where the object was to wear down the enemy, the Americans always proved the superior force.

In retrospect, Yorktown seems not so much a miscalculation on the part of a hapless commander surprised by a joint American and French land and naval force that outnumbered him two to one as a kind of providential delivery. In his memoirs, Clinton claimed that Cornwallis did not do enough to save himself at Yorktown, a classic siege which would have delighted Sterne's immortal Uncle Toby. Cornwallis countered that he chose not to fight his way out at Yorktown because he was waiting for relief from Clinton, which, of course, never came. (And, after all, it was Clinton who had ordered him to try to capture the tobacco port in the first place.) Yet the likelier explanation might be that this bedeviled man had simply had enough and yearned to be extricated from what had become an impossible war. As the French mortars exploded over this head, he might have said to himself what another British officer had told a newspaper earlier in the war: "Human exertion is a limited thing. Remember ... we do not contend with an army but with a country." And, in Cornwallis's own case, with the comte de Rochambeau, who had marched 400 miles down from New York with 7,800 troops, including some of the cleverest artillery officers in Europe.

After nine days of maddening artillery fire with 156 dead and 326 wounded, Cornwallis sent up the white flag. Later, although some in the colonies thought he should be executed for war crimes, Cornwallis was allowed to return to British headquarters in New York. Before departing, however, he was sumptuously fêted by his American captors, who vied with one another to wine and dine the defeated peer. Even in colonial America they loved a lord. That Cornwallis received a hero's welcome when he returned to England proved that this was a love shared by his countrymen. Later, he would go on to become both Governor-General of India and Lord Lieutenant of Ireland. After his death, the *Dictionary of National Biography* nicely summed up one of the most successful proconsuls of Britain's second empire: "If not a man of startling genius, he was a clear-sighted statesman and an able general, as well as an upright English gentleman."

The Men Who Lost America is the work of an historian in dazzling command of his sources who writes with admirable grace and acuity. Since this is only his second book, we can all look forward to many more good things from Andrew Jackson O'Shaughnessy.

Hopkins in His Letters:
The Importance of Being Earnest

The Collected Works of Gerard Manley Hopkins. Volumes I and II: *Correspondence 1852–1889*, edited by R. K. R. Thornton and Catherine Phillips. Oxford University Press. 1,057 pages.

ENGLAND PRODUCED SOME SUPERB LETTER WRITERS in the nineteenth century: Lord Byron, Emily Eden, John Keats, Charlotte Brontë, and Sydney Smith gave an altogether new charm and expressiveness to the epistolary art. Smith's letter to Miss Lucie Austin is a good example. "You are going to Boulogne," Smith told his young friend in 1835, "the city of debts, peopled by men who never understood arithmetic; by the time you return, I shall probably have received my first paralytic stroke, and shall have lost all recollection of you; therefore, I now give you my parting advice. Don't marry anybody who has not a tolerable understanding and a thousand a year, and God bless you, dear child." Swift, Johnson, and Horace Walpole all wrote splendid letters in the previous century, but they never achieved the sort of brilliant badinage that Smith achieved. Another figure who brought an inimitable gusto to his correspondence was the poet Gerard Manley Hopkins (1844–99), and in this magnificent edition of his letters admirably edited by Catherine Phillips and Kelsey Thornton, we can see the full range and exuberance of one of Victoria's best letter writers.

The central act of Hopkins's life was his conversion to Roman Catholicism when he was 22. Shortly thereafter he joined the Society of Jesus. Before converting, he wrote to his father how "the Catholic system ... only wants to be known in order to be loved – its consolations, its marvelous ideal of holiness, the faith and devotion of its children, its multiplicity, its array of saints and martyrs, its consistency and unity, its glowing prayers, the daring majesty of its claims".

This rhapsodic catalogue left his devoutly Anglican father aghast. His Oxford tutors were equally stunned. Henry Parry Liddon, the biographer of the Anglo-Catholic Edward Pusey, barraged him with letters, urging him to reconsider. Benjamin Jowett, Balliol's famous Professor of Greek, likened the appeal of Roman Catholicism that swept up Hopkins and so many others of his generation to a "commercial panic". In a letter to Florence Nightingale, Jowett wrote how "very miserable" it was that "at Oxford ... there should be so little moral strength and so little regard for truth".

Hopkins took the anti-Catholic bias of Oxford in stride. "Not to love my University", he said, "would be to undo the very buttons of my being". If John Henry Newman could say that it was Oxford that had made him a Catholic, it was even truer of Hopkins. Studying Greats at Balliol steeled him in both his faith and his art.

Considering how revolutionary so much of Hopkins poetry is, he had need of the confidence that only a place like Balliol could bestow. His bold, innovative syntax and his celebration of "the roll, the rise, the carol" of creation are like nothing in all English poetry:

> As kingfishers catch fire, dragonflies draw flame;
> As tumbled over rim in roundy wells
> Stones ring; like each tucked string tells, each hung bell's
> Bow swung finds tongue to fling out broad its name;
> Each mortal thing does one thing and the same:
> Deals out that being indoors each one dwells;
> Selves – goes itself; *myself* it speaks and spells,
> Crying *What I do is me: for that I came.*

Hopkins's delight in words is everywhere in his letters. He lived in the great age of philology and shared its fascination for what Matthew Prior called the "idiom of words". In fact, he was taught by the same headmaster who taught the etymologist Walter Skeat, who, with James Murray, launched the *Oxford English Dictionary* in 1879. "I am going to write to Skeat about *scope*", Hopkins says in one letter. "I have doubts about Skeat's treatment of *scope, cope, scoop, scape, cap*."

He was also fond of music, as his many observations on composers prove. "Do you like Weber", he asks one correspondent. "For personal preference and fellow feeling I like him of all musicians after Purcell. I feel as if I could have composed his music in another sphere" – which casts an intriguing sidelight on his own elaborately musical verse. Then, again, he knew the limits of his own decided taste: "The only good and truly beautiful recitative is that of plain chant ... It is a natural development of the speaking, reading, or declaiming voice, and has the richness of nature; the other is confinement of the voice to certain prominent intervals and has the poverty of an artifice. But Handel is Handel." As a Jesuit, Hopkins had many postings – proof that the Society of Jesus did not altogether know what to do with their extraordinary convert. From Blackburn, he writes of how "It seems likely that I shall be removed; where I have no notion", an uncertainty which led him to refer to himself as "Fortune's football". Nevertheless, Hopkins did his best to adjust. "It is our pride", he says, "to be ready for instant dispatch." Wales, the slums of Liverpool, Glasgow, Oxford, and, finally, dear, dirty Dublin all figure in both his letters and poetry.

"Museless" Liverpool produced his sullenest reflections: "The drunkards go on drinking, the filthy, as the scripture says, are filthy still: human nature is so inveterate. Would that I had seen the last of it." Once posted to Farm Street in London, he wrote, "I am so far as I know permanently here, but permanence with us is gingerbread permanence, cobweb, soapsud, and frost-feather permanence". No one – or only Sir Thomas Browne – ever expressed himself with such felicitous eccentricity.

Again and again the letters demonstrate the appeal that human distress held for Hopkins. In a letter to Robert Bridges, who became his sounding board and confidante, he wrote of how "a shocking thing ... has happened to a young man well known to our community. He put his eyes out. He was a medical student and probably knew how to proceed, which was nevertheless barbarously done with a stick and wire. The eyes were found among nettles in a field ... He was taken to a hospital and lay in some danger – from shock, I suppose ... It is not good to be a medical man in the making. It is a fire in which clay splits." This same concern for those in difficulties would lead Hopkins to recommend the practice of almsgiving to those, like Bridges, who were unsettled in their faith.

The letters also show what a shrewd literary critic Hopkins was. When someone praises Charles Doughty's *Arabia Deserta* (1888), he responds in allusive disbelief: "Is not Elizabethan English a corpse these centuries? No one admires, regrets, despairs over the death of the style, and the living masculine native rhetoric of that age more than I do; but 'tis gone, 'tis gone, 'tis gone."

The letters exhibit the great store that the artist in Hopkins placed on character, which was not a popular principle in the decadent ethos that his Balliol coach Walter Pater did so much to promote. Apropos what he calls "beautiful evil", Hopkins insists that "it is our baseness to admire anything evil. It seems to me we should in everything side with virtue, even if we do not feel its charm, because good is good". Indeed, for the poet, "without earnestness there is nothing sound or beautiful in character, and a cynical vein indulged coarsens everything in us" – an observation which the author of *De Profundis* would richly corroborate.

Another characteristic of the poet highlighted by the letters is his respect for failure. For the priest in Hopkins, the greatest exemplar of the power of failure was Christ:, since although "he would have wished to succeed by success – for it is insane to lay yourself out for failure... nevertheless he was doomed to succeed by failure; his plans were baffled, his hopes dashed, and his work was done by being broken off undone". With such an appreciation for the dignity of failure, it is perhaps not surprising that Hopkins should have told another correspondent that "his muse takes in washing". Such solicitude for human infirmity resulted in some unforgettably beautiful poetry.

> God, lover of souls, swaying considerate scales,
> Complete thy creature dear O where it fails
> Being mighty a master, being a father and fond

The letters also help illuminate Hopkins's highly experimental verse, especially such poems as "The Leaden Echo and the Golden Echo", and "The Wreck of the Deutschland". Moreover, in one letter, he defends his accustomed complexity by arguing that meaning in verse should be of two kinds: that which is immediately discernible and that which takes a while to emerge but then "explodes". It is perhaps only apt that the poets for whom he expresses most admiration should be John Milton and Walt Whitman, who may seem poles apart but whose meanings do often *explode* in the way Hopkins approves.

When it came to his own verse, Hopkins was human enough to miss fame. If he gradually reconciled himself to the fact that his poems would remain unpublished in his lifetime, he was deeply disappointed that *The Month* rejected his bravura Pindaric ode,

"The Wreck of the Deutschland", a rejection which severely tested the self-denial at the root of his vocation. But he was also devout enough to recognize, with Ronald Knox, that "waiting upon God alone and letting the world go its own way without you is an integral part of sanctity". W. B. Yeats's father once lamented that, with all his gifts, Hopkins should have become a priest. When this was reported back to Hopkins, he said: "You wouldn't only give the dull ones to Almighty God". Gerard Manley Hopkins was not one of the dull ones.

Much of his poetry in his last years was a wrestling with something Saint Ignatius Loyola says in his *Spiritual Exercises*: "Let him who is in desolation strive to remain in patience, which is the virtue contrary to the troubles which harass him; and let him think that he will shortly be consoled, making diligent efforts against this desolation". Unfortunately, some misrepresent Hopkins's spiritual difficulties, including Norman White, who wrote a misleading critical biography of the poet. The letters correct the view that Hopkins resented the religious order that forbade the publication of his verse. "When a man has given himself to God's service," Hopkins wrote to the poet Richard Watson Dixon in 1881, "when he has denied himself and followed Christ, he has fitted himself to receive and does receive from God a special guidance, a more particular providence ..."

> Now if you value what I write, if I do myself, much more does our Lord. And if he chooses to avail himself of what I leave at his disposal he can do so with a felicity and with a success which I could never command. And if he does not, then two things follow; one that the reward I shall nevertheless receive from him will be all the greater; the other that then I shall know how much a thing contrary to his will and even to my own best interests I should have done if I had taken things into my own hands and forced on publication.

Of course, this is not a point of view that most literary biographers can be expected to appreciate, but nevertheless, as these letters show, it was the point of view to which the poet himself subscribed, with whatever anguish. When it came to Hopkins's vocation, Newman provided the soundest gloss, telling the poet he converted: "Don't call the Jesuit discipline 'hard'. It will bring you to heaven."

Geoffrey Hill: The Light of Appraisal

Collected Critical Writings, Geoffrey Hill, edited by Kenneth Haynes. Oxford University Press. 816 pages.

In 1891, Henry James reaffirmed his respect for criticism by stressing what he might have called its exiguity.

> The critical sense is so far from frequent that it is absolutely rare, and the possession of the cluster of qualities that minister to it is one of the highest distinctions. It is a gift inestimably precious and beautiful; therefore, so far from thinking that it passes overmuch from hand to hand, one knows that one has only to stand by the counter an hour to see that business is done with baser coin. We have too many schoolmasters; yet not only do I not question in literature the high utility of criticism, but I should be tempted to say that the part it plays may be the supremely beneficent one when it proceeds from deep sources, from the efficient combination of experience and perception. In this light one sees the critic as the real helper of the artist, a torch-bearing outrider, the interpreter, the brother.

Into this exclusive club James would certainly have admitted the French critics who influenced him – Sainte-Beuve, Taine, Gautier, Daudet – but one suspects that he had English and American critics in mind when he spoke of his age having "too many schoolmasters". We are plagued with the same surplus, though our schoolmasters are infinitely duller. Nevertheless, we do have some proper critics still working: Ian Ker has written brilliantly about the writers of the Catholic Revival and Michael Alexander recently wrote an excellent book on medievalism and the history of modern England for Yale. Another good critic who has been at work for over a quarter century is the British poet Geoffrey Hill, whose learned criticism, like his poetry, revives something of the high seriousness of Modernism.

In this splendid collection of his critical writings, adroitly edited by Kenneth Haynes, which brings together three previous books, *The Lords of Limit* (1984), *The Enemy's Country* (1991), and *Style and Faith* (2003), as well as 13 hitherto uncollected pieces, Hill richly illustrates what James had in mind when he said that the good critic is "the helper of the artist". There are essays here on an extraordinary range of poets – from Shakespeare, Robert Southwell, Henry Vaughan, John Dryden, and Jonathan Swift to Gerard Manley Hopkins, Ralph Waldo Emerson, A. E. Housman, John Crowe Ransom, T. S. Eliot, Ezra Pound, Ivor Gurney, and Isaac Rosenberg, and each essay, in its way, examines what Hill refers to in one of his recent poems as "the pitiless wrench between truth and metre", a subject about which all diligent poets need all the help they can get.

The help Hill supplies is a constant summons to intelligence, which echoes James's advice to the young woman who asked him what she needed to do to become a proper novelist: "Be someone on whom nothing is lost." Very little is lost on Geoffrey Hill. In his introduction to *The Enemy's Country*, Hill declares: "I follow MacDiarmid in desiring "A learned poetry wholly free / From the brutal love of ignorance" and hold with John Berryman, that "all artists who have ever survived were intellectuals – sometimes intellectuals *also*, but intellectuals". Whenever Hill is critical of a poet, it is because he somehow fails his intelligence test, though, on the whole, he is a generous grader. Allowing Housman to have been more solipsistic than obtuse is one example of the quality of Hill's generosity.

The poet with whose later work Hill takes barbed exception is Eliot. After citing "the routine demands made, between 1940 and 1945, upon an author of Eliot's high reputation, for work of an appropriate public significance" he delivers the *coup de grace*:

> In the "Music of Poetry", though he says that the poet must, like the sculptor, be faithful to the material in which he works, Eliot's material is no longer primarily language but Christian Thought; or the People as he understands them. And how he understands people is still very much how he understood them in the pub scene of *The Waste Land*, only now, instead of saying, "Well, if Albert won't leave you alone, there it is, I said", they say, "that is how I should talk if I could talk poetry". This is not enhancement but impoverishment,

and the language of *Four Quartets* also is language that has suffered impoverishment. Making it part of the Anglican Lectionary is not going to amend that radical absence.

Some readers might balk at this: surely a case can be made for *Four Quartets*, Eliot's long good-bye not only to his varied influences but to art itself. His revels had ended and if the language in which he announced his farewell was, at times, tired, it was understandably so. He was "wore aht", as Bill tells Barbara in the Shaw play. Still, whatever claims can be made for the later poetry, it is difficult to deny that a good deal of Eliot's later criticism was marred by orotund superficiality, by what Hill calls "the ruminative, well-modulated voice of a man of letters". What gave Eliot's earlier criticism its zest was the satisfaction it drew from besieging the Georgian citadel. Once he became a citadel in his own right, he could only turn his guns on himself, which, in a late essay, he did to devastating effect: "Most men either cling to the experience of youth, so that their writing becomes an insincere mimicry of their earlier work, or they leave their passion behind, and write only from the head, with a hollow and wasted virtuosity. There is another and even worse temptation: that of becoming dignified, of becoming public figures with only a public existence – coat-racks hung with decorations and distinctions, doing, saying, and even thinking and feeling only what they believe the public expects of them." Here, one might say, Eliot was better at bashing Eliot than any of his critics.

Besides slack thinking, Hill castigates uncharitable feeling. Citing a passage in Matthew Arnold's "The Function of Criticism at the Present Time", he makes a point for which anyone saddled with an unfortunate surname will be grateful. Arnold had quoted a newspaper report in which a workhouse child named Wragg had been found murdered, which ended, "Wragg is in custody". The phrase offended Arnold "and rightly", says Hill, "because it speaks with the voice of the beadle, the complacent harshness of the penal code lopping off the superfluous Christian name, a process endorsed by the jubilant tribunes of the vox populi. However, the name Wragg itself strikes Arnold's sensitive ear as horribly vulgar; the critic who has warned against catch-words is caught by a word and, in an unguarded moment, righteous anger and unrighteous taste become compounded. The indignation of a just and compassionate man is degraded into a whinny of petty revulsion."

Hill is particularly good on Swift. "It is not altogether astonishing to find in Swift's poetic satire a certain amount of irritation at the spurious proscriptions of false delicacy", he writes. Yet "with many aspects of the consensus of taste Swift was undoubtedly able to agree, and it would be patronizing to suppose that he necessarily regarded himself as sacrificing original liberty on the altar of caste ... Swift's poetry gained more than it lost by his overall adherence to the major canons of his class." This dispels the still common view of Swift as a misanthropic exile repulsed by Yahoos. Elsewhere in the same superb essay, Hill remarks of the satirical dean's raillery, which was not universally appreciated, especially by those who bore its brunt.

> The casualty rate could, admittedly, have been higher; but the point would seem to be that, notwithstanding the precise distinction between fine raillery and coarse insult, mistakes were frequently made, even by... skilled practitioners. It may seem that infringements occurred through the necessity to turn in small tight circles of mutual exacerbation.

For so dazzlingly allusive a writer as Hill, it was perhaps inevitable that he should write about the most allusive of all writers, Robert Burton, whose *Anatomy of Melancholy* (1621) was the only book to get Samuel Johnson out of bed before noon. As in his brilliant essay on the poet Henry Vaughan, whom he commends for what he calls his "serene celebrations of indwelling... something within and withdrawn when all has been quantified and qualified", Hill finds much in Burton that sheds light on his own poetry, remarking in one passage how Burton "understands that sphere of action, which the Gospels and Epistles call 'this world', to be *Mundus foriosus*, the domain of stupefying monotony and purposeless energy". This is similar to much Hill country – for example, this, from *The Triumph of Love* (1998), his long jeremiad against history and its fallen architects:

> Admittedly at times this moral landscape
> to my exasperated ear emits
> archaic burrings like a small, high-fenced
> electricity sub-station of uncertain age

in a field corner where the flies
gather and old horses shake their sides.

Hill also reveals something of his own poetic *modus operandi* when he says "with Burton ... the active declares itself in plain, even severe statements of faith ... that stand out from the tragic-comic welter like inspirations of God's grammar". For example, he quotes this from Burton: "We must live by faith not by feeling, 'tis the beginning of grace to wish for grace: we must expect and tarry." Even when writing about other artists, Hill most illuminates the artist in himself. Perhaps one of the reasons why he has always cultivated a certain reticence in his poetry is that he is chary of the "plain, even severe statements of faith" to which he is otherwise drawn. As he says in one of his poems, "things unspoken as spoken give us away".

The tidy will find Hill wayward. Tangents and divagations pull him hither and yon, especially in a wonderful piece on rhythm, nicely entitled, "Redeeming the Time". He can never resist bypaths that promise sidelights on his subjects. In this he resembles the greatest of all digressers, Samuel Taylor Coleridge, who once remarked, "Of Parentheses I may be too fond – and will be on my guard in this respect ... But I am certain that no work of empassioned and eloquent reasoning ever did or could subsist without them – They are the drama of Reason – & present the thought growing, instead of a mere Hortus siccus."

Hopkins is perhaps the most congenial of the poets Hill takes up, sharing as he does his fascination with the music of verse, his close attention to words, and his impatience with the presumed lazy-mindedness of the common reader. In "A Postscript on Modernist Poetics", Hill quotes approvingly Hopkins's contention that "Plainly if it is possible to express a subtle and recondite thought on a subtle and recondite subject in a subtle and recondite way with great felicity and perfection ... something must be sacrificed ... and this may be the being at once, nay perhaps even being without explanation at all, intelligible". But is this persuasive? Shakespeare and Dante never had any difficulty treating the subtle and recondite intelligibly. Hopkins, conscious that he was vulnerable on this score, was trying to let himself off the hook. Hill can rehearse this feeble pleading to try to excuse his own impenetrability, but it won't wash.

Hopkins and Hill are good poets *despite* their unintelligibility, not because of it. Nevertheless, when the difficult demands they make on their readers pay off, the results can be exhilarating. Hill, for example, shows how Hopkins's stubborn eccentricity carries the day in "That Nature is a Heraclitean Fire":

> Suddenly there bursts in an uncouth anacoluthon: "Enough! The Resurrection!" It is a great moment, one of the greatest grammatical moments in nineteenth-century English poetry. It has been criticized for arbitrariness, but arbitrariness is the making of it. The Resurrection is a kind of eschatological anacoluthon; no amount of standard grammar can anticipate or regularize that moment.

This is the sort of close, useful criticism of which Henry James would have entirely approved. A good deal of disreputable acclaim has been lavished on Hill – he is, after all, touted by Harold Bloom – but readers should not be put off by his embarrassing admirers. For all his gratuitous obscurity, Hill is worth reading, and the brilliance of this collection demonstrates why.

Andrew Mellon:
The Imperative to Acquire

Mellon: An American Life, David Cannadine. Knopf. 782 pages.

"THERE ARE FEW WAYS in which a man can be more innocently employed", Samuel Johnson once said, "than in getting money". What he would have made of Andrew Mellon (1855–1937), the Gilded Age industrialist who probably devoted more time to getting money than anyone who ever lived, is an interesting question. In his superb new biography, the English historian David Cannadine meticulously recreates the career of a man who "was enthralled by acquisition and accumulation". Anyone interested in the rise of America's first plutocrats – or what Henry James called "the hard face of new aristocracies" – will find it fascinating.

Johnson approved of money making because he recognized that it obviates poverty, promotes charity, and enables men to follow other more liberal pursuits. As he wrote in his *Lives of the English Poets*, "A man, doubtful of his dinner, or trembling at a creditor, is not much disposed to abstracted meditation or remote enquiries". Mellon can certainly be credited with keeping the wolf from his own door – at his death, he was estimated to be worth $36 million (much less than many supposed) – though whether he kept it from those of his laborers is questionable. Cannadine vividly describes the lot of those who worked in the Mellon steel mills:

> Shifts in the mills were usually twelve hours long; the only holidays were the Fourth of July and Christmas; industrial accidents were frequent and ghastly; most workers were unable to continue beyond their forties; and unemployment was an ever present anxiety ... housing was squalid, unsanitary, and overcrowded, especially near the mills, the atmosphere, the streets, and the rivers were polluted with industrial effluent; and disease, especially typhoid, was endemic.

Whether Johnson would have approved of Mellon's money making on charitable grounds is perhaps less dubious. Although the son of a Scotch-Irish father who believed that charity thwarted enterprise and rewarded idleness, Mellon eventually came round to the view that there was merit to large-scale charity if it benefited the nation as a whole. Hence, his founding and endowment of the National Gallery in Washington with his own wonderful collection of paintings, some of which Knopf has nicely reproduced here.

Still, Johnson would have deplored the philistinism of Cannadine's hero, who rarely read other than for business and spent most of his meager spare time talking shop with other industrialists. As Gladstone once told Carnegie, "The desire to hoard is the lowest form of intellectual degradation". That Mellon found the theoretical puerilities of Herbert Spencer compelling was proof of his own degradation – though he would mitigate this somewhat by buying Old Masters with the help of the wily art dealer, Joseph Duveen.

Johnson would surely have approved of Mellon's belief that "real success comes from making others successful". The quintessential banker – dispassionate, circumspect, opportunistic – Mellon had the well-earned reputation of being "the best listener in Pittsburgh". He made many men millionaires and was instrumental, along with Heinz, Westinghouse, Carnegie and Frick, in building up his sooty, insalubrious hometown into one of the powerhouses of industry. Cannadine's book is as much a biography of Pittsburgh as it is of Mellon. A native of Birmingham, Cannadine brings not only sympathy but insight to his description of the place that Charles Dickens dubbed "the Birmingham of America".

The fourth son of Thomas Mellon, who settled in Pittsburgh from County Tyrone and made his fortune in law, business, and banking, Andrew was shrewd, hard-working, and indefatigable – the natural heir to his father's single-minded acquisitiveness. Unlike Carnegie, who made money to give it away, Judge Mellon made it to enrich the Mellon dynasty. Hence, Andrew's was not a rags-to-riches story. Yes, he became fabulously wealthy, but he began wealthy.

In his autobiography Thomas recalled "the luxuriant vegetation and luscious fruit" of the new world, which "gave the country the appearance of paradise". Andrew would pluck the industrial fruit of this paradise at a time of great industrial transformation in iron and steel, petroleum, natural gas, and aluminum, in all of which he built highly successful integrated businesses. Like his father, he accumulated his millions not by daring deals but safe bets. Alcoa, Gulf Oil, Koppers, Carborundum, and the Mellon National Bank were some of the more lucrative results.

Andrew also shared his father's contempt for the Catholic Irish and what he considered their superstitious, stultifying faith. When his son Paul contemplated marrying a Catholic, Andrew was aghast and warned his son against putting his future children at the mercy of priests. Paul broke off the romance and later married a Protestant allergic to horses, which could not have suited his passion for fox hunting. If the Mellons despised Catholics, their own Presbyterian faith was an odd stew of Calvin, Spencer, and Robert Burns, exalting, as Cannadine says, "canniness, practical wisdom and self-advancement: essential qualities for winning the struggles of life, which only the fittest would survive".

About Mellon's legendary reserve, one contemporary remarked that "had he got religion, he would not have told God". Cannadine is good at showing how "Mellon's strength as a banker derived from those very traits that inhibited his sociability, his shyness, his aloofness, his self-sufficiency, his calculating reticence, his inscrutable silences, his determination to keep his innermost thoughts to himself".

Mellon threw circumspection to the winds when he fell in love with an English woman less than half his age and succumbed to what T. S. Eliot called "The awful daring of a moment's surrender / Which an age of prudence can never retract". After reluctantly agreeing to marry the shy tycoon, Nora McMullen found Pittsburgh uninhabitably dull and her husband an undemonstrative drone. The marriage ended in divorce after Mellon discovered that his young wife had been cuckolding him with an English confidence man fond of preying on unhappy rich women.

Secretary of the Treasury from 1921 to 1932 under Harding, Coolidge, and Hoover, Mellon saw the boom he had helped create in the 1920s burst on 29 October 1929, when sixteen million shares changed hands and $26 billion in paper values vanished. Like his father, Mellon regarded cycles of boom and bust as inescapable: all one could do was keep one's head during the booms and ride out the busts. That this particular bust would last nearly a decade no one could predict. Nevertheless, Mellon stuck to his *laissez-faire* guns and could only have chuckled when FDR claimed in 1932 that "the day of the great promoter, or the financial Titan, to whom we granted everything if only he would build or develop, is over". It is a mark of Cannadine's balance that he should treat this aspect of his subject with such studied fairness. He does not downplay how FDR and his Justice Department wrongly tried to have Mellon indicted for tax evasion nor how Mellon was entirely exonerated.

Although full of illuminating detail and persuasive analysis, Cannadine's book finally mystifies. What could have induced anyone to give himself so thoroughly to such relentless money making? Here Johnson's description of a visit to the pyramids from *Rasselas* suggests one possible answer. After considering the extent and the exorbitance of the pyramids, the sage of the tale observes:

> I consider this mighty structure as a monument of the insufficiency of human enjoyments. A king, whose power is unlimited and whose treasures surmount all real and imaginary wants, is compelled to solace, by the erection of a pyramid, the satiety of domination and tastelessness of pleasures, and to amuse the tediousness of declining life by seeing thousands labouring without end, and one stone, for no purpose, laid upon another. Whoever thou art, that, not content with a moderate condition, imaginest happiness in royal magnificence, and dreamest that command or riches can feed the appetite of novelty with perpetual gratifications, survey the pyramids and confess thy folly!

Whoever imagines that making money can make happiness should read this brilliant, engrossing, sad book.

McKim, Mead, and White
and American Beauty

Triumvirate: McKim, Mead and White: Art, Architecture, Scandal and Class in America's Gilded Age, Mosette Broderick. Knopf. 582 pages.

TRYING TO IMAGINE NEW YORK without the architecture of McKim, Mead and White is like trying to imagine Paris without the architecture of Baron Hausmann. Of course, a good deal of that architecture is gone. We no longer have the wonderful old Pennsylvania Station that McKim modeled after the baths of Caracalla, or the Madison Square Garden that White based on the Cathedral of Seville, or the whimsical Herald Building that White modeled after the Loggia del Consiglio in Verona. But we do have the Metropolitan Club, the University Club, the Post Office, the Villard Houses, the Municipal Building, the Metropolitan Museum, and Washington Square Arch, to name only some of the firm's New York buildings. Without these, New York might still have some modest claim to architectural distinction, but it would have lost its greatest monuments to that acquisitive swagger that defined the Gilded Age, when the city was at the zenith of its confidence and creativity.

In *Triumvirate: McKim, Mead and White: Art, Architecture, Scandal and Class in America's Gilded Age*, Mossette Broderick revisits the three distinctly different personalities that founded the firm to show how their complementary strengths transformed architecture not only in New York but in all America at a time when the country was ripe for an aesthetic reawakening.

Charles Follen McKim (1847–1909) was born and raised a Quaker in southwestern Pennsylvania, the son of an abolitionist. If McKim *père* dedicated his life to freeing the slaves, his son dedicated his to giving his compatriots an architecture that would at once appropriate and renew European architecture. A scholarly, exacting, discriminating man, McKim lived in Europe for three years, where he studied at the École des Beaux Arts in Paris, after attending Harvard's Lawrence

Scientific School. On his return, he worked in the offices of Henry Hobson Richardson, the premier architect of the day, where he not only tapped his Harvard connections to obtain commissions but met White.

Stanford White (1853–1906) was the son of an impecunious Shakespeare scholar whose own literary ambitions would never be realized. Still, it was from his Anglophile dandy of a father that he acquired his passion for art. Although poorly educated, White was a quick study and brimming with talent. He was also an inspired draughtsman. For Richardson, who made the lively autodidact his personal assistant, White's contribution to the firm that he would help make famous was indisputable: "White", he recalled, "was the firebrand, eager to break precedent, to use new materials, to experiment with building form". He was also a consummate collector, whose avidity for furniture, rugs, hangings, plate, paintings, and antiques of all descriptions fed his flair for interior decoration. That some of these acquisitions were spurious never bothered White: they helped form his highly intuitive taste, and since it was his taste that brought in many of the firm's commissions, he learned to treat the impostures of dealers as simply another cost of doing business. Unfortunately, he also had a passion for showgirls, and Broderick vividly describes his murder atop the roof garden of Madison Square Garden by Harry Thaw, the jealous husband of Evelyn Nesbit. Interestingly enough, the murder occurred while one Harry Short was singing a popular tune of the day, "I Could Love a Thousand Girls", which might have been White's theme song. Yet, as Broderick notes, "The autopsy results shocked [White's] family almost as much as the murder ... White was in terrible health. Indeed, he was dying of kidney disease. Thaw never needed to shoot White. He would have died naturally in a few months' time." In all events, after pleading insanity, Thaw went scot-free.

William Rutherford Mead (1846–1928) was the down-to-earth engineer of the firm, who, unlike his partners, was happily married. If McKim was given to immobilizing depression and White to ringing the midnight bell, Mead was the reliable office man who, as Broderick notes, "ensured the completion of the projects and stability in the small, dark spaces of lower Broadway". Moreover, he saw to it that the often ambitious ideas of his partners were translated into structures that were as functional as they were beautiful. Taught his trade by the successful architect George Fletcher Babb in the offices of Russell Sturgis, Mead had no illusions about his own capabilities and deferred to the more original talents of his partners. Nevertheless, when he traveled to Florence as a young man he was disappointed by the architecture, which he considered too derivative, a criticism which the tribe of Le Corbusier would often level at the work of Mead and his confreres in the twentieth century.

What is striking about the borrowings of McKim, Mead and White is how they prefigure what T. S. Eliot had to say about the relationship between the artist and the past in "Tradition and the Individual Talent" (1919). There, he spoke of "the historical sense", the "perception", as he defined it, "not only of the pastness of the past, but of its presence", which makes the artist "most acutely conscious of his place in time" as well as "his own contemporaneity". In modeling their public buildings on past designs, McKim, Mead and White were not merely paying homage to the past: they were staking out claims for the present, which readjusted both past and present in precisely the way Eliot thought good traditional art must.

> The existing order is complete before the new work arrives; for order to persist after the supervention of novelty, the whole existing order *must* be, if ever so slightly, altered; and so the relations, proportions, and values of each work of art towards the whole are readjusted; and this is conformity between the old and the new. Whoever has approved this idea of order ... will not find it preposterous that the past should be altered by the present as much as the present is directed by the past.

McKim's appropriations of classical models in his designs for Pennsylvania Station brilliantly illustrate Eliot's understanding of the vitality of tradition. Eliot would also have enjoyed White's impish parody of White's Club in London, which James Wyatt designed in 1787–8, for his design of the Century Club, about which Broderick is nicely observant.

> Both have a rusticated base, pilaster strips that double on either side of the center of the building, five bays each, round ornament in four of the upper-story bays, and a crowing

balustrade. Lost at the Century was White's famous 1811 bow window [behind which Beau Brummell entertained his louche associates]. Instead, the Century has a tall central arched entrance. Above the entry at the Century was an open, Italian loggia formed by a great Palladian window. The resemblance is amazingly close, but the details vary, as do the materials.

One can see the same innovative use of models in the charming summer houses that the firm built in New Jersey and Rhode Island, which were inspired by the work of the English architect Richard Norman Shaw (1831–1912) and the Queen Anne Movement. Growing up around Elberon, New Jersey, where the firm built so many cottages in the shingle style, I vividly recall those breezy, capacious, ramshackle houses, with their wrap-around porches and witch-hat roofs. The book's photographs vividly recapture the now-vanished seaside of my childhood.

Although cosmopolitan, McKim, Mead and White always remained distinctly American – a trait they shared with Henry James. In *Sweetness and Light: The Queen Movement: 1860–1900* (1977) the architectural historian Mark Girouard notes how White's design for the Watts-Sherman house in Newport is "a brilliantly individual version of Shaw's 'Old English' manner – chimneys, sunflowers, oriels, overhanging gables, irregularity, and all. But 'Old English' tile-hanging is replaced by a lavish use of its American equivalent, wooden shingles, and the windows, instead of being glazed with leaded lights in the 'Old English' manner, have a close grid of wooden glazing bars." Moreover, White and his partners treated space differently because, as Girouard notes, "in America the social system which in England worked to separate men from women, grown-ups from children, and family from servants was less constrictive; spaces could open into each other without causing social embarrassment".

The loveliest of these shingle houses is the Robert Goelet House, which still stands in Newport. Goelet was the son of an old New Yorker of Huguenot stock who kept peacocks in his garden at 19th Street and Broadway. The house that White built for him is of a breathtaking beauty. To appreciate that beauty, one should keep in mind how unusual it was in most American residential architecture. H. L. Mencken is amusing on this score.

> On a winter day, not long ago, coming out of Pittsburgh on one of the swift, luxurious expresses of the eminent Pennsylvania Railroad, I rolled eastward for an hour through the coal and steel towns of Westmoreland County. It was familiar ground; boy and man, I had been through it often before. But somehow I had never quite sensed its appalling desolation. Here was the very heart of industrial America, the center of its most lucrative and characteristic activity, the boast and pride of the richest and grandest nation ever seen on earth – and here was a scene so dreadfully hideous, so intolerably bleak and forlorn that it reduced the whole aspiration of man to a macabre and depressing joke. Here was wealth beyond computation, almost beyond imagination – and here were human habitations so abominable that they would have disgraced a race of alley cats.

McKim, Mead and White were not unfamiliar with such noisome districts. When the firm built the Percy Rivington Pyne House on East 68th Street and Park Avenue, the neighborhood had only recently been transformed from a shanty town where locomotives made their fuliginous way to Grand Central. Broderick speaks of her subjects, so many of whom came from abolitionist backgrounds, as turning "the fervor of their parents' abolitionist zeal into the cause of beauty, carrying the banner of art forward as their parents had done with that of the freedom of the slaves". This is what made the firm great. McKim, Mead and White (and their junior associate Joe Wells) did zealously work to dissuade Americans from sating what Mencken called the "libido for the ugly" by introducing a new beauty into American architecture.

Broderick's command of the professional lives of McKim, Mead and White is admirably thorough. Indeed, she has made this material so much her own that she presents her narrative with few inclusions of secondary or primary sources. The absence of the former might be welcome; after all, she is writing for the general reader, not the academy. But the absence of primary sources – letters, memoranda, diary entries, news accounts, contemporary criticism – weakens her otherwise seamless narrative. The Gilded Age was neither a reticent nor a dull age: Broderick might have occasionally allowed it to speak for itself.

Nevertheless, anyone interested in architecture, history, New York, Newport, or that amusing thing, class will want to get hold of this engaging book. On the last item, Broderick is insightful, as here, where she speaks of McKim after his triumphant completion of the Boston Public Library.

> McKim could see himself now as a mature master, fostering the education of a future generation of American architects. He had joined those he had felt were his natural companions. In marrying into the Brahmin class, McKim had joined the Episcopal Church and let his family heritage of politically based idealism go. Indeed, when he was courting Julia [his second wife] and the family of William Lloyd Garrison had asked McKim to design the base for a monument to the great abolitionist, he declined the job. Instead, he gave it over to Joe Wells...

John Sloan and the Art of Painting in New York

John Sloan's New York, Heather Campbell Coyle and Joyce K. Schiller, with essays by Molly S. Hutton, Susan Fillin-Yeh, Katherine E. Manthorne, and Alexis L. Boylan. Yale University Press. 208 pages.

"The fun of being a New York painter," John Sloan told *Esquire* in 1936, "even today, is that landmarks are torn down so rapidly that your canvases become historical records almost before the paint on them is dry." Surely Sloan was being sardonic: chronicling the loss of the city's history could not have been *fun*. Yet, in fact, he took the depredations reshaping the city in stride. In this, he was the direct opposite of Henry James. In *The American Scene* (1905), describing his first visit to his native city in twenty years, James deplored the ethos of the skyscraper, what he called the "huge, continuous fifty-floored conspiracy against the very idea of the ancient graces". Sloan never objected to the development that James found so appalling. The ruthless impermanence of the city would always be central to his New York art.

One of the more interesting images in the catalogue accompanying the show of Sloan's work at the Delaware Art Museum, *Seeing the City: Sloan's New York* (20 October 2007 to 20 January 2008) is a photograph Sloan took in 1927 from his Washington Square apartment capturing One Fifth Avenue going up behind Washington Square Arch. In "Wet Night, Washington Square" (1928) Sloan would show the bold new high-rise towering over the Square with what appears smug remorselessness. It seems a clear protest – elegiac, unavailing – against the same sort of reckless development that robbed James of his birthplace at No. 21 Washington Place, a large block house off the Square near Greene Street. And yet Sloan welcomed One Fifth Avenue. As the curators of the Sloan show point out, the painter did not share Edmund Wilson's view that the object of this new development was "to crush, in Washington Arch and now in the row of red facades behind it, whatever they possessed of impressiveness and magnificence". For Sloan, the new buildings were grist to his artistic mill. Even when 53 Washington Square South, the old Judson Hotel, where he had an apartment on the fourth floor, was taken over by New York University, Sloan decamped willingly enough to a studio apartment atop the Chelsea Hotel, where he lived until his death.

Moving to the Chelsea Hotel was something of a homecoming since it was at 165 West 23rd Street that Sloan lived with his wife Dolly when he painted most of his greatest New York paintings. Edith Wharton was born two blocks to the east near Fifth Avenue in 1862 when the street was still fashionably residential. By the time Sloan moved there from Philadelphia in 1904, it was lined with shops and dominated by the Flatiron Building, which Alfred Stieglitz might have considered America's Parthenon but which the English Pre-Raphaelite painter Burne Jones described as "one vast horror, facing Madison Square ... distinctly responsible for a new form of hurricane, which meets unsuspecting pedestrians as they reach the corner". Sloan captured one of these "hurricanes" in "Dust Storm, Fifth Avenue" (1906), which gives his Madison Square neighborhood a dreamlike quality reminiscent of Giorgione. In real life, it was bustling, socially eclectic, and noisy (one could hear the Sixth Avenue El from Sloan's five-floor walk-up), the perfect base for an artist who wanted to paint Whitman's "Life immense in passion, pulse and power".

The English historian Macaulay once said that "it is only by walking on foot through all corners at all hours that cities can be really studied to good purpose". The diary Sloan kept from 1906 to 1913 records the wide-ranging attentiveness of his own perambulations. "Walked through the interesting streets of the East Side", he records in one entry. "Healthy-faced children, solid-legged, rich full color to their hair. Happiness rather than misery in the whole picture." In another entry, he observes: "A fire in the afternoon at 25th Street and 10th Avenue ... Boys thronging, the hook and ladder wagon, smoke, hot sun and all sorts of people". In another, "Dolly and I took a walk after dinner dishes were done, ending up on 8th Avenue, which is very interesting and different. The avenue life is different in each case. Sixth, tenderloin, fast. Eighth, neat lower class, honest. Third, poor, foreign. Each has its individual character." With John Butler Yeats, the poet's father and by all accounts a delightful conversationalist, Sloan "footed it down as far as Chambers Street". Afterwards, the pair "walked through Chinatown, his first visit, and then ... up to 6th St. and after a little lunch in a restaurant ... we went to the Astor Library" on Eighth Street and Lafayette, which now houses Joseph Papp's Public Theatre.

Sloan's "Scrubwomen in the Old Astor Library" (1910) exhibits the painter's delight in the ordinary at a time when the ordinary was spurned as *infra dig.*: scrubwomen might be seen but not shown. After exhibiting at Macbeth Galleries in 1908 with other like-minded artists, Sloan was consigned to the "Ashcan School", a label which has always misrepresented his considerable achievement. The Delaware show puts his paintings of New York – which represent that true achievement far better than his later nudes and landscapes – into well-distilled focus.

Sloan's influences were few but deep-rooted. One contemporary critic was astute enough to observe his kinship with Manet. Certainly Sloan shared the French painter's fondness for chiaroscuro, which he and Manet inherited from Velazquez. The passionate realist Robert Henri was another key influence, as were Daumier and Pissarro. However, it was from such preeminently urban writers as Balzac, Zola, and Whitman that he drew most inspiration. What contemporaries could not have seen was how much Sloan had in common with James Joyce. Both were gregarious, convivial men fascinated with cities, topography, and the humdrum details of life that many artists disdain. For both 1904 was pivotal: for Sloan, because it was the year he arrived in New York; and for Joyce, because it was the year he met his wife Nora Barnacle and in which he set *Ulysses* (1922). Sloan also illustrated a *deluxe* edition of the novels of the Parisian Paul de Kock, whose lubricious potboilers Molly Bloom enjoys in bed. Katherine Manthorne's essay "John Sloan, Moving Pictures, and Celtic Spirits" engagingly elaborates on these parallels.

If Walter Sickert saw the essence of Edwardian London in its music halls, Sloan saw the epitome of modern Manhattan in its elevated railroad. In "Six O'Clock, Winter" (1912) he shows a throng of pedestrians coming and going beside the headlong trajectory of the El. Here the time is dusk when the sharp sea-light of the city has faded, night is beginning to obscure the intent, inscrutable faces that animate the crowd, and Sloan sets before us the majesty of New York in all its transience. Much is made of Turner's "Rain, Steam and Speed – the Great Western Railway" (1844), as the herald of Impressionism. But Sloan's picture, which responds to Turner's with reaffirming humanity, has not received the attention it deserves. He did many other paintings of the El – "Sixth Avenue Elevated at Third Street" (1928) in the Whitney is probably the most well-known – but this earlier painting has a brooding power absent from the others.

No one can read Sloan's journals without remarking the compassionate fellow-feeling of the man. "While out for papers", he wrote in one entry, "I stopped on Fifth Avenue and stood for nearly an hour watching the Easter dressed throngs coming from their honorable Easter services – very funny humans. I didn't feel at all one of them, just then. But after all, I turned down a poor rum soaked bum who asked me for money – and regretted it and slunk home feeling below cost." This was no holiday remorse on Sloan's part. His wife Dolly was a confirmed drunkard, a source of continual embarrassment, and yet he was fiercely loyal to her. One of the reasons he was so fond of Yeats is that he recognized the goodness in Dolly, despite her problem. Proof that the humanity of the man did not elude the artist can be seen in "The Wake of the Ferry No. 2" (1907), which shows the back of a woman on the back of a ferry on a cold fogbound day. Compared to the forlorn back of this forlorn figure the backs of Watteau's beguiling ladies might be from a different universe. Sloan's painting was inspired by the sorrow he felt whenever his wife returned to Philadelphia where she often drank herself into a bedraggled stupor. Here the mystery of human suffering is faced with heart-rending honesty.

In this and other scenes, Sloan choreographed his own history of the city, culled from what James called the "great intricate frenzied dance, half merry, half desperate ... performed on the huge watery floor". There is his wonderful etching entitled "Arch Conspirators" (1917), showing Sloan, Marcel Duchamp, Charles Ellis, the set designer for the Provincetown Players, and others celebrating atop the Washington Arch. Discovering a staircase within the Arch, Sloan and his friends ascended to the top, where, with food, wine and hot water bottles, they declared the independence of Greenwich Village. Then there is his painting "Spring Rain" (1912) showing a young woman entering Madison Square Park, with the cupola of the Domestic Sewing Machine Building beckoning in the foreground. As the curators point out, the woman's black skirt and straw hat place her as a typical working woman. But as she enters the park, she hitches up her skirt to reveal stockings of a rich erotic red, which unites her with the red tulips blazing around the park's fountain, with what Whitman called "ever-returning spring". In "Sunset, West Twenty-Third Street" (1906–8), Sloan painted his wife pausing from hanging out laundry to admire a glorious red sunset from the roof of their apartment building. By preserving these moments of personal history, Sloan's profoundly human art preserved something of the indomitable life of the city, which, now, as then, defies the wrecking ball.

Faith and Failure in Graham Greene

Graham Greene: A Life in Letters, edited by Richard Greene.
W. W. Norton & Company. 446 pages.

IN 1981, IN A COLLECTION OF INTERVIEWS with Marie-François Allain later published as *The Other Man*, Graham Greene admitted: "My life is marked by a succession of failures which left their traces on my work. I think they're the warp and weft of it." The moral terrain of Greene's novels, which he described as "the narrow boundary between loyalty and disloyalty, between fidelity and infidelity, the mind's contradictions, the paradox one carries within oneself" corroborates this admission. *Graham Greene: A Life in Letters*, which has been adroitly edited by Richard Greene (no relation), shows how the novelist's personal life also confirms Greene's unsparing self-assessment.

Greene's sense of personal failure had deep abiding roots. He opened his autobiography, *A Sort of Life* (1971) with a memorable sentence: "If I had known it, the whole future must have lain all the time along those Berkhamsted streets." This was incisive self-knowledge, for the torment he endured as the son of the headmaster of Berkhamsted School left psychological wounds that never healed. He recalled being subjected to "a system of mental torture" so traumatic that he actually tried to kill himself, most spectacularly by playing Russian roulette. In 1950, in a letter that has the same vivid intensity that distinguishes his fiction, he recalled meeting one of his erstwhile tormentors

> Another queer encounter just before I came away. A man came up to me in the Cold Storage shop where I was buying drinks – a tall foxy faced rather heavy man, who introduced himself as Wheeler. Wheeler was at school with me & belonged to the bad period. We were in the junior school together & then in the same house ... The real misery of that time began when he was suborned onto the side of my

great enemy, Carter... What a lot began with Wheeler and Carter – suspicion, mental pain, loneliness, this damned desire to be successful that comes from a sense of inferiority, & here he was back again, after thirty-five years, in a shop in Kuala Lumpur, rather flash, an ardent polo player. And instead of saying "What hell you made my life 30 years ago", one arranged to meet for drinks!

The letters collected here reveal how frequently Greene reached out to members of his family, despite his frequent disavowals of family. Some of Greene's best letters were written to his mother, to whom he wrote with candor and warmth. As he admitted to Allain: "I loved and admired my mother precisely because she did not trespass on my privacy." Apropos his father, Greene wrote that he "never disputed by so much as a word my decision to become a Catholic", which was remarkable in an Englishman. After his father's death, Greene wrote his mother, "This may seem Popish superstition to you, or it may please you, that prayers are being said every day for Da in a West African church, & that rice is being distributed here in his name among people who live on rice & find it very hard to get".

In all his letters of condolence, whether to family or friends, Greene reaffirmed his Catholic faith. When a Russian friend's husband committed suicide, Greene wrote:

> I don't believe myself that death is everything, or rather my faith tells me that death is not the end of everything and when my faith wavers I tell myself that I am wrong. One can't believe 365 days a year ... There is a mystery which we won't be able to solve as long as we live. Personally even when I doubt I go on praying ... Why not try at night talking to your husband and telling him all you think. Who knows whether he mightn't be able to hear you and now with a mind unclouded.

The point is often made, mockingly, that Greene was a character in a Graham Greene novel, but here one sees that there was a truth to that which was anything but risible.

In 1926, Greene fell in love with Vivien Dayrell-Browning, a recent convert to Catholicism, who introduced Greene to the faith that he would keep for the rest of his life. When Greene confided in his young bride that "what I long for is a quite original marriage", she could scarcely have imagined the dance her husband would eventually lead her.

In 1929, Greene published his first novel, *The Man Within*, which sold 13,000 copies, an astounding amount for an unknown author's first novel. "And the funniest part of the absurd, joyful situation", Greene wrote his brother, "is that the book is quite terribly second-rate... How is the world fooled?" The world's applause brought out the truth teller in Greene. When he received the Hawthornden Prize in 1942 for *The Power and the Glory*, he wrote his mother: "I suppose at the bottom of every human mind is the rather degraded love of success. One feels ashamed of one's own pleasure." Susceptibility to failure never made him unwary of success.

After his debut, Greene wrote a total of 22 novels, three books of short stories, a biography of the notorious Second Earl of Rochester, four plays, and three books of travel. His greatest novels, *Brighton Rock* (1938), *The Power and the Glory* (1940), *The Heart of the Matter* (1948), and *The End of the Affair* (1951) all treat Catholic themes. Greene also wrote a series of what he called "entertainments", or thrillers, many of which, like *The Stamboul Train* (1932) and *The Third Man* (1949), were brilliantly adapted for film. In everything he wrote, moral failure takes center stage. As he remarked in one of his essays: "Goodness has only once found a perfect incarnation in a human body and never will again, but evil can always find a home there. Human nature is not black and white but black and grey."

When the elegant old house that Greene bought on Clapham Common was bombed during the Blitz, he treated its loss with tell-tale resignation. "Oddly enough," he wrote a friend, "it leaves one feeling very carefree." The bombing of the house (which would make a pivotal reappearance in *The End of the Affair*) marked the collapse of Greene's marriage, though he never divorced his wife. After bolting, he wrote Vivien, "you see, my restlessness, moods, melancholia, even my outside relationships, are symptoms of a disease ... & the disease, which has been going on ever since my childhood ... lies in a character profoundly antagonistic to ordinary domestic life. Unfortunately, the disease is also one's material. Cure the disease & I doubt whether a writer would remain." However fallacious, this was reasoning he never abandoned, as his many "outside relationships" attested.

Four mistresses gave Greene all the "material" he could require: Dorothy Glover, an English stage designer, who shared his fondness for Victorian detective fiction; Catherine Walston, a married Catholic from Rye, New York, whose passion for travel, drink, sex, and theology matched his own; the Swedish actress Anita Björk, whose youth and beauty infatuated the aging lothario; and Yvonne Cloetta, a married Frenchwoman, who set up part-time households with the novelist first in Antibes and Capri and then in Vevey. After making Greene his dinner, Cloetta would return home and make another for her husband. Greene's revolt against married domesticity might have begun in passionate defiance but it ended in farce.

Greene's letters to Walston make for embarrassing reading. In one, he tried to coax her into leaving her husband, Lord Walston, the British Labour politician, by promising, "I would tell the truth to you always". This must have sounded odd coming from the man who had one of his narrators say: "In human relations kindness and lies are worth a thousand truths." From Freetown, where Greene set *The Heart of the Matter*, he wrote: "A human relationship like ours has been is inextricably physical & mental. I have no real belief that the physical side is seriously wrong ... but you will remember that for the last two years I've urged you to go to confession & communion between our meetings. I can see a great benefit in that. Communion might help to reduce the occasions *happily*." How Walston took this counsel is anyone's guess, though she cannot have been flattered to hear her inamorato declare: "I never knew love was like this, a pain that only stops when I'm with people, drinking. Thank God, from tomorrow there are lots of engagements."

In other letters, he could almost be writing dialogue for a romance novel. "I drink Swedish akvavit out of the little silver beaker you gave me", he wrote Björk after their affair, "& always with thoughts of you." It was not as though he ever tried to conceal the vacuity of this illicit attachment. "A strange girl", he wrote one correspondent about Björk. "I won't ring up in case a stranger is now installed & I don't feel I can write again ... If you see or write her, you can indicate that she's still, unfortunately, in the blood stream & I'm quite unable to look for a successor." Here one sees something of the dreary promiscuity that would soon overtake an entire society.

Greene, like Evelyn Waugh, was one of the world's last great travelers, and there is much in these letters that captures his zest for place. In Haiti, he attended a voodoo ceremony with, of all people, Truman Capote, which he described with almost cinematic vividness. "The man carrying the hen swung it like a censer, & then would dash to this & that member of the congregation & plaster his face & body with the live bird ... More interminable prayers & then the bird's feet were cracked off like cheese biscuits & the attendant put the live bird's head in his mouth and bit if off – the body of course went on flapping while he squeezed the blood out of the trunk." If certain aspects of Greene's life portended the sexual revolution, here we see glimmers of that fascination with savagery that now enthralls the pagan West. Even Greene, however, wearied of these forays into the heart of darkness. To one correspondent, he admitted, "It's extraordinary how dull and boring the bizarre can be".

Waugh, to whom Greene wrote some of his warmest letters, deplored what he saw as the incoherence of *A Burnt-Out Case* (1961), Greene's novel about the erosion of faith in a leper colony. "God forbid I should pry into the secrets of your soul," Waugh wrote his friend. "It is simply your public performance which grieves me". Unnerved by Waugh's criticism, Greene confided in Walston, "I feel as though I've come to the end of a long rope with *A Burnt-Out Case* & that I'll probably never succeed in getting any *further* from the Church. It's like, when one was younger, taking a long walk in the country & at a certain tree or a certain gate or the top of one more hill one stopped & thought "Now I must start returning home". After this sad, unsatisfactory novel, Greene returned to the world of espionage that he had mined in earlier novels. *The Honorary Consul* (1972) and *The Human Factor* (1978) show the extent to which self-parody exercised his deteriorating talents.

Although muddled in many respects, Greene understood the true relation between literature and the Faith. "There are leaders of the Church who regard literature as a means to one end, edification", he writes in one letter. "That end may be of the highest value, of far higher value than literature, but it belongs to a different world. Literature has nothing to do with edification ... Catholic novelists (I would rather say novelists who are Catholics) should take Newman as their patron. No one understood their problem better or defended them more skillfully from the attacks of piety (that morbid growth of religion)." In an exchange of public letters about literature and society, Greene quoted Newman:

> I say from the nature of the case, if Literature is to be made a study of human nature, you cannot have a Christian Literature. It is a contradiction in terms to attempt a sinless Literature of sinful man. You may gather together something very great and high, something higher than any Literature ever was; and when you have done so, you will find that it is not Literature at all.

Pope Paul VI certainly sided with Newman's view of the matter when he told Greene in a private interview, apropos the Holy Office's condemnation of *The Power and the Glory*, "parts of all your books will always offend some Catholics ... you shouldn't pay any attention to that".

Greene might also have quoted something else Newman wrote in the same lecture: "One literature may be better than another, but bad will be the best, when weighed in the balance of truth and morality. It cannot be otherwise; human nature is in all ages and all countries the same ... Man's work will savour of man; in his elements and powers excellent and admirable, but prone to disorder and excess, to error and to sin. Such too will be his literature; it will have the beauty and the fierceness, the sweetness and the rankness, of the natural man ..." Such an unflinching understanding of man's fallen nature would have deeply appealed to Greene, who told Allain: "As for the human aspect ... well, there I've failed time and again! ... I've betrayed a great number of things and people in the course of my life, which probably explains this uncomfortable feeling I have about myself, this sense of having been cruel, unjust. It still torments me often enough before I go to sleep. This was forthright remorse, with which we can all empathize." But what can we make of Greene saying this, when asked if he received communion? "No ... I've broken the rules. They are rules I respect, so I haven't been to communion for nearly thirty years ... In my private life, my situation is not regular. If I went to communion, I would have to confess and make promises. I prefer to excommunicate myself."

This was the paradox that Greene carried within himself: he professed the reality of the Faith but chose not to practice it. The boundary he inhabited between fidelity and infidelity was very narrow indeed. In this excellent edition of the letters, Richard Greene maps out that boundary with unusual accuracy and verve.

The Ampthill Succession

The Virgin's Baby: The Battle of the Ampthill Succession, Bevis Hillier. Hopcyn Press. 282 pages. $25.00

Outrageous Fortune, Anthony Russell. St. Martin's Press. 303 pages.

IN HIS PREFACE to his well-researched and witty retelling of the famous Ampthill Succession case, Bevis Hillier, the biographer of John Betjeman recalls how he chose his subject after researching a proposed *Oxford Book of Fleet Street*. He went to a dealer of vintage newspapers in Covent Garden and came away with a sheaf of old tabloids, one of which had on its cover the headline: MRS CHRISTABEL RUSSELL WINS IN THE HOUSE OF LORDS, below which were photographs of the lady herself, her son, and her estranged husband, John Hugo Russell, third Baron Ampthill (1896–1973). Wondering "what all of that was about", Hillier read the story and was immediately drawn into the fascinating tale of family history and courtroom drama that constitutes the marrow of *The Virgin's Baby*.

The facts of the Ampthill Succession case can be readily set out, though "fact" is not perhaps the most apposite word to use to describe a case riddled with oddities. On 18 October 1918, Russell married Christabel Hulme (1895–1976), second daughter of Lieutenant Colonel John Hart, Leinster regiment, and his wife Blanche Anstruther Erskine of Sussex. They had one son, Geoffrey Denis Erskine, who was born on 15 October 1921. A year after the boy's birth, Russell sued his wife for divorce on the grounds of adultery, claiming that the boy was not his own, but that of one of two co-respondents. The jury acquitted the two-co-respondents (both erstwhile friends of Russell and his wife) and granted the petitioner a *decree nisi*. After Christabel's appeal was dismissed by the Court of Appeal, which found that Christabel was guilty of adultery with "an unknown man", she scraped together all she could from her Mayfair dress shop and appealed to the House of Lords, who by a majority of three to one found in her favor on the grounds that the evidence her husband had submitted to the lower court was inadmissible.

Among the Lords were Churchill's boon companion, F. E. Smith, Lord Birkenhead and Lord Edward Carson, whose cross-examining skills sent Oscar Wilde to Reading Gaol. The case established the principle (overturned in 1949) that no evidence could be given by a husband and wife in legal proceedings, if the result were to illegitimate a child born in wedlock. It also led to an act of parliament limiting the publication of divorce proceedings in England and Wales.

What made the case so sensational was that, by their own account, Russell and his wife had never consummated their marriage. The gynecologists to whom Christabel had gone after she found out that she was pregnant all confirmed that she was *virgo intacta*. When called upon to testify whether it was possible for a man and wife to conceive a child under such circumstances, the gynecological experts all testified that it was indeed possible, if "barely possible". Christabel, an unconventional, droll, impulsive woman, who was as mad about horses as she was repelled by sex, had forbidden her husband any connubial relations, short of the odd uncontrollable emission.

As my readers will appreciate, giving these travails precise expression is not easy. At the appeal trial, Lord Dunedin fared no better, referring to the likely circumstances in which the child was conceived as *"fecundatio ab extra"*. Nonetheless, it was a puzzle. Had baby Geoffrey been sired by Russell inadvertently or did Christabel give birth to him as the result of some adulterous encounter with an "unknown man"?

Russell resolutely refused to entertain the possibility that he had had sexual relations with his wife sufficient to account for the birth of a child, even though in the course of the gladiatorial courtroom trial it was at one point suggested by Christabel's counsel that this might have occurred when he was sleepwalking. Instead, Russell and his family went to their graves denying that he was the boy's father and even contested Geoffrey's right to the peerage after they lost the appeal in the House of Lords. When Geoffrey's contested right to assume the fourth baronage of Ampthill came before the Lords in 1973, they gave Christabel her crowning victory by upholding her son's claim.

One great virtue of Hillier's account is that he has had the good sense not to paraphrase the contemporary eye-witness record, which, as his generous quoting shows, is inimitably amusing. Anyone fond of courtroom drama will find the book an absolute delight. One exchange exemplifies the flavor of this testimony. When Russell's barrister, Sir John Simon asked Christabel "whether it wasn't 'unusual' for a young married woman to use the a bachelor's bathtub, she replied at once: 'Well, Sir John, isn't it better to be indiscreet than dirty?'"

Hillier also enriches his narrative with contemporary newspaper reaction to the highly dramatic courtroom trial. *Lloyd's Sunday News*, for example, spoke of the impact that the case had on the Law Courts. "Not within living memory", the paper reported, "have those sombre buildings where so many skeletons are dragged from the family cupboard, and where human wits are strained to the uttermost on the rack of cross-examinations, furnished a parallel to the questioning of this gently-nurtured society woman pitting herself against the trained intellect and forensic arts of one of the keenest intellects of the modern Bar".

Outrageous Fortune by Anthony Russell, one of Geoffrey's sons is a charming memoir of growing up in Leeds Castle, Kent. About Christabel, whom he calls "Granny A", he is affectionately vivid. "In keeping with her whirlwind character, Granny A was always a dashing dresser, and the day she took me, aged six, to my very first film at a cinema on Oxford Street, was no exception. She wore a hat, veil, scarf, jacket, flowing skirt, and high boots, all flung together with a superlative eye for cut and colour. Everything she did seemed to be done at breakneck speed; her thinking, riding, talking, cooking, arranging ..." One had to work hard to keep pace with her or "be prepared to be left trailing in her formidable wake". This is certainly the impression that Hillier gives of this volatile, imperious woman, whom Angelica Huston came to know and love when she was a child in Ireland. Indeed, she based her character, Mrs. Rafferty on Christabel in the film version of *A Handful of Dust.*

In one of the most evocative scenes of Russell's reminiscence, Christabel takes her young grandson to the London Odeon in 1964 to see the Beatles perform their Christmas show, intent, as he says, to see "what all the fuss was about". No sooner did the Fab Four take to the stage than "triple pandemonium" broke out. As Russell vividly attests, "Every teenage girl ... gave the distinct impression of having gone stark raving mad". When the band launched into their rollicking finale, "Long Tall Sally", the pandemonium became more hysterical still. However, after the show was over and the house lights came up, Anthony noticed how "Granny A gave the girl in the front of us a gentle prod with her umbrella and spoke to her in an angelic tone of voice: 'You know, my dear, only the plain girls scream'".

After that memorable evening, Russell vowed to become a rock star himself, though he never managed it, despite befriending Mick Jagger, who told the hapless aspirant that privilege and rock & roll were ill-suited. Still, Russell is a winning memoirist, who has a discerning eye for social history. "My parents were so far apart in their likes and dislikes, habits and personalities", he writes, "that sometimes their charm, good looks, and fondness for a stiff drink seemed to be all that they had in common. Smoking and drinking were pleasures their World War II generation indulged in, and they, along with practically everyone I saw around them, enjoyed both vices to the fullest." Many of my readers will recall that now superannuated conviviality in their own family histories, before bottled water and the mania for fitness locked up the drinks cabinet for good.

Both of these entertaining books should be read in tandem, though it is only a question of time before some film studio descends on Christabel and the Ampthill Succession case. If there is any justice in the world, the producers will commission Hillier to write the lucrative screenplay. In the meantime, it would be good to see Oxford University Press publish Hillier's *Oxford Book of Fleet Street*.

Whigs and Namierites: The History of English History

Modernizing England's Past. English Historiography in the Age of Modernism 1870–1970, Michael Bentley. Cambridge University Press. 245 pages.

TWO INAUGURAL LECTURES from Regius Professors of Modern History, one at Cambridge and the other at Oxford, measure the ground that Michael Bentley covers in his brilliant new book, *Modernizing England's Past: English Historiography in the Age of Modernism 1870–1970*. In 1903 J. B. Bury, the editor of Gibbon, told his Cambridge audience, "If, year by year, history is to become a more and more powerful force for stripping the bandages of error from the eyes of men, for shaping public opinion and advancing the cause of intellectual and political liberty, she will best prepare her disciples for the performance of that task ... by remembering always that, though she may supply material for literary art or philosophical speculation, she is herself simply a science, no less and no more." Here, Bury not only looked back to the Whig histories of the nineteenth century, with their preoccupation with the progress of liberty, but forward to the positivism of Lewis Namier (1888–1960) and the extravagant faith in archives of Geoffrey Elton (1921–94). Seventy-five years later, in 1981 the military historian Michael Howard told his Oxford audience, "There is no such thing as 'history'. History is what historians write, and historians are part of the process they are writing about. We may seek for what Jakob Burckhardt described as the 'Archimedean point outside events' which would enable us to make truly dispassionate judgments and evaluations, but we know we cannot find it, and ... we mistrust those of our colleagues in the social sciences who believe they can." Here the Rankean faith in archives has collapsed and no one can respectably claim that he can recreate the past *wie es eigentlich gewesen ist*. A new diffidence has entered history – or perhaps one should say a new humility, a new discipline – born of the recognition that finality in historical interpretation cannot be had. To quote Bentley, the days of imagining that "the historian of the future would be a computer programmer or he would be nothing" are dead and gone.

Bentley, Professor of Modern History at the University of St. Andrews, Scotland, fully grasps Howard's point that "historians are part of the process they are writing about". Again and again, he shows how that process influenced his historians, forming not only their ideological milieu but their understanding of their place within the tradition of their profession. And nowhere was that more evident than in their engagement with the legacy of their Whig forbears.

What was that legacy? The Whig history of the nineteenth and twentieth centuries, from Henry Hallam (1777–1859) to George Trevelyan (1876–1962), tended to depict English history as a triumphant tale of English freedom, progress, fair play, and continuity. Its great boasts were representative government and religious toleration – though Roman Catholics and Dissenters would always question the latter claim. Its upshot was that everything had happened for a reason and all the reasons put together spelled the superiority of liberal Protestant whiggery. If one doubted that, all one had to do was compare progressive Protestant England with backward Catholic Europe. In his famous essay, "The Whig Interpretation of History" (1931), Herbert Butterfield (1900–79) showed how the Whig tendency to see the past as "the ratification, if not the glorification of the present" was something to which all historians are prone. A West Riding Methodist, he also took exception to Whig historians indulging in what he nicely called "the luxury and pleasing sensuousness of moral indignation" – something which mars too much American history.

In considering the impact that Whig history had on his historians, Bentley looks at fundamental themes of constitution and nation, church and state, and war and empire. The constitutional historian William Stubbs (1825–1901) lay down the Whig terms of the first, declaring that after the Restoration, "out of the weakness and foulness and darkness of the time, the nation, church, peers and people, emerge with a strong hold on better things; prepared to set out again on a career which has never, since the Revolution of 1688, been materially impeded". F. W. Maitland (1850–1906) and later Elton would reject Stubbs's reading of parliamentary development but not his contention that, for the English, "the continuity of life, and the continuity of national purpose, never fails". The durability of the Whig point of view is one of Bentley's major themes.

The Whig reading of church and state first appeared in the pages of Henry Hallam, whose *Constitutional History of England* (1827), made no bones about the matter: Roman Catholicism had been shown the door in England because it was corrupt, foreign, and treacherous. Apropos Thomas Cromwell's dissolution of the monasteries, Hallam would provide a ready rationale for the extirpation of the old faith.

> Cromwell, in his desire to promote the Reformation, advised the king to make this partition of abbey lands among the nobles and gentry, either by grant, or by sale on easy terms, that, being thus bound by the sure ties of private interest, they might always oppose any return to the dominion of Rome ... But if the participation of so many persons in the spoils of ecclesiastical property gave stability to the new religion, by pledging them to its support, it was also of no slight advantage to our civil constitution, strengthening, and as it were infusing new blood into the territorial aristocracy, who were to withstand the enormous prerogatives of the Crown.

In other words, robbing the English of their Catholic faith had been justifiable because it gave an opportunistic oligarchy the power to check despotic monarchy. This is a perfect epitome of Whig history rigging the past to justify the present.

Bentley is particularly good on the anti-religious bias that informed much of the English history of the twentieth century, noting of A. L. Rowse (1903–97), for example, the popular Elizabethan historian, "once pointed out that [Lytton] Strachey did not merely dislike religion but had no idea of what it might be like to have a religious experience. One may be moved to add that it takes one to know one, though Rowse himself occasionally found religious sites personally moving before snapping out of his reverie with a dismissive sneer." Llewellyn Woodward (1890–1971), author of *The Age of Reform 1815–1870* (1938) in The Oxford History of England, was even less sympathetic: "Is there no end to the procession of medicine men," he asked in a private journal, "witch doctors, weavers of spells, masters of rain, prophets and prophetesses of runes and oracles, augurs of good and evil fortune?" This bias, however, was offset by the brilliant work of David Knowles (1896–1974), the monk and monastic historian, whose three-volume *The Religious Orders in England* (1948–59) is one of the glories of twentieth-century history.

About the impact of the First World War on English historiography and on English society as a whole, Bentley is rather sweeping. Speaking of the trenches in Flanders, he says, "Brutality and cynicism, squalidness and despair: these products of that environment did nothing to sustain the values of liberal gentlemen; and they received such an amplification over the next two decades from those who wrote about the war that to claim a permanent element of cultural collapse in English values does not seem hyperbolic" – a diagnosis which echoes Ford Madox Ford's *Parade's End* (1924–8). What Bentley does not mention – understandably, since they fall outside his period – are the many brilliant books on the war written by English historians, including Denis Winter's *Death's Men: Soldiers of the Great War* (1978) and J. M. Bourne's *Britain and the Great War 1914–1918* (1989) which hardly support his thesis of "cultural collapse". Nevertheless, it is interesting that it was the Whig historian Macaulay who said that "the essence of war is violence, and moderation in war is imbecility".

On the theme of empire, Bentley shows how J. R. Seeley's *The Expansion of England* (1883) revealed the extent to which the British Empire was more than the exploitative swindle that so many Marxists would later claim. For the Victorians themselves, as Bentley persuasively argues, "It radiated mission; it embraced a destiny. The mission and destiny might imply a form of racial superiority. They might assert a Darwinian inevitability. They asserted no less however (and to a degree rarely observed through the lenses of a later age), a view of Christian involvement in the world ... The white man's burden transcended the taking of responsibility and insisted on the importance of witness with its symbols and sacraments." Now that the Procrustean frames into which Marxists tried to fit empire have had their day, it will be interesting to see what less biased historians do with a theme that cries out for more balanced treatment.

For Namier, the star iconoclast of Bentley's book, the idea that empire had anything to do with Christian witness would have been laughable; place and power, together with their guarantors, money and possessions, not anything as intangible as Christian faith, drove empire, as they drove domestic politics. Discussing Clive of Plassey in a review of his student Lucy Sutherland's *The East India Company in Eighteenth-century Politics* (1962) Namier wrote:

> Clive returned home in 1760, determined to cut a great figure in the country. The *jagir*, the fee of a purely nominal office under the Mogul, became his dominant concern. "My future power, my future grandeur", he wrote to a friend, "all depend on the receipt of the jaghire money"; and again: "Believe me there is no other interest in this kingdom but what arises from great possessions" – had he stayed in India and acquired a yet greater fortune, he might have been "an English Earl with a Blue Ribbon."

For Namier, this would have been proof positive that his materialist reading of history was not only right but incontestably right. The Christian missionaries in India, whom the Anglican clergyman Sydney Smith (1771–1845) took seriously enough to attack in the pages of the *Edinburgh Review* as "insane and ungovernable" were never given even so much as a nod in Namier's astringent calculus.

Namier is a fascinating figure. Born Ludwik Bernstein in Poland in 1888 of Jewish parents who converted to Roman Catholicism, he spent a year at the London School of Economics before taking a first in modern history at Balliol. Then he took a post with one of his father's business partners in America, where he began researching eighteenth-century parliamentary history. When he returned to England he worked in the Foreign Office from 1915 to 1920 in its political intelligence department, taking a particular interest in the resolution of Polish affairs at the Treaty of Versailles. From 1920 to 1921 he worked as a tutor at Balliol, which reinforced his infatuation with the English ruling class. "All I've done", he later admitted, "I owe to Balliol." To gain financial independence, Namier left his Balliol paradise and became the European representative of a firm of Manchester cotton manufacturers based in Czechoslovakia and a journalist with the *Manchester Guardian*. From 1924 to 1929 he amassed the research for the two groundbreaking books that made his reputation, *The Structure of Politics at the Accession of George III* (1929) and *England in the Age of the American Revolution* (1930). Bentley nicely captures their unsettling impact:

The tale, such as it was, was emphatically not one told by idiots, but the whole signified something close to nothing. It did so still more obnoxiously if one began with the view that history had to be conceived as a humanizing subject that laid the foundations among young people for an appreciation of citizenship and its obligation. Butterfield stood among those who wanted to see the study of eighteenth-century history function as a form of "political education". To accomplish that objective it had to show statesmen to be better than crooks and wastrels, and to provide a story whose denouements would reveal improvement even when leadership had proved lacking.

Throughout the 1930s, Namier himself was a strong supporter of the anti-appeasement leadership of Churchill. In 1939, he became adviser to Chaim Weizmann, though he later repudiated Zionism as ineffectual. From 1931 until 1953, he held the chair of modern History at the University of Manchester. In 1946 he published what is probably his best book, *1848: The Revolution of the Intellectuals*. The last nine years of his life, despite growing deafness and paralysis of his right hand, he dedicated to writing biographies of MPs for the period 1754–90 for an official history of Parliament that embodied his exacting, static approach to the past.

According to his research assistant John Brooke, Namier was convinced that "the reasons men give for their actions are rationalizations designed to cloak their deeper purposes", which led him "to distrust ideas as the explanation of historical movements and to stress the determinism underlying history". Accordingly, Edmund Burke's political philosophy was so much "cant". Yet Burke's understanding of history, which, he said, consisted "of the miseries brought upon the world by pride, ambition, avarice, revenge, lust, sedition, hypocrisy, ungoverned zeal, and all the train of disorderly appetites" had more in common with Namier's than is perhaps often realized. In all events, A. J. P. Taylor, who taught with Namier at Manchester, was not being entirely facetious when he said that his friend had taken the mind out of history. Still, if Namier was adamant about excluding dogma from his pages, he never stooped to using history to advance the interests of Soviet Marxism as did the egregious Eric Hobsbawm, Christopher Hill, and E. P. Thompson. Nor was his distrust of ideas as unreasonable as it may sound. As J. L. Talmon pointed out, "far from denying the potency of political and social ideologies, [Namier] was frightened by their power to disturb, and he was inclined to regard them as the neurotic symptoms of a society, as traumatic visitations". Those who have lived to see the ideas of multiculturalism and political correctness addle whole swathes of American and European public opinion can readily see how ideas might become "neurotic symptoms".

In summing up his period, Bentley sees an era of increasing professionalism that became too professional, too specialist, bearing out Tolstoy's quip that "historians are like deaf people who go on answering questions that no one has asked them". The history that has succeeded Bentley's period may be less rigorous but it is more attentive to the interests of readers. Bentley deplores the behavior of "academic publishers [who] now lead historians with a cheque-book towards the banality of the television script or door-stop biography". But this is hardly fair to first-rate historians – Andrew Roberts comes most readily to mind – who have written brilliant biographies. In any case, most readers will agree with Bentley that "one stands in awe" of what historians in his period accomplished. "The skill and assiduity that they brought to their monographs meant that their writing will never be superseded ... because new reckonings must engage with their work."

Good books about historiography are rare. J. W. Burrow's *A Liberal Descent: Victorian Historians and the English Past* (1981), Gertrude Himmelfarb's *The New History and the Old* (1987), and John Clive's *Not By Fact Alone* (1989) were all superb additions to this slender literature. One can now add Bentley's *Modernizing England Past*, which is at once a very shrewd and a very witty book. It should appeal to a wide audience, not only to students of history but to those of theory as well. On the issue of theory, broadly defined, Bentley quotes Arnold Toynbee (1889–1975), author of the monumental ten-volume *History of the World* (1934–54) who claimed that "pattern history" was a "dangerous game". Why? "The pattern becomes clear in one's own head", the great historian explained, "without any guarantee that it isn't nonsense."

Unsquashable: Churchill the Author

Mr. Churchill's Profession: The Statesman as Author and the Book that Defined the "Special Relationship", Peter Clarke. Bloomsbury. 352 pages.

THE OTHER DAY I was in Boston browsing the stacks of that legendary emporium, the Brattle Bookshop when I chanced upon *Winston Spencer Churchill: Servant of Crown and Commonwealth*, a collection of tributes to the parliamentarian, war leader, historian and wit, which his long-standing English publisher Cassell brought out in 1954 to celebrate the great man's eightieth birthday.

Included among the contributors are some notably diverse figures, all of whom had lively things to say about the august honoree, including Lord Norwich, who resigned his post at the Foreign Office after Munich; Viscount Cecil, whose abounding faith in the League of Nations proved such a pitiable illusion; Aga Khan, the sybaritic imam, who shared Churchill's passion for the turf; Bernard Baruch, who helped put Churchill back on his feet after the crash of 1929; and Clement Attlee, who, in his many years in the Commons, prized Churchill not only as a worthy colleague but as an even worthier opponent.

Yet the contributor whose tribute captured the essence of Churchill best was Violet Bonham-Carter, Asquith's daughter. Describing meeting young Churchill at a dinner party when she was 19 and he 33, she recalled that "with his dramatic South African exploits behind him, and a political career in the making, [he] was already on the high road to fame", though his critics were quick to dismiss it as mere self-seeking "notoriety". Still, Violet was shrewd enough to see it as something that would hold Churchill in good stead throughout his tumultuous career.

"His unabashed confidence, unsquashable resilience, his push and dash and flair for taking short cuts through life, his contempt for humdrum conformity, have always challenged stuffy, stolid, stick-in-the-mud opinion here and elsewhere." For Violet, no one knew better "how to perform the public service known as "putting the cat among the pigeons". Readers of Violet's memoir about her famous friend, *Winston Churchill as I Knew Him* (1965), will also recall that it was at this same dinner that Churchill turned to his young dinner companion and quipped, "We are all worms, but I do believe that I am a glow-worm".

In *Mr. Churchill's Profession*, Peter Clarke attempts to dim the lustre of Violet's friend by disparaging not only the writing of the man but the man himself. The author of a recent study of John Maynard Keynes and a survey of the end of empire for the Penguin History of Britain, he might seem the perfect person to take on this peculiar work of demolition.

Rather than studying Churchill's literary work as a whole, Clarke's book limits itself to a sustained attack on *A History of the English-Speaking Peoples*, which Churchill wrote from 1932, when his political career seemed finished, to the late 1950s, when he finally handed the conservative baton off to the eternally natty Anthony Eden. Clarke does take up aspects of Churchill's four-volume life of Marlborough (1933–8) but there is very little about his life of Lord Randolph Churchill (1906), his history of the Great War, *The World Crisis* (1923–9), his autobiography, *My Early Life* (1930), his history of the Second World War (1948–54), or his charming collection of pen portraits, *Great Contemporaries* (1936).

Clarke spends a good deal of the book discussing the assistance Churchill obtained for his *History of the English-Speaking Peoples* from a number of brilliant editors, most of whom were good historians in their own right, including Keith Feiling, the biographer of Neville Chamberlain; G. M. Young, the author of that wonderful study of the Victorians, *Portrait of an Age* (1936); Alan Bullock and William Deakin, who would go on to edit the "Oxford History of Modern Europe" series; Denis Brogan, the Cambridge don who wrote a number of books on American history; Alan Hodge, Robert Graves's co-author of the classic inter-war social history, *The Long Weekend* (1940); and J. H. Plumb, the high-living head of Cambridge's history faculty and biographer of Sir Robert Walpole.

Clarke only deviates from his niggling account of Churchill's history for momentary digressions. For example, apropos *Frontiers and Wars* (1962), the omnibus edition of Churchill's early imperial histories, Clarke notes how the book "is still readable today for its lucid and bold exposition", though the real reason he commends "its mordant asides" is that they underscore "the intractable nature of the resistance to Western dominance in Afghanistan".

Similarly, Clarke is full of praise for Churchill's private secretary Jock Colville, when Colville initially confides in his journal how "the country believes that Winston is the man of action who is winning the war and little realise how ineffective, and indeed harmful, much of his energy is proving itself to be"; but when he has a change of heart and sees the morale-boosting point of Churchill's *modus operandi*, Clarke quickly turns against Colville. In response to Colville's remarking how "refreshing" it is "to work with somebody who refuses to be depressed, even by the most formidable danger that has ever threatened the country", Clarke writes with censorious disdain, "The lack of executive substance here now seems to be no problem for Colville".

The gist of Clarke's dossier against the *History of the English-Speaking Peoples* is threefold: Churchill did not deliver the book on time; he did not deliver the book that he had contracted to deliver; and the finished book was largely written by other hands, Churchill himself only contributing Volumes 1 and 2 and the history of the American Civil War in Volume 4.

Then, again, Clarke takes issue with Churchill's view of Oliver Cromwell. For Churchill, Cromwell should be "condemned as representative of the dictatorships against which all the whole movement of English history has been continuous". For Clarke, this position amounts to little more than "a sort of class action against dictatorship" and Cromwell is "thus an unlucky defendant against an indictment neither entirely generated by nor faithful to a purely seventeenth-century context". But if one compares Churchill's Cromwell to that of Christopher Hill, the Marxist historian who viewed Cromwell in much the same light as the international left viewed Joseph Stalin – as a necessary, even salutary autocrat – we can see that Clarke's charge that Churchill was guilty of ahistorical special pleading is blatant table turning.

Clarke also slags Churchill for preferring the old-fashioned Whig history that he read in his youth to the Marxist history that came into vogue in the 1930s. For Clarke, that Churchill never ceased delighting in the narrative histories of Gibbon and Macaulay is proof of his sentimental amateurism, though he omits to mention that this was the same history on which Trevelyan, Young, and Plumb were weaned.

Another strike against Churchill in Clarke's estimation is his admiration for William Pitt, Lord Chatham (1708–78), the brilliant orator and war leader who led his countrymen to victory against the French not only in India, Africa, and Canada, but on the Rhine as well. For Clarke, Churchill's attempt to differentiate the inspired leadership of Pitt from the usurpatory tyranny of Oliver Cromwell only reinforces their similarities. Indeed, in Churchill's own account of the two men, Clarke sees an unwitting hypocrisy: "Many of the qualities denounced as dictatorial in Cromwell become admirable qualities in Chatham's unique personal command". And Clarke goes further. In response to Churchill's observation, made during his broadcast of 8 August 1939, that "it is curious how the English-speaking peoples have always had this horror of one-man power", Clarke writes, "A lot depended, of course, upon which man was being judged by these elastic historical standards". In other words, Churchill could not warrantably take Cromwell to task – or Hitler, for that matter – because Cromwell, Chatham, and Hitler were "all one-man powers". Here is the same equivalence that John Le Carré and his friends made so fashionable during the Cold War, which excuses true tyrants while discrediting the opponents of tyranny.

Another target at which Clarke trains his scattershot fire is the "special relationship", which he treats as an offshoot of Churchill's "sentimental vision of the unity of the English-speaking peoples", a vision without any discernible root in reality. For Clarke, "Churchill surely asked too much of sentiment. American policy towards Britain, whether under Roosevelt or his successors, was based on more substantial considerations". But this criticism misses its mark: Churchill's writings on the special bond between America and Great Britain are valuable precisely because they reaffirm the shared democratic values of the two countries, their commitment to liberty. Clarke's Hobbesian contempt for such values, his dismissal of them as so much sentimentality, is typical of his crude, reductionist view of his subject.

Yet there is something even more distasteful about Clarke's handling of the "special relationship". After calling Churchill's respect for Anglo-American collaboration into question, he suggests that Churchill only advocated collaboration between the two countries "to turn his soft words into hard cash, dollars and pound alike". In this aspersion, there is more envy than spite. As Clarke himself admits, Churchill was consistently well-paid for his work, but surely this is no reason to claim that he only advocated the "special relationship" to swell his bank balance.

Clarke may fleer at Churchill for not paying attention to his publisher's deadlines or for failing to deliver on the agreed scope of the work (at a time when he was defending Great Britain against the full fury of Nazi aggression) but he cannot fault him for casting aspersions on the character of those with whom he disagreed. The eloquent eulogy that Churchill delivered in the Commons for the much-reviled Neville Chamberlain after his death was moving proof of that. Readers seeking a more balanced and incisive study of the "special relationship" should read Andrew Roberts's *A History of the English-Speaking Peoples Since 1900* (2006), which exposes the folly of the sort of sophisticated cynicism that is evident on nearly every page of Clarke's book.

One clear proof of Winston Churchill's continuing fascination for our otherwise distracted age is the number of genuinely good books that continue to roll off the presses about him. Doubtless, my readers will have their own favorites among these more recent books. Mine are Paul Addison's brilliant short biography, *Churchill: The Unexpected Hero* (2005) and Max Hastings's *Winston's War: Churchill 1940–1945* (2010), both of which are packed with insightful commentary about a subject that will probably go on resisting definitive study with the same obduracy that Churchill refused to yield to Hitler and the Nazis.

Despite its strenuous attempts to debunk Churchill, *Mr. Churchill's Profession* will never find its way onto any reliable list of good books about Churchill. Besides lacking critical sympathy, it is poorly conceived and dully executed. Why Clarke bothered to write the book in the first place is a nice question. Despite begrudging Churchill his considerable commercial success, Clarke might have sought to achieve some commercial success of his own by writing more sympathetically about a figure who still commands a huge readership in America. Instead, he chose to berate Churchill for, of all things, his profound respect for liberty. This same respect, after all, is what gives his life and work its unity and appeal. Anyone who revels in Violet Bonham-Carter's unsquashable glow-worm will not fork over $30 to read a tout for Keynes belittling that altogether admirable virtue.

Andrew Roberts and the Vital Impulses of Victory

A History of the English-Speaking Peoples Since 1900, Andrew Roberts. Harper Collins. 736 pages.

READERS FAMILIAR with the work of Andrew Roberts will know that he is one of the very best historians now working. His books on Lord Halifax, Churchill and Hitler, Napoleon and Wellington, and Waterloo all showcase his ebullient originality. His magisterial biography of the conservative Prime Minister Lord Salisbury is a dazzling portrait of a fascinating man whose exemplary statesmanship is too little studied by present-day conservatives. Roberts is also a prolific reviewer who brings to his reviews the same rigor and panache that he brings to his books. His sequel to Churchill's great work should delight his fans and win him many new readers. It deserves as wide a readership as it can get.

A History of the English-Speaking Peoples Since 1900 is a superb reappraisal of the achievements and lost opportunities of the "special relationship", which persuasively makes the case that America and the United Kingdom are "infinitely stronger than their constituent parts" – a truth that needs retelling at a time when the freedom not only of the English-speaking peoples but of all peoples is so clearly threatened by Islamic terrorists.

Divided, the English-speaking peoples saw their worst reversals: Roberts cites Dunkirk, Pearl Harbor, Suez and Vietnam. Together they accomplished their greatest victories: the 1918 summer offensive, North Africa 1942, the liberation of Europe 1944–5, the Berlin airlift, the Korean War, the Falklands, the collapse of Soviet Communism, the Gulf War, the liberation of Kosovo, and now the overthrow of Saddam Hussein. This, by any standard, is an impressive record. As Winston Churchill put it, "the English-speaking nations ... almost alone, keep alight the torch of Freedom. These things are a powerful incentive to collaboration. With nations, as with individuals, if you care deeply for the same things, and these things are threatened, it is natural to work together to preserve them."

The nineteenth-century English wit Sydney Smith once confessed that he entirely understood why an American might say "I will live up to my neck in mud, fight bears, swim rivers, and combat with backwoodsman, that I may ultimately gain an independence for myself and children". This is why Smith was what he called a Philoyankeist. "I doubt if there ever was an instance of a new people conducting their affairs with so much wisdom". Roberts, too, can be described as a *Philoyankeist*. He writes with unusual sympathy and balance about a people whom many of his English compatriots simply do not understand.

Nevertheless, he is unsparing when it comes to what he regards as American folly. Jimmy Carter, of course, is an easy target but Roberts nonetheless hits the bulls-eye when he reminds his readers that there was no justification for an American president responding to the fall of the pro-American Shah in 1979 by warning Americans against "the temptation to see all changes as inevitably against the interests of the United States, as a kind of loss for 'u' and a victory for 'them' ... We need to see what is happening not in terms of simplistic colors of black and white, but in more subtle shades." Robert's riposte is unanswerable: Khomeini "turned out not to be an aficionado of subtle shades". In the 2004 American presidential election, Americans heard the same pseudo-subtle defeatism from John Kerry, the candidate whom Mark Steyn nicely dubbed the "Nuancy Boy".

Roberts is no more tolerant of British folly. Apropos the fall of Singapore on 15 February 1942, in which a garrison of over 110,000 troops surrendered to a Japanese assault force of 35,000, Roberts remarks: "As so often happens in chaotic military debâcles involving civilians, there were many appalling scenes in which the sang-froid of the British and Australians completely disappeared, to be replaced by inexcusably disgraceful behavior." In societies where "face" was paramount, this unedifying sauve qui peut unmasked the mystique of British rule and heralded the collapse of the British Empire in Asia. Roberts quotes a New Zealander on the sudden demise of the port that Sir Thomas Stamford Raffles had established in 1824: "Seems rather appalling, all that labour and those millions of pounds worth nothing in a few days. Maybe all concerned did their best, but it seems to me that there must have been some rank inefficiency somewhere, after the lessons of the Maginot Line, not to mention Pearl Harbor and the Philippines and Hong Kong."

Churchill, being Churchill, was rather more upbeat about this colossal snafu: "Singapore has fallen. All the Malay Peninsula has been overrun... This is one of those moments when the British race and nation can show their quality and their genius. This is one of those moments when it can draw from the heart of misfortune the vital impulses of victory. Here is the moment to display that calm and poise combined with grim determination which not long ago brought us out of the very jaws of death... So far we have not failed. We shall not fail now. Let us move forward steadfastly together into the storm and through the storm." Compared to our own senatorial class braying for retreat in Iraq, Churchill's wartime speeches sound a note of serene indomitability.

Roberts shows how Munich tested the English-speaking people's commitment to freedom. Proponents of Munich often argue that Chamberlain was right to let Hitler devour Czechoslovakia in 1938 because it gave Britain time to rearm. Opponents argue that defending Czechoslovakia was the right thing to do in any case and might very well have averted the Second World War by preempting Hitler's Wehrmacht. Following Chamberlain's return from Berchtesgaden, the Lord Chancellor Lord Maugham (Somerset Maugham's brother) argued that "according to the principles of Canning and Disraeli, Great Britain should never intervene unless her own interests are directly affected..." Duff Cooper, First Lord of the Admiralty, disagreed. Britain's main interest in foreign affairs had always been preventing "any one power from gaining undue predominance in Europe". Neither Canning nor Disraeli would have disputed that. Resisting Nazi Germany – "probably the most formidable power that had ever dominated Europe" – was therefore a direct British interest. Of course, Chamberlain and most of those who would later scapegoat him thought otherwise. But Duff Cooper honorably held his ground. Speaking of the interview he had with Chamberlain when he tendered his resignation, he recalled: "I found it a relief to be in complete agreement with him for once. I think he was as glad to be rid of me as I was determined to go." For the old diplomatist the lesson of Munich was one Chamberlain had grossly failed: "Sweet reasonableness is no match for the mailed fist."

Roberts observes that the themes debated by Maugham and Duff Cooper on 17 September 1938 "have reverberated through the history of the English-speaking peoples ... right up to the invasion of Iraq in 2003. They can be separated into the distinct yet overlapping foreign policy strands of isolationism, prestige, the thin-edge-of-wedge, the domino theory and the importance of coalition." The one strand he omits to mention is preemption.

Most Americans are grateful to Tony Blair for showing such support for the War on Terror in the wake of 9 / 11 when it was neither popular nor profitable. Yet in England Blair is loathed, more so perhaps than any prime minister since Sir Robert Peel, another statesman vilified for opposing his party's consensus. This leads to another of Robert's points: that the English-speaking peoples, "Like the Romans ... would at times be ruthless, at times self-indulgent" but they "would sometimes find that the greatest danger to their continued imperium came not from their declared enemies without, but rather from vociferous critics within their own society".

Roberts is particularly good on the vociferous Marxists that still exert a pernicious influence on British education, "teaching Western culture in terms of a series of crimes against humanity". These are also the people who have convinced the British electorate that the Islamic terrorist attacks perpetrated against the West in the last 50 years have been the result not of Islamic extremism but Western imperialism. The relativism of multiculturalism only reinforces this grotesque table-turning.

Blair acknowledged this in the speech he gave at the Foreign Policy Center in September 2006, when he said, "We will not win the battle against global extremism unless we win it at the level of values as much as force. We can only win by showing that our values are stronger, better and more just than the alternative."

Robert's book shows these better values in action. Reagan, for example, "framed the issue of anti-communism in stark, black-and-white terms, entirely eschewing the nuanced chiaroscuro of Détente". Why? The New York Times political columnist Anthony Lewis was convinced that he was set on instigating a nuclear standoff with the Soviets. But Roberts offers a different explanation. Reagan "possessed something that those who scoffed at him did not: an instinctive belief in America's capability to win the Cold War, because of the desire of those trapped behind the Iron Curtain to live in liberty".

What sets *A History of the English-Speaking Peoples since 1900* apart is its passionate sincerity. Yes, it is admirably researched and enviably well-written. It is full of revisionist fireworks. It is, in parts, laugh-aloud funny. (See Robert's animadversions on Harold Wilson's Foreign Secretary, George Brown.) But it is also a cry from the heart. Roberts believes in Anglo-American collaboration because he believes in freedom. He believes in what Churchill told Harvard in 1943:

> Law, language, literature – these are considerable factors. Common conceptions of what is right and decent, a marked regard for fair play, especially to the weak and poor, a stern sentiment of impartial justice, and above all a love of personal freedom... these are the common conceptions on both sides of the ocean among the English-speaking peoples... Tyranny is our foe, whatever trappings or disguise it wears, whatever language it speaks, be it external or internal...

What Harvard would make of such sentiments today is anyone's guess but it is encouraging nonetheless to have someone as capable as Andrew Roberts going to bat for them in this rousing, unputdownable, brilliant book.

A. W. Pugin: "Like Arthur Come to Life Again"

God's Architect: Pugin and the Building of Romantic Britain,
Rosemary Hill. Yale University Press. 602 pages.

In Disraeli's *Contarini Fleming* (1832), the hero is advised by his father: "Read no history, nothing but biography, for that is life without theory." In the nineteenth century, the notion that biography is superior to history because it is more faithful to life enjoyed a certain vogue. Emerson would go so far as to say that "there is properly no history, only biography". This was not entirely untenable: biography can have an actuality that thesis-driven history lacks. Boswell's *Life of Johnson*, for example, may not put its subject in much historical perspective, but in capturing the minutenesses of the great lexicographer, poet, essayist, and critic it captured the tone of eighteenth-century society far more reliably than the histories of Macaulay, Carlyle, or Lecky. Yet, ideally, biography and history go hand in hand, and in *God's Architect: Pugin and the Building of Romantic Britain*, Rosemary Hill has written an admirably rich life steeped in history. In addition to delineating the development of Pugin's prodigious talent, Hill's narrative interweaves histories of English architecture and society at a time when "the railway and the Gothic revival, those two great Victorian enterprises, were gathering steam together".

One of Hill's themes is how an inspired autodidact scathingly critical of the architectural consensus of his youth gradually brought his contemporaries round to appreciating his own decidedly passionate vision of Gothic – a "sacred style", as Hill describes it, "infused with inner truth, an architecture that did not merely evoke 'pleasing associations' but that embodied, in its very fabric, a metaphysical, divine reality". Another is how Pugin recovered from the middle ages principles which, when applied to his own buildings – including Saint Chad's (1838) in Birmingham, Saint Giles (1841–6) in Cheadle, Staffordshire, and Saint Augustine's (1846–51) in Ramsgate, as well as the interior of the House of Lords (1847) and the wonderful clock tower (1852) of the Palace of Westminster (otherwise known as Big Ben) – helped him to go beyond the "limitations of literal revivalism" to achieve a supple, eclectic, eminently inventive approach to the challenges of architectural design and use. In his mature style, Hill writes, "form and meaning, what an object was, how it was made and what it was made for, all were interwoven".

Born at 39 Keppel Street, Bloomsbury, in 1812, Pugin was the only child of the architect and drawing teacher Auguste Charles Pugin, and his wife, Catherine Welby. His father came to London from France and worked in the offices of John Nash, who would become one of Pugin's prime satirical whipping boys, synonymous with jobbery and false refinement. If his father instilled in Pugin his skill in draughtmanship, his mother gave him his unflappable self-confidence, once remarking how, "if he only knew how to dress I would consider him a universal genius". However brilliant, her son was a confirmed sloven, always preferring filthy sailor smocks to more conventional attire. Such anti-dandyism was sustained by extravagant pride in his putatively noble birth. He was convinced that his father had been "le Comte de Pugin", who fought for the king and escaped from the Bastille before sailing to England. Hill treats this with a genial grain of salt: "The legend of the émigré Count wandering the streets of London in his tricorn hat, with his muff and gold-topped cane, was handed down by pupils and passed into myth. It became entwined with the romance of the Gothic revival, where history and fiction mingle easily." The great turning point in Pugin's life occurred when he made a tour with his parents of the Gothic architecture of Lincoln, York, Boston, Tattershall, Grantham, Petersborough, and Hull. There, he beheld the Gothic that would ever afterwards epitomize for him a kind of lost childhood, a prelapsarian ideal of true faith and good order. Later, the precocious bilingual Pugin would accompany his parents on visits to France, where he acquired his lifelong passion for antiquities. After the French Revolution, which stripped so many nobles of their estates, bargains were ubiquitous. "In the first half of the nineteenth century it was possible", Hill remarks, "even with the limited pocket money of a twelve-year old to buy world-class works of medieval art, for few people knew or cared about them." Many of the objects Pugin picked up for a song are now in the Victoria and Albert, the British Museum, and the Metropolitan Museum in New York.

In 1832, while designing stage sets at Covent Garden, he met his first wife, Anne Garnet, an actress, who died one week after giving birth to their daughter. A year later, both his parents were dead. In 1833, he married Louisa Burton, another actress. About his hasty remarriage, Hill remarks: "To marry on the very day that his parents' effects were sold was a gesture of defiance ... The trauma of the twelve months that began with his first wife's death ... and ended with his second marriage resonated throughout his life. He could never bear to look back at it directly, but the past, though he scarcely spoke of it, found expression, obliquely, throughout his work." After the death of Louisa in 1844, Pugin fell in love in rapid succession with two beautiful women much younger than himself, both of whom first returned and then rejected his attentions, one because of his class and the other because of his religion. "Those who never knew him", one colleague wrote, "may smile at his being able to fall in love again and again but it is the truth, he was always young through vitality and would be happy or miserable like a boy." About his third wife, Jane Knill, whom he married in 1848 when he was 36 and she was 21, he wrote a friend, "I have got a first-rate Gothic woman at last, who perfectly understands and delights in spires, chancels, screens, stained glass, brasses, vestments, etc." For all his amorousness, Pugin was a contented family man and never the aloof paterfamilias: when six of his young children came down with measles (which was then life-threatening) he nursed each of them back to health. His domestic architecture, however, was not flawless. "I have made a horrid mistake in building this house", he complained of the Grange, his family home in Ramsgate. "There are no nurseries cut off from the rest the consequence is that living in a Pig market is less terrible the perpetual screams that proceed from every room in the house are distracting ... incessant powerful screeching ... oh dear."

In 1835, Pugin converted to Catholicism, writing a friend: "I can assure you after a most close & impartial investigation I feel perfectly convinced the roman Catholick church is the only true one – and the only one in which the grand & sublime style of church architecture can ever be restored." As this makes clear, his conversion – a particularly bold one for any Englishman to make twelve years before Newman went over – was inspired as much by aesthetics as faith. His journals document his impatience with the more easy-going Anglican Church, noting in one entry how "Rev. Wm. Cooper wore top boots & white breeches on Sunday", and in another, "I can see the time ... rapidly approaching when there will be only the catholick & the infidel: the power of the church of England is rapidly on the decline".

Still, what is remarkable about Pugin's faith was how reticent he was about it. "Of the interior, spiritual experience of these months," Hill observes, "Pugin himself, who was not by nature introspective, said nothing, and there is nothing that a biographer can properly say either." This is true: Pugin was never shy about castigating those who did not share his principles – he was particularly vituperative towards Robert Smirke and Charles Cockerell, the architects, respectively, of the British Museum and the Ashmolean Museum – but when it came to articulating his own faith, he was mum, preferring to let his buildings speak for him, which was just as well, because on the few occasions that he did try to describe his faith, he baffled most English Catholics. For Pugin, Catholicism had little to do with Rome, nothing to do with the pope, and everything to do with rood screens. In light of these eccentric views, it is not surprising that Newman should have looked askance at Pugin, though he was never impervious to the brilliance of his work. About Saint Giles, Cheadle, one of Pugin's most dazzling works, Newman wrote: "The chapel ... is, on entering, a blaze of light. I could not help saying to myself, Porta Coeli."

In 1835, Pugin met the architect Charles Barry, with whom his name will always be linked. It was on the strength of Pugin's drawings that Barry won the commission for the rebuilding of the Palace of Westminster after it burned down in 1834. Once it was time to begin work on the interior, Barry recognized, as Hill points out, that "he could not possibly design Gothic detail of the quantity and quality required and in so many different media. Nobody except Pugin could". Barry pleaded with Pugin to help and Pugin agreed. "Thus began a commitment that lasted, and, he often felt, blighted the rest of his life." Because of his Roman Catholic faith, which posed problems for England's Protestant Establishment, Pugin's role in the collaborative work was always kept quiet. Consequently, "the nature of his employment made it invidious from the beginning for both Pugin and Barry. It ensured that while Pugin would never in his lifetime get the credit he deserved, Barry would always be suspected of owing him more than he did". Still, the results of Pugin's contribution were magnificent. The House of Lords, the Peers' Lobby, and Big Ben are some of the loveliest things in all of English architecture.

In 1836, Pugin published *Contrasts*, the success of which helped launch his architectural career. In this rollicking polemic, Pugin contrasted the England of Nash with medieval England to show how inferior the former was. In thus attacking what Hill calls "the world of the Regency, that Vanity Fair of stucco-fronted manners, high taste and low principles", Pugin argued what William Cobbett had argued in *Rural Rides* (1830): that the English Reformation had robbed the English of their traditional faith and their traditional liberties. In the 1830s and 40s, when England was reeling from the Industrial Revolution and the First Reform Bill, such critiques commanded serious consideration. Afterwards, as Hill shows, a more liberal consensus took hold.

> The England of Prince Albert and the Great Exhibition did not feel the romantic pull of the olden times so strongly. The dream of "reunion" with Rome that had faded through the 1840s now vanished. Between the Evangelical and High Church parts of the Established Church, a Liberal, Broad Church movement was emerging anxious that England, having escaped the Continental revolutions of 1848, should now avoid the reaction to those revolutions which has seen the Catholic Church reassert itself already in Belgium and Austria, as it would soon in France.

In 1845, the year of Newman's conversion, Pugin built a grim barracks-like structure for the Catholic seminary at Maynooth outside Dublin, but after this his architectural commissions dried up, and he did much of his later work in textiles, wall paper, furniture, and stained glass. Apropos these piece-meal commissions, Pugin complained: "This is all very well if one is architect to the whole job but architect to one grate or one fireplace is worse than keeping a fish stall." Still, even if Pugin never was given the freedom or the scope he needed to develop his genius fully, his output remains impressive.

Readers looking for a good guide to his work as a whole should track down Paul Atterbury and Clive Wainwright's *Pugin: A Gothic Passion* (1994), which accompanied the first major exhibition of Pugin's work at the Victoria and Albert.

When Pugin and his brilliant collaborators showed their Medieval Court at The Great Exhibition (1851), it was an unexpected success. "No other designer", Hill writes, "embodied Pugin's vision of home and hearth and God. It was a vision that appealed powerfully to the mid-Victorian mind." Proof of the vindication of his principles could also be seen in the fealty he commanded from such leading lights of the Gothic Revival as Gilbert Scott, George Street, and William Butterfield, as well as from William Morris and members of the Arts and Crafts Movement, though Ruskin, who perversely insisted that the Gothic had nothing to do with Catholicism, belittled Pugin in *The Stones of Venice*. When a family member asked Pugin what he thought of Ruskin, the architect replied, "Let the fellow build something himself", and returned to his work.

In 1852, after putting the final touches to the great clock tower for the Palace of Westminster, which recalled his first commission in 1837 for Scarisbrick Hall, Pugin remarked, "I am the machinery in the clock". Thereafter, he grew increasingly psychotic and on 13 September 1852, at the age of forty, he died mad, probably of syphilis contracted when he worked in the theatre. His body was that of a seventy-year-old.

Apropos the early nineteenth century, Hill observes: "These were years of revivalism in the positive sense, not of nostalgia or lack of confidence in the present but a time when for many the past was experienced as a living source of inspiration from which England could regenerate itself, like Arthur come to life again." This creative understanding of the past was one of Pugin's greatest legacies and Hill's book emulates it, for she too mines the past in an attempt to regenerate the present. In her prologue, she writes: "We feel, once more, that there is something wrong with our cities and that perhaps this has something to do with ourselves." Pugin's life and work repay critical study but to imagine that they can help us set right what afflicts our cities and ourselves is to ask too much of them. To cure those deeply related ills we need a much stronger medicine.

Life of Bertie

The Heir Apparent: A Life of Edward VII: The Playboy Prince,
Jane Ridley. Random House. 726 pages.

In 1871, when Albert Edward Prince of Wales (1841–1910) and his wife Alexandra lost their youngest child, after a premature birth, Queen Victoria advised that they go into prolonged mourning. Bertie's response exhibited one of the great differences between him and his notoriously woeful mother:

> Want of feeling I never could show, but I think it's one's duty not to nurse one's sorrow, however much one may feel it ... You have no conception of the quantity of applications we get ... to open this place, lay a stone, public dinners, luncheons, fetes without end ... and all these things have increased tenfold in the last 10 years ... It is however gratifying that this wish exists in these Democratic days, as one must show oneself in public.

If, after the death of Prince Albert, Victoria secluded herself, Bertie was ubiquitous, making the rounds not only of country houses and ceremonial dinners but theatres, operas, and music halls. As Jane Ridley shows in her superb biography, Bertie's gregarious delight in people uniquely fitted him for his royal role, which he played with consummate brio.

Although sent for his education to Oxbridge, Bertie was the reverse of studious. After being found out with a prostitute, he so scandalized his father that Victoria believed that her son's "fall" had actually killed Albert. She never forgave him, and for the rest of her life made sure that he received no government dispatches. Bertie responded by giving himself up to a life of pleasure, eating, drinking, shooting, and fornicating on a truly Olympian scale.

Paying for this sybaritic life, which he led for 60 years before ascending the throne, required continual loans, but Bertie could always tap rich financiers, most of whom never required their loans to be repaid. Whenever he needed urgent rescue, he would write his friend Nathaniel Rothschild, always beginning his begging letters, "My dear Natty...". Consequently, when he became king he could boast to Parliament that "for the first time in history the heir apparent comes to you without a single penny of debt".

There have been two full-dress biographies of Bertie, an unduly reticent one by the biographer of Gladstone, Sir Philip Magnus, and a far superior one by a former Master of Eton, Giles St. Aubyn, which takes stock not only of Bertie's political and diplomatic achievements but the peculiar moral character of Victorian England. In one memorable passage, which Ridley substantiates again and again in her own biography, he observes:

> There can be no advantage in pretending to virtue unless society values it. Hypocrisy only flourishes where standards are high. In permissive ages, where few things are unacceptable, there is little to hide. Because the Victorians made such strenuous moral demands they did not always practice what they preached. The dominating idea of English society was not to cultivate virtue but to avoid scandal. "Everything was all right", claimed Lady Warwick, "if only it was kept quiet, hushed up, covered."

However excellent, St. Aubyn's life lacks the richness and panache of Ridley's magisterial work. Her command of her sources is masterly; she holds up the folly of her characters with patient tongs; and she recreates their plutocratic world with gusto. About Sandringham, Bertie's country house, for example, she writes:

> It was hardly a normal country house... Lunch at two thirty (the clocks were half an hour fast) was followed by tea, when the King scoffed poached eggs, petits four, cakes and shortbread. A twelve-course dinner followed at nine, and the King would cheerfully swallow several oysters in minutes, and then devour at high speed course after course of pheasant stuffed with truffles, chicken in aspic, sole poached in Chablis, or quails and boned snipe packed with *foie gras*, the richer and creamier the sauce the better.

Together with good food, good cigars, and impeccably cut clothes, Bertie reveled in the society of beautiful women. Ridley vividly recaptures his affairs with Lillie Langtry, Jennie Churchill, Daisy Warwick, Mrs. Keppel, and many others, all of whom prized their royal inamorato. Still, as Ridley points out, the prince did not have as many affairs as he was rumored to have had. One of the revelations of the book is the extent to which the prurience of nineteenth-century England actually required Bertie to be more debauched than he was. As Ridley nicely puts it, Bertie was popular with his compatriots precisely because he stood for "an ideal of illustrious misbehavior absolutely beyond their reach".

Still, Ridley has no illusions about the real character of adultery. The Countess of Warwick might claim that society made too much of sexual infidelity, but Ridley does not skirt over how the Countess's own infidelities damaged both her children and other people's marriages. Nor is she mum on how destructive Bertie's philandering was. Lady Harriett Mordaunt, whose dalliance with the prince led to her husband taking the unusual step of suing her for divorce, after she gave birth to a child of dubious paternity, actually went insane as a result of the opprobrium she suffered at the hands of a society that might relish scandal but was often unmerciful to those caught out in it. As for Sir Charles Mordaunt, Ridley is surely right to blame him for neglecting the good advice that Rosa Lewis always gave to would-be litigious cuckolds: "No letters, no lawyers and kiss the baby's bottom."

Something of Ridley's wit, as well as the charm of her style, can be seen in her description of Queen Alexandra at Bertie's coronation: "She was fifty-six, heavily made up, allegedly bald, and almost stone deaf, but she seemed like a queen from a fairy tale." For this demure Danish princess, Bertie could be forgiven everything. Indeed, she met her husband's chronic infidelity with regal unflappability. Towards the end, however, after Bertie's death, she "metamorphosed into a monster", as Ridley notes, becoming "a spoiled and willful child", who turned her unmarried daughter Victoria into a "glorified maid" – the same daughter to whom Rosebery had proposed, before Alexandra refused to give her consent.

As king, Bertie broke with his mother's example by refusing to allow his family life to become the focus of his reign; instead, he made pageantry its centerpiece. His affairs might be public knowledge, but their details would always remain sketchy. That Elizabeth II chose to emulate Victoria and make her less-than-ideal family the focus of her reign accentuates the wisdom of Bertie's decision.

Bertie also differed from his mother and indeed from the Hanoverians by never quarrelling with his heir. As Ridley remarks, "an obsession with punctuality, an addiction to smoking, a passion for uniforms, and a devotion to the competitive slaughter of game birds" was as characteristic of Bertie as George V.

Another of Bertie's virtues was his flare for diplomacy. According to the diplomatic historian Harold Nicholson, Bertie was a "supreme diplomatist". His profound understanding of the German, French, and Russian courts, acquired during his time as Prince of Wales, as well as his gift for languages, gave him great insight into those often elusive subtleties that make comity possible, though his greatest diplomatic achievement, the *Entente Cordiale*, struck with France in 1904 after Britain had become isolated during the Boer War, was also his greatest liability, since it exacerbated the estrangement of Wilhelm II and Germany, which led to the First World War.

The spectre of the Great War hovers over nearly every page of this brilliant biography. After Wilhelm II dealt Bertie a deliberate diplomatic snub by refusing to meet him in Vienna in 1888, Alexandra wrote her son, the future George V, of his tetchy uncle: "Oh he is mad and a conceited ass – who also says Papa and Grandmamma don't treat him with proper respect as the Emperor of all and mighty Germany! But my hope is that pride will have a fall someday!! Won't we rejoice then." Nothing could better exemplify the tragic irony of history.

One corollary of Bertie's continental *savoir-faire* was his marked distaste for many of his compatriots' xenophobic prejudices, especially their Anti-Semitism and No Popery. At the same time, he was adamant about respecting the different traditions of his subjects. When his First Sea Lord, Jackie Fisher, marveled at his concern for the socialist Keir Hardy's health, Bertie responded, "You don't understand me. I am the King of ALL the people."

Proof of this can be seen in the many charitable institutions he founded, including the Royal Society of Arts, the Royal College of Music, the Imperial Institute, St. Bartholomew's Hospital, and the Putney Hospital for Incurables. He was often criticized for honoring millionaires like the tea merchant Thomas Lipton, but, as Ridley sensibly observes, "the social sovereignty of wealth was not unconditional; the plutocrat must be validated by charitable works before he was rewarded at court". In Lipton's case, he gave £25,000 to Alexandra's fund to feed the London poor in 1897, and then another £100,000 for her poor people's restaurant. Another of Bertie's rich friends, Sir Ernest Cassel, donated a good deal of his vast fortune to build the London underground. Clearly, Edwardian plutocracy produced more than self-indulgence and frivolity.

Although Bertie worked well with his ministers, who appreciated his business-like efficiency, he often found them a trial. When the absent-minded Marquess of Salisbury showed up for an official function improperly dressed, Bertie exploded, asking his courtiers, "What can the Europeans think of a premier who can't put his clothes on?" Rosebery often struck him as an inscrutable eccentric; Churchill, as a crude radical. Asquith was clever but vulgar; Balfour was clever but arrogant. Campbell-Bannerman annoyed him by supporting the Suffragettes. As for Lloyd George's fabled oratory, Bertie dubbed it "Celtic gas".

"Few kings have come to the throne amid lower expectations", Ridley remarks. Victoria certainly had no high hopes, confiding to her daughter Vicky, "I often pray he may never survive me, for I know not what would happen". Yet Bertie confounded his critics by proving an exemplary king. In rediscovering the tradition of monarchy, he reformed and modernized it.

He was also deeply appreciative of the obligations of constitutional monarchy. Unlike his mother, who sided with the Tory Disraeli against the liberal Gladstone, Bertie was punctiliously impartial. Once, in response to a letter from Churchill, he wrote how "His Majesty is glad to see that you are becoming a reliable Minister and above all a serious politician which can only be attained by putting country above party". In his own dealings with successive governments, Bertie always put country before party, as he proved in 1909 in his even-handed response to Lloyd George's Finance Bill, which rifled so many of his friends amongst the landed aristocracy.

If Bertie's inner circle consisted of the roués and financiers associated with Marlborough House, he came to personify the life of his people as a whole, even though the middle classes did not always know what to make of him. The poet Wilfrid Blunt recognized this when he wrote of the newly crowned king: "He has certain good qualities of amiability and of philistine tolerance of other people's sins and vulgarities, which endear him to rich and poor, to Stock Exchange Jews, to the Turf bookmen and to the Man in the Street." The equerry Fritz Ponsonby agreed, recalling how Bertie "was intensely human and ... a great enough man to show his friends his true self with all the weaknesses of a human being. He never posed and never pretended to be any better than he was. The upper and lower classes loved him."

When Bertie died, the British people mourned him in unprecedented numbers. Certainly, as Ridley shows, for all of his cosmopolitanism, he had a very English sense of humor, which always endeared him to his compatriots. At the Paris opera one night, the French police asked him if they should remove a brazen courtesan, who had made no bones about her familiarity with the playboy king. "Not at all," replied Bertie. The Parisians should never think it necessary "to ignore the laws of gallantry in order to avoid offending my well known taste for austerity."

London Lives

Lived in London: Blue Plaques and the Stories behind Them,
Emily Cole. Yale University Press. 637 pages.

Leigh Hunt, the littérateur and friend of Byron, Shelley, Keats, and Lamb might now be little read, but his autobiography vividly recalls early nineteenth-century Chelsea. Of 22 Upper Cheyne Row, where he lived with his wife and seven children, Hunt wrote:

> The house was of that old-fashioned sort which I have always loved best, familiar to the eyes of my parents, and associated with my childhood. It had seats in the windows, a small third room on the first floor, of which I made a *sanctum* ... and ... a few lime trees in front, which in their due season diffused a fragrance.

After years spent eluding creditors – literary journalism then being no more remunerative than it is now – Hunt welcomed the peacefulness of Chelsea. "I felt for some weeks", he wrote, "as if I could sit still for ever, embalmed in the silence." Only the songs of street sellers broke the riverside quiet. Hunt particularly recalled "an old seller of fish ... whose cry of 'shrimps as large as prawns' was such a regular, long-drawn, and truly pleasing melody, that in spite of his hoarse and, I am afraid, drunken voice, I used to wish for it of an evening, and hail it when it came".

This is precisely the sort of domestic history that the blue plaques, set up throughout London by the Greater London Council, London County Council, and English Heritage, were created to evoke. When Hunt lived in Chelsea in the early 1830s it was a cheap, uncrowded, unfashionable district. His neighbors Jane Welsh Carlyle and her combustible husband paid £35 a year for their rambling house at 24 Cheyne Row, which is now the Carlyle Museum. Later the district would cater more to plutocrats than bohemians. Still, the list of Chelsea residents who have received blue plaques is impressive, including as it does Lillie Langtry, Arnold Bennett, Dame Sybil Thorndike, Sir Stafford Cripps, Augustus John, Sylvia Pankhurst, Hilaire Belloc,

George Eliot, Mark Twain, Scott of Antarctica, and Brunel, the great civil engineer.

In *Lived in London*, her wonderful *tour d'horizon* of the blue plaque scheme, Emily Cole relates how the idea for the plaques, first floated by the reformer William Ewart in 1863 and carried out by the civil servant Laurence Gomme, grew out of the same solicitude for preserving England's past that inspired the founding of the National Portrait Gallery (1856), the Society of the Arts (1866), and the Dictionary of National Biography (1882).

Since Gomme took over the project, honorees have been chosen in accordance with simple criteria: they must have been dead at least twenty years and made some signal contribution to their profession. Of course, there have been exceptions: Gladstone, Gandhi, Marconi, and John Galsworthy all got plaques sooner than twenty years after their deaths. And, beginning in 1954, the practice ended of marking sites rather than actual residences where honorees lived.

Ideally, plaques commemorate both biographical and architectural history. Apropos the plaque at 91 Gower Street for the architect George Dance, who designed Newgate Prison and the Royal College of Surgeons, Cole quotes a plaque historian who pointed out: "it is no doubt fitting that the architect should have chosen as his London home for many years one of the simple but excellently proportioned brick built terrace houses that were such an important contribution to the Georgian townscape". Dance was also responsible for the circus and crescent layouts that would become so characteristic of the city's town-planning. And he drew up ambitious plans for the redevelopment of London's waterfront, which, of course, were never executed. Another plaque of architectural interest is the one affixed to the former residence of W. S. Gilbert at 39 Harrington Gardens in South Kensington, where the dramatist wrote *The Mikado*, *The Yeoman of the Guard*, and *The Gondoliers*. On the gable of this fantastic dwelling Gilbert requested his architects to insert a sailing ship to commemorate his descent from the seafarer Sir Humphrey Gilbert. When one guest assumed that the ship was an allusion to *HMS Pinafore*, the dramatist curtly corrected him: "Sir, I do not put my trademark on my house."

Cole includes much out-of-the-way biographical and historical detail in her book and a rich gallimaufry of prints, photographs, drawings and paintings illustrating the people and places described in the text. She deserves high praise for putting together such an inspired history. Coffee table books rarely come packed with so many good things. The book's maps are particularly good. Splendidly hand-drawn by Malcolm Fowler, they nicely locate the whereabouts of the plaques and quantify their number by district.

Hackney, for example, may only have five blue plaques but they commemorate an arresting array of famous Londoners. There is a plaque for Marie Lloyd, the great Music Hall artist, whom T. S. Eliot admired for "her understanding of the people and sympathy with them, and the people's recognition of the fact that she embodied the virtues which they genuinely most respected in private life". Another for Joseph Priestley, the Presbyterian minister and Enlightenment philosopher whose support for the French Revolution eventually led to his leaving England and taking up residence in Pennsylvania, where he died waiting for the Second Coming. And still another for Daniel Defoe, the author of *Robinson Crusoe*, whose hero James Joyce considered "the true symbol of British conquest" because, "shipwrecked on a lonely island, with a knife and a pipe in his pocket, [he became] an architect, carpenter, knife-grinder, astronomer, baker, shipwright, potter, saddler, farmer, tailor, umbrella-maker, and cleric". As these Hackney plaques show, even in one of London's least glamorous locales, history abounds.

In fashionable Mayfair, 45 plaques recall some of the most powerful figures in English history, including Lord Clive, Lord Palmerston, and Lord Nelson. Then there are plaques commemorating the great dandies Beau Brummel and Benjamin Disraeli, the former of whom ended his days in a French lunatic asylum after running up huge gambling debts. And there is a plaque for a man who proved that in England there are not only second acts but third and fourth and fifth acts. General John Burgoyne, "Gentleman Johnny" as he was called, may have surrendered to the Americans at Saratoga in October 1777, but he went on to have a lucrative playwriting career after joining Charles James Fox and the Whigs in parliament and serving as Commander-in-Chief in Ireland. The house he had Robert Adam furnish for him at 10 Hertford Street was originally designed by Henry Holland, who also designed Carlton House, Brooks Club, and Brighton Pavilion.

Richard Brinsley Sheridan, the Irish playwright who had huge successes with *The Rivals* and *The School for Scandal*, also lived in Hertford Street until his beloved theatre Drury Lane burned down and he had to sell his furniture to keep the bailiffs at bay, only escaping debtor's prison, as Cole remarks, because his doctor insisted that moving the distressed playwright would kill him.

Sheridan recalls something that the perennially hard-up Cyril Connolly came to recognize: that London "was created for rich young men to shop in, dine in, ride in, get married in, go to theatres in, and die in as respected householders. It is a city for the unmarried upper classes, not for the poor". This has always spurred London's enterprising poor to escape poverty. George Leybourne, a.k.a. "Champagne Charlie", was the poor son of a currier, who got his start, together with Gracie Fields and Charlie Chaplin, at Collins Music Hall, Islington Green, when he was still in his teens. After scoring hits with "Champagne Charlie" and "The Daring Young Man on the Flying Trapeze" in the 1860s, Leybourne was paid the unprecedented annual salary of £1500 – mostly by men in the drinks trade eager to have him tout their bubbly. At the age of 42, however, after nearly thirty years on the Music Hall stage, Leybourne was dead of cirrhosis of the liver. A plaque commemorates his fizzy rise and fall at 136 Engelfield Road, Islington.

That so many dedicated to amusing London came to smash would not have surprised Dickens. In his moving essay "Night Walks", describing the noctambulatory forays he made through the city after the death of his father, whose own reversals landed him in the Marshalsea, Dickens described the misery that gives so much of London its bleak distinction. There are no blue plaques to mark the sleeping places of London's poor, whose houseless heads and unfed sides, whose looped and windowed raggedness inspire no memorials. But there is a magnificent blue plaque commemorating Dickens's residence at 48 Doughty Street, Bloomsbury, where he wrote *The Pickwick Papers, Oliver Twist,* and *Nicholas Nickleby*. Erected in 1903, it predates the opening of the Dickens Museum on this site in 1925.

The wretchedness that Dickens encountered in the city at night is one reason why London has always produced a high proportion of good popular writers with no interest in bothering readers with life's grimmer realities. In Mayfair, blue plaques commemorate such popular "middle-brow" authors as Somerset Maugham, who shared a flat with his wife Syrie Wellcome, the interior decorator, at 6 Chesterfield Street before he took up with Gerald Haxton, an exuberant alcoholic who was fond of diving into empty swimming pools; Nancy Mitford, who worked at Heywood Hill's bookshop at 10 Curzon Street, before winning fame and fortune with her best-selling novels and biographies; and P. G. Wodehouse, who wrote ten of his 90 odd novels, including *Summer Lightning, Very Good, Jeeves*, and *Right Ho, Jeeves* at 17 Dunraven (formerly Norfolk) Street. Wodehouse's stepdaughter described the house as full of servants with strict orders never to disturb their literary master. "It is understood that he is thinking deep thoughts and planning great novels, but when all the smoke has cleared away it really means that he is either asleep or eating an apple or reading Edgar Wallace."

If the blue plaques are a kind of historical stock-taking, they recall the personal stock-taking of the residents they memorialize. Cardinal Manning, for example, who followed Newman into the Roman Church in 1851, has a plaque in Westminster commemorating his residence at 22 Carlisle Place, a forbiddingly austere palace, which remained the residence of the archbishops of Westminster until 1901. From his bedroom window, Manning, who toyed with the idea of entering politics as a young man, could see the Houses of Parliament, which caused him to reflect in old age: "If I had been able to have my own way and to go there, what a rascal I should have been by this time!"

DEAR DIRTY HISTORICAL DUBLIN

Dublin: The Making of a Capital City, David Dickson. Harvard University Press. 718 pages.

IN 1732, DEAN SWIFT wrote a friend that while he had lost all hope of favor with those in power in Dublin, and "drawn above one thousand libels on himself", he had won "the love of the Irish vulgar" and inspired "two or three dozen signposts of the Drapier in this city..." Here, he was referring to the great gratitude the people of Dublin felt for the eloquent stand he took against Wood's debased halfpence, which constituted some of the first stirrings of Irish nationhood, albeit a distinctly Anglo-Irish nation.

> A people long used to hardships, lose by degrees the very notions of liberty; they look upon themselves as creatures at mercy; and that all impositions laid on them by a stronger hand, are... legal and obligatory. Hence proceed that poverty and lowness of spirit, to which a kingdom may be subject, as well as a particular person. And when Esau came fainting from the field, at the point to die, it is no wonder that he sold his birthright for a mess of pottage.

When an award of £300 was offered to anyone who could identify the author of the anonymous Drapier letters, and Swift let it be known that he was the author, the Lord Lieutenant did nothing, fully aware that if he tried to arrest Swift the Dublin poor would have torn him limb from limb. In all events, Wood's coins were revoked and Swift had his victory, about which the great Irish parliamentarian Henry Grattan would later remark: "Swift was on the wrong side of England but in Ireland he was a giant."

This episode says a good deal about the city in which Swift developed so much of his satirical genius. Dublin has always reveled in its great men, even if they tend to repay the compliment by abusing the city. Swift, for example, liked to tell his English friends Gay and Pope that he had left England for Dublin because he preferred to be "a freeman among slaves, rather than a slave among freemen". And James Joyce famously wrote *Dubliners* (1914) "to betray the soul of that ... paralysis which many consider a city". Dublin has always been fond of good writing and good talk, though its "notions of liberty" have tended to be fitful. Consequently, its history has always been one of promise unfulfilled. Elizabeth Bowen saw this when she referred to the city being "full of false starts and dead ends, the store plan of something that never realized itself". The beautiful buildings of Georgian Dublin might have been built to accommodate the Irish Parliament, but, in one stroke, the Act of Union (1800) made most of them superfluous. Here, as in so many other instances, venality trumped "notions of liberty".

Many of these elegant Georgian buildings – most notably, James Gandon's Custom House and the Four Courts – were commissioned by John Beresford (1764–1840) in his thirty-year tenure as head of the Irish revenue. That Beresford, the descendant of a powerful political dynasty rooted in the Londonderry plantation should have also been instrumental in passing the Act of Union was an irony with an altogether Irish twist. Working behind the scenes with William Pitt to subvert the Irish Parliament, Beresford paved the way for the sectarian divisions that would undo much of what he helped the Georgian city to accomplish. "Union will leave Dublin but a splendid ruin," Dickson quotes one patriot prophesying as early as 1795, "the fallen and impoverished and crumbling capital of a province", and so it proved for much of the nineteenth and twentieth centuries. Lawyers, it is true, always made a good living in the post-Union city; the Anglo-Irish, after all, were incorrigibly litigious; and doctors never went broke humoring the city's legion hypochondriacs; but nearly everyone else was hard up. As for Beresford, although an inspired town planner, he epitomized all that was most treacherous about the Ascendancy, and there was fine poetic justice in Daniel O'Connell and the Catholic Association defeating a Beresford for the County Waterford seat in 1826, which led not only to Catholic Emancipation (1829) but the eventual destruction of the Anglo-Irish ruling class.

If the Protestant Dublin of Swift and Grattan left little behind but memorials of betrayal, the Catholic Dublin of Fianna Fáil fared no better. When De Valera's government opted for neutrality, its claims to be acting in the interests of Irish nationalism rang with comical hollowness. Considering the "might-have-beens" contingent on neutrality, J. J. Lee asked in his brilliant study, *Ireland: 1912–1985* (1989) whether a Nazis invasion, with all its attendant atrocities, could have "disturbed the complacent certainties of hereditary hatreds", to which he gave an answer that Swift himself might have enjoyed: "It is precisely because these things did not happen, as they could so easily have happened if the fortunes of war had shifted, that the citizen of a small state must be grateful, not so much for neutrality, which in itself could do little to prevent such horrors, but for the most important event in the history of Irish neutrality, Allied victory."

For his all-encompassing history of the city from medieval times to the end of the twentieth century, David Dickson has chosen the subtitle, "The Making of a Capital City", which is an intriguing choice, given that so much of the book chronicles Dublin's failure to become a capital city. Indeed, now that the city has ceded much of its sovereignty to the European Union, in the wake of the collapse of the Celtic Tiger, its capital status is more dubious still. Certainly, this recent abdication of sovereignty smacks of the same fecklessness that led to Ireland's neutrality, which was itself the *dénouement* of centuries of subjugation. As Lee points out, "The 'success' of neutrality fed . . . the popular fantasy that Ireland achieved it merely by proclaiming it", and as a result, the Irish would continue to "evade the responsibilities of sovereignty. . ."

Dickson gives an amusing example of Dublin's peculiar insouciance in this line when he notes how the Hibernian city passed the day that inaugurated so much misery elsewhere. "When the singing cowboy Gene Autrey riding Champion the Wonder Horse came up the steps of the Theatre Royal on 3 September 1939 to launch his latest singing Western, he drew a crowd of many thousands."

If Dublin was largely indifferent to World War II, the city was equally indifferent to the outbreak of the Eastern Rebellion (1916), when a band of romantic insurrectionists occupied key points of the imperial city, proclaiming how "In the name of God and of the dead generations from which she receives her old tradition of nationhood, Ireland, through us, summons her children to her flag and strikes for her freedom". It was only when the rebels had caused a good deal of their city to be burned down that Dubliners began to take notice. And it was only when the English began shooting the rebels that what had hitherto been hostile public opinion swung round in favor of the Volunteers.

Dickson's account of the rebellion is a model of evenhandedness. Certainly, one can agree with the author that when General Maxwell took command of over 20,000 troops throughout the city, "There was some but not a great deal of abuse of that overwhelming power". It is true that Maxwell eventually shot 15 of the rebels but it is also true that they were guilty of treason when the British were fighting the same Germans on the Somme that had supplied the rebels with their guns. In all events, the undeniable courage of the rebels is evident from the fact that while Crown forces suffered 103 fatalities, the greatly outnumbered Volunteers had only 60, which is all the more impressive when one considers that the Mauser rifles that Germany supplied the 3,500 rebels were no match for the Lewis guns of the British.

In his account of the Anglo-Irish Civil War that followed the Easter Rebellion, so much of which took place in and around Dublin, Dickson points out that when the IRA killed 15 alleged "spies" – in point-blank executions that were expressly designed to provoke politically useful reprisals from the Black and Tans – most of the men murdered had no link to espionage. For Dubliners familiar with their city's violent past, this chapter would have recalled an earlier one in 1798, when the United Irishmen staged their uprising, in response to which, as Dickson relates, every street was turned into a Golgotha, lampposts served as gibbets, and the bridges across the Liffey were festooned with "the trophy corpses of rebels". If, as Dickson says, this was a "barbaric coda to an era that had promised so much", it also prefigured the even greater barbarity that the IRA would carry out in the increasingly indefensible name of nationalism in the years beyond the founding of Éire, as the southern state styled itself after 1937.

Dickson is revelatory about the shrewd and enterprising Catholic bishops who presided over the city's Catholic faithful, including Archbishop Daniel Murray (1823–52), Cardinal Paul Cullen (1803–78) and Archbishop John Charles McQuaid (1895–1973), all of whom strengthened the city's impressive network of Catholic schools. If the literacy levels in Dublin after the Union remained high, much of that is attributable to the resourceful work undertaken by the Catholic bishops with dedicated lay people, especially Frances Teresa Ball (1794–1861), the daughter of a well-to-do silk merchant, who set up convent schools for both upper-class and poor women not only in Dublin but throughout the empire from Calcutta to Toronto. Critics of the Irish Catholic hierarchy often argue that it was the dictatorial sway the bishops held over the laity (in addition to various abuses and scandals) that ultimately impelled the Irish (and particularly Dubliners) to repudiate the Catholic faith, but Dickson shows that the historical relationship between the hierarchy and the laity was much more cooperative than previously appreciated.

Regarding the trade unionist James Larkin (1876–1947) and the Dublin lockout of 1913, Dickson persuasively rehabilitates William Martin Murphy (1844–1919), the owner of the city's extensive tramways, who, far from being the cardboard villain of Marxist caricature, was one of the fairest employers in the city, a genuine patriot and the principal sponsor of the 1907 Irish International Exhibition, which drew over 2 million spectators. It was the Liverpudlian Larkin who injected class warfare into disputes which could have been amicably negotiated without such gratuitous warfare. As it was, not only were the city's transport workers adversely affected but those in the building trades and the main coal yards as well. Predictably, it was the generous support of Britain's trade unions that kept Larkin's strike alive and when that ended, Larkin retired to America, where he joined the American Communist Party, but only after leaving much unnecessary hardship behind amongst Dublin's working poor. Tellingly, there was no support for Larkinism in the Dublin press, either nationalist or Unionist, though Dickson quotes Yeats's friend, the poet AE fulminating against Dublin's employers for being "blind Samsons pulling down the pillars of the social order", proof that no demagoguery can compete with the demagoguery of poets.

What is remarkable about Dublin is how little class warfare figured in its history, especially considering its slums, which were some of the worst in Europe and had consistently appalling rates of overcrowding and child mortality. According to the 1926 census, 39, 615 families were living in two-room tenements and the average death rate per 1,000 for children aged 1–5 was 25.6. Shaw's response to this deplorable record is amusingly barbed. "If the United States, instead of asking its immigrants silly questions as to whether they are anarchists and the like, so as to make sure that all of her foreign anarchists shall also be liars, were to refer to the statistics of infant mortality in the country or city from which the immigrants came, and send them back contemptuously if the rate were anything like so infamously high as it is in the slums of Dublin, such a step would... call the attention of Irishmen to the disgrace of their annual Slaughter of the Innocents..." However, since Shaw zealously advocated not only contraception but eugenics, he was hardly a champion himself of vulnerable children.

Despite the relative amity between the different classes in Dublin, some, like the journalist D. P. Moran (1869–1936), an atrabilious Waterford man who had come to Dublin from London, were intent on exacerbating the differences of Dubliners. Convinced that the Irish and Anglo-Irish were locked in what he characterized as a "battle of two civilizations", Moran urged his Gaelic neighbors to repudiate what he saw as the degrading influence of the Anglo-Irish. In his weekly, *The Leader*, he was particularly dismissive of the Ascendancy's last literary hurrah. "Mr. Yeats does not understand us", Moran complained, "and he has yet to write even one line that will strike a chord in the Irish heart. He dreams dreams. They may be very beautiful and 'Celtic', but they are not ours." In another piece, Moran even deplored the lovely Georgian terraces along Merrion Square. "Their day is done", he fumed. "The Georgian era is over, and there is little sense in seeking to perpetuate it... nothing is left for them but demolition." Thanks, in part, to Desmond Guinness, Diana Mosley's son, and the Irish Georgian Society, Moran's exhortation did not go entirely heeded, which spared Dublin from what might have been more of the sort of ghastly office blocks that Dublin Corporation put up in the 1960s, one of which, Hawkins House, was nicely described by one aggrieved conservationist as "easily the most monstrous pile of architectural rubbish ever built in Dublin".

The only shortcoming of this otherwise admirable book is that it includes too little primary documentation, without which no piece of history can have the texture of history. In his introduction, Dickson states that his aim in writing the book was "to try to understand the past rather than recreate it". Fair enough, but the book would have been richer if he had recreated more of what he elucidates. For example, no history of Dublin should be without Grattan's stinging rejoinder to the venal men who dissolved the Irish Parliament in favor of the Union.

> You will be taught by the debates of the Imperial Parliament that you have grievances, and you will be further taught by the abortive consequences of those debates that you have no Parliament to redress them. You will find that to deprive a nation of hope is not the best method to prevent her becoming desperate; and that you least of all secure the peace of your country by taking away that Constitution which the Country has pledged herself to support.

Then, again, to determine whether Grattan had the best of the argument, it might be best to give the last word to the attorney-general, Lord Clare, a passionate advocate of Union, though also an unsparing critic of both the Anglo-Irish and the Irish.

> When I look at the squalid misery, and profound ignorance, and barbarous manners and brutal ferocity of the mass of the Irish people, I am sickened with this rant of Irish dignity and independence. Is the dignity and independence of Ireland to consist in the continued depression and unredeemed barbarism of the great majority of the people, and the factious contentions of a puny and rapacious oligarchy, who consider the Irish nation as their political inheritance, and are ready to sacrifice the public peace and happiness to their insatiate love of patronage and power? ... If we are to pursue the beaten course of faction and folly, I have no scruple to say, it were better for Great Britain that this island should sink into the sea, than continue connected with the British Crown on the terms of our present Union. ...

Here are good examples of the brilliant talk of Dublin without which one cannot begin to understand the city's vexed history. Dickson's narrative includes too few of these inimitable voices. Nevertheless, such omissions notwithstanding, David Dickson's history of Dublin is an insightful, deeply researched, witty book, which anyone interested in Ireland, England, Georgian architecture, or the misadventures of nation building will find fascinating.

The Quick and Piercing Word

A People of One Book: The Bible and the Victorians, Timothy Larsen. Oxford University Press. 326 pages.

THE POPULAR VICTORIAN NOVELIST and travel writer Georgiana, Lady Chatterton (1806–76), describing the bafflement she felt when reading the Bible as a girl, recalled how "one governess considered me unteachable, because I could not say the second Psalm by heart, and especially the verse, 'Why do the heathen so furiously rage?' which she used to repeat over and over again ... The fact is, I was wondering all the time why the heathen did so furiously rage, and who they could be; so that the more my mind was made to dwell on the words, the more puzzled I became ...'." It is difficult imagining the children of our own England puzzling over the Bible because it is difficult imagining them reading the book in the first place. Yet children in Victorian England were profoundly different. In his sprightly new study, *A People of One Book: The Bible and the Victorians*, Timothy Larsen, Professor of Christian Thought at Wheaton College, richly documents the appeal the Bible had not only for Victorian adults but for their children as well.

Indeed, Larsen quotes Thomas Huxley (1825–95), the agnostic biologist, who was convinced that "if Bible-reading is not accompanied by constraint and solemnity ... I do not believe there is anything in which children take more pleasure". Gladstone and Disraeli devoured Scripture as children, as did the great art critic John Ruskin (1819–1900). "My mother forced me, by steady daily toil, to learn long chapters of the Bible by heart," he recalled; "as well as to read it every syllable through, aloud, hard names and all, from Genesis to the Apocalypse once a year; and to that discipline – patient, accurate, and resolute – I owe, not only a knowledge of the book, which I find occasionally serviceable, but much of my general powers of taking pains, and the best part of my taste in literature .... Once knowing the 32nd of Deuteronomy, the 119th Psalm, the 15th of 1st Corinthians, the Sermon on the Mount, and most of all the Apocalypse, every syllable by heart, and having always a way of thinking with myself what words meant, it was impossible for me, even in the foolishest times of youth, to write entirely superficial or formal English."

The deep regard of English Protestants for the Bible can be traced back to John Foxe's *Book of Martyrs* (1563), in which those put to death by Queen Mary were commemorated not only as martyrs to Protestantism but to the authority of Scripture. By the beginning of the nineteenth century, William Cobbett might claim that Foxe's martyrs were "most wicked wretches, who sought to destroy the Queen and her government ... under the pretense of conscience and superior piety", but this was not the majority view. Queen Victoria spoke for an entire Protestant civilization when she referred to Mary's Catholic faith, which, after the Reformation, de-emphasized the Bible, as "sacerdotal tyranny". More to the taste of free-born Englishmen was John Milton's *sola scriptura* Christianity, which he defended against the proponents of episcopacy with impassioned eloquence.

> Let them chant while they will of prerogatives, we shall tell them of Scripture; of customs, we of Scripture; of Acts and Statutes, still of Scripture, till the quick and piercing word enter to the dividing of their souls, and the mighty weakness of the Gospel throw down the weak mightiness of man's reasoning.

The most brilliant of all Victorian churchmen, John Henry Newman (1801–90) never accepted the notion that the Bible alone could encompass Christianity – there was nothing in the Bible, after all, about the Trinity or, for that matter, about the Bible being the sole repository of the faith – yet he recognized that the Bible was "the best book of meditations which can be, because it is divine". He also recognized that Catholic countries negligent of the Bible were in peril of losing their faith. France and Italy, for example, risked succumbing to apostasy precisely because, as he said, "they have not impressed upon their hearts the life of our Lord and Saviour as given us in the Evangelists. They believe merely with the intellect, not with the heart".

About Newman's great friend, Edward Pusey (1800–82), Prof. Larsen is revelatory, seeing him not merely as a controversial champion of episcopacy but a first-rate biblical scholar. It is true that most of his English contemporaries took issue with him for being too Roman, but Larsen suggests that this might have been misconceived criticism. Bishops, after all, never meant as much to Pusey as the Bible, about which he wrote with such learned zest. When he threw in his lot with the Tractarians, he might have missed his true calling. In fine, as Larsen nicely puts it, Pusey was a "Bible man, who led an exegetical life", and had, in this respect at least, more in common with the Evangelicals than the Anglo-Catholics.

Larsen's book is far-ranging. He has chapters on what a vital role the Bible played among Evangelicals, Roman Catholics, Anglo-Catholics, Methodists, Quakers, Unitarians, dissenters, agnostics, even atheists; and what is more impressive, he manages to show each of these different traditions true critical sympathy.

There is also much lively biography in the book. In taking up the case of Elizabeth Fry (1780–1845), for example, the Quaker who devoted her life to prison reform, Prof. Larsen shows how the Bible was an integral part of her ministry at a time when not everyone approved of Scripture. On one occasion, the French press characterized the Bible passages that she was attempting to distribute to prisoners as "controversial tracts". Perhaps the greatest accomplishment of this enterprising woman was to supply Bibles to the English coastguard. Certainly, the sailors for whom she cared so deeply would have been amused to know how opposed their benefactress was to teetotalism. In response to Romans 14:21, which dissuades the faithful from taking wine if it cause scandal or offence to another, Fry wrote in the margin of her own Bible: "We must on one hand be very careful not to offend a weak brother & on the other we must not unite in scruples that we think contrary to the will of God."

Larsen is particularly good on Huxley, who, for all his contempt for what he regarded as the credulity of Christian belief, loved the Bible. Indeed, he was adamant that, for educational purposes, Scripture was incomparable.

> Take the Bible as a whole; make the severest deductions which fair criticism can dictate for shortcomings and positive errors; eliminate ... all that is not desirable for children ... and there still remains in the old literature a vast residuum of moral beauty and grandeur. And then consider the great historical fact that, for three centuries, this book has been

woven into the life that is best and noblest in English history, that is has become the national epic of Britain, and is as familiar to noble and simple, from John-o-Groat's House to Land's End.

At the same time, Huxley was fond of quoting the Bible to tease Bible thumpers. In 1870, for example, he spoke of how "the green bay tree of bibliolatry flourishes as it did sixty years ago" because, as he said, "whoso refuses to offer incense to the idol [of the Bible] is held to be guilty of 'a dishonor to God', imperiling his salvation".

There is much to praise in Larsen's book. Deeply researched and deftly presented, his chapters capture the ubiquity of the Bible in Victorian culture without ever becoming sidetracked by those two fashionable bores that stultify so much academic history, Gender and Class. Instead, he allows his subjects to speak for themselves and never takes them to task for failing to conform to the dictates of political correctness. He also uncovers a good deal of endearing absurdity in his subjects, as in this passage, in which he writes of Charles Haddon Spurgeon (1834–92), the celebrated preacher:

> When he was at Mentone, Spurgeon would convince himself that he was seeing life as it was in biblical stories. "I often fancy that I am looking upon the Lake of Gennesaret, or walking at the foot of the Mount of Olives, or peering into the mysterious gloom of the Garden of Gethsemane. The narrow streets of the old town are such as Jesus traversed, those villages are such as He inhabited." One can safely assume that this tells us more about Spurgeon's biblically saturated imagination than it does about the French Riviera.

What lies outside the compass of Prof. Larsen's study is how the English lost their attachment to the Bible. In this, the German biblical criticism that emerged in England in the 1830s and finally took hold at the end of the century was a factor, as was the general waning of Christian belief that followed. But perhaps the severest blow to the authority of the Bible came from the work of geologists like Sir Charles Lyell (1797–1875), which cast doubt on so many biblical certainties. In 1851, Ruskin wrote to a friend, "You speak of the Flimsiness of your own faith. Mine, which was never strong, is being beaten into mere gold leaf, and flutters in weak rags from the letter of its old forms; but the only letters it can hold by at all are the very old Evangelical formulae. If only the Geologists would let me alone, I could do very well, but those dreadful Hammers! I hear the clink of them at the end of every cadence of the Bible verses."

If some blamed the geologists and their physical science for the eventual desuetude in which the Bible fell, others blamed the liturgical reformers. Regarding these energetic vandals, the conservative MP for Aldershot, Julian Critchley, spoke for many when he wrote in the *Listener* in 1982:"The statue of the Virgin is no longer the target of the iconoclasts' hammer; it is those two distinctive treasures of the English language, James I's Authorised Version of the Bible and Cranmer's Book of Common Prayer. Now they are seldom heard in church, having been translated into Sunday Supplement Prose. The transfiguration is unforgivable."

At the same time, Larsen makes a vital point when he observes how our own contemporary scholars have "overlooked or distorted" the primacy of the Bible for the Victorians "by a preoccupation ... with critical approaches to the Bible". These scholars have also tended to minimize the extent to which the Bible was taken up for devotional purposes. Diverging from these ahistorical accounts, Larsen succeeds admirably in showing how the Victorians "experienced the Bible first and foremost as a ... life-giving source of spiritual comfort and divine promises". Nevertheless, if the Victorians refused to "ignore or sidestep the Bible", the same cannot be said for their successors.

In August of 2011, in the towns and cities of England, a fair sampling of those successors regaled the world with scenes that posed anew the question that baffled Lady Chatterton – *Why do the heathen so furiously rage?* Prof. Larsen's study does not answer that rather involved question, but it will send many readers back to the book that more than any other defined the English when they had a common culture.

Guinness Backstage

Alec Guinness: The Authorized Biography, Piers Paul Read.
Simon & Schuster, 624 pages.

Apropos biography, Samuel Johnson once said that "the business of the biographer is to pass lightly over those performances and incidents, which produce vulgar greatness" in order "to lead the thoughts into domestic privacies, and display the minute details of daily life, where exterior appendages are cast aside and men excel each other only by prudence and by virtue". In *Alec Guinness: The Authorized Biography*, Piers Paul Read does not neglect the performances that won his subject "vulgar greatness". Read's observations on Guinness's acting career are incisive and shrewd. But he puts them into perspective and shows how Guinness's moral development played out in the "minute details of daily life" constituted his true career.

Read fully appreciates the centrality that Catholicism came to have for Guinness. Two years before he converted at the age of 42, Guinness confided to his diary: "My soul, my body, my brain longs for religion. The world is too bleak and blank without a sense of worship." Even in his twenties, while an officer in the Royal Navy, he recognized Catholicism as "the crack regiment", though at the time he felt he could not afford its "expensive uniforms". When his son Matthew fell ill with polio in 1952, Guinness made a pact with God that if Matthew recovered, he would convert. Matthew recovered and Guinness converted. Or so he recalled in his autobiography, *Blessings in Disguise* (1985). Read shows that his conversion was much more gradual, taking root slowly but tenaciously in a nature avid for the life of faith.

Guinness's childhood was rackety. Born in London in 1914 and educated at private schools, he never knew his father and grew up in lodgings with a mother who was as improvident as she was unpresentable. "My mother was a whore", Guinness told John Le Carré. "She slept with the entire crew on Lord Moyne's yacht at the Cowes Regatta and when she gave birth she called the bastard

Guinness but my father was probably the bloody cook." She drank. She stole things. She also turned her son into something of a sybaritic precisian. The delight Guinness took in Savile Row suits, shopping at Asprey's, and hosting Lucullian dinners at the Connaught Hotel, as well as his legendary punctiliousness, can all be traced back to his determination to distance himself from his incorrigible mother.

If Guinness was fond of having things just so, he also enjoyed the louche society of homosexuals. He had homosexual leanings himself, though he appears to have resisted them. One of his best friends, Peter Glenville, the director, was homosexual and Catholic. On the topic of homosexuality, Read is refreshingly sensible. He admits to a certain bafflement as to how Glenville could reconcile a life-long homosexual liaison with the Church's teaching on the sinfulness of sexual relations outside a marriage between a man and a woman. But he acknowledges that the very fact that Glenville saw the sacrament of confession as "necessary for his salvation suggests faith in Christ and acceptance of, if not obedience to, the disciplines of the Church". Guinness felt that such passions "could be controlled, if not cured, by prayer, repentance and the Grace of God".

Once Guinness left school he worked as an advertising copywriter for a year before training for the stage under Martita Hunt, a friend of John Gielgud's, who had "the voice and demeanor of a dowager duchess". At their first lesson, after asking Guinness to mix her a martini, she told him that an actor should emphasize the verb and leave the nouns and adjectives to look after themselves. (Robert Graves gave the same advice to young poets.) It was a lesson Guinness never forgot. When Gielgud took pity on the pitiably thin young actor and gave him the role of Osric in his 1934 production of Hamlet, his acting career was launched. Sixty years later, when Gielgud turned 90, Guinness handsomely honored his first employer by giving him a lavish luncheon at the Connaught.

During the Second World War, Guinness embraced Anglo-Catholicism "flittingly", as he says, before wearying of what Lytton Strachey called "the tight-rope of High Anglicanism". For Guinness, it was "a psychological bulwark against the uncertainties of war and fear of the future and it stood me in good stead". Indeed, after marrying, he even toyed with the idea of becoming an Anglican priest. But gradually he came to believe that by remaining in the Church of England he was "quite definitely in enemy territory".

Several factors went into Guinness's conversion. An unusually intelligent man, he reveled in the intellectual richness of the Catholic tradition. After converting, he wrote to his wife, "One of the recent things I've discovered is that now there is always something to think about. Never a dull moment in heaven or hell."

Then, too, he needed his faith to be therapeutic. Catholic devotion healed the wounds of illegitimacy. "My prayers are always full of my requirements and not true prayers at all", he once said. And yet he could also write: "I accept absolutely now and with no effort that I am in the actual presence of God on the altar". About the villainies of Rome, he was broadminded: "If you *are* to come in to the Church then it'll be useless your trying to resist – all the horrors that have been and are perpetrated in Christ's name will be so skillfully outweighed by God." Edward Hermann, the American actor, claimed that the English Catholic Church appealed to his friend because it was posh. But it was no more posh in the 1950s than it is today. What attracted Guinness to the Catholic faith was its truth, not its trappings.

After converting, Guinness regularly renewed his faith with spiritual reading, devouring the works of Newman, Chesterton, Belloc, Knox, Charles de Foucauld, and Saint Teresa of Avila. In the first volume of his journals, *My Name Escapes Me* (1997), he quotes a passage from Julian of Norwich's *Revelations of Divine Love*, where Julian speaks of a vision she had in which she saw:

> A little thing, the quantity of a hazelnut, in the palm of my hand, and it was as round as a ball. I thought, "What may this be?" And it was answered me, "It is all that is made". I marveled how it might last and not fall to nothing for littleness. I was answered, "It lasts, and ever shall last, for God loves it".

Guinness was so enamored of this image that he kept a hazelnut in his makeup box: "it was the first thing to be laid out on my dressing-table when I came into the theatre". When the brewery heiress Honor Guinness rejoined the Church, she gave the actor a hazelnut of rare gold to mark the occasion, which prompted him to observe that "something had come full circle, as I have often found in life, giving the lie to my earlier concept of accident, meaninglessness and chaos".

The fact that Honor was convinced that Guinness had been sired by one of her more rambunctious uncles must also have given the bauble special appeal. Another favorite author was Saint Francis de Sales. For Guinness, who could say the most wounding things, it must have been chastening to open *The Devout Life* and read: "Derision or mockery always involves contempt and so is gravely sinful, so that theologians rightly hold mockery to be the worst sin of the tongue we can commit against our neighbor."

De Sales's methods for identifying and resisting sin led Guinness to call him "the most comfortable of saints". As he told a friend, "I have returned to his friendly wisdom and greatness with more understanding and a better resolution, I hope, to follow his methods ... I come and go in fits and starts – so to speak – in my religious life, but it deepens I believe and pray and trust." No one struggling to live the devout life will fail to recognize that prayer. But Read shows that Guinness's Catholic faith was not simply the faith of a reader of apologetics. Grace touched him directly, personally. "I think most ... human beings have that once in their lives ... in greatly varying degrees of course," he wrote his wife. "And of course it is ... God giving each man and woman, according to their capacity, a glimpse of His promise to them, an impression of what eternity could mean, a glimpse of their adoption as Sons of God, and by its withdrawal a realization of what the Fall of man means. We are all left with a feeling of exhilaration, and yet at the same time, hand in hand with its happiness, a sadness that we are unlikely to encounter it again in this life. It's a golden carrot held up to donkeys – who could be gods."

In his autobiography, Guinness says that whenever people found out that he was Catholic they would congratulate him on his good fortune, "as if my Premium Bonds paid in a handsome dividend". He was grateful for the dividends but also acknowledged "the constant failures", which were "painful, when not just laughable, and boringly repetitive". Failure, come to think of it, was also the theme of most of his films – the failure of soldiers and spies, bank clerks and salesmen, Cambridge scientists and hapless peers. In his spiritual life, it was his recognition of the failure of natural virtue and the abiding need for sacramental grace that strengthened his faith.

As dutiful as Read is about retailing Guinness's personal characteristics – his hypochondria, his delight in his Hampshire home, his tart tongue, and refusal to suffer fools gladly – there was an essential inscrutability about the man. Ronald Neame, who directed him in *The Card* (1952), *The Horse's Mouth* (1958), and *Tunes of Glory* (1960) told the *Independent* after his death: "The diffident, the introvert side of him is something that's been slightly questioned. Was he doing a Greta Garbo, telling the world he wanted to be alone but wanting to be a star? No. Alec was self-effacing, and that was genuine. But he was an extremely difficult person to know. There is a kind of loneliness in his performances, which is him in life. I very much doubt even if his wife really knew him. I got fairly close to him, but I didn't really know him. Nobody did." His wife, Merula, would have disputed that. As she jotted down in a memorandum before her death: "With all the contradictions of his makeup, there was always the rod of truth up the middle which was what I recognized when we first fell in love. I knew I could always trust him."

Merula comes out admirably in the book. Guinness constantly found fault with her, belittling her children's books, her artwork, her cookery. Yet Merula saw her husband's flaws as the result of his compulsive fussiness and forgave him. Read praises her forbearance: "To a number of the Guinnesses' closest friends, while Alec remained his old difficult self, it was Merula who gained in wisdom and goodness ... achieving the genius of sanctity that had eluded Alec."

In "the minute details of daily life, where men excel each other only by prudence and by virtue" Guinness did not altogether shine. Yet, to be fair, if at times he was insufferable, he was a loyal friend and a faithful husband. He was grandly munificent. He recognized his faults and sought to combat them. In summing up his character, Read compares him to Evelyn Waugh, who once said "I know I am awful. But how much more awful I should be without the Faith". Guinness could have said the same. As could many readers of this brilliant book.

John Osborne: Mum's the Word

John Osborne: The Many Lives of the Angry Young Man, John Heilpern. Knopf. 527 pages.

When John Osborne's *Look Back in Anger* opened at The Royal Court on 8 May 1956, the initial response was dismal. To an audience fond of the witty badinage of Nöel Coward, the clever plot twists of Terrence Rattigan, and the modern morality plays of T. S. Eliot, the scattershot invective of Jimmy Porter, Osborne's hero, seemed tedious and offensive. Osborne himself recalled the first night audience as "mostly adrift, like Eskimos watching a Restoration Comedy". Many walked out.

The reviewers were equally unsympathetic. One found Porter "a caricature of the sort of frustrated left-wing intellectual who, I thought, died out in the war". Another took Osborne himself to task: "When he stops being angry – or when he knows what he's angry about – he might write a very good play." Others were more straightforwardly abusive, calling the play "putrid", "sickening", and "self-pitying". But then Kenneth Tynan ran his review claiming: "I doubt if I could love anyone who did not wish to see *Look Back in Anger*: it is the best young play of its decade", and the production was saved. Osborne became famous overnight.

When Osborne followed up his unexpected success with *The Entertainer* (1959) and *Inadmissible Evidence* (1964) – which gave memorable expression to his sense of loss and futility – he proved his staying power, though later he would write several plays that should never have left his notebooks.

In his entertaining new biography John Heilpern looks squarely at the many flaws of the first Angry Young Man without losing sight of his good points. Like Piers Paul Read's brilliant biography of Alec Guinness – another flawed man of talent – Heilpern's book shows his subject unusual compassion. In many respects, Osborne was a monster, but he could also be remarkably generous and good-hearted. Heilpern's evenhandedness underscores the radical contradictions of the man.

To try to describe Osborne the playwright, Heilpern quotes Artie Shaw describing how he approached playing music: "You're trying to make a sound that no one ever got before, creating an emotion. You're trying to take notes and make them come out in a way that moves you. If it moves you, it's going to move others." Yet Osborne's plays exhibit too much emotion. Structurally ramshackle and devoid of any sustained thought, they are often little more than staged jeremiads. If there is an apt jazz parallel to Osborne's work, it is not the swinging aplomb of Artie Shaw but the cacophonous banality of Ornette Coleman. Nevertheless, even for those skeptical about the merits of Osborne's work, Heilpern's book is worth reading. It recreates a theatre that has all but vanished and an exuberant life hobbled by hate.

John James Osborne (1929–94) was born an only child in Fulham. His mother, Nellie Beatrice Grove, was an enterprising Cockney who began work as a charwoman in an orphanage, did a stint as cashier in Lyons Corner House in the Strand, and finally became a popular barmaid known for her lewd patter.

Osborne's father, Thomas Godfrey, was a frail, asthmatic, feckless Welshman, a commercial artist who had wanted to be a real artist, but never managed it. In the all-important calculus of class, he married beneath himself and regretted it. Every time his wife opened her mouth, he winced. Like many of the artists Osborne admired – Chekhov, Beardsley, D. H. Lawrence, Orwell – he died young of TB.

Osborne went to his grave adoring his father, even though his most vivid memories of him were of his coming home "after supper full of Waterloo buffet whiskey, Guinness or Moussec playing the upright piano and singing 'Red Sails in the Sunset'". On such crumbs did Osborne feed his filial love. In *Look Back in Anger*, he has Jimmy Porter say: "For twelve months I watched my father dying when I was ten years old ... You see I learnt at an early age what it was to be angry – angry and helpless. And I can never forget it."

Osborne claimed that he hated his mother because she was "the grabbing uncaring crone of my childhood", berated him publicly when he was growing up, and showed no grief when his beloved father died. What most galled him was her refusal to show him the maternal love he craved. When Nellie Beatrice died at age 87, he began an article for *The Times*, "a year in which one's mother died can't be all bad". He repaid her Cockney cruelty with something of his own Cockney vindictiveness.

After being expelled from school for punching out one of his masters, Osborne worked as a copy editor for a trade magazine called *Gas World*. Most of his days were spent poring over the huge office dictionary. Notebooks from this period abound with word lists: "Acolyte, addled, alchemy, blancmange, bumbling, burgeon, bollocks, clammy, coverture, conk..." But it was not until he escaped journalism for repertory theatre that he put his love of words to the test. *Look Back in Anger* was not his first but his fourth play and drew on much that he had learned as a repertory actor.

When it came to marriage Osborne's motto was "Eat, Drink and Remarry". In trying to account for why he was such a repeatedly poor husband, he explained: "I often confronted problems like an improvising chimpanzee faced with the dashboard of a jumbo jet." That many in England and America spent decades trying to turn this chaotic man into a spokesman for the benefits of social revolution says volumes about the judgment of our friends on the left.

Osborne's first marriage to fellow actor Pamela Lane supplied most of the materials for *Look Back in Anger*. Lane's middle-class parents strenuously opposed the match and Osborne pursued it largely to spite them, just as Jimmy Porter marries Alison to spite her parents. When Lane saw the play, she was amazed by its fidelity to their marital nightmare. After they divorced, Osborne married Mary Ure, his beautiful leading lady, who was playing Alison at the time. Osborne later admitted that he married Ure because she reminded him of Lane, which prompts Heilpern to remark: "The man who thinks of his first wife while marrying his second gives nostalgia a bad name." Although a talented actress, Ure would later descend into madness. (It is remarkable how many of his wives came to bad ends.)

It was with his third wife, Penelope Gilliatt, the film critic for *The New Yorker*, that Osborne had his only child, Nolan, whom he would later disown after he discovered that she preferred the company of her teenage girlfriends to his. Worse, she reminded him of his stony, mocking mother. She spent most of her adult life telephoning William Shawn with late edits and drinking herself to death. The man who brought up Osborne's castoff daughter was the old *Times* film critic Vincent Canby, who when asked for comments about the playwright replied: "I've nothing to say about the bastard!"

Wife number four was another of Osborne's leading ladies, Jill Bennett, with whom he would have a bruisingly destructive marriage fueled by drink and venom. After its collapse, Osborne formed *Adolf's Anonymous*, Adolf being his nickname for Bennett. Anyone tempted to marry Jill Bennett could ring the organization day or night and be talked out of it. Bennett would eventually commit suicide.

Before leaving Bennett, Osborne had a nervous breakdown, during which he mused: "'Things fall apart, the centre cannot hold.' Is that right? It feels just right at this moment in time. I feel like a figment. A pretty awful fiction. I take back what I have said about the Irish." Osborne's fifth and final wife was Helen Dawson, arts editor for the *Observer*, with whom he shared estates in Shropshire and Clun, A. E. Housemanland, about which Osborne would remark "I may be the poorest playwright in England but I've got the best view".

That Osborne should have been virtually bankrupt in the last decade of his life was proof of his extravagance. His lavish homes in London and the country, his cars, his wives, his many generous handouts to friends and colleagues down on their luck, his drink bills ("Osborne and champagne", Heilpern says, "were as inseparable as Fortnum and Mason.") and his bills from his Savile Row tailor whittled away a sizable fortune. In his prime, he made money hand over fist. Several of his plays were box office hits in the UK and around the world. *Tom Jones* (1963), for which he wrote the screenplay, was one of the most successful films ever made. Today its profits would be the equivalent of $247.7 million. Since half the profits went to Woodfall Films, owned jointly by Osborne and the director Tony Richardson, Osborne was a multi-millionaire by the time he was 35.

After his talent for writing plays dried up, he was forced to write columns for *The Spectator* to keep the local tradesmen at bay, which prompted the Angry Old Man to complain: "That's how you end up: A f—g journalist!" Nevertheless, the columns collected in *Damn You England!* (1994) are full of salutary diatribes against the English nanny state.

What, in conclusion, can one say of such an impossible, gifted, unhappy man? Heilpern sums up matters rather lamely in his otherwise insightful biography when he says, "His cause was always the triumphant domain of the English language where words alone are certain good and man grapples with defeat and sadness". Osborne himself was nearer the mark when he said: "At least a man who hates his mother has a standard of excellence in mind." Like Archie Rice in the film version of *The Entertainer*, whom Laurence Olivier played so brilliantly, Osborne could never resist seeing his life as a bad Music Hall gag.

THE NATIONAL GALLERY AT WAR: A DEFIANT OUTPOST OF CULTURE

The National Gallery in Wartime, Suzanne Bosman. Yale University Press. 122 pages.

IN SEPTEMBER 1938, at the height of the Munich crisis (which would result in Neville Chamberlain giving Herr Hitler *carte blanche* to help himself to Czechoslovakia – Churchill put it nicely when he said that "the German dictator, instead of snatching his victuals from the table, has been content to have them served to him course by course"), the Assistant Keeper of the National Gallery, Martin Davies, made a tour of country houses to see whether they would be suitable for storing the museum's art collection for the duration of what even then the English knew would be a frightful bombing from the Luftwaffe. After sojourning to each house, Davies made notes, remarking of one visit: "The owner is nice, ruled by his wife, a tartar, anxious to have NG pictures instead of refugees or worse." Of another, "Owner ... seems obliging in a haughty way". However obliging, most owners did not have what was necessary to store paintings: their houses lacked the requisite size (doorways had to be of an immense height to accommodate larger paintings), fireproofing, or the proper temperature. Penrhyn Castle, a huge neo-Norman pile built in Wales in the early nineteenth century, was one of the few exceptions. Davies transported two shipments of paintings to the castle on special trains and stored them in its massive dining room and garage, where the ghosts of the West Indian slaves whose labor had built the castle must have welcomed them with sardonic amusement.

In *The National Gallery in Wartime*, Suzanne Bosman has written a fascinating account of how Director Kenneth Clark and his staff arranged for the wartime storage of the museum's contents first in country houses like the sham castle and then in the capacious repository of a disused quarry in the Welsh mountains. The book is wonderfully illustrated, including photographs of solitary railway vans negotiating the long and winding roads of Wales on their way to the quarry – scenes worthy of the old Ealing comedies in which English pluck always carried the day. There is certainly an Ealing touch to one of Davies's concerns: "One of our troubles at Penrhyn Castle", he wrote, "is that the owner is celebrating the war by being fairly constantly drunk. He stumbled with a dog into the Dining Room a few days ago; this will not happen again. Yesterday, he smashed up his car, and, I believe, himself a little – so perhaps the problem has solved itself for the moment."

In his autobiography, *Another Part of the Wood* (1974), Clark vividly recalled this tense time. "By 1938 it did not require Mr. Churchill's eloquence, nor the muddled, hysterical support of the left for Czechoslovakia, to arouse in the minds of ordinary men and women a sense of shame and foreboding. We realized at last that the pandering of successive governments to the peace-loving inclinations of the country in which, for once, materialism and idealism were united, had left us impotent. No one, not even Mr. Churchill, knew exactly how weak we were." Coincidentally, Chamberlain was a friend of Clark's. He and his wife Jane often dined with him at Chequers. However, he had no illusions about Birmingham's most famous son. "I was educated as an historian," Clark wrote, "and so have a certain prejudice in favour of those who can think historically. Mr. Chamberlain although he had a fund of information on unimportant matters (he occupied a whole luncheon at Chequers in 1938 by giving Jane the history of every famous gem), had no conception of what Gibbon called 'The vicissitudes of fortune, which spares neither man nor the proudest of his works, which buries empires and cities in a common grave'. This sweep of historical imagination was one of the supreme gifts of Mr. Churchill." In times to come, Clark's supreme gift may be seen not as his glorious television series or his incomparable monogram on Leonardo or his critical work on Piero della Francesca and Rembrandt, but the work he did to keep the National Gallery's collection out of that common grave.

Now that many in the West begin to forget their own vulnerability to attack from assailants that make Hitler's ruffians look like choir boys, it might be a salutary reminder to read of how Clark and his staff protected the Gallery's riches. What strikes one most about this undertaking is how tremendously efficient it was. Once the English ascertained that the sites of the country houses where National Gallery paintings were stored – Bangor, Aberystwyth, Caenarvon, and Penrhyn – would be within the flight path of German bombers headed for targets in and around the Liverpool docks, they realized that they would have to transfer most of the paintings to some securer place, and it was then that they moved their treasures to the Manod quarry near Blaenau Ffestiniog. One thousand and seven hundred feet above sea level, it was only accessible by four miles of mazy, mountainous road. To ensure that there was an opening big enough into the quarry, five thousand tons of rock had to be blasted away. Moreover, within the quarry, temperature-controlled rooms had to be constructed to house the paintings, narrow-gauge railway tracks had to be put down to ensure their easy transportation, and special wagons had to be designed by the London, Midland and Scottish Railway Company to protect the paintings from fluctuations of humidity and temperature. Hygrometers monitored the effects of temperature on the paintings with unprecedented accuracy. In addition to paintings, the National Gallery's library was also transferred to the underground quarry, for which controlled temperature was also imperative. One unexpected scholarly benefit of the transferal was that it allowed Davies to assess the collection afresh, and as a result pioneering new editions of *The Early Netherlandish School*, *The British School*, *The French School*, and *The Early Italian School* were all brought out at this time.

Ian Rawlins, a railway expert, was responsible for seeing that the truly heroic removal of the paintings went smoothly. At every turn unforeseen challenges tested his ingenuity. In the case of Van Dyck's *Equestrian Portrait of Charles I*, one of the largest paintings in the collection, Rawlins and his team had to hollow out a road leading to the quarry to enable the special cart expressly designed to transport the painting, dubbed the "Elephant Case", to pass under a low bridge, and then it was only possible after the cart's tires were deflated. Here truly was a close-run thing.

That the paintings and library were stored underground made them vulnerable to other threats besides aerial bombardment. As Bosman observes, "the brick chambers protected the pictures from minor falls, but there was always the possibility of the whole collection being buried in a catastrophic collapse". Davies was fully cognizant of this. "It would have been useless to save the pictures from bombs, only to crush them in Wales with tons of slate falling on them. Manod quarry roofs are safer than most; nevertheless, the pictures could not walk away like a gang of quarrymen from any doubtful section." When a section was identified as liable to give way, three hundred paintings were removed within seven hours. Engineers later concluded that the temperature-controlled heating of the chambers had made the rock above more than usually friable. However, this would be Manod's only failure. Once the success of the transfer spread through England's cultural grapevine, other museums joined the National Gallery in making Manod their wartime home, including the Courtauld, the National Portrait Gallery, the Soane Museum, and the Victoria and Albert Museum.

In his autobiography, Clark paid Davies witty tribute:

> He had always been a solitary character, and was said by his contemporaries in Cambridge to have emerged from his rooms only after dark; so this sunless exile [working underground at Manod] was not as painful to him as it would have been for a less unusual man. In the morning he would emerge, thin and colorless as a ghost, and would be driven up to the caves, carrying with him a strong torch and several magnifying glasses. With these he would examine every square millimeter of a few pictures. In twelve years I hardly ever saw him look at a picture as whole, but at a series of small areas of paint, which he usually found to be more or less damaged ... These revealed to him how insecure was the evidence for all attributions in early art, and for the very existence of certain painters. It is indeed true that the history of art, like all history, is to a large extent an agreed fable, and perhaps only someone as passionately skeptical as Martin Davies could have exposed so many convenient fallacies.

Not only did Clark save the National Gallery collection, he also saw to it that the museum remained "a defiant outpost of culture right in the middle of a bombed and shattered metropolis". Accordingly, in 1941, with all the Old Masters in storage, Clark mounted an exhibition of contemporary painting, which was not, however, to everyone's taste. One diarist wrote: "Another bomb there might save posterity lighting a few bonfires in the future." Also key to keeping the museum's cultural life going was Clark's hiring of the pianist Myra Hess, whom, he later recalled, had "a jolly, rolling walk, and a strong element of the old trouper". When Clark broached the idea of having lunchtime concerts, Hess thought they might be periodic; Clark insisted that they be daily; Hess took a deep breath and agreed. Three quarters of a million people eventually attended the concerts. About the music she chose for the concerts, Hess remarked: "Everybody was very busy during the war and there was nobody to tell the people that this sort of music was over their heads. So they came and liked it." The courage it took to sit and listen to Hess can only be appreciated by remembering that in October 1940, a large bomb fell on the Gallery, ruining Room XXVI (where Room 10 is today). The fact that the building next door, which now holds the Sainsbury Wing, was completely demolished shows how close the Gallery came to a similar fate.

Whatever jubilation Clark felt at war's end was fleeting. Although he took some pleasure in personally choosing the first paintings to be transported back to the museum, including Bellini's *Doge Leonardo Loredan* and Titian's *Noli Me Tangere*, events beyond London gave the war's sequel an inexpellable gloom. "The brutal Russian occupation of Berlin, the discovery and visible documentation of the German extermination camps, these and a dozen other ghastly revelations filled my mind", he wrote. "I felt that European civilization could never again recover its confidence and its equilibrium." Whether this will have been proved right is anyone's guess, though the response Europe has so far made to the gathering threat of Islamic terrorism does not augur well.

The National Gallery in Wartime is an entertaining, informative, cautionary book, which everyone interested in London, the Battle of Britain, or art will enjoy.

Honest Chronicler: Joseph Liebling

Liebling at War. World War II Writings, A. J. Liebling. Library of America. 1089 pages.

Towards the end of his life, A. J. Liebling (1904–63) summed up his experience of war with characteristic incisiveness. "I know that it is socially acceptable to write about war as an unmitigated horror, but subjectively at least, it was not true, and you can feel its pull on men's memories at the maudlin reunion of war divisions. They mourn for their dead, but also for war." This shows something essential about Liebling: his readiness to trust experience, even when it confounded his suppositions – an indispensable attribute in any good reporter. He also saw a certain comedy in baffled supposition. In 1941 he recounted boarding a train for London.

> When I went down to my train the next day I was pleasurably impressed to find nearly all the seats in the first-class carriage occupied by private soldiers and aircraftsmen. The head porter of the hotel had sent a lad along half an hour ahead of time to get a place for me. I decided that the British social revolution, of which we had heard a good deal in America, had at last arrived. One minute before train time all the "other ranks" yielded their seats to officers and got out. They were batsmen who had been sent to hold the places. "Obviously," I thought to myself, "in this country it is unwise to jump to conclusions."

Earlier, he witnessed an exchange between two Scots – a scene, as he described it, straight out of a Waverly novel – but rather than jump to conclusions, he pondered the episode: "I went to bed ... trying to figure whether they had framed me with some amateur theatricals. But it had all been on the level. The first fact one must accept about Britain is that all British literature, no matter how improbably it reads, is realistic. You meet its most outrageous models everywhere you turn ..." Here, again, Liebling was the consummate reporter, albeit with a twinkle in his eye.

The human aspect of war, not grand strategy, was his forte. Like Robert Graves, Liebling often treated war as though it were the stuff of light comedy. His description of an encounter in an apple orchard riddled with snipers is a good example.

> The Colonel who reassured me about the snipers was an Ozark type; he saw they couldn't have done much shooting before they got into the army, since they didn't know how to lead a moving target. "If you keep walking, they almost always shoot behind you," he told me. I looked around, and it was the most perambulatory headquarters ... I had ever seen ... "We got some old Missouri squirrel-hunters in this outfit, and we are hunting the snipers down pretty good," the Colonel said. "But we could do better if we had dogs."

At the same time, Liebling never spared his reader the grislier aspects of war. In Western Tunisia, he witnessed the ministrations of a field doctor who had set up shop along the roadside.

> He had a tanned giant perched on the camp stool, a second lieutenant in the Corps France d'Afrique. The man's breasts were hanging off his chest in a kind of bloody ruff. "A bit of courage now, my son, will save you a great deal of trouble later on," the doctor said as he prepared to do something or other. I assumed, perhaps pessimistically, that he was going to hack off bits of flesh as you would trim the ragged edges of an ill-cut page. "Go easy, Doctor," the young man said. "I'm such a softie." The traffic jam started to move, so I don't know what the doctor did to him.

Liebling's masters were the great English journalists Daniel Defoe, William Hazlitt, and William Cobbett. He also admired George Borrow, who wrote the picaresque *Lavengro* and *The Romany Rye*, as well as many paeans to prize-fighting. ("Let no one sneer at the bruisers of England", begins one section of *Lavengro*.) From these models he took away not only a respect for exuberance and intellectual honesty but an approach to style that illustrated Swift's definition of good writing: "proper words in proper places". The war writings collected in this Library of America edition – including *The Road Back to Paris* (1944), *Normandy Revisited* (1958), *Mollie and Other*

War Pieces (1964) and many uncollected pieces – exhibit Liebling's strengths on nearly every page. Raymond Sokolov's lively biography, *Wayward Reporter: The Life of A. J. Liebling* (1980), still available from online booksellers, makes a good companion to the collection.

Liebling's war, like war itself, was a whirlwind, interspersed with anxious waiting, though it was also a preeminently literary war. In 1939, Harold Ross sent him to Paris, where he covered *la drôle de guerre*. After Paris fell in June 1940, he had no alternative but to fly back to New York. In July 1941, he flew to London on an RAF bomber and wrote "Paddy of the RAF", about a middle-class Dubliner whose defiance of his country's ignominious neutrality endeared him to a reporter who was never taken in by the rationalizations of the dishonorable. In December 1941, after sailing to the United States on a Norwegian tanker, Liebling wrote "Westbound Tanker", which Joseph Mitchell considered the best of his war pieces. In July 1942, he sailed back to England and covered the Allied troops in London. In 1943, he stayed with US fighter squadrons in Algeria and Tunisia. In April 1943 he traveled to Tripoli and in May 1943 he sailed from Casablanca to New York. In 1944, he returned to England and accompanied a B-26 bombing mission over France. In that same year, he published "Notes from the Kidnap House", a three-part story on the press in occupied France, in which he dryly observed that "the treason of a writer is explicit, because he puts it in words", something not all war correspondents sufficiently grasp. On D-Day, 6 June, Liebling crossed the English Channel in a large landing craft transporting troops to Omaha Beach, an experience he recalled vividly in "Channel Crossing". Going ashore on 9 June, he spent the next two months with American troops in Normandy and Brittany. In September, he dispatched a "Letter from Paris" announcing that "for the first time in my life and probably the last, I have lived for a week in a great city where everybody is happy". In December he returned to New York, where he took rooms at the Fifth Avenue Hotel to draft "Mollie", perhaps his best known war piece.

Before and after the war, Liebling wrote brilliantly about low life, the press, boxing, and, his two favorite subjects, food and drink. In *Between Meals: An Appetite for Paris* (1959), he vividly described the year he spent at the Sorbonne after he was thrown out of Dartmouth for refusing to attend chapel. In one passage, he recalled Ives

Mirande, a *farceur* who was also one of the great gourmands.

> In the restaurant on the Rue Saint-Augustin, M. Mirande would dazzle his juniors ... by dispatching a lunch of raw Bayonne ham and fresh figs, a hot sausage in a crust, spindles of filleted pike in a rich rose sauce Nantua, a leg of lamb larded with anchovies, artichokes on a pedestal of foie gras, and four or five kinds of cheese, with a good bottle of Bordeaux and one of champagne, after which he would call for the Armangac and remind Madame to have ready for dinner the larks and the ortolans she had promised him, with a few langoustes and a turbot – and, of course, a fine civet made from the marcassin, or young wild boar that the lover of the leading lady in his current production had sent up from his estate in Sologne.

Liebling admired gourmands partly as the result of his upbringing: his father, a successful furrier, took his family on frequent trips to Europe, where his insatiable son, familiar only with the beer gardens of New York, found the gastronomy of the old world irresistible. Yet Liebling also admired gourmands because they had something heroic about them. What ruined the old gargantuan appetites was a preoccupation with the liver, and for Liebling, "the liver was the seat of the Maginot mentality".

Although of German Jewish ancestry – his Jewish father arrived in New York from Austria and later married a Jewess from San Francisco – Liebling was an unabashed Francophile who downplayed his Jewishness and abominated the Germans. In "Madame Hamel's Cows" about the Americans' capture of Saint Lô in 1944, Liebling observed of the retreating enemy.

> During the last days of the battle, I had been heartened by the number of abandoned German bodies in the road; it showed that the survivors were moving backward a lot faster than they wanted, or they would have carried their dead with them. They were unlikable people and they had no business in that part of France anyway.

Germans were not the only nationals Liebling skewered. He was particularly withering about the Italian prisoners he encountered on the beach after D-Day. "They were fine, rugged specimens," he wrote, "as they should have been, because since the Italian surrender they had undoubtedly had plenty of exercise swinging pick-axes for the Todt organization." Disarmed by the Germans in Greece, they had been given the choice of either fighting with their Axis allies or doing labor service for them. "They had all chosen labor service ... They seemed to expect to be commended for this choice ... 'We wouldn't fight for Hitler,' they assured me. I thought that the point had already been pretty well proved. Now they were digging for us ..." Liebling's Francophilia had fully acquainted him with the pitiable shifts of *amour-propre*.

When Liebling went to war he took his peacetime enthusiasms with him. There was his interest in cookery: "Among troops actively engaged, a K ration beat nothing to eat, but it was a photo finish. These components were a round tin of alleged pork and egg, ground up together and worked to a consistency like the inside of a sick lobster's claw, and tasting like boardwalk cotton candy without any sugar in it ..."

Horse-racing also showed up in his dispatches. At Auteuil, he noticed: "Steeplechasing here has the same picaresque attraction that flat racing has in America – an identical atmosphere of engaging skullduggery motivated by avarice." Then there was his delight in women. Describing the liberation of Paris in September 1944, Liebling recalled "hundreds of bicyclists" peddling towards his jeep and among them "pretty girls, their hair dressed high on their heads". Like Ford Madox Ford, another fat man whom women found irresistible, Liebling attracted women by making no secret of how attractive he found them.

> These girls show legs of a length and slimness and firmness and brownness never associated with French womanhood. Food restrictions and the amount of bicycling that is necessary in getting around a big city without any other means of transportation have endowed these girls with the best figures in the world, which they will doubtless be glad to trade in for three square meals, plentiful supplies of chocolate, and a seat in the family Citroën ...

One reason why Liebling's marriage to Jean Stafford never went south was that she found the pedestal he put her on an agreeable perch. Robert Lowell never bought her fur coats. She also liked the foul-mouthed, hard-drinking, raffish company he kept.

Liebling also took to war his respect for good reporting, which he exhibited brilliantly in "Mollie", a piece about a legendary soldier killed in Morocco after allegedly taking 568 Italians prisoner. Mollie fascinated Liebling because he was Times Square gone to war, in much the same way as Evelyn Waugh's Basil Seal, the hero of *Put Out More Flags*, was Mayfair gone to war.

Mollie also fascinated Liebling because he was a dreamer, a sort of proletarian Jay Gatsby. Liebling was a dreamer himself. He loved dive bars, boxing rings, and race tracks because they were the fastnesses of dreams, where he could cultivate his rakish ideal of the man about town. However, in these and other louche locales he kept up the regimen of excess that killed him at 61. (Gout was his constant companion.) Mollie was cut out of the same cloth. As one of his company described him, he treated the Army as though it were his own personal stage set:

> There will never be anybody in the division as well-known as him. In the first place, you couldn't help noticing him on account of his clothes. He looked like a soldier out of some other army, always wearing them twenty-dollar green tailor-made officer's shirts and sometimes riding boots, with a French beret with a long rooster feather that he got off another prisoner for a can of C ration ... He had the biggest blanket roll in the Ninth Division, with a wall tent inside it and some Arabian carpets and bronze lamps and a folding washstand and about five changes of uniform, none of them regulation, and he would always manage to get it on a truck when we moved. When he pitched his tent, it looked like a concession at Coney Island ...

Mollie proved to Liebling how a soldier from his own stomping ground – a dime-store dreamer – could help preserve the dreams of all free men. This was what gave him his special heroism. He was the common man of uncommon bravery rescuing Europe from the nightmare of Prussian militarism. In *Brideshead Revisited*, Waugh might have faulted Hooper for slackness and vulgarity, but Liebling had nothing but praise for Mollie and his plebeian derring-do.

When it came to politics, Liebling did not go in for elaborate exegesis: "I think democracy a most precious thing, not because any state is perfect, but because it is perfectible." If American democracy passed Prohibition it also passed the repeal of Prohibition. After Germany invaded Russia, in the summer of 1941, Liebling found himself walking through Union Square, where "all the free-style catch-as-catch-can Marxist arguers hang out, and all the boys who two days earlier had been howling for Churchill's blood were now screaming for us to get right into the war. 'Well,' I thought, 'we are on the same side of a question for once, any way.'"

This was the extent of what Liebling called "my ideology".

Editors whose ideology compels them to oppose war often have no qualms running pieces designed to demoralize the home front. They will not see their defeatism in any of Liebling's pages. He was too intent on victory. As he wrote in *The Road Back to Paris*: "Some people like to live in a good neighborhood. I like to live in a good age. I am a sucker for a happy ending – the villain kicked in the teeth, the stepchildren released from the dark basement, the hero in bed with the heroine." Thanks to the heroism of people like Mollie, Liebling got his happy ending, which, as this description of the liberation of France shows, he chronicled with an admirable honesty.

> The Fourteenth of July apparently found everybody in the liberated zone happy. Tricolors that had not seen the light since the Petain armistice fluttered over houses and draped window sills everywhere, usually along with homemade American flags and often with signs saying "Vive l'Amerique" or "Merci a Nos Liberateurs". . . . As one thick-waisted old farmer, an ex-cuirassier said, "An armored formation has cut up my best pasture, a promising heifer has gone up with a mine, and a bomb has removed most of the tiles from the roof of my house, but, Monsieur, I assure you, I was never so happy in my life".

The Ghost of George Lansbury

The Lights that Failed. European International History 1919–1933, Zara Steiner. Oxford University Press. 938 pages.

VIRGINIA WOOLF ONCE REMARKED of Gibbon's great work that "few people can read the whole of the *Decline and Fall* without admitting that some chapters have glided away without leaving a trace ... many pages are no more than a concussion of sonorous sounds ... and innumerable figures have passed across the stage without printing even their names upon our memories".

Readers might feel similarly stupefied by Zara Steiner's new history of international relations between 1919 and 1933, *The Lights that Failed*, the latest volume in the Oxford History of Modern Europe series launched by Allan Bullock back in the 1950s. A sequel, *The Triumph of the Dark 1933–1939* will follow. The ground the present book covers in its 900-odd pages is enormous. It provides a comprehensive account of the Treaty of Versailles, showing how this and related treaties played out in Western and Eastern Europe, as well as in the Middle East and Asia. It charts in detail the diplomatic history of the League of Nations. There are also chapters on the repartitioning of the Middle East after the collapse of the Ottoman Empire; the rise of Mussolini; the diplomacy of the depression; the Manchurian Crisis; and the hapless fortunes of disarmament in a world never convinced that internationalism would root out militarism. Preparedness, not pacifism carried the day – though too late for millions who never survived the Second World War that Versailles was convened, in part, to prevent.

Despite its daunting length, the book is worth reading. One does not have to share Steiner's affection for the League of Nations to recognize the usefulness of a book that studies so closely the *supple confusions* – to use Eliot's memorable phrase – that often inform even the best-laid plans of diplomatists.

The plans that Georges Clemenceau, David Lloyd George, and Woodrow Wilson laid at Versailles were never entirely coherent. Clemenceau insisted that the Treaty give France security from German *revanche*; Lloyd George was equally insistent that it enable Germany to rejoin the economic and diplomatic comity of nations; Wilson, the wild card of the peacemakers, whose Fourteen Points generated so much unfulfilled promise, initially spoke of the need for a "just peace" but eventually proved nearly as unmerciful as Clemenceau. "Paris was a nightmare, and every one there was morbid. A sense of impending catastrophe overhung the frivolous scene; the futility and smallness of man before the great events confronting him; the mingled significance and unreality of the decisions; levity, blindness, insolence, confused cries from without – all the elements of ancient tragedy were there." This was how the peace conference struck John Maynard Keynes, the glib economist whose book *The Economic Consequences of the Peace* (1919) popularized the notion that the Treaty was too punitive to be constructive. Steiner contests this, persuasively arguing that the Treaty "was not a "Carthaginian peace". Nor was Germany brought to her knees. Indeed, as Steiner notes, Germany's recovery might have been deliberately delayed "in order to obtain a reduction in reparations". One need only recall the truly vindictive peace that the Germans exacted from the Russians at Brest-Litovsk (1918) to see how comparatively magnanimous the Versailles Treaty was.

Steiner concedes that the Treaty had its inconsistencies and contradictions: "It failed to solve the problem of both punishing and conciliating a country that remained a great power despite … its military defeat. It could hardly have been otherwise, given the very different aims of the peacemakers, not to speak of the multiplicity of the problems they faced, many well beyond their competence or control." The Congress of Vienna (1815) proved more durable, but it had only one architect in Metternich and nothing like the fundamental problems that exercised the "Big Three" at Versailles. When one considers those problems – the fierce ethnic enmities that the collapse of the Austro-Hungarian Empire unleashed in the Balkans, the question of what to do with Poland vis-à-vis France and Germany, the disposition of the Rhineland and the Saar – it is surprising that the Treaty accomplished as much as it did. With all its shortcomings, until Adolf Hitler came to power in 1933, the Treaty did create, as Steiner demonstrates, "a legitimate post-war order that the defeated as well as the victor nations could accept" – though Lloyd George must have spoken for many when he said that "we shall have to do the whole thing over again in twenty-five years at three times the cost".

What is less persuasive is Steiner's contention that "the establishment of the League of Nations, whatever the reservations of the victor powers, held out the promise of a more just international regime which the excluded could one day join".

The League of Nations was the brainchild of Lord Robert Cecil (1864–1958), who once recalled that it was the absence of the rule of law at Eton that first gave him the idea for an international body that would prevent war and promote peace. The chivalrous son of Lord Salisbury could no more abide the bullying of little boys than the bullying of little states. Readers interested in the prototype of the United Nations should read Kenneth Rose's witty biography of Lord Cecil and his siblings, *The Later Cecils* (1975), which highlights the widespread skepticism that the new body inspired. As Rose relates, "The intruder at a meeting of the League of Nations, who declaimed through his megaphone, 'Robert Cecil, you are a bloody traitor', was both rude and wrong. But he echoed the suspicions of very many Tories who felt that dependence on the whims of any international assembly was both corrosive of national sovereignty and an insult to the millions who had fought, died and suffered for their country during four years of war." Churchill, although fond of Cecil, never extended that fondness to the League.

> It seems a mad business to confront these dictators without weapons or military force, and at the same time to try to tame and cow the spirit of our people with peace films, anti-recruiting propaganda and resistance to defense measures. Unless the free and law-respecting nations are prepared to organize, arm and combine, they are going to be smashed up.

In fairness to Cecil, if he was passionate about doing what he could to promote peace, he was free of the pacifism that muddled so many League supporters. He never advocated dismantling Europe's defenses in pursuit of a peace that would only have served the dictators. For Cecil, the League was simply another means to rein in Germany. He made no grandstanding claims for its moral imperative. On this score he was shrewd enough to take Wilson's measure: "I do not quite know what it is that repels me: a certain hardness, coupled with vanity and an eye for effect. He supports idealistic causes without being in the least an idealist himself." When it came to the claims many liberals made on behalf of the League, and still make, Cecil would have agreed with his cousin, the historian Algernon Cecil, who exclaimed: "God help the world ... if the League of Nations is its only hope!"

It has to be said that the thesis of *The Lights that Failed* is trite. It amounts to this: the Treaty of Versailles did not cause the Second World War. Steiner quotes an article from *The Economist* claiming that the "harsh terms" of the Treaty "would ensure a second war" to suggest that this view is somehow widely accepted and needs refuting. Yet readers will not find it in the pioneering work that Ian Kershaw did on Hitler and the Nazis. They will not find it in Hew Strachan's definitive history of the First World War, where he says explicitly that "there was no inevitable link between [the Treaty of Versailles] and the outbreak of a second world war twenty years later". The only person who consistently argued that the Treaty of Versailles caused the Second World War was Hitler. Steiner's thesis is a non-thesis. It is reminiscent of the *ignoratio elenchi* that propels so much academic debate, or what the *Oxford English Dictionary* defines as an "argument that appears to refute opponent while actually disproving something not advanced by him".

This caveat aside, *The Lights that Failed* is a welcome book at a time when we must decide ourselves whether we shall meet the threats of proven aggressors with happy talk or preemption. For those who find the book a little overwhelming, I would recommend reading it in tandem with Ronald Blythe's *The Age of Illusion* (1963), which is at once very insightful and very funny. In studying what Steiner calls "the crooked path to Armageddon" one needs the odd laugh. For true gallows humor, there is nothing better than this from the once hugely popular Labourite George Lansbury, who told the House of Commons on the day that the Second World War began:

> The cause that I and a handful of friends represent is this morning going down to ruin. But I think that we ought to take heart and courage from the fact that after two thousand years of war and strife, at least those who enter upon this colossal struggle have to admit that force has not settled and cannot settle anything.

What is not so funny is that the ghost of George Lansbury haunts us still.

Samuel Johnson: "True, Evident and Actual Wisdom"

The Supplicating Voice: The Spiritual Writing of Samuel Johnson, Samuel Johnson. Vintage. 352 pages.

WHILE TRAVELING IN THE HEBRIDES with Johnson in 1773, Boswell enlivened an otherwise dull afternoon outside Banff by suggesting that members of Johnson's famous Club "come and set up in St. Andrews, as a college, to teach ... in the several departments of learning and taste". Boswell could teach civil and Scotch law; Edmund Burke, politics and eloquence; David Garrick, the art of public speaking; Bennett Langton, Greek; Sir Robert Chambers, the law of England; Topham Beauclerk, natural philosophy; Oliver Goldsmith, poetry and ancient history; and Johnson, logic, metaphysics, and scholastic divinity. He would trust theology to nobody but himself.

This was only fitting. With his prodigious learning, Johnson was something of a Renaissance man in the tradition of Saint Thomas More and Erasmus in an England that had long ago renounced its spiritual inheritance by renouncing the Faith. It was certainly no longer the pillar of Christendom that it had been before Henry VIII went off the rails. So by insisting on teaching theology in Boswell's ideal academy, Johnson was harking back to a world in which theology naturally enjoyed the intellectual preeminence that Newman would reclaim for it a century later in his *Idea of a University* (1873). That Johnson would have made a good professor of theology is clear from this new collection. His spiritual writings are exhilaratingly insightful. Of course, all Johnson's writing could be described as "spiritual". Although a poet, critic, essayist, journalist, travel writer, biographer, diarist, and lexicographer – this year marks the 250th anniversary of the publication of his great *Dictionary of the English Language* (1755) – he was at heart a moralist. As he said in his life of Milton, "We are perpetually moralists but we are geometricians only by chance". To have so many of his sermons, prayers, and meditations together in one inexpensive volume is cause for celebration. "The only end of writing", he once wrote, "is to enable the reader better to enjoy life, or better to endure it." The writings included in *The Supplicating Voice* accomplish both ends.

Catholic readers might be surprised to discover how sympathetic Johnson was to Roman Catholicism at a time when the Faith in England was still synonymous with what William Cobbett called "monkish ignorance and superstition". In Boswell's *Life* (1791), Johnson is quoted as saying that, "a good man, of a timorous disposition, in great doubt of his acceptance with God, and pretty credulous, might be glad to be of a church where there are so many helps to get to Heaven. I would be a Papist if I could. I have fear enough; but an obstinate rationality prevents me." In one sense, no man was less timorous than Johnson – he knocked down the impudent bookseller Osborne with a folio, and Osborne was a big man – but, in another, deeper sense, he recognized how holy fear, which for Johnson was always the beginning of wisdom, might dispose a man to put rational misgivings aside and embrace "a church where there are so many helps to get to Heaven".

On Purgatory, the defining issue of the continental Reformation, about which English Protestants have always been understandably ambivalent, Johnson showed how little he credited the distortions of Protestant reformers. "Why, Sir, it is a very harmless doctrine. They [Roman Catholics] are of an opinion that the generality of mankind are neither so obstinately wicked as to deserve ever-lasting punishment, nor so good as to merit being admitted into the society of blessed spirits; and therefore that God is graciously pleased to allow of a middle state, where they may be purified by certain degrees of suffering". Johnson's own belief in the doctrine is evident from his prayers for his wife, Tetty: "O Lord, so far as it may be lawful in me, I commend to thy fatherly goodness the soul of my departed wife; beseeching thee to grant her whatever is best in her present state, and finally to receive her to eternal happiness." One of the best things in the present collection is Johnson's sermon for Tetty's funeral, in which he enjoins his auditors to "remember that the day of life is short, and that the day of grace may be much shorter; that this may be the last warning which God will grant us, and that, perhaps, he who looks on this grave unalarmed, may sink unreformed into his own". Like all good sermon writers, Johnson is adamant about doing the good deed now, not tomorrow.

On Confession, Johnson told Boswell: "Why, I don't know but that is a good thing. The scripture says, 'Confess your faults one to another', and the priests confess as well as the laity." He was equally sympathetic about what might be thought the sins of the Roman Church. In the Harwich stage coach one afternoon in 1763, Johnson and Boswell encountered a woman who was railing against the Inquisition. Johnson, to what Boswell describes as the "utter astonishment of all the other passengers", defended it, maintaining that "false doctrine should be checked on its first appearance; that the civil power should unite with the church in punishing those who dared to attack the established religion, and that such only were punished by the Inquisition". Indeed, Johnson routinely spoke so well of the Roman Church that Bennet Langton's father believed he was actually Catholic.

Some will always attribute this partiality to sophistry, to what Boswell refers to as Johnson's "spirit of contradiction". By recommending the unpopular doctrines of Catholicism Johnson only wished to exhibit what an ingenious advocate he could be. But this is to deny him his accustomed independence. He was, after all, very High Church and loyal to the Stuarts. It would have been strange if he had not been partial to Catholicism.

Fear loomed large in Johnson's faith. The notion now prevalent, even in Catholic circles, that God is really an easy-going Latitudinarian who wishes somehow to spare us the unpleasantness of fear would have struck him as presumptuous folly. Still, he never neglected charity. Boswell's *Life* abounds with examples of his kindness to those in distress, from the mad poet Christopher Smart, who insisted on people praying with him in the street, to one of his old schoolfellows down on his luck, whose face, Boswell recalled, "had the ruddiness of one who is in no haste to leave his can". In one of his sermons, Johnson takes the respectable to task for withholding alms from a misguided aversion to vice. "It is always to be carefully observed that we are not to refuse any man relief, because he is wicked, but to afford it in such a manner, as may not contribute to confirm his vices; the crime and the criminal are always to be carefully distinguished, and the detestation that we may properly indulge against the one, ought never to harden our hearts against the other."

About the consequences for those who omit charity, Johnson is appropriately lurid. "At that day, when all the generations of the earth shall stand forth in the immediate presence of God ... they, who have looked with indifference upon the calamities of others, who have scoffed at the mourner and insulted the captive; who have diverted the uneasiness of sympathy by vicious enjoyments, and suffered others to languish in pain or poverty ... shall be condemned to an everlasting society, with those beings, whose depravity incites them to rejoice at the destruction of mankind."

The current *Concise Oxford Dictionary* now treats the word *alms* as an historical word, proof, if we needed proof that Johnson's appeals to his countrymen on this score have not met with the receptivity he might have wished.

A surprising omission from *The Supplicating Voice* is essay Number 185 of *The Rambler*, Johnson's great periodical where his best essays ran twice weekly between 1750 and 1752. The theme of the essay is forgiveness and it is one of the noblest things he ever wrote. It ruthlessly exposes the tragic self-love that impedes forgiveness. "He who has often brooded over his wrongs, pleased himself with schemes of malignity, and glutted his pride with the fancied supplications of humbled enmity, will not easily open his bosom to amity and reconciliation, or indulge the gentle sentiments of benevolence and peace." Here one detects something of the resentment that Johnson himself must have felt when he was a Grub Street writer seething under the condescension of lesser, more powerful men. But Johnson repudiates all embittered pride. "Of him that hopes to be forgiven it is indispensably required, that he forgive. It is therefore superfluous to urge any other motive. On this great duty eternity is suspended, and to him that refuses to practice it, the throne of mercy is inaccessible, and the Saviour of the world has been born in vain."

DR. JOHNSON AT 300

Samuel Johnson: A Life, Peter Martin. Harvard University Press. 608 pages.

Samuel Johnson: The Struggle, Jeffrey Myers. Basic Books. 528 pages.

James Boswell's *Life of Johnson* (1791) may be the greatest biography ever written but it is also uneven, unbalanced, and anything but definitive. In the last sixty years, many Johnsonians have sought to round out Boswell's account: James Clifford recreated his pugnacious youth; Walter Jackson Bate explored his moral vision; Donald Greene took up his politics; Jonathan Clark meticulously delineated his essential Toryism; Robert DeMaria reassessed his literary achievement; Henry Hitchens revisited his lexicographical innovations; and Ian McIntyre just completed a study of his relationship with Hester Thrale. Now, to mark Johnson's 300th birthday, Peter Martin and Jeffrey Myers have written new biographies of the poet, moralist, lexicographer, essayist, critic, biographer, and editor who dominated the later eighteenth century and has fascinated readers ever since.

Johnson's life can be seen best as a study in indomitability. He was born in the cathedral town of Lichfield in 1709, half-blind and scarred with scrofula. His father was a bookseller and his mother a peevish, implacable woman who married beneath herself and lived to regret it. Johnson's struggles began in the cradle: "I was born almost dead," he recalled, "and could not cry for some time." At Lichfield Grammar School, he related having Latin beat into him by a schoolmaster, who would cry out as he thrashed his charges: "this I do to save you from the gallows". Johnson escaped the gallows but not debtor's prison. Poverty dogged him all his days until George III awarded him a pension in his fifties. Johnson could only afford to spend a year at Oxford and when he returned dejectedly to Lichfield he suffered the first of his two crack-ups, which nearly relieved him of his sanity. After failing to make a living as a schoolmaster, he moved to London and put himself to school to the arts of Grub

Street, where he gradually established himself as "that great Cham of literature", as Smollet called him.

The works on which Johnson's literary reputation is based include the pioneering *Life of Savage* (1744); the long poem, *The Vanity of Human Wishes* (1749), which T. S. Eliot thought superior to Gray's *Elegy* and "the perfect theme for his abilities"; his great *Dictionary* (1755), on which Noah Webster and James Murray based their dictionaries; *Rasselas: The Prince of Abyssinia* (1759), an Oriental tale featuring some of Johnson's wittiest prose, which he polished off in two weeks to bury his mother; *A Journey to the Western Isles of Scotland* (1733), a caustic account of his trip to the Hebrides with Boswell; a fascinating edition of the works of Shakespeare (1765); and his magnificent *Lives of the English Poets* (1779–81), which Oxford recently released in a superb five-volume set edited by Roger Lonsdale. Johnson also wrote some of the greatest essays in the language, including a series of moral essays for a periodical called *The Rambler* (1750–2) and a series of more light-hearted essays for two other periodicals, *The Adventurer* (1754) and *The Idler* (1758–60).

In 1735, Johnson married Elizabeth Porter, a widow 20 years his senior, who fell in love with the genius of her unlikely suitor, if not his grotesque person, telling her daughter: "This is the most sensible man that I ever saw in my life." Her death inspired Johnson's greatest sermon, which he wrote to bear the seemingly unbearable trial of bereavement. "The only end of writing", he once wrote, "is to enable the reader better to enjoy life, or better to endure it." In his sermon for Tetty, he practiced what he preached.

Since one of Johnson's deepest convictions was that "a decent provision for the poor is the true test of civilization", he made his successive London homes a haven for strays and misfits and often walked the streets at night to put pennies in the palms of sleeping homeless children. Still, when it came to poverty, and the problems that perpetuate poverty, Johnson was no "liberal"; he believed in alms, not government hand-outs. And he also believed in something our own liberals abominate: personal responsibility. "Resolve not to be poor," Johnson urged the extravagant Boswell, "spend less. Poverty is a great enemy to human happiness; it certainly destroys liberty, and it makes some virtues impracticable."

On Monday, 16 May 1762, Boswell met Johnson in Tom Davies's

bookshop and it is from that momentous day that he began to draft his own largely eye-witness account of Johnson's life in London, which he lived in company with some of the greatest figures of the age, including Edmund Burke, Joshua Reynolds, Oliver Goldsmith, David Garrick, and Edward Gibbon, all of whom were also members of Johnson's famous Club, where Boswell heard and recorded many of the brilliant conversations that give his biography so much of its exuberant life.

To show the extent to which Boswell honored Georgian proprieties, Myers quotes several diary entries that Boswell suppressed from his *Life*. These include Johnson's conviction that "unless a woman has amorous heat she is a dull companion" and his revelation that his wife had told him "I might lie with as many women as I pleased provided I loved her alone" – an offer Johnson apparently never took her up on but which nonetheless shows that the two may not have enjoyed conjugal relations. Still, if Boswell bowdlerized the more salacious aspects of Johnson's life, he had no qualms about pumping his hero's inner circle. He particularly hounded Elizabeth Desmoulins, one of Johnson's indigent lodgers, who admitted that "she actually got into bed with Johnson while Tetty was sleeping in the next room", though Johnson "commanded his passion". Most biographers would have been content with this but Boswell probed further, until Desmoulins finally confessed: "I have many times considered how I should behave, supposing [Johnson] should proceed to extremities ... [Though he was] so terribly disgusting ... such was my high respect for him, such the awe I felt of him, that I could not have had resolution to have resisted him". Myers cannot resist adding: "Tetty and Desmoulins, his two Elizabeths, were the closest he ever came to realizing his fantasies about having a Turkish seraglio."

Myers is good on Johnson's condemnation of the slave trade at a time when many of the 20,000 blacks living in London were poorly-paid servants. Francis Barber, Johnson's Jamaican servant, whom Myers believes might have been the son of Johnson's good friend Richard Bathhurst, was a notable exception: Johnson made him his principle heir, after rescuing him from the navy and paying his fees for five years of schooling at Hertfordshire – to the tune of £300. "A black man and naval veteran in his late twenties", Myers observes, "must have been wildly out of place among rural English schoolboys".

Readers of Myers's earlier biographies know that if he is not always fair – he was particularly unmerciful to poor, drink-addled, lugubrious Scott Fitzgerald – he does at least endeavor to present new interpretations of the lives he undertakes. For example, in his life of Somerset Maugham, he showed how the novelist was never entirely comfortable with his homosexuality, which caused him as much pain as his stammer.

Myers departs from the general consensus on Johnson by arguing that he was anti-Catholic. Specifically, he cites Johnson's translation of the seventh-century Portuguese Jesuit Father Lobo's *Voyage to Abyssinia* (1735), in one passage of which Johnson excoriated the Jesuit missionaries on the grounds that they "preach the Gospel with swords in their hands, and propagate by desolation and slaughter the true worship of the Peace of God . . ." Myers infers from this and from Johnson's lifelong contempt for the Catholic French that his subject regarded the Roman Church as "cruel, insolent, and oppressive . . ."

Those who consult Boswell's *Life* will know that this was not Johnson's settled view. Indeed, he clearly saw the appeal of Catholicism, about which he wrote: "A man who is converted from Protestantism to Popery may be sincere: he parts with nothing: he is only superadding what he already had. But a convert from Popery to Protestantism gives up so much of what he has held as sacred as any thing that he retains: there is so much laceration of mind in such a conversion, that it can hardly be sincere and lasting." Then, again, Johnson shared the old religion's respect for holy fear, precisely because, as he said, it "implicitly condemns all self-confidence, all presumptuous security; and enjoins a constant state of vigilance and caution, a perpetual distrust of our own hearts, a full conviction of our natural weakness, and an earnest solicitude for divine assistance".

Myers may be quick to expose Boswell's suppression of evidence – indeed, he is convinced that "biographers, like lawyers, should be required to take a course in evidence" – but, as his handling of Johnson's religious views shows, he is ready to suppress evidence himself when it suits his purposes. Still, Myers has written an engaging book. Thoroughly in command of his sources, he writes with brisk efficiency and has genuinely new things to say about the life and work. He includes a lively epilogue on the influence Johnson had on such writers as Jane Austen, Nathaniel Hawthorne, Virginia Woolf, and Samuel Beckett. And he appreciates how it was often Johnson's vulnerability that prompted his truculence: "the loud explosions were guns of distress", as Boswell nicely put it.

Still, one criticism needs to be made: Myers plays fast and loose with the historical record by claiming that Johnson was "progressive". Simply because he abhorred the "race of wretches ... whose favorite amusement is to nail dogs to tables and open them alive..." or felt that there should be a "more rational and equitable adaptation of penalties to offences" in English courts of law does not make Johnson a "progressive". In the continuing debate over Johnson's politics, Myers sides with Greene, who disputed Clark's claim that Johnson's Toryism consistently proceeded from his lifelong commitment to "order, rank, and subordination". Yet even Greene recognized that Johnson tended to a kind of "skeptical conservatism" and distrusted fashionable shibboleths. The very word "progressive" would have struck Johnson as delusive.

Martin follows Myers in trying to make Johnson more sympathetic by making him more acceptable to our own contemporaries. Yet, in his preface, he admits that he has his work cut out for him: "Paradoxically, in spite of Johnson's iconic status and occasional programs about him on television and on the radio, I have been surprised from spot interviews in the high streets of several English towns that only about a quarter of people I spoke to could identify him. Some wondered whether he was a boxer, or a contemporary of Shakespeare's, or a Canadian sprinter convicted of drug-taking, or a leading Conservative MP."

By saddling Johnson with something as preposterous as "iconic status" Martin signals the tone he means to take with his reader. If Johnson treated his "common reader, uncorrupted with literary prejudices", with straightforward respect, Martin treats his as though he were as ill-informed as the high street English. For example, he makes the claim that "when one reads Johnson, one is struck by how modern he is. Far from being rigidly conservative, backward-looking and authoritarian, he was one of the most advanced liberals of his time." That the word *liberal* as a term of political affiliation and conviction only entered the language in 1801, seven years after Johnson's death, does not stay Martin from making such a preposterous assertion. Were Martin's Johnson alive today, he would subscribe to the *Guardian* and champion the nanny state. This anachronistic misrepresentation may flatter the high street English but it will be of no use to those interested in the real, historical Johnson. Simply because the great moralist was not an inveterate Tory does not make him a liberal, advanced or otherwise.

Martin, in his earlier biography of Boswell, looked beyond his subject's wenching and carousing to focus on the scrupulous biographer and the improbable family man. His present biography is good on Johnson's friendship with Mrs. Thrale and other women – a topic that cries out for more balanced, scholarly treatment – but rather less good on many other matters. In his preface, Martin chides Boswell for neglecting his hero's literary achievement but the incorrigible Boswell certainly understood the force of Johnson's moral essays and made at least one observation that nicely sums up all of Johnson's writing. "His superiority over other learned men", Boswell wrote, "consisted chiefly in what may be called the art of thinking, the art of using his mind; a certain continual power of seizing the useful substance of all that he knew, and exhibiting it in a clear and forcible manner; so that knowledge, which we often see to be no better than lumber in men of dull understanding, was, in him, true, evident, and actual wisdom."

When Martin takes up the work he is either banal or fatuous. About *London: A Poem*, which rehearses so many of Johnson's major themes, Martin can find nothing more to say than that it possesses "energy", "animus", and what he calls "currency in the present political situation". Of the *Life of Savage* he offers this baffling gloss: "Johnson was enraged by society's obtuse, clumsy, ill-conceived philanthropy that organized Savage's 'miseries of dependence' and coerced him to go west" – that is to say, into Wales, whenever the improvident poet ran out of money. Martin's is a characteristically muddled sentence – how does one *organize* misery? – but if what he is trying to say is that Johnson blamed society for Savage's follies, he needs to reread the book.

Martin makes a similar hash of the great moral essays of *The Rambler*. "Complicated human behaviour cannot be reduced to easy choices," he writes. "Nobody can attain perfection, so to judge others is a dangerous and misguided business." For Martin, this is the essence of what the moralist in Johnson had to say to his readers:

don't be judgmental. He sees the import of Johnson's literary criticism in similarly simple-minded terms: "Literature was not for him a rarefied aspect of human expression but part of ordinary and endlessly complicated life itself; it was another of life's pleasures." How can Harvard University Press expect anyone to fork over $35 to read such things?

Granted not all biographers are obliged to be critics, but even on strict biographical grounds Martin is slapdash. Of all the events in Johnson's fascinating life, none is more moving than the amends he made for his filial ingratitude. When Johnson was a proud, frustrated, bitter young man, and without the necessary fees to remain at Oxford, he had no alternative but to rejoin his father in his failed bookshop. But rather than help salvage the business, the young Johnson spent most of his time in idle brooding. Fifty years later, as Johnson told Boswell, "I desired to atone for this fault; I went to Uttoxeter in very bad weather, and stood for a considerable time bareheaded in the rain, on the spot where my father's stall used to stand. In contrition I stood, and I hope the penance was expiatory." Martin's response is the reverse of scintillating. "The scene has been pictorially represented and cited so many times that it has been certified as one of the great images of Johnson's troubled soul." This impatience with his material is characteristic of how he treats many of the pivotal events of Johnson's life.

Readers who expect a modicum of good English from their authors will look askance at Martin's odd use of the word "certified" here. But, then, Martin misuses words on nearly every page. He writes of a "fresh boost to his disaffection and alienation". He claims that the Christian doctrines of original sin and damnation constitute what he calls "Protestant fundamentalism". He refers to Michael Johnson's bankrupt bookshop as "a bookish bower of bliss". Worse, in a feeble attempt to be jocose, he calls the conversations that Boswell so brilliantly recreates in the *Life* "bull-sessions". The *Oxford English Dictionary* defines *bull* as "trivial, insincere, worthless talk". If this is how Martin regards the conversation of Johnson and his friends, why should he bother sharing it with anyone?

There is nothing wrong with trying to make Johnson sympathetic to contemporary readers; but he should not be treated as though his greatness were somehow reliant on whether he shares – or can be made to appear to share – the prejudices of current readers. There is a contemptible vanity in this approach to literature, of which neither Martin nor Myers is entirely free. The literary critic A. D. Nuttall saw the same narcissism in those who wish "to be handed not Milton, but a Miltonised version of their own features". What make Johnson great are not his views about this or that political issue – "Why, Sir, most schemes of political improvement", he told Boswell, "are very laughable things" – but his genius, good-heartedness, courage, wit, and, of course, his profoundly enjoyable, profoundly instructive writings. In one of his greatest books, *A Journey to the Western Islands of Scotland*, Johnson defined the historical sense that gives all learning – including biography – its universal appeal. After visiting Iona, the birthplace of Christianity in Scotland and northern England, Johnson wrote:

> Whatever withdraws us from the power of our senses; whatever makes the past, the distant, or the future predominate over the present, advances us in the dignity of thinking beings. Far from me and from my friends, be such frigid philosophy as may conduct us indifferent and unmoved over any ground which has been dignified by wisdom, bravery, or virtue. That man is little to be envied ... whose piety would not grow warmer among the ruins of *Iona*!

Johnson recommended these ruins not because they flattered the eighteenth-century English but because they testified to a wisdom, bravery, and virtue noble in their own right. Biographers should endeavor to recommend Johnson with the same imaginative humility and stop trying to turn him into nothing more than a mirror for their own self-satisfied faces.

Painted Faces

Renaissance Faces: Van Eyck to Titian, Lorne Campell, Luke Syson, Miguel Falomir, Jennifer Fletcher. Yale University Press. 304 pages.

Towards the end of the first act of *Macbeth*, Duncan asks after the traitor Cawdor and is told that he died confessing his treachery, to which the too trusting king replies:

> There's no art
> To find the mind's construction in the face:
> He was a gentleman on whom I built
> An absolute trust ...

Whereupon Macbeth strides into the royal presence and Duncan exclaims: "More is thy due than more than all can pay."

It is a moment of supreme irony. And yet we can be grateful that the artists featured in *Renaissance Faces* did not agree with Duncan. Van Eyck, Pisanello, Giovanni Bellini, Baldovinetti, Hans Memling, Hans Holbein, Lorenzo Lotto, Ghirlandaio, Raphael, Pontormo, and Titian would all have insisted that there *is* "an art to find the mind's construction in the face" and their portraits prove it.

Curators of London's National Gallery have arranged the portraits of *Renaissance Faces* topically under "Remembering", "Identity, Attributes, Allegory", "Courtship and Friendship", "Family", "Love and Beauty", "Drawing Portraits", and "Portraits of Rulers". Yale has outdone itself in the book's production and the catalogue commentary brims with curatorial insight. If nothing fascinated the Renaissance more than the human in all its abundance, nothing exhibits this fascination better than the Renaissance portrait. Taken together, the book constitutes a kind of illustrated history of that fascination, which nicely complements more full-dress histories.

On exhibit here is Giovanni Bellini's portrait of Leonardo Loredan (1504), which captures the Venetian doge five years before the League of Cambrai went to war against Venice "to extinguish, like a great fire", as Pope Julius put it, "the insatiable rapacity of the Venetians".

Once war was joined, Loredan used the customary state banquet held on the Feast of Saint Mark to urge his compatriots to forget their differences and unite to save the Republic; he even donated his private plate to the Treasury and gave back more than half his salary. As it happened, Venice lost the war, and a good deal of its Italian empire, but Loredan managed to recoup some of his personal losses by extracting 500,000 ducats from Pope Julius – a huge sum in those days. In Bellini's portrait we can see not only the subtlety but the serenity of the man about whom Lord Norwich wrote: "Unlike so many of his predecessors, he could boast no glittering record as admiral or diplomat ... he spent virtually all his active life in Venice." There, he learned the intricate protocols of a state that was notoriously insistent on keeping its rulers in their place. For all the sumptuousness of his horned hat and white and gold silk mantle, Loredan resembles nothing so much as a ship's figurehead – a witty pun on the Venetian ship of state's real figurehead. But in all the years he spent in that magnificent sea-girt cage, Loredan also acquired a certain world-weary sense of humor – and in Bellini's portrait it is just palpable in the smile that plays along his subject's otherwise impassive lips, a smile that must have flashed into a triumphant grin when Julius forked over.

Raphael's great *Portrait of Pope Julius II* (1511) is also included here, showing the imperious patron looking uncharacteristically vulnerable, though Vasari attests that when the portrait was first shown, "it was so lifelike and real that it made the onlooker shrink from it in fear, as if the pope were truly alive". Julius, for all of his enduring achievements, was hardly a popular pope. He was known as *il terrible* – which might be translated, "holy terror". There was little that was pious about him. For Julius, the papacy was a power to be extended and enriched and he saw himself, above all, as charged with its worldly aggrandizement. That he was, on the whole, an able administrator did not spare him from criticism. In her lively history of the building of Saint Peter's, over so much of which Julius presided, R. A. Scotti observes how "few popes provoked more vitriol in their lifetimes. Anti-Julius fury was pitiless. Scurrilous plays, cartoons, pasquinades and diatribes of every sort condemned the della Rovere pope for his bellicosity, his wily politics, and his duplicitous power grabs". Yet Raphael shows that the man who goaded Bramante,

Raphael, and Michelangelo into remaking Rome into what Jacob Burckhardt called "the Classical City of the World ... and the Papacy [into] the pioneer of civilization" was not incapable of introspection. With his downcast gaze and air of being at once a million miles away and imprisoned in his pontifical setting, Julius does indeed seem, as the curators describe him, "a man too preoccupied to perform for the artist for whom he is sitting". No pontiff had ever been shown in so human a light.

An equally revealing portrait is that of Mary I of England (1554), the daughter of Henry VIII and Katherine of Aragon, by the Netherlandish painter Antonis Mor, which was commissioned by Mary's Spanish husband Philip II in the year of their ill-fated marriage. When still a young woman, Mary refused to swear the Oath of Supremacy, rejecting her father's claim to be head of the English Church, an act of extraordinary courage, considering that such defiance cost Thomas More and many others their lives. Withstanding years of court intrigue, she ascended the throne in 1553, after the death of Edward VI, reconciled England to Catholicism in 1555, and died three years later of influenza at the age of 42. The curators point out how "when Philip would not return to England, [Mary] vented her rages on his portraits. On one occasion she was reported to have kicked a portrait of Philip from her privy chamber, on another, to have scratched at his portraits in her chamber". In the portrait here, the look of cold impatient contempt that she turns to painter and viewer alike is arresting. (Could the painter's reformed religion have annoyed her?) Her regal glower confirms the impression left by a Venetian ambassador that her "eyes are so piercing as to command not only respect but awe from those on whom she casts them". Equally arresting is the fact that she scarcely sits on her red and gold upholstered throne, which is shown at a precarious diagonal. Instead, her tense, menacing figure seems merely to shadow it. And to the left of her, beyond the immediate setting, a brooding darkness awaits. Altogether, the portrait is a study in unease and uncertainty, made all the more poignant by the fact that when Mary sat for the painting she was convinced (delusively) that she was pregnant. Of course, she produced no heir. And yet at the very center of the portrait Mor pointedly positions a reliquary set with a Jerusalem cross of diamonds, hanging from Mary's girdle, surrounded by figures of the four Evangelists. For Mary, alone on a throne that she could hardly hold, the only stable thing in her otherwise unstable life was her faith. Philip, for his part, detested the painting. As the curators point out, the English portraits of the queen are much more flattering. Yet in refusing to idealize his subject, Mor got at something deeply true about Mary and her predicament.

These are portraits of well-known figures. But just as engaging are portraits of unknowns. For example, there is Ghirlandaio's *Portrait of a Lady* (1480–90), which shows a young woman before a walled city in an idyllic countryside complete with winding roads, a river, cypress trees, and blue mountains. As the curators note, everything about the young woman seems to exemplify the "grave demeanour and self-restraint" that Leon Battista Alberti, the great Renaissance architect, painter, poet, musician, and philosopher, commended in respectable brides; and yet at the bottom left of the painting the subject's fingers are shown carelessly holding, or perhaps letting go, an orange blossom, symbol of chastity. This sweet-faced, blond, Botticellian woman looks beyond the viewer, intent on keeping her own counsel, but those fingers have a mind of their own.

In stark contrast, there is a joint portrait by Jan Gossaert called *An Elderly Couple* (1520), showing an old man and his wife, looking respectively exasperated and resigned – a Flemish Darby and Joan. The young woman in Ghirlandaio's painting would never begin to fathom the regrets that exercise these two venerable souls. Gossaert concedes as much by showing two sprightly nudes in a badge the old man wears in his cap, proof of the immeasurable divide between youth and age. If one purpose of portraits was to commemorate the living, another was to disillusion the dying.

Still another was to moralize. In *Portrait of a Collector* (1523), Parmigiano, the great Mannerist, shows an acquisitive, hard-nosed connoisseur grasping a jewel-encased Book of Hours (still extant in the Biblioteca Berio, Genoa), while before him a statuette of Ceres, goddess of fertility, lies grotesquely on its back and behind him a marble relief of Mars and Venus shows the God of War taking Venus in his arms for what promises to be a passionate kiss. The moral here is unmistakable: the art the collector accumulates has more life in it than he does, which makes a travesty of the productivity enjoined by Ceres. We must not confuse the amassing of fine things with living. Yet if Renaissance collectors had taken Parmigiano's apologue entirely to heart, we would never have had the hoard of antique art that made the Renaissance possible.

Renaissance Faces includes good essays on the history of Renaissance portraiture by, among others, Luke Syson, Curator of Italian Paintings at the National Gallery ("Witnessing Faces, Remembering Souls"), and Jennifer Fletcher, formerly Senior Lecturer at the Courtauld Institute ("The Renaissance Portrait: Function, Uses and Display"). Syson observes how the genre developed as a result of the rediscovery of antique portraiture – which can be seen at its best in the busts of such imperial monsters as Caligula and Caracalla – and the Renaissance study of physiognomy. Dante, Dürer, Holbein, and Erasmus all followed Pomponius Gauricus in seeing physiognomy "as a way of observing by which we deduce the qualities of souls from the features of bodies". The Milanese art theorist, Gian Paolo Lomazzo recognized that it was the peculiar charge of portrait painters to identify the *passioni dell' animo* (the "passions of the mind") in the features of the face. Fletcher makes an even more fundamental point when she says, "In the context of expanding collecting and connoisseurship, portraits were often valued not for a sitter's identity, which might be unknown, but rather for their technique, rarity, good looks and execution". The people of the Renaissance, in other words, liked these portraits for the same reason that viewers today like them: they make for wonderful art.

Henry's Way

The King's Reformation: Henry VIII and the Remaking of the English Church, G. W. Bernard. Yale University Press. 736 pages.

FOR THE THE MID-VICTORIAN ENGLISH, A. J. Froude's account of the Reformation in England must have come as something of a relief. For the Whig historian, everything about that complex, calamitous history was so reassuringly clear-cut. Henry had freed England of oppressive popery, of what he called "a hocus pocus ... a conglomerate of half truths buried in lies". He had "carried the commonwealth securely through the hardest crisis in its history". Yes, he had been a tyrant, but surely an enlightened tyrant. The English had been under the tutelage of papal religion for too long. Henry broke its spell. "And now", as Froude wrote in a memorable passage, "it is all gone – like an unsubstantial pageant faded."

In *The King's Reformation*, G. W. Bernard revives the Carlylean hero that bestrides the pages of Froude. Henry is once again master of events, intent not only on breaking with Rome but establishing his own Erasmian faith, a *via media* between Wittenberg and Rome. Yet unlike Froude, Bernard doesn't excuse his hero's sins. In this respect, his Henry is reminiscent of the one that rampages through the *Short History* of J. R. Green, who summed up Henry's reign as one in which "all sense of loyalty to England, to its freedom, to its institutions, had utterly passed away".

Bernard is right to return Henry to center stage of his Reformation, though his main contention that Henry was motivated by religious scruples and ready to break with Rome as early as 1527 is unpersuasive. Henry did cite religious scruples, but only to advance his dynastic interests. He was only ready to apostatize in 1533, after several attempts at securing an annulment from Catherine of Aragon had failed. Bernard goes to great lengths to present a consistent, conscientious Henry. But the record is against him. In the progress of Henry's royal apostasy, there was more blundering than premeditation.

Bernard, the editor of *The English Historical Review*, treats his readers to an inordinate amount of historiographical criticism. About one historian of the Pilgrimage of Grace, he writes, with comic even-handedness: "To be fair ... he was writing in the mid-1960s when quasi-Marxist materialistic interpretations were at the height of their influence, and to have given religion even as much of a place as he did was itself boldly iconoclastic." That is an odd use of the word *iconoclastic*. In all events, thanks to Eamon Duffy's *Stripping of the Altars* (1992) and Christopher Haigh's *English Reformations* (1993), we can all be grateful that it is no longer fashionable to treat the English Reformation as though it had nothing to do with religion.

The historian with whom Bernard takes most issue is Sir Geoffrey Elton, who dominated Tudor studies for decades by arguing that the real genius behind the Henrician Reformation was not Henry but Thomas Cromwell, *malleus monachorum*, "hammer of the monks" – though Bernard ends by giving Cromwell too little credit. The immense work of demolition that the dissolution of the monasteries required could never have been carried through without Cromwell's exceptional administrative skills.

As Bernard shows, Elton was not the first to argue that Henry's responsibility for his Reformation was dubious. As early as 1535, the monk John Rochester of Hull Charterhouse claimed that Henry "hath been deluded and defamed by them that have provoked and enticed his grace to take upon him the authority of supreme head and confessed his grace to be of right the only supreme head of the church of England ...". This reluctance to hold Henry accountable for his assault against the Faith and to argue instead that he was the dupe of courtiers grew out of the reverence with which kingship was regarded. Kings were not supposed to be impious or base. It also accounts for the relatively weak opposition that Henry faced. Again and again, when required to swear the oath affirming Henry as supreme head, his subjects acquiesced, even though they knew the oath was heretical. Their tongues swore but their hearts were unsworn.

Apropos the men who did oppose Henry, Bernard is not entirely reliable. He claims, for example, that More opposed Henry not on his break with the papacy or with the Catholic Faith but with Christendom – which is a distinction without a difference. The papal

Catholic Faith was Christendom. Bernard also misreads the spirit in which the imprisoned More sparred with Henry's agents. What motivated him was not any uncertainty as to whether Henry was justified in breaking with Rome but a lawyer's determination to deny his captors grounds for conviction. The ophidian Rich did his level best to coax treason from More, but More continually baffled him. (Joseph Koterski, SJ, wrote a brilliant essay on this sad business in the popular Vintage edition of More's selected works.)

While choosing to make Henry the hero of his Reformation, Bernard neglects to paint a convincing portrait of the man himself or of the period that produced him. As regards the man, in all his six hundred pages there is nothing as revealing as this from Henry's greatest biographer, Jack Scarisbrick:

> Henry was a huge, consequential and majestic figure. At least for some, he was everything that a people could wish him to be – a bluff, confident patriot king who was master of his kingdom and feared no one. By the end of his long reign, despite everything, he was indisputably revered, indeed, in some strange way, loved ... Yet, for all his power to dazzle, for all the charm and bonhomie which he could undoubtedly sometimes show ... it is difficult to think of any truly generous or selfless action performed by him and difficult not to suppose that, even those who enjoyed his apparently secure esteem, like Jane Seymour or Thomas Cranmer, would not have been thrown aside if it had expedient to do so.

Nor is Bernard altogether satisfactory on the period itself. For this, readers might wish to consult David Knowles's *The Religious Orders in England* (1959), which shows how "in no other epoch of English history have purely material interests had such a monopoly ... Readers of the letter-books of the time – of the Pastons, the Plumptons, the Celys and the Stonors – are familiar with this. The cash value of a young man or young woman is canvassed more eagerly than qualities of character or personal inclinations ... The code of chivalry had gone; the code of loyalty and honour had yet to come. It was an earthly, selfish, grasping age." And yet Bernard is right to insist that it was also an age for which religion was vital. Too often historians have assumed that Henry dissolved the monasteries – 550 houses and 7,000 religious, by Powicke's estimation – merely to enrich his courtiers. It might be true, as the Whig historian Hallam argued, that "the participation of so many persons in the spoils of ecclesiastical property gave stability to the new religion by pledging them to its support", but this is to take an incidental for the main purpose of the dissolution, which was to rid England of monasticism. The men whom Henry sent out to report on the monasteries, described by Knowles as "adulatory, pliant, time-serving... ready to accuse or ruin any man... in order to retain the favour of Henry or Cromwell", had told him what he wanted to hear: that the monks were irredeemably corrupt. But since he had already made his mind up on these melancholy matters, it was evidence he hardly required. When it became clear, after the rising in the North, that monasteries would continue to be rallying points of popular rebellion, he only became more determined to destroy them.

Reservations aside, Bernard's book is worth reading. He is good at analyzing the evidence of the visitations, showing that statistical integrity was not their strong suit. He is also good on the degree to which Henry was prepared to play pope in the theological formulation of his new religion, a role which has not spared the Church of England centuries of division and turmoil.

Penelope's Odyssey

Penelope Fitzgerald: A Life, Hermione Lee. Chatto & Windus. 508 pages.

IN WRITING THE LIFE OF PENELOPE FITZGERALD, Hermione Lee has had to face a number of considerable hurdles. Fitzgerald only began publishing when she was sixty; she left an exiguous body of letters behind; and in *The Knox Brothers* (1977), her joint biography of her father and uncles, she wrote an account of the men who had the greatest influence on her that no biographer can hope to rival. Still, her subject also offered blessings. Fitzgerald was a supremely autobiographical writer, all of whose books, even her historical novels, draw heavily on her life. She was not only an author but a teacher and mother, and these other roles greatly enriched her literary art. And since she has still not received the critical attention she deserves, she is an ideal subject for a full-dress, critical life.

Lee turns most of these blessings to account by presenting her biography as a family history, with Fitzgerald as the indomitable heroine whose misfortunes only prove her mettle. She also plots the biography as a kind of odyssey: a homecoming through very rough seas. Apropos this, there is a funny bit in Fitzgerald's book on the Knox brothers where she recalls how all four brothers were invited to speak at the Oxford Union in response to the proposition that "There's No Place Like Home", and yet none of the brothers showed because they were detained in London by an impenetrable fog. In this quintessentially Knoxian anecdote, both droll and poignant, we can see the same note that animates all of Fitzgerald's work.

Fitzgerald's preoccupation with home grew out of an idyllic childhood. Born in 1916, she grew up in a now vanished Hampstead, where, as she recalled, sheep grazed on Hampstead Heath, "poets, conspicuous in their broad-brimmed hats, roamed the streets" and "lamplighters walked at dusk from gas lamp to gas lamp". Her father was Edmund, "Evoe" Knox, the editor of *Punch*, about whom Malcolm Muggeridge observed: "He was a hard man to get to know, an enigmatic person altogether". As a girl of seven

Fitzgerald was sent into "exile and imprisonment" to a preparatory boarding school in Eastbourne, before entering Somerville College, where she studied with J. R. R. Tolkien and won a First in English Literature. After university, and throughout the war, she worked at the BBC, where she met her husband, a handsome soldier in the Irish Guards, who was later called to the Bar as a barrister in the Middle Temple. Although well liked, Desmond drank too much and was disbarred after he was caught stealing from his chambers. Later, he swallowed his pride and took a job as a travel agent, which enabled his wife to visit the foreign countries – especially Italy and Russia – in which she set her historical novels. In 1959, Evoe argued in his Leslie Stephen Lecture that the best approach to the twentieth century was one of "self satire, the ability to see humour in the constant small defeats of life". Desmond was one of the big defeats in Fitzgerald's life, in whom she could find little humor, though she never turned against him. In this, the only thing that matched her fortitude was her loyalty.

In 1941, the couple settled in Hampstead and had three children, all of whom, in their different ways, were deeply attached to their exceptional mother. Some of the funniest pages in Lee's book are descriptions of the tensions between Fitzgerald and her son's pretty Cordoban wife, of whom Fitzgerald was keenly jealous. From 1950 until 1953, Fitzgerald and her husband co-edited the *World Review*, a cultural journal which published, among others, Henry Treece, Robert Conquest, Max Beloff and Walter de la Mare. They also published J. D. Salinger a year before *The Cather in the Rye* (1951) appeared. Raleigh Trevelyan, who would publish Fitzgerald's first book, recalled the husband and wife team of editors with amused affection: "They seemed very different types – Desmond Etonian, she more housewifey. He did most of the talking, but she was the brains". In 1957, to flee their creditors, the family moved to Southwold, on the east coast of England, "a flat, sandy, Holland-like coast", as Fitzgerald remembered it, "with wide skies and bright clouds, beloved of painters and a temptation to those who think they can paint but can't". There Fitzgerald worked in a haunted bookshop not unlike the one she describes in her second novel, where "the Unseen ... could no more mind its business than the Seen".

One of her projects that never panned out was a history of the Poetry Bookshop, the proprietor of which, Harold Monro edited the immensely successful *Georgian Poetry* series before being deserted by the poets whose careers he helped launch. Dying of drink in his early fifties, Monro epitomized the sort of failure that would always appeal to Fitzgerald's interest in life's losers, those whom she nicely dubbed "exterminatees". Indeed, her very first published story, "The Axe" (1974), a brilliantly funny *jeu d'esprit*, reaffirmed the dignity of castaways.

In the early 1960s, again in financial straits, Fitzgerald and her family moved back to London where they lived on a barge on Chelsea Reach – a "battered, patched, caulked, tar-blackened hulk", as she later described it, "heaving up with difficulty on every rising tide". Irresistibly for this novelist of faith, the name of the old wooden barge was *Grace*. After the barge sank, the family moved into a council estate, where they continued to endure much squalor and penury. To help keep the family from total destitution, Fitzgerald taught at the Italia Conti, a school for child actors. She also managed to get all three of her children into Oxford, no small feat at a time when entrance into her *alma mater* had become unusually competitive.

In 1975 her first book was published, a biography of the pre-Raphaelite painter, Edward Burne-Jones, followed in 1977 by *The Knox Brothers*. That same year, at the age of 61, to amuse her dying husband, she wrote her first novel, *The Golden Child*. In 1984 her biography of Charlotte Mew appeared. From 1978 to 1995, she wrote eight more novels: *The Bookshop* (1977); *Offshore* (1979), based on her life on Chelsea Reach; *Human Voices* (1980), based on her BBC experiences; *At Freddy's* (1982), one of the few good theatre novels in English; and then, in stately succession, *Innocence* (1986), *The Beginning of Spring* (1988), *The Gate of Angels* (1990) and *The Blue Flower* (1995), all of which ingeniously renovate the historical novel. A book of short stories, *The Means of Escape* (2000) – which includes "At Hiruharama", a marvelous pro-life story – and a posthumous collection of her literary journalism, *The Afterlife* (2003) rounded off a remarkably prolific career.

Although influenced by aspects of the work of others – the epistemological comedy of Samuel Beckett, the moral intelligence of Mrs. Oliphant and George Eliot, the impassioned didacticism of

Ruskin and William Morris – Fitzgerald learned most from her extraordinary family. Her mother, Christina Hicks, was "a gentle, spirited, scholarly, hazel-eyed girl, a lover of poetry and music, a determined, though not a militant, suffragette". However, months before her daughter entered Somerville – her own college – Christina died. The loss that haunts Fitzgerald's fiction originated from this first irreplaceable loss.

Fortunately there was a tradition of faith in the family. Her mother's father, Edward Hicks, fell under the influence of Ruskin at Oxford, became an authority on Greek inscriptions and worked for years as a rector in grim industrial Salford before being appointed Bishop of Lincoln. Throughout his life, his daughter recalled, his religion remained "the beauty of holiness, quiet worship, and the steady discharge of common duties". Her paternal grandfather, Bishop Edmund Knox was equally devout. Apropos his adolescent religious doubts, he recalled: "When the testing came, and when I heard the question put to my soul, 'Wilt thou also go away?' I was able to see that unfaith could not satisfy my deepest needs." Nevertheless, he was baffled by the faith of his two younger sons, confiding in his daughter: "Between ourselves, Winnie, I cannot understand what it is that the dear boys see in the Blessed Virgin Mary." The "dear boys" were Fitzgerald's uncle Wilfrid, an Anglo-Catholic priest, who was an authority on the apostle Paul, and her uncle Ronnie, the great Catholic convert. Her father, in his retirement, after decades of indifference, returned to the Anglican Church. Her uncle Dilly was the family's sole atheist. With this background, it is not surprising that Fitzgerald should have made questions of faith the core of her books.

In *The Beginning of Spring* (1988), for example, set in Moscow in 1913, about an Anglo-Russian printer whose wife deserts him, the narrator describes an Eastern Orthodox blessing on the feast of St. Modestus, which inspires uncomfortable soul-searching in the hero:

> The priest offered a prayer for the God-protected Tsar and his family, for the Imperial Army ... for the city of Moscow ... for those at sea, for travelers, for the sick, for the suffering, for prisoners, for the founders of the Press and the workers there, for mercy, for life, peace, health, salvation, visitation, pardon and remission of sins. Because I don't believe in this, Frank thought, that doesn't mean that it is not true. He tried

> to call himself to order. Thomas Huxley had written that if only there was some proof of the truth of religion, humanity would clutch at it as a drowning man clutches at a hencoop. But as long as mankind doesn't pretend to believe in something they see no reason to believe, because there might be an advantage in pretending – as long as they don't do that, they won't have sunk to the lowest depth. He himself could be said to be pretending now, still more so when he had attended the Anglican chapel... Why he had felt alarmed when Dolly [his daughter] told him that her teacher said there was no God, he didn't know. The alarm suggested that as a rational being he was unsuccessful...

Here, Fitzgerald captures not the bravado of atheism but the sad uncertainty of unbelief. For herself, she never abandoned the broad church Anglicanism that she had inherited from her family, though considering her fondness for the work of her uncle Ronnie, she also had a soft spot for the Church of Rome. Indeed, during a visit to the Holy Land in 1992, as Lee relates, Fitzgerald took outdoor communion at St. Peter's Church and then "took a perfectly flat, smooth, pale red pebble home to remind herself of it. "I think it may have some jasper in it, and it shines a little in a good light".

Since Lee's book is a critical biography it has to be said that it offers no real insight into the thematic import of Fitzgerald's work. Like Frank Kermode, Lee neglects everything but the highly finished surface of Fitzgerald's fiction. Consequently, she misses the work's deep preoccupation with faith and, even more, the inability of rationalism in all its guises to replace faith.

After winning the Booker Prize for *Offshore*, Fitzgerald became a regular on the literary circuit, attending literary festivals, giving literary interviews, judging novels for literary prizes. If Lee's later chapters include too much of this unedifying folderol – Evelyn Waugh referred to such things as "the penances of eminence which real writers shirk" – they do show how literary fame brought out the rivalrous in Fitzgerald. For instance, she did her best to keep poor Beryl Bainbridge out of the running for the Booker Prize, and this despite the fact that Bainbridge was a loyal friend, whose books brilliantly exemplify Fitzgerald's contention that "Novels arise out of the shortcomings of history".

Fitzgerald's greatest achievement was to show human failure the solicitous attention it deserves. "I am drawn to people who have been born defeated or even profoundly lost", she once remarked. Her books chart the history of that fascination in all its fellow feeling. For anyone interested in entering into and understanding that history Lee's biography will be a helpful though not an indispensable guide.

No Holiday for the Huguenots

The Huguenots, Geoffrey Treasure. Yale University Press. 468 pages.

IN HIS LIVELY ESSAY, "Forgotten English Worthies" (1852), the historian James Anthony Froude had occasion to speak of the seventeenth-century ethos that produced the Huguenots. "The Catholic faith had ceased to be the faith of the large mass of earnest, thinking, capable persons." the good Protestant in Froude claimed, and as a result a tenth of France's population, largely from towns, turned away from their traditional faith and adopted the *sola scriptura* faith of John Calvin, set out in his *Institutes* (1542), the purpose of which, as the Genevan divine observed, was "to prepare students of sacred theology for the study of God's word that they might have easy access into it and be able to proceed in it without hindrance". After very violent hindrances arose from a Catholic France convinced that the Huguenots were not only heretics but traitors, some Huguenots migrated to America, where they could worship without fear of stake or gibbet. Froude relayed the case of one Huguenot, John Ribault, who, with 400 co-religionists, settled in Florida.

> They were quiet inoffensive people, and lived in peace there several years, cultivating the soil, building villages, and on the best possible terms with the natives. Spain was at the time at peace with France; we are, therefore, to suppose that it was in pursuance of the great crusade, in which they might feel secure of the secret, if not the confessed, sympathy of the Guises [a noble French Catholic family], that a powerful Spanish fleet bore down upon this settlement. The French made no resistance, and they were seized and flayed alive, and their bodies hung out upon the trees, with an inscription suspended over them, "Not as Frenchmen, but as heretics". At Paris all was sweetness and silence. The settlement was tranquilly surrendered to the same men who

had made it the scene of their atrocity; and two years later, 500 of the very Spaniards who had been most active in the murder were living there in peaceable possession, in two forts which their relation with the natives had obliged them to build. It was well that there were other Frenchmen living, of whose consciences the Court had not the keeping, and who were able on emergencies to do what was right without consulting it. A certain privateer named Dominique de Gourges, secretly armed and equipped a vessel at Rochelle, and, stealing across the Atlantic and in two days collecting a strong party of Indians, he came down suddenly upon the forts, and, taking them by storm, slew or afterwards hanged every man he found there, leaving their bodies on the trees on which they had hanged the Huguenots, with their own inscription reversed against them, "Not as Spaniards, but as murderers". For which exploit, well deserving of all honest men's praise, Dominique de Gourges had to fly his country for his life; and, coming to England, was received with honourable welcome by Elizabeth.

Here we can see not only the passion but the cosmopolitan intricacy that came to characterize the history of the Huguenots. In his admirably researched and deftly plotted book, Geoffrey Treasure, a former master of Harrow, has written a fascinating study of this resourceful Protestant sect, which reaffirms the central importance of religion in any understanding of French history.

The Huguenots were largely comprised of literate artisans and tradesmen, who, like their counterparts in Protestant Europe, opposed what they regarded as the sacerdotalism of papal Catholicism and embraced instead a deeply personal Bible-based religion, as well as an ethic of studied piety, industriousness, and austerity. They derived their name from the German word *Eidgenossen*, meaning "confederates", which hearkened back to a medieval Swiss federation formed for mutual protection. Residing in a swath of France stretching from La Rochelle to Valence, with impressive majorities in Nîmes and Montauban, these redoubtable reformers were joined by ambitious nobles, especially the house of Montmorency, who set themselves up against the Catholic house of Guise. When Louis de Condé, the brother of Antoine de Navarre, leader of the Bourbons, sought to contest the regency of François II, which had the support of the duc de Guise and the cardinal de Lorraine, both uncles of François's wife, Mary Queen of Scots, a civil war ensued between Catholics and Protestants that would become known as the Wars of Religion. Out of this increasingly bitter divide the Huguenots took shape.

At first, the French monarchy sought to conciliate the Huguenots. After the Colloquy of Poissy (1561), the king passed the Edict of January to try to ensure the religious liberty of the French Calvinists. But the duc de Guise retaliated by slaughtering Protestant worshippers at Wassy and the civil war intensified. When Charles IX again sought to placate the Huguenots by granting them favorable peace terms in 1570, the Guise responded by attempting to kill one of the most capable of the Huguenot leaders, Gaspard de Coligny, a gifted soldier and devout Calvinist. When the plot to kill Coligny was unmasked, Catherine de Medici and her younger son, the future Henri III, prevailed upon Charles IX to retaliate against the Huguenots, and in the ensuing Saint Bartholomew's Day Massacre (1572) thousands of Huguenots were murdered, first by the king's men and then by the Paris mob before the killing extended to the provinces.

The Wars of Religion took another turn for the worse in 1584 when the Protestant Henry of Navarre (the future Henry IV) became heir presumptive, which inspired the house of Guise to form the Catholic League to counteract members of the *noblesse d'epee* rallying round the Protestant cause and to reinforce Catholic support for the beleaguered French crown. Henry of Navarre, for his part, undercut the Catholic League by converting to Catholicism, famously declaring that *"Paris vaut bien une messe"*. Nevertheless, by passing the Edict of Nantes (1598), which ensured limited but significant freedom of worship for the Huguenots, he ushered in not only the absolutist monarchy of Louis XIV, but Richelieu's revocation of the Edict of Nantes (1685), which would trigger the tragic diaspora of the Huguenots from France and leave the country as shorn of administrative and entrepreneurial talent as the diaspora of the Sephardic Jews left Spain.

To this complex history, Treasure brings many psychological, social, and religious insights. For example, far from ascribing the violence of the time to mere fanaticism, as Froude tended to do, Treasure sees it in more nuanced terms.

Religious division led quickly to violence because there were vital issues at stake, but also because men and women were used to settling differences by force. As in the Huguenot's beloved Psalms, as in the Catholic tales of saints, there is a nobility of aspiration, an exalting of the good, of heroic action for the just cause. There are also – as again in the Psalms – recurring notes of anger, calls for vengeance, prophecies of destruction, even torture for those who do not recognize the true God.

Then, again, Treasure is brilliant when it comes to describing the exhilarating sense of discovery that literate artisans in places like Rouen found in the reformed faith. "Huguenots could readily identify with the Old Testament's central theme of a covenant between God and chosen people; with the idea that they were the Children of God, the obligation and the assurance that are conveyed by the common inscription on their temples: *Dieu est avec nous, qui sera contre nous*. They responded to the New Testament's picture of the early church as a distinct community in an indifferent or hostile world ..." For such perfervid acolytes. the traditional faith of the French simply had no appeal.

And yet this is precisely why the Huguenots so deeply offended the French. Contemptuous alike of devotion to the Blessed Virgin and the saints, in which so much French civilization reveled, they struck their Catholic neighbors as worse than heretical: they were unFrench. (Henry Adams amusingly quantified the Virgin's attraction for the French in terms of the huge monetary investment that they had made over the centuries in churches and cathedrals dedicated to her honor, a calculation that would have appealed to Balzac, for whom the bottom line always had an almost mystical allure.) After the Edict of Nantes, the charge of disloyalty may have been relaxed but, as Treasure remarks, "the implication was always there ... the Huguenot did not belong to the France of Clovis, Charlemagne, St. Louis, Philip the Fair and the Maid".

Although Treasure shows the Huguenots and their cause unflagging sympathy, he is never blind to their excesses. For example, he notes how profoundly Catholic Orléans, with its glorious cathedral, became a continual target of Protestant vandalism. "The iconoclastic mob was not content with stripping the churches of relics and 'superstitious' images", Treasure observes, "but went on to damage even the buildings themselves. Behind the theology, the intelligible argument against false ways of worship one sees the irrational rage and greed that would evoke a terrible revenge."

Ironically enough, in making Scripture the center of their faith, the Huguenots were willy-nilly reliant on the inelegant Geneva Bible, which had nothing of the resonance for the French that the King James Bible had for the English. As Treasure remarks, "Huguenots did not have in their Bible the Englishman's opportunity to read what has been called the greatest book in the language, capable of high eloquence yet not far removed from the talk of kitchen, forge or marketplace".

However, this was a trifling stumbling block to the spread of the faith compared to the savagery that greeted the Huguenots on Saint Bartholomew's Day. Treasure nicely sums up the impact of that sectarian bloodbath when he says that it "decapitated" French Protestantism. Only Henry of Navarre was spared and he eventually renounced the Huguenot's Calvinist faith. Many others followed suit, convinced, like the Huguenot minister Hugues Sureau, that the massacre was somehow proof of God's displeasure with the Huguenots and their astringent faith.

If this was the result of persecution on the Huguenots' native French soil, there was another result in England, which Treasure catalogues with understandable zest.

> At a time when England was poised, benefitting from the Dutch model and from its natural resources, to take a leading position in capitalist enterprise and industrial productivity, Huguenots were coming to a land of opportunity. They brought their work ethic with the entrepreneurial spirit that enabled them to found family firms and to respond to increasing demand. They found and catered for the growing taste of the prospering classes for the decorative and luxurious. Among their number were artists, engravers, and print-sellers, printers, paper-makers, booksellers, and bookbinders; furniture makers, wood carvers, sculptors, gun-makers, goldsmiths and jewelers; clock and watch-makers; painters, glassmakers, ceramicists, ivory turners; silk and other textile workers.

Then, again, the Huguenots who found their way to England also contributed to the fields of medicine, law, literature, science, banking, and commerce. George Courtauld, Sydney Smith, John Everett Millais, and Walter de la Mare were just a few of the distinguished Englishmen of Huguenot ancestry. By 1700, 40,000 Huguenots had settled in England – a fifth of the entire Huguenot Diaspora. What Treasure omits to mention is that the Huguenots also produced England's greatest churchman, John Henry Newman, whose mother, Jemima Fourdrinier came of a talented Huguenot family of engravers and paper makers from Normandy. But this is an altogether forgivable omission in an otherwise magnificent book.

G. K. CHESTERTON: ANTI-MODERNIST

Chesterton and the Romance of Orthodoxy: The Making of GKC 1874–1908, William Oddie. Oxford University Press. 401 pages.

"THE FIRST USE OF GOOD LITERATURE", wrote G. K. Chesterton (1874–1936), "is that it prevents a man from being merely modern". When Chesterton said that he doubtless had in mind some of his own favorite authors – exuberant optimists like Dickens, Browning, Whitman, and Stevenson, who had little in common with the decadents fashionable in his youth, or with the modernists who succeeded them. Yet he might just as well have been describing his own work, for *anti-modernity* characterizes nearly everything Chesterton wrote from his paean to the local and the small and the limited in *The Napoleon of Notting Hill* (1904) to his celebration of holy reason in *Saint Thomas Aquinas* (1933).

Of course, one of the paradoxes of Chesterton's work is that its distrust of modernity is what continues to make it modern. T. S. Eliot recognized this when he observed: "Even if Chesterton's social and economic ideas appear to be totally without effect, even if they should be demonstrated to be wrong – which would perhaps only mean that men have not had the goodwill to carry them out – they were *the* ideas for his time that were fundamentally Christian and Catholic. He did more ... than any man of his time ... to maintain the existence of the important minority in the modern world."

In his brilliant new study *Chesterton and the Romance of Orthodoxy: The Making of GKC 1874–1908* William Oddie revisits Chesterton's formative years to show how his critique of the modern culminated in *Orthodoxy* (1908), one of his finest books, in which he set out his distinctly Christian vision, celebrating God over nihilism, joy over despair, the common man over Superman, wonder over sophistry. Taking it as a given that, "we need so to view the world as to combine an idea of wonder and an idea of welcome", Chesterton saw in the Christian tradition a means of acquiring that view by discovering the "romance of orthodoxy". "It is always easy to be a modernist," he wrote, "as it is easy to be a snob. To have fallen into any of those open traps of error and exaggeration which fashion after fashion ... set along the historic path of Christendom ... would indeed have been simple ... But to have avoided them all has been a whirling adventure; and in my vision the heavenly chariot flies thundering through the ages, the dull heresies sprawling and prostate, the wild truth reeling but erect." If *Orthodoxy* is Chesterton's conversion story, Oddie's book is its illuminating exegesis.

Apropos Chesterton's happy childhood, E. C. Bentley wrote: "Family affection ... was the cradle of that immense benevolence that lived in him." Chesterton was the son of an estate agent and his wife, whom Maisie Ward described as an untidy but kind woman, whose "blackened and protruding teeth ... gave her a witchlike appearance". Both parents shared and encouraged their son's literary and artistic interests. He was equally fortunate in his wife, Frances Blogg, a devout Anglo-Catholic, who not only familiarized him with doctrinal Christianity but helped him negotiate the puzzles of daily living. She also saved him from the clutches of Fleet Street's pubs. For years the Cheshire Cheese and Cock Tavern had been his home away from home.

After attending University College and the Slade School, Chesterton abandoned art for journalism and all his life prided himself on keeping the pot boiling. On this score, Oddie is right to argue – with his principal reader, Ian Ker, Newman's biographer – that the greatest paradox of Chesterton's career may be that this tremendously funny journalist was also the author of such first-rate reads as *Charles Dickens* (1906), *The Victorian Age in Literature* (1913), and *The Thing* (1929), which, together with his autobiography and his superb works of Christian apology, rank him with the best serious writers of the nineteenth century, including Carlyle, Ruskin, Arnold, and Newman.

Although indissolubly linked with Catholicism, Chesterton remains a fuzzy figure. Too little is known about the formation of his mind before he converted and about the ways in which he came to prize what he called the "rock of reality" by contrasting it with what Nietzsche and Schopenhauer had to offer. He could see the smash of their philosophies, he said, "as clearly as an inevitable railway smash from a balloon". Another arresting thing about his development was that he came to his faith without benefit of Christian apologetics. "There had come into my into my mind", he says in *Orthodoxy*, "a vague and vast impression that in some way all good was a remnant to be stored and held sacred out of some primordial ruin. Man had saved his good as Crusoe saved his goods: he had saved them from a wreck. All this I felt and the age gave me no encouragement to feel it. And all this time I had not even thought of Christian theology." So it was an instinctive grasp of the Fall that turned the key for Chesterton, not Christian theology or modernism. Oddie is the first biographer to pay these matters the scholarly attention they deserve.

Whether familiar or unfamiliar with Chesterton, readers will benefit from Oddie's insightful researches. The battle between reason and rationalism still rages; and no one measures the stakes of that fight more compellingly than G.K.C. "To understand the development of his ideas in the context of his own age", Oddie shows, "is not only to begin to understand why Chesterton came to write as he did; it is also to deepen our understanding of what it is to live in the modern world."

Foxhunting at Bay

Blood Sport: Hunting in Britain Since 1066, Emma Griffin. Yale University Press. 283 pages.

In *Hunting the Fox* (1920), his celebrated handbook, Lord Willoughby de Broke praised the resiliency of foxhunting.

> When we declared war upon Germany in 1914, many people thought, some perhaps hoped, that foxhunting in the British Isles was doomed. It would appear that the former are likely to experience a pleasant shock ... while the latter ... may be disappointed ... Never were cavalry so quickly or so well mounted as those regiments of Regulars and Yeomanry who embarked for France in August 1914 ... Foxhunting will surely survive from its own innate qualities. The manner in which it has lived through all the obstacles of war time is a sufficient testimony to its vitality.

Lord Willoughby, a Tory radical who owned 18,000 acres in Warwickshire and once threatened to lead a cavalry charge up Whitehall if Asquith and the Liberals granted Ireland Home Rule, might have somewhat exaggerated the contribution of foxhunting to England's war effort, but he was right about what would ultimately decide its future. "Hunting", he said, "depends for its existence on the support of public opinion".

In *Blood Sport: Hunting in Britain Since 1066*, Emma Griffin confirms the accuracy of Willoughby's analysis. Since the eighteenth century, fox hunting had survived any number of immense social upheavals – the industrial revolution, the coming of the railways, the great reform bills, two world wars, the spoliation of the English countryside to make way for the suburb and the automobile – but what it could not survive was a campaign to subvert its public support, fully backed by Labour parliamentarians.

When Willoughby tried to call to mind the typical opponent of foxhunting, he could only see a spoilsport. "Anti-social and un-English in whatever rank of life he is to be found ... he could best be described as the spiritual descendant of that often-quoted band of reformers who wished to put a stop to bear-baiting not because it gave pain to the bear, but because it gave pleasure to the spectators." With the passing of the 2004 Hunting Act, this anti-social, un-English, priggish creature was in the saddle: he had the whip hand; and foxhunting found itself finally at bay.

Behind this reversal of fortune Griffin contrives to see moral principle. "The most enduring argument to come from the anti-hunting lobby was their belief that it was wrong for people to take pleasure in the act of killing. It was not simply the fact of cruelty that offended them ... It was the human participation, and indeed delight, in the act of killing that consistently underpinned their opposition to hunting." But her research shows that there was no consistent argument underpinning opposition to hunting: the argument against cruelty was always alloyed with misinformed class envy, party politics, and, worse, criminal mayhem. Nevertheless, though she ascribes more coherence to the anti-hunt lobby than it possesses, *Blood Sport* is not only a scholarly but an entertaining book, which covers enormous ground with deft succinctness. Professor of History at the University of East Anglia, Griffin is that rare thing: a talented scholar who is also a gifted writer.

Blood Sport opens with the Normans introducing their new vassals to a hunting technique that would permanently change British hunting: the *par force* hunt, which matched a small group of hunters against a single wild animal. The Normans usually hunted a deer or a boar, though the single animal changed over the centuries. In contrast to a drive hunt, where hunters drove their quarry to an ambush, the *par force* hunt pitted human skill against animal guile more sportingly by allowing the animal to dictate the chase. And since no one knew where the animal would lead, the chase became all the more exhilarating.

Griffin sees how this innovation continues to animate the present: "The pastime that grand landowners, pig-farmers, agricultural laborers and elderly ladies congregated in London to preserve in March 1998 may in fact be directly traced to the *par force* hunting introduced by the Norman nobility". The Countryside Alliance, forged to repel Labour's assault on country life, of which foxhunting is so central a part, has indeed immemorial roots.

Between the Norman Conquest and the Civil Wars, wild deer were the preferred quarry of hunters, prized as much for their majesty as their delectable flesh. But since they required large tracts of woodland and rich landowners were unable to keep such lucrative land for such unprofitable purposes, deer became scarce. This was compounded during the Civil Wars by the wanton slaughter of deer by republican rebels intent on flouting the game laws. "A fine meal of venison on the plates of the poor signified the world turned upside down," as Griffin nicely puts it, "a motif endlessly reworked in the tales of Robin Hood". By the eighteenth century deer had become so scarce that deer hunting could only be had in deer parks or in out-of-the-way Exmoor and Scotland.

Foxhunting proved the perfect antidote to this paucity of deer. Of course, foxes, being vermin, lacked the éclat and edibility of deer, but once the enclosures of the 1760s added hedges and fences to the formerly open hunting field, the quality of chase that the fox provided, which now included breakneck jumping, could be much more challenging than the chase the deer provided. Moreover, for a commercial people, necessarily committed to a certain plebeian inclusiveness, the fox had advantages deer lacked: he could be hunted in more places at more times by more hunters and, like foxhunting itself, he was eminently adaptable to different terrains.

This is why the greatest of all foxhunting heroes was not an aristocratic landowner but John Jorrocks, R. S. Surtees's Cockney grocer, who, as Griffin remarks, "took advantage of the opening of each train line to visit new hunting country, each time combining hunting with business – 'hunting one day and selling teas another'".

Lord Willoughby understood the importance of the sport's inclusiveness when he affirmed one of the great principles of foxhunting, which the town-bred supporters of the Labour party continue to dispute: "If [foxhunting] is to retain its vigor, it must never become the privilege of any particular class. Like all other really good things it is either national or it is nothing." For the time being, Labour has made sure that foxhunting is nothing. But there are many other people in the country who are intent on demonstrating that it is as national now as it has always been – perhaps more so, when so much of the traditional fabric of English society is being unraveled by barbarous politicians.

Griffin questions Prince Charles's claim that he "met more farmers and more ordinary blokes [foxhunting] than in any other exercise or sport". For the author, Charles's "assessment surely tells us more about the rarefied social circles in which he customarily moved than about the openness of hunting in the Shires in the 1990s". But the Countryside Alliance, made up of all classes, corroborates Charles's claim. The class argument against foxhunting is founded on misconceptions of class, not on any familiarity with the men and women actually attached to the sport.

Griffin may favor the cruelty argument, but she knows as a good historian that the cry against what one critic called "amateur butchery" had never been popular. "Through much of the twentieth century, the animal protection cause had been confined to the realms of literature, art and liberal intellectual thought; the protectionists' goal to free hares and foxes from the tyranny of hunting was no more than a dream". With Labour backing, however, anything was possible. "When Parliament became involved at the very end of the century ... their dreams were turned into reality; their idealized vision of humane and civilized England proved more powerful than any had expected."

Of course, to claim that Labour's England is a "humane and civilized England" because it has outlawed foxhunting is risible. The 200,000 unborn children that the NHS aborts each year, including children with special needs, exposes the hollowness of that impudent claim. A more balanced approach to the debate can be found in *Child of the Twenties* (1959), the autobiography of Frances Donaldson, Freddie Lonsdale's daughter, who hunted the same country in Sussex that Siegfried Sassoon described in his classic *Memoirs of a Fox-Hunting Man* (1928). "A lot has been written about hunting," she says,

> but much of it is without knowledge. It is too late now to set out to defend the hunting of the fox, but what can be defended is the attitude of the people who take part in it. This is not, as is so often believed, in the least sadistic, although it may be completely callous. Country people have a necessary callousness which is not understood by townsfolk. Anyone who has ever seen a fox pause and look about him as he crosses a ride in a wood in front of the hounds, knows full

> well that his fear is not nearly so great as is that of a sheep every time the shepherd catches him to trim his feet or inject him against some disease. A sheep is cornered and caught often in his life, and whenever this happens he suffers the extreme of hysterical fear. Every time his fear is quite irrational except the last time; and then he is right, because he is on his way to the butcher. When a pig is killed he is caught and held, and a vein in his throat is cut, so that he shall bleed slowly to death to make a meal for animal-lovers. And all the time he is dying he screams, a harsh and blood-curdling scream that everyone on the farm dislikes to hear. He is not screaming because he is dying a slow and tragic death, but because he is being held ... And the pig and the sheep and rabbits disturbed playing in a hollow in the evening sun seem to experience a fear unknown to the fox, who is wily and brave, except in the last extremity, when, of course, one does not know. But death comes to everybody in the end.

What hunt saboteurs most oppose is not cruelty to foxes but Old England, traditional England, the unbiddable English countryside. The hunting debate, at its heart, is about English identity. Griffin is not unaware of this. "Underneath all the hyperbole", she admits, "the defenders of hunting had a clear vision of British society ... [They] stood for the Old England of traditional values, for a society in which individuals, not government, made decisions for themselves, a place above all where tradition triumphed over progress."

But that tendentious "progress" is misleading. The question is not whether England should embrace tradition or progress but whether any progress is possible without tradition. Too many in the Labour camp see Old England as something static, reactionary, superannuated. But Old England, like any good tradition is a living thing. Roger Scruton makes an eloquent case for the vitality of England's rural tradition in his excellent *On Hunting* (2001). Still, Griffin is surely right when she says: "Whether a change in political winds will reverse the fortunes of this ancient sport in the new millennium remains to be seen."

Fascinating Rhythm: A Rave for Wilfrid Sheed

The House that George Built: With a Little Help from Irving, Cole and a Crew of about Fifty, Wilfrid Sheed. Random House. 335 pages.

The novelist and critic Wilfrid Sheed calls his new book "a labor of love, not a work of scholarship, which means that I have been researching it for most of my life". A lifetime's research into the work of Jerome Kern, Irving Berlin, George Gershwin, Duke Ellington, Cole Porter, and Richard Rogers, as well as Harold Arlen, Hoagy Carmichael, Jimmy Van Heusen, Johnny Mercer, Frank Loesser, and many others has provided him with unusually rich materials. That he has gathered them together into a book that reads like inspired conversation will surprise none of his fans and win him many new readers. Full of astute judgments about the music itself and the tunesmiths who knocked it into shape, *The House that George Built* is a delightful companion to an inexhaustibly fascinating subject.

Where did this wonderful music come from? It came from Stephen Foster and Scott Joplin, from Tin Pan Alley and Dixieland, from Basin Street and the Great White Way, from the European waltz and the twelve-bar blues, from the Jazz Age and the Crack-Up, from two World Wars and a Depression, from the American dream and an American patriotism that saw America, not any Old Country as "home sweet home". But mostly it came from the fascination that the Jews of New York's Lower East Side had for the jazz of Harlem. Understanding that fascination is crucial to understanding the great popular music that flourished in America from the 1920s to the 1950s, and Sheed misses nothing of its momentous import. "Music is not produced by whole groups, but by one genius at a time," he says, "and it may be significant that the two families that gave us Irving Berlin and George Gershwin both fled Russia on the same great wave of czarist pogroms, only to find American black people not only singing about a similar experience, but using the Hebrew Bible as their text." There was another factor that made this music possible, which, sadly, has all but disappeared from most American homes, rich or poor.

> Whether it bounced up the staircase or jangled its way over the fire escape and in through the windows, the neighbors knew about it all right, and would be reminded again every time Junior hit the keys and shook the building. Short of a Rolls-Royce or carriage and horses, there was never such a status symbol, with the consequence that although "all the families around us were poor," as Harry Ruby recalled, "they all had pianos". For such important matters, time-payments were born.

Sheed refrains from those flights of indignation that feature in so many accounts of this music. He does not cite Edward Said on the evils of cultural imperialism or bewail the enormities of blackface. He does, however, allow himself one modest sociological observation when he says: "It speaks wonders for those parents in that era that they knew that being a lawyer or a doctor wasn't enough in life. If you weren't a person of cultivation, you were still a bum".

Less a formal history than a series of witty profiles, the book is particularly good at showing the crucial role that the Cotton Club played in helping America find her native wood-notes wild. Apropos Arlen, for example, the man who wrote "Stormy Weather", "Over the Rainbow", "Last Night When We Were Young", and "Between the Devil and the Deep Blue Sea", Sheed stresses that "the rough-and-ready give-and-take of the bandstand had been his finishing school, and the Cotton Club was the name on his diploma, not the Julliard or the Sorbonne".

Arlen's father was an Orthodox cantor who tried hard to separate his son from the secular music that he brought back from Harlem, but Arlen would not renounce his newfound love. Sheed remarks with aphoristic élan:

> Nature had never intended him to be a rebel; it was a triumph of vocation. When I met Harold Arlen in person years later, I could only wonder, as many people must have, how such a mild, unimposing little man could have produced such powerful and turbulent music.

Once MGM beckoned, Arlen obliged with the score for the *Wizard of Oz* (1939). He found Hollywood almost too good to be true. "They brought us money on bicycles", he recalled, prompting Sheed to remark that: "the image of a kid tossing a check onto your porch as casually as an evening newspaper must have packed a positively Norman Rockwell enchantment to eyes used to Depression New York".

Irving Berlin got his start on the Bowery in a Chinese saloon called Nigger Mike's where he worked as a singing waiter. His piano playing would always remain rudimentary. "If the best in the business is that bad", Hoagy Carmichael quipped, "there's hope for us all". Yet the jazz song found its classic expression in Berlin: the score he wrote for *Top Hat* (1935) would become the standard for all standards. Sheed points out:

> At least a part of Irving Berlin was an intuitive jazzman, who had once heard the sounds of Harlem as clearly as those of Hester Street and had, so to speak, finally hatched out the embryonic sounds of his early rags into the swinging majesty of "Cheek to Cheek". "Heaven", as he puts it perfectly, "I'm in heaven".

Sheed is good at showing what a defining influence Berlin had on Cole Porter. The well-heeled Porter envied Berlin his apprenticeship on New York's Lower East Side – "the Vienna of American song", as Sheed calls it – and when he returned to New York in the mid 1930s after living it up in Paris and Venice he was determined to give his cosmopolitanism a rest and write, as he put it, "little Jewish songs". If Berlin, Kern, and Gershwin worked hard to emulate the jazz of blacks, Porter worked even harder to emulate his Jewish colleagues. As a result, Porter's songs took on a new depth – or, perhaps one should say, a liberating vulgarity. For "Just One of Those Things", for example, he lifted the line, "A trip to the moon on gossamer wings" from an ad for mattresses. The sophisticate was putting away his smoking jacket and tuning into the radio, though the WASP element in Porter always gave the wannabe Jewish element an undertone of ironic wit. Berlin repaid Porter's admiration with a touching note after seeing *Can-Can* (1953): "It's a swell show and I still say, to paraphrase an old bar-room ballad, 'Anything I can do, you can do better.'" For Porter the Berlin ballad would always be the top.

Longing was Hoagy Carmichael's great theme. "Star Dust", "Skylark", "Georgia on My Mind", and "Lazy River" all exude a hunger for the unattainable. His songs also teem with an itinerant restlessness. Carmichael, like Porter, might have been born in Indiana, but his music abounds with evocations of other places, from Harlem and Baltimore to Memphis and Hong Kong. Carmichael's nostalgia for places that were *not* his home was characteristic. After leaving Indiana, he moved to Chicago, then New York, then Palm Springs, and finally California. (That this dapper vagabond was a lifelong Republican did not endear him to Hollywood's liberals. It was only their wives who prevented him and Humphrey Bogart from coming to blows.) "Rockin Chair", which became a staple of Louis Armstrong's shows, describes a kind of vagabond's nightmare, where there will be no more wandering, only flies, the front porch, and Judgment Day. Sheed sums up this versatile composer nicely: "Hoagy Carmichael was, like many Americans, a divided soul, part nomad and part homebody, who seemed a little bit at home everywhere, but was probably more so someplace else, if he could just find it."

Sheed has a soft spot for the first of Richard Rogers's collaborators. His take on Larry Hart's fondness for the jug is worth quoting, though it would probably cause certain expulsion from any AA meeting:

> The one thing that dwarfs really can't do is drink as much as the Jolly Green Giant, and Hart's attempts to do so would lead to most of the grief that followed. In the cramped world of psychohistory, nobody has ever gotten drunk just for fun, but only to escape from some problem he or she can't face. So the possibility that Hart might have had an inspired and highly productive capacity for enjoying himself is simply squeezed into a box marked "manic-depressive", from which nothing good or beautiful has ever emerged.

"My Funny Valentine", "Bewitched, Bothered and Bewildered", "Love Never Went to College", and "I Didn't Know What Time It Was", to name just a few of Hart's gems, prove that Sheed has a point. Hart's demons could never stop him from writing like an angel. And he was not alone in his drink problem. His collaborator Rogers could not handle the stuff, nor could Johnny Mercer, whom Sheed calls the "meanest, cruelest of drunks this side of James Thurber". Porter never became a drunk, but that was only because he knew how to abstain now and again. ("For when you lay off the liquor / You feel so much slicker".)

Sheed gives pride of place in his book to George Gershwin, whom he regards as the *capomaestro* of the golden age of American popular music. "You can subtract any other great name from the story", he says, "and it would be basically the same story. Without Gershwin, or his godfather, Irving Berlin, it would be unrecognizably different." Moreover, many of the songwriters "looked up to [Gershwin], as the closest thing to a role model that this happy-go-lucky profession would allow itself".

Ellington was an exception. He may have admired Gershwin's music, but he hardly looked up to him. The model for the Duke's royal ways was closer to home. As Sheed points out, Ellington's father James "had been at various times a butler and a chauffeur to the Washington, DC, elite, both positions that could teach one an awful lot about irony and the way the world works, and perhaps James imparted some of this outlook to his son". It was certainly the case that Ellington "didn't 'beat down doors' but 'he walked through them'". Sheed also notes that what Ellington took exception to about *Porgy and Bess* (1935) was not that it appropriated black experience (the man who wrote *Such Sweet Thunder* (1957) had no problem with anyone appropriating things) but that it didn't make sufficient allowance for the Christian faith of blacks. Ellington disliked Gershwin making light of the Good Book in "It Ain't Necessarily So".

Gershwin, for his part, always let it be known that he envied the bridge of Ellington's "Sophisticated Lady". He was never slow to acknowledge the brilliance of others, citing Kern and Berlin in particular as principal influences. He also gave such younger talents as Arlen and Vernon Duke a leg up. Duke, a.k.a. Vladimir Dukelsky, was a White Russian Cossack, a child prodigy with an aristocrat's belief in his own superiority. Gershwin put up with his airs for the sake of his talent and inspired him to write some of the loveliest standards in the canon, including "Autumn in New York", "April in Paris", "Taking a Chance on Love", and my father's all-time favorite, "I Can't Get Started". (Whenever I had dinner with my father at P. J. Clarke's in New York, we always played Bunny Berigan's classic version on the juke-box.) Sheed points out that Duke could not find a lyric for the song and went to Gershwin for help, whereupon George put his brother Ira on the case, who delivered the immortal goods. ("I've been consulted by Franklin D / Greta Garbo has had me to tea...") Apropos Gershwin's generosity to beginners and rivals alike, Sheed says: "It was as if George wanted all those great songs to be written by *somebody*, preferably by himself, of course, but not exclusively."

The number of truly great songs that Gershwin wrote is impressive, considering his early death at 39. "A Foggy Day", "They Can't Take That Away from Me", "Embraceable You", and "Things Are Looking Up" are just a few of many. He might have done Vernon Duke a favor when he told him: "Try to write some real popular tunes – and don't be scared about going low-brow. They will open you up." (Kern was another starchy composer who gained from "going low-brow".) But what set Gershwin apart was that he was never afraid of going high-brow. *Rhapsody in Blue* and *An American in Paris* show how right he was to recognize that his unique understanding of popular music opened up a special place for him in classical music. Ralph Vaughn Williams paid him a compliment that Gershwin himself would have relished.

> We must not make the mistake of thinking lightly of the very characteristic art of Gershwin or, to go further back, the beautiful melodies of Stephen Foster. Great things grow out of small beginnings. The American composers who wrote symphonic poems for which they were not emotionally ready, are forgotten, while the work of those who attempted less and achieved more has become the foundation on which a great art can rise.

Gershwin did not live to build that great art himself, but what an art it would have been if he had! Still, we can be grateful for the riches that he and all the other famous and not so famous songwriters left behind. *The House That George Built* should inspire younger readers to give those riches a listen and remind the rest of us who prize the great American standards that our love is here to stay.

Organ Grinders: The Italian Front in the Great War

The White War: Life and Death on the Italian Front 1915–1919, Mark Thompson. Basic Books. 480 pages.

The First World War: A Short History, Norman Stone. Basic Books. 226 pages.

In May 1915 Margot Asquith, the British Prime Minister's wife, asked "Jackie" Fisher, Lord of the Admiralty (whom his friends called "the old Malay" because of his oriental appearance) how things were going with the war: "As badly as they can," Fisher replied, "30,000 casualties in the Dardanelles... I was always as you know against this mad expedition." Trying to say something positive, Asquith remarked the recent entry of the Italians into the war on the side of Britain and France. "Mere organ grinders!" was the naval Lord's response. "No use whatever."

Besides showing how blithely oblivious the subjects of George V were to political correctness, this exchange points up how the Italian role in WWI was denigrated from the outset. War historians have only compounded matters by tending to cede coverage of the Italian front to Ernest Hemingway, whose *A Farewell to Arms* (1929) takes place against the backdrop of the battle of Caporetto. In *The White War: Life and Death on the Italian Front 1915–1919*, Mark Thompson, a young Cambridge historian, remedies this neglect with a study that is as pioneering as it is consistently brilliant.

Drawing on an impressive array of English, Italian, and Austrian sources, including fascinating interviews with survivors of the war, Thompson recreates the Italo-Austrian conflict in all its facets, including the diplomatic haggling that preceded it, the character of the two armies, their senior staff, the battles themselves, the home front, and the harsh mountainous conditions in which the armies fought.

When war broke out in 1914, Italy opted for neutrality. A titular ally of Germany and Austro-Hungary, the country that had just celebrated 50 years of unification was still divided. Most people living under Italian rule were illiterate peasants for whom the idea of going to war to recover putatively "Italian" lands under Austrian rule was meaningless. Irredentists, sustained by the cult of Garibaldi, had their hearts set on recovering Trento and Trieste. The Socialists initially resisted a war that they held would only serve capitalists, though, with Mussolini, they eventually joined with interventionists to take what they could of the imperialist booty promised by war.

Giovanni Giolitti, prime minister in 1914, urged his countrymen to sit out a fight for which they were unprepared, but was branded a defeatist and driven from power. His successor Antonio Salandra, a lawyer from a rich landowning family in Puglia, together with his foreign minister, Sidney Sonnino, the son of a Jewish Protestant father and Scottish mother, pressed for intervention. The compliant king, Victor Emanuel III, threw in his lot with his opportunistic ministers. Following a policy of *"sacro egoismo"*, Sonnino sounded London and Vienna to see what each would offer in the way of territorial incentives. The Austrians refused even to consider ceding territory: it would only encourage other nationalists to start making their own demands. Sonnino then turned to London and asked for control of the Adriatic, including the South Tyrol up to the Brenner Pass, Trieste and Gorizia, Dalmatia, Valona in Albania, and the Dodescanese Islands between Greece and Turkey. Asquith, reeling from the Dardanelles fiasco, overrode Russia and instructed his foreign secretary Edward Grey to give Sonnino what he wanted: Italy must be brought in "at once, greedy and slippery as she is". Winston Churchill summed up the Entente's view of their new ally when he referred to her as "the harlot of Europe".

Besides territorial greed, what motivated the Italian interventionists was fear of borderland upstarts. As Thompson points out, "the Slovenes were powered by the unstoppable energy of youth. Many educated Italians worried that their own civilization was torpid and exhausted; in Trieste, this worry sharpened into paranoid fear. History's next winners would prove their strength by trampling on the has-beens" – a fear with which Republicans are now not entirely unfamiliar.

Thompson provides rich portraits of the commanding officers of both armies. Franz Conrad von Hotzendorf was a charming, popular, intelligent man, who nevertheless recognized that Austria's chances of victory were negligible: "Our purpose", he wrote his Italian mistress, "will be only to go under honorably . . . like a sinking ship". As Thompson points out, Hotzendorf "was under no illusion about Austria's ability to win on three fronts . . . When the short, victorious campaign of his public predictions did not come to pass, he blamed the politicians for dragging the empire into war before it was ready".

Luigi Cordona was a careerist who had entered military school in Turin at the age of ten. His ascent was swift: captain in 1880, major in 1883, colonel in 1892, major general in 1898, lieutenant general in 1904, and chief of general staff in 1908. When the king stepped aside and urged him to become supreme commander in 1915, Cordona insisted on and was given absolute powers. There would be none of the rivalries that bedeviled Garibaldi in 1866. Cordona's plenary powers ensured that his ruthlessly unimaginative approach to war met with no opposition.

Of course, in the Great War strategic unimaginativeness was not exactly uncommon. On the Western Front, after the French suffered 143,567 casualties at Loos (1915), Marshal Joffre resolved to intensify the fight: "We shall kill more of the enemy than he can kill of us." Thus was born attrition, "that last resort of paralyzed strategy", as the poet Charles Sorley put it, who was killed himself at Loos. Toleration for huge casualties became a staple of the war. Verdun was attrition personified, killing 700,000 men along a front of fifteen miles. "The folly, the waste, and the stupendous courage of the men who fought at Verdun seem to belong to an age a thousand years removed from our own", wrote the historian Alistair Horne.

The same could be said about the numbing attrition that the Italians suffered in the battles of the Isonzo (eleven in all and all defeats) along the 400-mile mountainous front, which the Austrians carefully fortified before the Italians entered the war. Three-hundred thousand of the six-hundred thousand men the Italians lost were lost in these dreadful battles, which followed an invariable pattern: the Italians attacked and the Austrians mowed them down from their higher, defensive positions. At times, the carnage became so revolting that the Austrians had to urge the Italians to desist. "Italians! Go back! We don't want to massacre you", survivors recalled the Austrians calling out. As Thompson remarks: "If there is any proof that such scenes played out on other fronts I have not found it." They attest to the unique odds against which the Italians fought – which were compounded by the singularly unforgiving mountainous terrain of the largely static battlefields. Lack of camouflage, avalanches, and snow-blindness were persistent killers. On 13 December 1916, Thompson points out, 10,000 soldiers were killed in avalanches.

The historian John Keegan puts the whole campaign leading up to Caporetto, when the Austrians, led by Rommel, finally went on the offensive and routed the Italians, in dispassionate perspective: "In the circumstances it was highly creditable that the Italian army had persisted in eleven costly and fruitless assaults on Austria's mountain borderland. The incidence of an offensive every three months, between May 1915 and August 1917, was higher than that demanded of the British and French armies on the Western Front ... shellfire on the rocky terrain caused 70 percent more casualties per rounds expended than on the soft ground in France and Belgium."

Moreover, the discipline meted out to the Italians was Draconian. After each defeat, Cordona practiced the old Roman policy of "decimation", randomly picking men from the ranks and executing them in a mad attempt to deter slackers. As Keegan remarks, "it is unlikely that the British or Germans would have stood for such 'normal persuasion' and it is a tribute to Italy's sorely tried and dumbly uncomplaining peasant infantrymen that they did". Why the Italians put up with Cordona and his stupid brutality – what Thompson elegantly calls "mystical sadism" – was explained by Carlo Sforza: "The Italian middle classes wanted to believe that a harsh mask and hermetic silence were the signs of genius, and that brutality was energy." Later, Mussolini would harness this same brutality to establish fascism.

The statistics of Caporetto speak for themselves: the Italians lost 12,000 dead with 30,000 wounded; 294,000 were taken prisoner, and 350,000 deserted. Only half of the army's 65 divisions survived the rout intact, and half the artillery was lost, including 300,000 guns, 300,000 rifles, and 3,000 machine guns, as well as 1,600 motor vehicles. Caporetto was an unmitigated disaster, and as Thompson points out, "the prime fear of dissolution" to which the defeat gave rise "survives in metaphor. Corruption scandals are still branded 'a moral Caporetto'. Politicians accuse each other of facing an 'electoral Caporetto.' ... This figure of speech stands for more than simple defeat; it involves a hint of stomach-churning exposure – rottenness laid bare."

What is remarkable, however, is that even after this shattering collapse, the Italians still emerged victorious. In all the annals of war there have been few reversals of fortune more phoenix-like than the Italian victory at Vittorio Veneto. In November 1918, Armando Diaz, a modest, humane, cautious man, with strong administrative skills, succeeded Cordona and with the help of the British 48th Division under Lord Cavan, successfully directed the advance of his armies deep into Austrian territory as far as the Tagliamento River. The spoils of victory were immense: Italy appropriated Trieste, the South Tyrol, Tarvisio, the Isonzo Valley, Gorizia, Istria, western Carniola, and Dalmatia, most of which, however, the Treaty of Versailles would revoke, thus opening the door to Mussolini's belligerent demagoguery.

Outmanned and outgunned, the Austrians lost what would be the Habsburg Empire's last battle. Thirty thousand Austrian soldiers were killed and from three-hundred to five-hundred thousand were taken prisoner. Thompson quotes one Austrian referring to the retreat as terrifying but not chaotic: a "semblance of order" was "maintained by sheer force of habit, a march into nothingness".

The legacy of the Italian experience in WWI continues to ramify. If some historically minded Italians choose to see the war as completing the Risorgimento, many others see it as confirming the deep-seated Italian hostility to statism. It also revived the Italian cynicism of Machiavelli and Guicciardini. In this respect, the most perceptive commentator of the war remains Hemingway, who has his hero in *A Farewell to Arms* confide: "I was always embarrassed by the words sacred, glorious, and sacrifice ... I had seen nothing sacred, and the things that were glorious had no glory ... There were many words that you could not stand to hear and finally only the names of places had dignity." This captures perfectly the regional revulsion from nationalist war.

If *The White War* is the work of a bright young historian proving his mettle, Norman Stone's *The First World War* is that of an established historian resting on his laurels. Readers familiar with his previous work will not be surprised by the excessive attention he pays to the Eastern Front, or by his often spellbinding narrative. Still, for readers unfamiliar with the war, and even for aficionados, much of what Stone writes in this glib overview will be of dubious use in helping them to understand why and how the war was fought. Like A. J. P. Taylor before him, Stone includes much here about railway timetables; he even makes Taylorish noises about the glamour of German power, citing Caporetto and the March offensive of 1918 against the British as "displays of panache of which the plodders on the Allied side were utterly incapable". And yet Stone omits to explain why the plodders won the war, or indeed why they fought it in the first place. Hew Strachan's one-volume overview is far superior.

The Glory of the War Poets

Poetry of the First World War: An Anthology, edited by Tim Kendall. Oxford University Press. 312 pages.

IN 1755, IN HIS MAGNIFICENT PREFACE to his *Dictionary*, Samuel Johnson declared that "the chief glory of every people arises from its authors". Barely 160 years later, after England had entered the First World War, the very notion of glory began to take a beating from which it has never recovered. Wilfrid Owen was perhaps its most savage critic.

> If in some smothering dreams you too could pace
> Behind the wagon that we flung him in
> And watch the white eyes writhing in his face,
> His hanging face, like a devil's sick of sin;
> If you could hear, at every jolt, the blood
> Come gargling from the froth-corrupted lungs,
> Obscene as cancer, bitter as the cud
> Of vile, incurable sores on innocent tongues,
> My friend, you would not tell with such high zest
> To children ardent for some desperate glory,
> The old Lie; *Dulce et Decorum est*
> *Pro patria mori.*

In the trenches, Owen fought alongside the Manchester Regiment, with whom he saw ghastly action. As Tim Kendall, the superb editor of *Poetry of the First World War: An Anthology* points out, "in March, 1917, Owen fell in the dark into a ruined cellar, suffering severe concussion; the following month, several days after experiencing the 'extraordinary exultation' of going over the top, he was blown into the air by a shell and landed amid the exploded remains of a fellow officer whose corpse had been disinterred by the blast". In such horrifying circumstances, it is only natural that Owen should have turned against "*la gloire du guerre*". And yet by recording so meticulously and so faithfully the ingloriousness of war, Owen actually bore out Johnson's contention, for without Owen's poetry and that of the other poets collected in Kendall's excellent anthology we should never know the true human cost of the war. In this respect, we owe these admirable poets a special debt: they mobilized their ancient art to show how this most unmerciful of wars was an assault not only on life and limb but on the very sacredness of the human. Their theme was the betrayal of man's true glory.

Now that we have lived to see assaults on the human ramify in our pro-abortion, pro-euthanasia culture, we can see in the trenches rehearsals of that dehumanization that defines so much of our own society. Yet the poets of the First World War counter-attacked this dehumanization by celebrating the human, often with heartbreaking tenderness. May Wedderburn Cannan, an Englishwoman who spent the war in a canteen in Rouen, exemplifies this in her lovely lyric, "After the War".

> After the War perhaps I'll sit again
> Out on the terrace where I sat with you,
> And see the changeless sky and hills beat blue
> And live an afternoon of summer through.
>
> I shall remember then, and sad at heart
> For the lost day of happiness we knew,
> Wish only that some other man were you
> And spoke my name as you used to do.

That this counter-offensive was conducted in poetic forms that had celebrated the human for centuries made it all the more arresting. Over Ivory Gurney's sonnet, for example, the ghosts of Sidney and Shakespeare hover as a kind of ironic chorus, though the import of the poem could not be more laceratingly modern.

> Pain, pain continual; pain unending;
> Hard even to the roughest, but to those
> Hungry for beauty ... Not the wisest knows,
> Nor most pitiful-hearted, what the wending
> Of one hour's way meant. Grey monotony lending
> Weight to the grey skies, grey mud where goes
> An army of grey bedrenched scarecrows in rows
> Careless at last of cruellest Fate-sending.
> Seeing the pitiful eyes of men foredone,
> Or horses shot, too tired merely to stir,
> Dying in shell-holes both, slain by the mud.

> Men broken, shrieking even to hear a gun. –
> Till pain grinds down, or lethargy numbs her,
> The amazed heart cries angrily out on God.

Gurney arrived with the Gloucesters in France in May 1916, two months before the cataclysmic battle of the Somme began. Previously, he had been enrolled at the Royal College of Music under Charles Stanford, who, although charged with teaching Bliss, Holst, Ireland, and Vaughan Williams, thought Gurney the most talented of his pupils, though scarcely "teachable". The music of his verse has a headlong, colloquial urgency:

> O, but the racked clear tired strained frames we had!
> Tumbling in the new billet on to straw bed,
> Dead asleep ...

Gurney also recognized that the Tennysonian music that had dominated the verse of the Georgian poets before the war could not be simply kitted out for service in the trenches: it would need to be replaced with something altogether different to reflect the dissonant new reality. So in one of his poems about the false euphoria before the Marne, he writes of how

> High over London
> Victory floats
> And high, high, high
> Harsh bugle notes
> Rend and embronze the air.

Kendall's anthology, although dedicated to Jon Stallworthy, who edited the Penguin book of World War I poetry, is in many ways a welcome departure from previous collections. Kendall includes introductions to each of his 27 poets; he adds selections from several unjustly neglected poets; and he appreciates that the war was not simply an exercise in senseless carnage. For all of its ravage, it was a war of liberation. Neither the Belgians nor the French nor the English was willing to live under King Billy's jackboot: each fought to protect their respective sovereignty.

In his moving autobiography, *The Weald of Youth* (1942), Siegfried Sassoon captured this widely shared sentiment, albeit with bitter irony.

> The years of my youth were going down for ever in the weltering western gold, and the future would take me far from that sunset-embered horizon. Beyond the night was my beginning. The Weald had been the world of my youngness, and while I gazed across it now I felt prepared to do what I could to defend it. And after all, dying for one's native land was believed to be the most glorious thing one could possibly do!

Kendall illustrates a far less ironical instance of this same love of country by quoting one of the lesser known poets of the war, Mary Borden, an American heiress from Chicago, who worked as a nurse in the French Red Cross. Recalling the *poilus* among whom so much of her life-saving work was carried out, she observed how "I see them still, marching up the long roads of France in their clumsy boots and their heavy grey-blue coats that were too big for them; dogged, patient, steady men, plodding to death in defence of their land. I shall never forget them." At the same time, Kendall includes lines from Thomas Hardy that profoundly question this otherwise straightforward *casus belli*: "The Sinister Spirit sneered, 'It had to be!' / And again the Spirit of Pity whispered 'Why?'"

In his excellent study, *Modern English War Poetry* (2006), which should be read in conjunction with his anthology, Kendall stresses the ambivalence of the war poets. Contrary to received opinion, they were not simply anti-war. Poets, rather than polemicists, their poetry has to be read with the same care that one would read any other poetry. As he writes in his bracing study of war poetry:

> The truths told by war poets continue to disconcert, not least because they encompass what Wilfrid Owen called the "exultation" of war as well as the futility, the imaginative opportunities as well as the senseless horrors. War poets cannot wholly regret even the most appalling experiences, as they transform violence, death, atrocity, into the pleasing formal aesthetics of art. Poetry, we never cease to be told, makes nothing happen; but war makes poetry happen.

Then, again, Kendall understands what often lay behind the formal aesthetics of war poetry. By including such popular trench songs as "Pack Up Your Troubles in Your Own Kit Bag" and "Oh, It's A

Lovely War!" in the anthology, Kendall shows how their often jaunty defiance of war and war's despair influenced many of the poets in his collection, Edgell Rickword perhaps most strikingly.

> I knew a man, he was my chum,
> but he grew darker day by day,
> and would not brush the flies away,
> nor blanch however fierce the hum
> of passing shells; I used to read,
> to rouse him, random things from Donne –
> like "Get thee with child a mandrake root".
> But you can tell he was far gone,
> for he lay gaping, mackerel-eyed,
> and stiff and senseless as a post
> even when that old poet cried
> "I long to talk with some old lover's ghost".

The youngest of the war poets, Rickword crossed the Irish Sea to join the newly formed Berkshires in Dublin in 1918. For carrying out a highly dangerous reconnaissance mission he received the Military Cross and later almost died after succumbing to a bad case of septicaemia, which cost him his left eye. Although he would publish books of verse after the war and contribute critical reviews to journals, he spent most of his long life (he died in 1982) touting the benefits of Bolshevism. Robert Graves might have had Rickword in mind when, in a powerful piece called "Recalling War", he sought to make sense of his own harrowing experiences in the trenches.

> And we recall the merry ways of guns –
> Nibbling the walls of factory and church
> Like a child, piecrust; felling groves of trees
> Like a child, dandelions with a switch.
> Machine-guns rattle toy-like from a hill,
> Down in a row the brave tin-soldiers fall:
> A sight to be recalled in elder days
> When learnedly the future we devote
> To yet more boastful visions of despair.

In *Goodbye to All That* (1929), his memoir of the war, Graves offended his friends Siegfried Sassoon and Edmund Blunden by turning his wartime experiences into the knockabout comedy of the music halls.

In a typical passage, Graves described how a platoon commander "whistled the advance..." but none of his men seemed to notice.

> He jumped up from his shell-hole, waved, and signaled "Forward!"
> Nobody stirred.
> He shouted: "You bloody cowards, are you leaving me to go on alone?"
> His platoon-sergeant, groaning with a broken shoulder, gasped, "Not cowards, sir. Willing enough. But they're all f—ing dead".

If Graves chose to satirize the conduct of the war, he was never unreceptive to its unexpected blessings.

> And have we done with War at last?
> Well, we've been lucky devils both,
> And there's no need of pledge or oath
> To bind our lovely friendship fast,
> By firmer stuff
> Close bound enough,
>
> By wire and wood and stake we're bound,
> By Fricourt and by Festubert,
> By whipping rain, by the sun's glare,
> By all the misery and loud sound,
> By a Spring day,
> By Picard clay.
>
> Show me the two so closely bound
> As we, by the wet bond of blood,
> By friendship blossoming from the mud,
> By Death: we faced him, and we found
> Beauty in Death,
> In dead men, breath.

Reading this or David Jones's moving *In Parenthesis*, in which he speaks of how "No one sings: Lully lully / for the mate whose blood runs down", one is not so quick to dismiss lines from Laurence Binyon, a Red Cross volunteer, who, before and after the war, was Keeper of the Prints and Drawings at the British Museum and an expert on British, Japanese and Persian art.

Solemn the drums thrill: Death august and royal
Sings sorrow up into immortal spheres.
There is music in the midst of desolation
And a glory that shines upon our tears.

The Angry Governess: Ruskin on Venice

Ruskin on Venice: Paradise of Cities, John Hewison. Yale University Press. 460 pages.

In one of his essays on Venice, Henry James spoke of John Ruskin's writing on the city as that of "an angry governess"; it might be worth reading but it was "pitched in the nursery key". James took particular issue with the construction of *The Stones of Venice* (1851–3), about which he observed: "There is an inconceivable want of form in it, though the author has spent his life in laying down the principles of form and scolding people for departing from them." Then, again, James was unsparing about the idiosyncrasies that riddled Ruskin's views on Venice – "the narrow theological spirit, the moralism *à tout propos*, the queer provincialities and pruderies". Nevertheless, the great novelist loved the city too much himself not to recognize the depth of Ruskin's love. "Among the many strange things that have befallen Venice, she has had the good fortune to become the object of a passion to a man of splendid genius, who has made her his own and in doing so has made her the world's."

In *Ruskin on Venice*, Robert Hewison has written a fine tribute to that passion in a book that is a model of lively critical scholarship. In the first part, he revisits the influences that formed Ruskin's decided but often erratic taste. In the second, he recounts the research, writing, and reception of *The Stones of Venice*. And in the third, he discusses Ruskin's return to the city in 1876–7 and the obsession with Carpaccio's Saint Ursula paintings that prefigured his descent into madness.

There are many good books on Ruskin – Mary Lutyens, John Rosenberg, John Batchelor, John Pemble, and Tim Hilton have all done good work on him – but Hewison's book deserves to be accounted one of the very best. An incisive amalgam of biography, art history, and literary criticism, it is written with infectious gusto and does its complex subject proud.

Ruskin's interest in Venice was first fired by Byron. "Shakepeare's Venice was visionary; and Portia as impossible as Miranda", he wrote in his autobiography, *Praeterita* (1885); but Byron told him of "the real people whose feet had worn the marble I trod on" and bade him seek out "the ruined houses of Foscari and Faliero". When he first visited those houses as an adult in 1841, his response was ecstatic: "Thank God I am here! It is the Paradise of cities and there is moon enough to make half the sanities of earth lunatic ..."

His passion was also fed by artists. In Carpaccio, Jacopo Bellini, Giorgione, Titian, Veronese, and Tintoretto, Ruskin observed how "the preciousness of the luminous sky ... is nearly constant", though he was surprised that the great Venetian painters "should have left us no instance ... of any marine effects carefully studied". In *Modern Painters* (1843–60), he supplied this deficiency with a marvelous vividness.

> Could I but place the reader at early morning on the quay below the Rialto, when the market boats, full laden, float into groups of golden colour, and let him watch the dashing of the water about their glittering steely heads, and under the shadows of the vine leaves; and show him the purple of the grapes and the figs, and the glowing of the scarlet gourds carried away in long streams upon the waves; and among them, the crimson fish baskets, plashing and sparkling, and flaming as the morning sun falls on their wet tawny sides; and above, the painted sails of the fishing-boats, orange and white, scarlet and blue, and better than all such florid colour, the naked, bronzed, burning limbs of the seamen, the last of the old Venetian race, who yet keep the right Giorgione colour on their brows and bosoms in strange contrast with the sallow sensual degradation of the creatures that live in the cafes of the Piazza, he would not be merciful to Canaletto any more.

Turner was another matter. Looking at his *Campo Santo* when it was first exhibited at Somerset House in 1842, Ruskin came away enraptured. "Detail after detail, thought beyond thought, you find and feel them through the radiant mystery, inexhaustible as indistinct, beautiful, but never all revealed." The very inimitability of Turner's Venice convinced Ruskin that he must see the city through his own eyes.

Seeing things for himself meant a good deal to Ruskin. During his extended stay in the city, between 1849 and 1850, which resulted in *The Stones of Venice*, his wife Effie described her husband leaving the Danieli each morning to study his architectural subjects stone by stone. "Nothing interrupts him," she wrote, "and whether the Square is crowded or empty he is either seen with a black cloth over his head taking Daguerreotypes or climbing about the capitals covered with dust, or else with cobwebs exactly as if he had just arrived from taking a voyage with the old woman with a broomstick." Such forays were essential if Ruskin was to make his readers see with the same acuity that he saw. "Senses, fancy, feeling, reason, the whole of the beholding spirit, must be stilled in attention or stirred with delight; else the labouring spirit has not done its work well", he insisted.

It is true that he often had highly questionable things to say about what he saw. As Jan Morris notes in her introduction to the handsome Folio Society edition of *The Stones of Venice*: "Whether he was very mad or very wise would puzzle people always and everywhere, for Ruskin was a character of fluctuating extremes and contradictions, now displaying all the symptoms of the genuine sage, now behaving like a perfect ass."

Yet he was least asinine when sharing the discoveries of his passionate scrutiny, whether of arches or traceries, capitals or cornices, and it was in Venice that he realized that he must make these discoveries central to his criticism. "The greatest thing a human ever does in this world", he declared in *Modern Painters*, "is to see something, and tell what it saw in a plain way. Hundreds of people can talk for one who can think, but thousands can think for one who can see. To see clearly is poetry, prophecy, and religion – all in one."

The problem was that when Ruskin looked at Venice, so much of which was Catholic, the Evangelical in him found a good deal of it abominable; and as Hewison notes, "the violence of his hostility to Renaissance Venice was a form of atonement for the sensual spell the city had cast upon him as a young man". Indeed, Ruskin's reading of Venetian architecture was often unabashedly sectarian, a fact which still baffles many English writers. Sarah Quill, for example, in her useful book *The Stones Revisited* admits, apropos Palladio's churches: "It remains ... something of a mystery that [Ruskin] should have felt so much contempt for both the interiors and exteriors of such beautiful works."

Yet Hewison shows that in this there was no mystery. Palladio's churches were contemptible to Ruskin because they were Catholic. Of San Giorgio Maggiore, he wrote: "It is impossible to conceive a design more gross, more barbarous, more childish in conception, more servile in plagiarism, more insipid in result . . ." He hated Palladio for the same reason he hated Pugin because, as he said, they "lured" people "into the Romanist church by the glitter of it . . . like larks into a trap of broken glass".

For Ruskin, "the entire doctrine and system of that Church is in the fullest sense anti-Christian, its lying and idolatrous Power is the darkest plague that ever held commission to hurt the Earth . . ." Later, he excised this passage but it nevertheless captures his antipathy to the faith that inspired so much of Venetian architecture. Hewison is right to see *The Stones of Venice* as Ruskin's No Popery response to the period known as Papal Aggression in 1850 when the English Catholic Church reconstituted its hierarchy. Ruskin's message was blunt: if the English allowed themselves to be Romanized, they would suffer the same fate as the decadent Venetians.

This is why, as Hewison shows, when Ruskin wrote *The Stones of Venice*, "he set out to make Venice Protestant" by arguing not only that the only authentic Venetian art was Gothic but that Gothic itself was Protestant. Yet by insisting that buildings "are not Gothic unless the pointed arch be the principal form adopted", Ruskin contradicted his own thesis. As the architectural historian of Venice, Deborah Howard notes, "according to this definition virtually none of the Gothic palaces of Venice would qualify as 'true Gothic'"; indeed, "his elaborate structural justification of the Gothic style has little validity in Venice, where Gothic forms in civil architecture are primarily decorative".

The theses of art historians are not invariably cogent – Burckhardt prevented generations from understanding the true spirit of the Renaissance in Italy by denying its Catholic inspiration – but few are as self-evidently preposterous as the one Ruskin pursued.

Still, for all their contradictions, Ruskin's Venetian studies bore rich fruit. As Howard concedes, "it is to Ruskin's sensitive writings, and his delicate wash drawings" – many of which Yale nicely reproduces in Hewison's book – "that we owe the nineteenth-century 'rediscovery' of Venetian Gothic architecture, undervalued since the onset of the Renaissance". Ruskin's work on Venice also enriched the Neo-Gothic Movement. Then, again, Ruskin was a pioneer in deploring the outrages that could result from misguided restoration. Hewison's inclusion of photographs of the Byzantine Fondaco dei Turchi is a case in point. The earlier of the two photographs shows the "ghastly ruin" that Ruskin encountered; while the latter shows the building "restored" twenty years later beyond recognition. Ruskin's campaign for true restoration was incalculably salutary. Indeed, as Hewison shows, it was Ruskin, together with the Venetian Count Zorzi, who prevented a plan of restoration going forward in 1877 that would have ruined Saint Mark's.

But the greatest thing about *The Stones of Venice* remains its prose. It is often elaborate, purple with a capital "P", even rhapsodic, but as Kenneth Clark remarked: "only the puritanical enemy of eloquence could object". Certainly, it seldom failed the majesty of its subject. Ruskin's description of the interior of St. Mark's is as good an example as any.

> Under foot and over head, a continual succession of crowded imagery, one picture passing into another, as in a dream; forms beautiful and terrible mixed together; dragons and serpents, and ravening beasts of prey, and graceful birds that in the midst of them drink from running fountains and feed from vases of crystal; the passions and the pleasures of human life symbolized together, and the mystery of its redemption; for the mazes of interwoven lines and changeful pictures lead always at last to the Cross, lifted and carved in every place and upon every stone; sometimes with the serpent of eternity wrapt round it, sometimes with doves beneath its arms, and sweet herbage growing forth from its feet; but conspicuous most of all on the great road that crosses the church before the altar, raised in bright blazonry against the shadow of the apse.

Whatever else can be said of this "angry governess", he could turn a phrase and set the treasures of Venice to an incomparable music.

WILLIAM TREVOR: KEEPING FAITH

Cheating at Canasta, William Trevor. Viking. 232 pages.

NO ONE NOW WRITING has put together a more consistently brilliant body of work than William Trevor. Wit, inventiveness, artful economy, and profound insight into human failure distinguish alike his novels and his short stories. If in *Cheating at Canasta*, his twelfth collection of stories, he falls short of earlier collections – and any collection should have to be very good indeed to top *The Day We Got Drunk on Cake* (1967), *Angels at the Ritz* (1979), *Lovers of Their Time* (1980), *After Rain* (1996), or *A Bit on the Side* (2004) – it is only because he has set himself a new and more exacting standard. Where once he might have been content to anatomize his Irish characters ("A Choice of Butchers", "Teresa's Wedding", "The Piano Tuner's Wives") or his English characters ("Broken Homes", "Matilda's England", "Torridge") with brisk definitiveness, as if to prove what whole lives stories can reveal, in this latest collection he looks at those things about his characters that baffle the storyteller's art, and finds that it is the stories about them that cannot be told – or will not be told – that are most worth telling.

In "Olivehill", about an Irish Catholic family that sells off the family land to a golf-course developer, Trevor shows how conspiracies of silence undermine families. After the sons of the family broach the sale, their mother Mollie swears them to silence: their father James must not know that they intend to part with lands that have been in the family since penal times. Mollie herself finds her sons' insistence on the sale mystifying. "It was foolish ... Yet her sons weren't fools. It was graceless, even a vulgarity ... yet they were not vulgar." Still, she refuses to protest. Then James dies and the consequences of her silence become plain. What her sons have done, and what she has helped them to do, will destroy Olivehill. Her silence has been accessory.

"Are we at one?" was a favorite phrase of Mollie's husband's and an emblem of the family's presumed accord. Now it comes back to upbraid her. "He loved to use that old expression. He loved to be reassured ..." All the more reason "he would hate what she had protected him from". How "chilling and loathsome it would seem to him, how disappointing". The living may refuse to speak to one another but they cannot stop the dead from speaking. Mollie has a dream in which James tells her that to put a request into the county-council for such a sale will expose the family to ridicule; but still she says nothing, preferring collusion to confrontation. When one of the servants comes and tells her that the family oaks have been felled, she withdraws for good into the "artificial dark" of her drawing room.

Silence is a character in its own right in this and all the stories gathered here. In "A Perfect Relationship", about a December and May affair between compatible misfits, "the reticence they shared was natural to them, but they knew – each as certainly as the other – what was not put into words". In "An Afternoon", Trevor remarks of the adolescent girl who does not realize that the man with whom she is infatuated is a sex offender, "She didn't break the silence when they walked on, knowing that it was special, and better than all the words there might have been". In "Cheating at Canasta", the narrator speculates about a couple doing their all to keep up appearances in Harry's Bar. "It was their stylishness, their deportment, the young wife's beauty, her silence going on, that suggested Scott Fitzgerald, a surface held in spite of an unhappiness". Trevor has never neglected the surface – much of his comedy springs from what Henry James once called "the anguish of exasperated taste" – but it is the unhappiness below that interests him most, the unspeakable grievances that thrive in silence.

V. S. Pritchett, Trevor's only peer in the art of the short story before he died in 1997, once wrote that "unselfing oneself, speaking for others, justifying those who cannot speak, giving importance to the fact that they live, is especially the privilege of the storyteller". This describes what Trevor accomplishes in his fiction, though to say he *justifies* his characters would be saying too much. Like Joyce, Trevor is fascinated by the psychology of baseness. In "Men of Ireland", a story about an Irish exile who returns to his native land to shake down a priest who tried to reform him when he was a boy, he describes a rogue's progress which even the most forbearing storyteller would have difficulty justifying.

The heroine of "The Room" is another hard case. After finding out that her husband has been linked to the death of a young prostitute, Katherine begins a nine-year affair with another married man. Rather than leave her husband, she vouches for him, even though she knows his alibi is false. When police incompetence results in his acquittal, she continues to live with him, only sharing "the room" of her adulterous lover for certain set assignations. How?

> For all nine years there'd been restraint. There'd been no asking to be told, no asking for promises that the truth was what she heard. There'd been no asking about the girl, how she'd dressed, her voice, her face, and if she only sat there talking ... There'd been no asking if there had really been the usual misery on the Northern line, the waiting for a taxi in the rain. For all nine years ... there had been silence in their ordinary exchanges, in conversation, in making love, in weekend walks and summer trips abroad. For all nine years love had been there, and more than just a comforter, too intense for that ...

Here again we encounter silence. The travesty of love that Katherine cobbles together out of her moral bewilderment is indeed ineffable.

"The Children" shows marriage in a less sordid light. When Connie, a young girl, loses her mother, her father Robert notices that her opposition to his remarriage is stronger than he had expected. It brings him and his fiancée up short to see such fierce undiminishing love. It forces Teresa, the fiancée, to recognize not only her step-daughter's sensitivities but her own insensitivities. "Teresa confessed that nothing was as tidy as she'd imagined. There were no rights that cancelled other rights, less comfort than she'd thought for the rejected and the widowed, no fairness either." It also forces Robert to undergo a crash course in empathy. "Time would gather up the ends, and see to it that his daughter's honouring of a memory was love that mattered also, and even mattered more."

"Faith" provides another look at family relations. Bartholomew, a Church of Ireland clergyman, is marched about by Hester, his domineering sister, who puts asunder what she considers his "silly" engagement, secures for him the living of a well-endowed, if sparsely attended church, where "they're managing with a recorded service", and takes charge of his new residence. About this singular hero,

Trevor remarks, "Often he didn't want to talk about what had to be talked about, hoping that whatever it was would go away of its own accord". Bartholomew can hardly be blamed for not wanting his story told.

But then Hester falls mortally ill and he begins to face what he has spent a lifetime dodging. He acknowledges that Hester scared off his fiancée deliberately for her own selfish purposes; he admits that he is losing his faith. He admits how unfamiliar he finds the sister who has held such sway over his life. "He didn't know her; that thought came, which never had before. Her severity, the outspokenness that was natural to her, told too little". Yet the imminence of death changes that. His own faith might be rattled, but he recognizes that "the intensity of her faith, the sureness of her trust, was unaffected by the pain she suffered". In his sister's acceptance of death, the brother comes to admire "the mercy of her tranquility", which he finds "a miracle that was real ... Heaven enough, and more than angels". Here is a droll twist on the bedside conversion.

The last story in the collection, *"Folie a Deux"*, is about two estranged friends, bound by an act of youthful ignominy, who accidentally meet up again in Paris. Wilby tries to mitigate what Anthony recognizes is immitigable.

> For Anthony, the betrayal matters, the folly, the carelessness that would have been forgiven, the cruelty. It mattered in the silence – while they watched, while they clambered over the shingle and the rocks, while they passed through the gorse field. It matters now. The haunted sea is all the truth there is for Anthony, what he honours because it matters still.

Some regard guilt as chimerical; Trevor recognizes that without it there would be neither penance nor redemption. In "Old Flame", a story about the often thankless demands of loyalty, Trevor remarks about his beleaguered hero: "No one told him that keeping faith could be as cruel as confessing faithlessness." By endeavoring to tell stories that his characters wish untold or tell falsely or cannot tell, Trevor keeps faith with the art of storytelling. He also lays bare the treachery of the human heart. *Cheating at Canasta* is a superb collection and splendid proof that the old master has new life in him yet.

The "Buried Life" of T. S. Eliot

T. S. Eliot, Craig Raine. Oxford University Press. 202 pages.

For the bookmen who ruled literary London in the years after the First World War T. S. Eliot was an absurdity. Arthur Waugh spoke for many of his generation when he wrote mockingly of the poet: "It was a classic custom in the family hall, when a feast was at its height, to display a drunken slave among the sons of the household, to the end that they, being ashamed at the ignominious folly of his gesticulations, might determine never to be tempted into such a pitiable condition themselves. The custom has its advantages; for the wisdom of the younger generation was found to be fostered more surely by a single example than by a world of homily and precept." In *A Little Learning*, Evelyn Waugh remarked of his father's not altogether facetious jest: "This was the function he predicted for the future idol of the academies."

From the 1920s until the 1960s, Eliot's influence was indeed immense. As poet, critic, and publisher, he set the literary standards of his age as decisively as Samuel Johnson had set those of his. Poets and critics around the world put themselves to school to his exacting discriminations. Then, with the collapse of academic standards in the 1960s and the rise of grievance as the postmodernist university's sole governing principle, Eliot fell out of favor. If Arthur Waugh wanted him exhibited as a literary delinquent whose antics should dissuade the young from unseemly experimentation, the custodians of the new political correctness continue to hold him up as an example of anti-Semitism, misogyny, and fascism.

The editor of Oxford's Lives and Legacies series should be commended for commissioning the poet and critic Craig Raine to revisit Eliot's work. If there is any justice in the world, Raine's contribution will usher in a more balanced assessment of a man who hardly deserves the obloquy to which he has been subjected. In the same series Paul Addison rescued Churchill from his unfair detractors; Raine has done an equally adroit job of rescuing Eliot.

Raine is a shrewd, learned, entertaining critic. His readings of "The Waste Land" (1922), "The Hollow Men" (1925), and "Ash Wednesday" (1930) reacquaint us with a dazzling poet. Over the years, Eliot has attracted many good commentators. For a figure who is supposed to be riddled with misogyny, it is interesting that two of his very best commentators have been women: Helen Gardner and Lyndall Gordon. Raine now joins that distinguished company.

He shows Eliot's work preoccupied first and last with the "buried life", a theme which Eliot borrowed from a poem by Matthew Arnold, whom Raine convincingly depicts as Eliot's "poetic father figure". From *Prufrock* (1917) to *The Elder Statesman* (1958) Eliot plumbed what Arnold called "the unregarded River of our Life". But whereas Arnold saw only unfelt emotions in the "buried life", Eliot saw things "more distant than the stars and nearer than the eye"; "time present and time past"; "motives late revealed"; "the intolerable wrestle with words and meanings"; and perhaps most insistently, "the loud lament of the disconsolate chimera". Here is a thesis that elucidates the full range of Eliot's art.

Eliot rebelled against Arnold's influence by extolling what he considered the classical virtues of reason and objectivity against the romantic vices of emotionalism and subjectivity. This is why Eliot called himself a "classicist in literature". It is also at the heart of his idea of the "objective correlative", his insistence, as Raine says, that "the emotion of a character should be bodied forth in the action" – as Lady Macbeth's guilt is bodied forth in her sleepwalking. In *After Strange Gods* (1933) Eliot described some of the characteristic fallacies of romantic art: "it is a cardinal point of faith in a romantic age to believe that there is something admirable in violent emotion for its own sake". Worse, "many people act upon the assumption that the mere accumulation of 'experiences', including literary and intellectual experiences, as well as amorous and picaresque ones, is – like the accumulation of money – valuable in itself". For Eliot this would ensure, as it has ensured, a meretricious art judged not on its objective merits but on the acceptability of its experiences, its "point of view". And, indeed, it is in accordance with such subjective standards that Eliot's own art is now misjudged.

Eliot never depreciated emotion *per se*. As a young man he might have famously asserted that "Poetry is not a turning loose of emotion, but an escape from emotion; it is not the expression of personality, but an escape from personality". Yet even in that early essay, "Tradition and the Individual Talent" (1919), he was careful to qualify: "But, of course, only those who have personality and emotions know what it means to want to escape from these things." Eliot was skeptical of emotions not because he felt them too little but because he felt them too much. This is why renunciation had such an appeal for him, and why, in so many of his poems, that appeal is met with prayer. For example, in "Marina" (1930):

> This form, this face, this life
> Living to live in a world of time beyond me; let me
> Resign my life for this life, my speech for that unspoken,
> The awakened, lips parted, the hope, the new ships.

Many have been baffled or repulsed by Eliot's spirituality. His conversion to Anglo-Catholicism in 1930 continues to be seen in many quarters as an act of reactionary deviance. Some have even suggested that between the subversive poet and the orthodox critic there was something almost schizophrenic. In the undeniable inconsistencies of Eliot's work Raine sees not schizophrenia but honesty.

> His attitude to religion was publicly uncompromising: he didn't want religion to make any compromise with the secular impulse. In "Religion and Literature" (1935), he is certain that modern literature is "simply unaware of, simply cannot understand the meaning of, the primacy of the supernatural over the natural life". *Ash Wednesday* argues precisely this position – the primacy of the supernatural over the natural life – and *fails*. It is possible to argue that, therefore, the poetry is truer to reality than Eliot's theoretical position. But the difficulty of true religion was precisely what attracted Eliot. Its requirements are intractable, absolute – and difficult to fulfill. Were they not difficult, they would not be worth struggling towards.

Regarding the charge of anti-Semitism leveled at Eliot by Anthony Julius, George Steiner, and Louis Menand, Raine demonstrates that the charge has been brought by malice. In addition to being sloppy prosecutors, Julius and his friends are incompetent literary critics. "Burbank with a Baedeker: Bleinstein with a Cigar" (1917), for example, as Raine shows, "is not an anti-Semitic poem, but a poem about anti-Semitism". Eliot's critics need to familiarize themselves with the dramatic monologue. (If their reasoning were applied to other poets, the authors of "My Last Duchess" and "The Farmer's Bride" would have to be charged with very dark tendencies.)

Raine's sympathy for his subject is not unqualified. He scoffs at what Eliot called "dissociation of sensibility" or his theory that between Donne and Tennyson thought and feeling parted company and never reunited. For Raine, "Eliot's theory is surely a myth – almost Wildean in its sacrifice of rigour to éclat..." Most readers will agree. The poetry of Pope, Johnson, Clare, Wordsworth, Coleridge, Keats, Browning, and even Tennyson makes mincemeat of such a theory.

Raine is equally dismissive of Eliot's theory that "genuine poetry can communicate before it is understood":

> If you do not speak a language, you may communicate by bodily gesture – smiling or tearing your hair – because these gestures are understood. But without *any* understanding, no communication is possible. You are in Tbilisi airport. You don't speak Georgian. An announcement in Georgian on the (expressionless, unsmiling) public address system tells you that your luggage has gone to Riga rather than Heathrow. At that moment, you won't get the joke. You won't see the funny side until much later.

This is amusing but unconvincing. Poetry is not analogous to an announcement on a public address system, and its meaning extends beyond the whereabouts of bags. Poetry that also happens to be difficult – Eliot's own poetry is a good example – *must* communicate before it is understood. Not, perhaps, all or even most of its meaning but enough to prompt the reader to reread, attend more closely, delve more deeply. Understanding, like the knowledge it attempts to acquire, is a matter of degrees. If the meaning of poetry could be communicated only *after* it was understood, our aesthetic experience should be radically impoverished. Not knowing a thing, after all, finding it mystifying, finding it intriguing but baffling is often as much a part of understanding as knowing a thing. We know that we do not know. But this is a minor quibble.

Raine is more frequently right than wrong. He is right to see that what the postmodernist academy finds most objectionable about Eliot is the "fundamental polarity" he proposes between "a theological view of the world, in which every action is significant and carries moral consequence, and a humanist view of the world, in which every action is drained of significance because there is neither salvation nor damnation, neither a heaven nor a hell, only moral opinion". Elsewhere he says, accurately enough: "I think Eliot writes acutely about sex – in all its variety. He does acute justice to the variety of its disappointments". There is no more honest catalogue of the sorrows of sex than *The Waste Land*. In another passage he says, "Eliot's religious writings demonstrate the angularity and awkwardness, the unbiddable intransigence of sincere belief". This is true: there was nothing of the Vicar of Bray about Eliot. As his *Selected Essays* (1951) abundantly shows, he enjoyed going against the grain.

In excavating the buried life of Eliot's art, Raine uncovers the unfamiliar compound ghost of genius. He has written a book that all Eliot fans and all Eliot foes will find an instructive, witty read.

Reclaiming the Age of Chivalry

Medievalism: The Middle Ages in Modern England, Michael Alexander. Yale University Press. 306 pages.

In *Medievalism: The Middle Ages in Modern England*, Michael Alexander has written a superb study, showing how differing versions of the Middle Ages helped shape the art, architecture and literature of modern England. This is a subject of enormous scope; yet rather than march his readers through an exhaustive survey, Alexander provides a witty overview of representative painters, architects and writers whose medievalism helped them negotiate their modernity. Printed on good heavy paper and handsomely illustrated, the book nicely complements Alexander's sprightly commentary.

The former chair of the English department at St. Andrews, Alexander traces the modern fascination with things medieval to the late eighteenth century, to the antiquarianism of Horace Walpole and Thomas Percy, Macpherson's *Ossian* (1760), and Burke's rococo elegy to Marie Antoinette in his *Reflections on the French Revolution* (1790–1).

> Oh! What a revolution! And what a heart I must have to contemplate without emotion that elevation and that fall! ... little did I dream that I should have lived to see such disasters fallen upon her in a nation of gallant men, in a nation of men of honour, and of cavaliers. I thought ten thousand swords must have leaped from their scabbards to avenge even a look that threatened her with insult. But the age of chivalry is gone. That of sophisters, economists, and calculators, has succeeded and the glory of Europe is extinguished for ever ...

This pitting of the present against an exemplary past set the stage for Sir Walter Scott, Pugin, the Pre-Raphaelites, Ruskin, and the Gothic Revival. If the age of chivalry was gone in France, it could be revived in England. As Alexander remarks, "the Medieval Revival was always interested in how people should live now in the present as well as how they had lived in the past". The revival could simply have been an episode in the history of nostalgia – always compounded by the ambivalent legacy of the English Reformation – but, as Alexander deftly shows, it issued in genuinely new art in the work of, among others, Keats, Tennyson, John Everett Millais, Gerard Manley Hopkins and David Jones.

Many English readers agreed with Burke on the revolutionary French but doubted whether he understood their own history. Rockingham's friend exaggerated the achievements of the Whig aristocracy and glossed over its sins. The English history described by the great constitutional historian William Stubbs rang truer. F. W. Maitland, the greatest of all constitutional historians, realized this later when he wrote:

> Dr. Stubbs saw English history and taught others to see it in a manner, which if I am not mistaken, was somewhat new. Somewhere about the year 1307 the strain of the triumphal march must be abandoned; we pass in those well-known words "from the age of chivalry, from an age ennobled by devotion and self-sacrifice to one in which the gloss of superficial refinement fails to hide the reality of heartless selfishness and moral degradation". It was no small feat for an historian who held this opinion to keep us reading while the decades went from bad to worse, reading of "dynastic faction, bloody conquest, grievous misgovernance, local tyrannies, plagues and famines unhelped and unaverted, hollowness of pomp, disease and dissolution".

If such horrors characterized the national history, it was understandable that artists should want to go in search of less unpalatable themes. One sees the same thing with recent English novelists. Surveying a society that has lost its manners with its moral bearings, they sidestep the present and go to the past for settings and characters. The historical novels of Beryl Bainbridge and Penelope Fitzgerald demonstrate this. Many of the Victorian English felt a similar reluctance to tackle the enormities of their present society. Medievalism might have begun as an antidote to those enormities but along the way it reshaped English history and became a permanent part of English identity.

Keats is a good example of an artist who took the prevailing vogue for things medieval – wrought to a certain finish by Coleridge and Scott – and used it for his own original purposes. "La Belle Dame sans Merci" (1820) could almost have been written to prove what natural bedfellows genius and pastiche are. Listen to the poem as Sir Ralph Richardson recites it and you will hear a love song of timeless power. In his decidedly *unmedievalist* poem, "Modern Love" (1817), Keats asked: "And what is love? It is a doll dress'd up / For idleness to cosset, nurse and dandle / A thing of soft misnomers..." Well, in what Keats's knight-at-arms relates, alone and palely loitering, on that cold hill's side, there are no misnomers, soft or otherwise.

Keats's medievalism had a lasting influence on Tennyson. From "The Lady of Shalott" (1832) to "The Idylls of the King" (1891), he viewed the modern world from a disenchanted remove, convinced that the living, like Gawain's ghost, were "blown along a wandering wind / And hollow, hollow, hollow, all delight..." In "The Lotos-Eaters" (1833), he describes a people beset with duties that they can neither honor nor shun, who sound very much like his own contemporaries – and ours.

> What pleasure can we have
> To war with evil? Is there any peace
> In ever climbing the climbing wave?
> All things have rest, and ripen towards the grave
> In silence; ripen, fall and cease;
> Give us long rest or death, dark death, or dreamful ease.

If Tennyson saw labor as a curse for spiritual sloth, Gerard Manley Hopkins followed the Middle Ages in extolling its dignity. Apropos his inimitable claim, "sheer plod makes plough down sillion shine", from "The Windhover" (1877), which Hopkins thought his best poem, Alexander is brilliant:

> "Sillion" is "furrow", archaic in English but familiar in French. It comes in the refrain of the first verse of *La Marseillaise*, the revolutionary anthem of the French Republic, which encourages *citoyens* so to defend themselves against their enemies "*Qu'un sang impur / Abreuve nos sillons*" – "That an impure blood / Should slake our furrows". The Christian Hopkins associates the furrow made by the plough not with the blood of enemies but with daily sweat for daily bread: the lot of mankind since Adam. For medieval social thought, as seen in *Piers Ploughman*, this gave physical work a special

value: hence the medieval maxim, *laborare est orare* – "to work is to pray". It also made the ploughman an archetype of man: the labourer whose labour provides the archetypal food for all. That is why, for Hopkins, the ploughman's hard work makes the earth turned over to shine in the eye of heaven.

The drudgery that Hopkins knew as an examiner in Greek at University College Dublin gave his respect for labor a hard-earned credibility. There was nothing sentimental or condescending about it: "557 papers on hand", he once remarked, "let those who have been thro' the like say what that means."

Alexander might have also pointed out how this Christian conception of labour was shared by Virgil. In his essay, "Virgil and the Christian World" (1951), T. S. Eliot explained that this was why Dante had made the poet of the *Eclogues* and the *Georgics* his guide to the ancient world. Unlike Homer, who regarded labour as *infra dig*, "Virgil perceived that agriculture is fundamental to civilization, and he affirmed the dignity of manual labour. When the Christian monastic orders came into being, the contemplative life and the life of manual labour were conjoined ... Christianity established the principle that action and contemplation, labour and prayer, are both essential to the life of the complete man." These truths must have particularly haunted Hopkins as he made his way through the rookeries of Liverpool, Glasgow and Dublin, where he witnessed first-hand how unemployment turned labouring men into animals: "This, by Despair, bred Hangdog, dull; by Rage, Manwolf, worse; and their packs infest the age."

Medievalism can also be seen in the work of twentieth-century artists, including the Anglo-Welsh poet, David Jones, whose long poem about the trenches, *In Parenthesis* (1937), received high praise from Eliot, Auden and Evelyn Waugh. Alexander shows how controversial Jones's take on the Great War was. In refusing to see it as pointless, Jones cited his Roman Catholic faith, to which he converted after the war. Here was a medievalism in deadly earnest.

> Though the point may not have been evident to those who fell, their sacrifice is presented as not without meaning. The kind of heroism implied is not especially valorous, more a question of putting up with things – Milton's "the better part

of patience and heroic martyrdom", where "martyr" means "witness". The cause is obscure, the motive is a sense of duty rather than the need to resist Prussian militarism; and the kind of Christianity implied is of the most inclusive sort. Jones's notion of the Catholic Church was that it included "many chaps who did not know that they were in it"... The broken texture of *In Parenthesis*, its relapse into prose, is related to the intense strain of finding any formal analogy in human and sacred history to the dire actuality of a subject matter which did not easily yield sense, still less grandeur. Yet the soldiers of the First World War were not the first soldiers, or men or women, to feel themselves godforsaken. On the cross, Jesus himself repeated the opening of Psalm 22, traditionally attributed to King David, of a thousand years earlier: "My God, my God, why hast thou forsaken me?"

Alexander's book is primarily a work of literary criticism but he is also incisive on medievalist architecture and painting, particularly Millais's *Christ in the House of his Parents* (1849), which he persuasively judges "an unusual and rather successful painting". Depicting a boyish Christ with his family in a carpenter's shop, the painting entirely eschews the glamour that we find in Burne-Jones. The simplicity of the scene is underscored by the simplicity of the technique, which nevertheless appeals by its very unpretentiousness. But this was not how it was seen by contemporaries. A popular magazine described Millais's Jesus as a "hideous, wry-necked, blubbering, red-haired boy in a night-gown", and his mother as a woman "so horrible in her ugliness ... that she would stand out from the rest of the company in the vilest cabaret in France or in the lowest gin-shop in England". This attack on modern medieval art was written, not in an outraged Letter to the Editor, but by the magazine's Editor himself, Charles Dickens ...

Dickens's critique exemplifies how the merits of medievalism would be disputed. Even Eliot, in his polemical youth, charged Chesterton's "The Ballad of the White Horse" (1911), surely one of the triumphs of medievalism, with deadening English poetry. Yet only captious readers would dispute the merit of Michael Alexander's book. Deeply researched and stylishly written, *Medievalism* is an unalloyed delight that will instruct and amuse a wide readership.

Samuel Johnson and the Idiom of Words

Defining the World: The Extraordinary Story of Dr. Johnson's Dictionary, Henry Hitchings. Farrar, Straus and Giroux. 304 pages.

On 18 June 1746 over breakfast at the Golden Anchor near Holborn Bar, the thirty-seven year old Samuel Johnson contracted with the publisher Robert Dodsley to compile a new dictionary of the English language. He was to be paid 1,500 guineas, or what would now be £150,000. Nine years later, in 1755, when he was forty-six, the *Dictionary* finally appeared – *vasta mole superba*, as he described it to Thomas Warton, "proud in its great bulk". In 1779, Boswell asked him if he knew what he was undertaking when he entered into the contract, and Johnson responded, "Yes, Sir, I knew very well what I was undertaking – and very well how to do it, – and have done it very well". This was well-earned pride in an achievement that would have usually required the industry of academies. When Johnson initially told Williams Adams that he was confident he could get the job done in three years, Adams reminded him that it had taken the French academy's forty members forty years to complete their dictionary. Johnson was unimpressed. "Sir, thus it is. This is the proportion. Let me see; forty times forty is sixteen hundred. As three to sixteen hundred, so is the proportion of an Englishman to a Frenchman". "With so much ease and pleasantry", recalled Boswell, "could he talk of that prodigious labour ..."

In *Defining The World: The Extraordinary Story of Dr. Johnson's Dictionary*, Henry Hitchings proposes to show how the great book was compiled and why it is "the most important cultural monument of the eighteenth century". He succeeds brilliantly, showing how Johnson's two folio volumes "tell us more about the society of this period – lustily commercial, cultivated but energetic, politically volatile yet eager for consensus – than any other work". The reviews from England have been unusually glowing: Not since Andrew Robert's biography of Lord Halifax has an author's first book received such rapturous praise. It is praise that the book entirely deserves. Well-researched, well-written, stylish and witty, it is a model introduction not only to the *Dictionary* but to Johnson himself and the entrepreneurial literary London that he came to epitomize. In his excellent popular biography of Johnson, published in 1974, the poet John Wain lamented that "Young people for the most part still think of Johnson, when they think of him at all, as a stupid old reactionary". It is reassuring to be able to observe, in the whirligig of time, that Mr. Hitchings, who was born in 1974, has written a book that invites us to think of "the old philosopher ... in the brown coat with the metal buttons ...", as Macaulay famously referred to him, not as a stupid old reactionary but as a brilliant pioneer.

It is no discredit to Mr. Hitchings that he has relied heavily on the work of others. If there is one thing that makes reading books about Johnson such a lifelong pleasure, it is the unusual distinction of most Johnsonians. He has inspired brilliant commentary. Mr. Hitchings builds on the work of the two of the most brilliant recent Johnsonians: Robert DeMaria's *Johnson's Dictionary and the Language of Learning* (1986) and Allen Reddick's *The Making of Johnson's Dictionary 1746–1773* (1996).

Writers will especially enjoy Mr. Hitchings's account of the genesis of the *Dictionary*. Before taking it on, Johnson had done the often anonymous and ill-paying donkey work of Grub Street, reporting parliamentary debates for Edward Cave's *Gentleman's Magazine*, translating Lobo's *Voyage to Abyssinia*, reviewing, cataloguing. "London furnished Johnson with plenty to write about", Hitchings observes, but "he had yet to fix on a single project that could draw together his skills and synthesize the many strands of knowledge he had accumulated. This was what he wanted – a substantial enterprise which would put him on a par with the Renaissance scholars he admired." Only Samuel Johnson, looking for a big book with which to make his reputation, would have settled on something quite as big as a dictionary. In all events, it was entirely characteristic that he should resolve to climb his way out of Grub Street by taking its accustomed drudgery – the harmless drudgery of lexicography – and elevating it to the level of art.

We know that with Mr. Hitching we are in capable hands when

he reminds us of the brilliance of so much of the miscellaneous work that Johnson did before and during the compiling of the *Dictionary*. Beginning in the early twentieth century, Johnsonians from R. W. Chapman and L. F. Powell to Bertrand Bronson and Donald Greene objected to the fact that the real Johnson – especially Johnson the writer – was being supplanted by the Johnson who appears in the pages of Boswell's *Life*. This was ironic because it was hardly Boswell's fault. What first attracted him to Johnson was not his personality but his moral essays. Boswell, of course, was no saint. "It would be difficult to find a more shattering refutation of the lessons of cheap morality than the life of James Boswell", as Lytton Strachey observed. "One of the most extraordinary successes in the history of civilization" – Boswell's incomparable *Life* – "was achieved by an idler, a lecher, a drunkard, and a snob". But it was precisely his frailties that led Boswell to appreciate the great moral force in Johnson. Accordingly, he never underrated Johnson the writer. It was Boswell's Romantic and Victorian readers – Coleridge, Hazlitt, Carlyle, Macaulay – who first put about the heresy that the talker in Boswell was somehow superior to the real writer of *The Vanity of Human Wishes* (1749), *Rasselas* (1759), *The Rambler* (1750–2), *A Journey to the Western Islands of Scotland* (1775), and *The Lives of the Poets* (1781).

Mr. Hitchings has shrewd things to say about this often neglected writer. About Johnson's parliamentary debates, he remarks: "The semi-fictional accounts of debates ... were an education in working to order. They taught him how to draw disparate materials together into an organic whole; how to work at speed (he would sometimes turn out as many as 10,000 words in a day); how to construct and balance arguments; how to reconcile or juxtapose dissonant points of view: and, above all, how to make the most of an unpromising task." That last item shows how deftly Mr. Hitchings relates what in another writer might appear merely tangential information to the central object of his study. The *Dictionary* was indeed the culmination of everything Johnson had done previously.

About *The Rambler*, Johnson's great periodical essays, which Johnson considered some of his finest things, Mr. Hitchings writes that they gave Johnson "an opportunity to try out words he had encountered during his reading for the *Dictionary*, words like *adsciti-*

tious, effloresence, equiponderant, quadrature, superinduce and *terraqueous*". While some of these terms might be of questionable use, it is undeniable, as Mr. Hitchings points out, that Johnson "remains an influential figure in giving the specialized terms of natural philosophy a real public currency". In this regard, it is telling that one of the books that Johnson cited most heavily was Sir Thomas Browne's *Pseudodoxia Epidemica or Enquiries into Vulgar and Common Errors* (1646), from which Johnson culled 2,000 quotations. As Mr. Hitching observes, in Johnson's *Dictionary*, "Browne's natural philosophy enjoys an afterlife as literature". The sheer quotability of Browne was also a factor. My favorite of Browne's many good things is from *Christian Morals* (1716): "Despise not the obliquities of younger ways, nor despair of better things whereof there is yet no prospect" – words to live by for anyone who has had to recover from a misspent youth.

Johnson's was not the first English dictionary. Prior to his, there had been more than twenty, beginning with Sir Thomas Elyot's *Latin-English Dictionary* (1538). The dictionary with which the British reading public would have been familiar before Johnson began work on his own was *An Universal Etymological English Dictionary* compiled by Nathan Bailey, a schoolmaster from Stepney, about whom East Enders must take some modest pride. The book was first published in 1721 and went through thirty editions. As Mr. Hitchings observes, "its definitions were often poor: *cat* was "a creature well known" ... *strawberry* "was a well-known fruit" and so on. It was also "full of bizarre digressions, red herrings and cack-handed attempts to explain popular sayings". Despite its incidental crudity, Bailey's *Dictionary* supplied not only ordinary Britons with an understanding of their increasingly cosmopolitan language but even the Eton-educated William Pitt, the first earl of Chatham with his command of rhetoric, which so dazzled the eighteenth-century House of Commons. Chatham gratefully admitted to reading the entire *Dictionary* twice. In any case, there was a clear need for a new and improved dictionary when Johnson set to work.

One of the best aspects of Mr. Hitching's book is how vividly he describes the actual process of compilation that the *Dictionary* required. "To alleviate the inevitable drudgery of the work", he points out, "Johnson employed six amanuenses, who attended to the more menial and mechanical tasks. No more than four were with him at any one time, but he was seldom without at least one in the first four years, and dispensed with their services only when money was short and there was truly nothing they could usefully do... The amanuenses were his servants, but also his companions – dogsbodies with the status of intimates, hirelings who doubled as friends. Their presence in the background is a reminder of the giant effort of compilation". No visitor to Johnson's house behind Fleet Street can fail to be moved when he climbs the narrow stairway to the top floor and sees the room where the *Dictionary* was compiled. There, what Mr. Hitchings refers to "as the camaraderie of the garret" is still palpable.

Apropos the amanuenses, Boswell made a point of acquainting his readers with their nationality. "Let it be remembered", he wrote in the *Life*, that they were "natives of North Britain, to whom [Johnson] is supposed to have been so hostile". Jack Lynch, in his excellent abridgement of the *Dictionary*, quotes Reddick's description of the amanuenses as "a rag-tag group of predominantly Scottish ne'er-do-wells".

We cannot speak of the Scotch without remembering the greatest of all dictionary makers. In *Caught in the Web of Words* (1977), her delightful biography of her grandfather, James Murray (1837–1915), the Scotch son of a tailor who would go on to edit the first edition of the *Oxford English Dictionary*, Elisabeth Murray describes how "in memory of descriptions of Dr. Johnson at work at his Dictionary, seated at the end of the table supervising his assistants, [Murray] constructed a foot-high dais for his own table and placed another at a lower level for the sorters". The Scriptorium where Murray and his assistants labored day after day had need of Johnson's great tutelary spirit – though Murray was fond of sharing with friends the dream he had of Johnson, in which:

> Johnson was speaking of his *Dictionary* and Boswell, in an impish mood, asked "What would you say, Sir, if you were told that in a hundred years' time a bigger and better dictionary than yours would be compiled by a Whig?" Johnson grunted. "A Dissenter". Johnson stirred in his chair. "A Scotsman." Johnson began, "Sir...," but Boswell persisted – "and that the University of Oxford would publish it." "Sir," thundered Johnson, "in order to be facetious it is not necessary to be indecent."

Hints of the onerous tedium of dictionary writing found their way into *The Rambler*, where, in one essay, Johnson wrote: "As any action or posture long continued, will distort and disfigure the limbs; so the mind likewise is crippled and contracted by perpetual application to the same set of ideas." Mr. Hitchings's comment on this revelation is characteristically insightful: "No one reading this would have seen it as self-critique but it was. The more he pushed himself, the more his mind bumped and jolted. While other kinds of work made him feel vigorous, his enthusiasm for lexicography was flagging."

Still, he persevered. What held his attention most, besides the odd rewarding entry, was the reassessment he was gradually making of what ought to be the object of lexicography. In the Plan he initially drew up, he conceived of the lexicographer's role as essentially one of fixing the language, purifying it of adulteration. This prescriptive object was one he shared not only with his absentee patron, Lord Chesterfield but with Jonathan Swift, who, earlier in the century, had vehemently censured such neologisms as *speculation, operation, preliminary, ambassador, palisade, communication, circumvallation* and *battalion*. "These two evils, ignorance and want of taste", Swift declared, reminding us of our own John Simon, "have produced a third; I mean the continual corruption of our English tongue, which, without some timely remedy, will suffer more by the false refinements of twenty years past..."

The imagery that Johnson used to portray the object he initially set himself was appropriately martial. About his prescriptive undertaking, he wrote, "I am frighted by its extent, and like the soldiers of Caesar, look on Britain as a new world, which it is almost madness to invade... Though I should not complete the conquest, I shall, at least, discover the coast, civilize part of the inhabitants, and make it easy for some other adventurer to proceed further, to reduce them wholly to subjection, and settle them under laws." But the exuberant unruliness of the language proved too much for him, and he was forced to describe what he could neither repel nor subdue. As he would later concede in the great Preface that he wrote to the *Dictionary*,

> Those who have been persuaded to think well of my design will require that it should fix our language and put a stop to alterations which time and chance have hitherto been suffered to make in it without opposition. With this

consequence I will confess that I flattered myself for a while; but now begin to fear that I have indulged expectation which neither reason nor experience can justify. When we see men grow old and die at a certain time one after another, from century to century, we laugh at the elixir that promises to prolong life to a thousand years; and with equal justice may the lexicographer be derided, who being able to produce no example of a nation that has preserved their words and phrases from mutability, shall imagine that his dictionary can embalm the language and secure it from corruption and decay, that it is in his power to change sublunary nature, and clear the world at once from folly, vanity and affectation.

Johnson famously exhorted the would-be writer to give his days and nights to the study of Addison to acquire "an English style, familiar but not coarse, and elegant but not ostentatious". His own Preface supplies a far superior model. In its periods we can hear what Hilaire Belloc meant when he said that Johnson's prose was "like the rhythmical swell of deep water".

Johnson's understanding of the descriptive role of the lexicographer profoundly influenced the dictionaries of James Murray and Noah Webster (1758–1843), even though the latter inveighed against Johnson for choosing Shakespeare as one of his main authorities. "Play-writers", Webster complained, "in describing vulgar scenes and low characters use low language, language unfit for decent company." Nevertheless, for all his objection to the indecency of Shakespeare, the Yale-educated Webster was sensible enough to recognize that "Johnson's writings had, in Philology, the effect which Newton's discoveries had in Mathematics". Accordingly, as Mr. Hitchings shows, Webster pinched hundreds of Johnson's definitions and adopted many others with only slight modifications. Murray helped himself to even more of the spoils of his illustrious predecessor, reproducing around 1,700 of Johnson's definitions in the *Oxford English Dictionary*, which continue to be denoted with a simple [J]. As Hitchings points out, "Murray worked with Johnson's *Dictionary* open on the table beside him in his Scriptorium; it was an invaluable point of reference..." Johnson's innovative use of illustrative quotations, which amount, as Mr. Hitchings remarks, to "a giant commonplace book", also gave

Murray the idea of using quotations to chart how the usage of each word defined evolved over time.

Mr. Hitchings shows how Johnson's moral preoccupations prompted his choice of illustrations: He would not cite authors of whose philosophy he disapproved. Consequently, there are no citations from Hobbes. As Mr. Hitchings remarks, "In his eyes, Hobbes, who had savaged the Church in *Leviathan* (1651), was unambiguously wicked, and excluding him was a pleasure". Nor are there any citations from the sermons of the latitudinarian churchmen Samuel Clarke or Isaac Barrow. He excluded Bernard Mandeville, despite the fact that he had read *The Fable of the Bees* (1723) with great admiration as a young man. The more mature Johnson considered the main contention of the book – that "private vices are public benefits" – as dangerously sophistical. Mr. Hitchings makes an interesting observation when he remarks that in showcasing quotations that promoted virtue, Johnson was actually following a long Islamic tradition of "infusing dictionaries with moral teaching". However, unlike Webster, where Johnson might have been inclined to censure – the word *cant* pops up repeatedly in the definitions – he resisted censorship. It would be a welcome change to see our universities exercise similar restraint.

Relying heavily on the historical work of John Brewer, especially *The Pleasures of the Imagination: English Culture in the Eighteenth Century* (1997), Mr. Hitchings shows how Johnson's *Dictionary* reflects the spread of luxury in British society. This can be seen in his entries for *toyshop, mezzotint, spa town, tobacconist, tulip, japan,* and *vase*. It is important to remember that the spread of luxury was something with which Johnson was entirely comfortable. "Riches, without goodness" he might assert, "cannot make us happy". But that was no argument for the inherent evil of riches. In fact, Johnson saw the abundance of private charity in eighteenth-century England as directly linked to the spread of luxury. "The present age, though not likely to shine hereafter, among the most splendid periods of history, has yet given examples of charity, which may be very properly recommended to imitation. The equal distribution of wealth, which long commerce has produced, does not enable any single hand to raise edifices of piety like fortified cities, to appropriate manors to religious uses, or deal out such large and lasting beneficence as was scattered over the land in ancient times, by those who possess counties or provinces. But no sooner is a new species of misery brought to view, and a design of relieving it professed, than every hand is open to contribute something, every tongue is busied in solicitation, and every art of pleasure is employed ... in the interests of virtue." A lively essay on this fascinating aspect of Johnson's thinking is John H. Middendorf's "Johnson on Wealth and Commerce" which can be found in *Johnson, Boswell and Their Circle: Essays Presented to Lawrence Fitzroy Powell* (1965).

What will always win the *Dictionary* new readers, despite the unavoidable obsolescence of many of its components, are its wonderful definitions. For what Matthew Prior called "the idiom of words" Johnson had an uncanny flair. Thus, he describes *rake* as "a loose, disorderly, vicious, wild, gay, thoughtless fellow". *Heart* he defines as "The muscle which by its contraction and dilation propels the blood through the course of circulation and is therefore considered as the source of vital motion. It is supposed in popular language to be the seat sometimes of courage, sometimes of affection." *Vermicelli* is "a paste rolled and broken in the form of worms" – which is an accurate, if oddly unappetizing definition. *Nice* is defined as "accurate in judgment to minute exactness; superfluously exact. It is often used to express a culpable delicacy". *Chess* is defined as "a nice and abstruse game, in which two sets of men are moved in opposition to each other". In the nicety of Johnson's definitions, one can see why writers as different as T. S. Eliot and Samuel Beckett read him so closely.

Another reason why the *Dictionary* will never lack readers is that it is so emblematic of the man who wrote it – his prejudices, his hopes, his fears, his loyalties. As we all know, Johnson was both a great and a good man, and his goodness is evident throughout the *Dictionary*. Mr. Hitchings shows how in defining *lich* ("a dead carcass"), Johnson took the opportunity to remark that his birthplace, Lichfield was named after the Christians who were once martyred there and that it meant "the field of the dead". This etymology, like so many in the *Dictionary*, sounds plausible but it is wrong. Lichfield probably comes from the Celtic *luitcoit*, meaning "grey wood", or from the Roman name of the place, which was *Letocetum*. Nevertheless, after his definition, Johnson saluted his birthplace with the touching phrase, *Salve magna parens*, "Hail, great parent". His readiness to pay his respects to his place of birth was characteristic of a man whose provincialism was an important part of his genius: it enabled him to see London for the incomparable city that it was, it fired him, as it fired David Garrick, with consummate ambition, and it gave him a humility which his often truculent exterior was assumed to protect. This humility, which is not without a certain warranted pride, is given noble expression in the Preface, where he says:

> In hope of giving longevity to that which its own nature forbids to be immortal, I have devoted this book, the labor of years, to the honor my country, that we may no longer yield the palm of philology without a contest to the nations of the Continent. The chief glory of every people arises from its authors: whether I shall add anything by my own writings to the reputation of English literature must be left to time: much of my life has been lost under the pressures of disease; much has been trifled away; and much has always been spent in provision for the day that was passing over me; but I shall not think my employment useless or ignoble if by my assistance foreign nations and distant ages gain access to the propagators of knowledge, and understand the teachers of truth; if my labors afford light to the repositories of science, and add celebrity to Bacon, to Hooker, to Milton, and to Boyle.

All good Johnsonians know how much the parable of the talents hounded Johnson. Acutely aware that his own talents were of an exceptional order, he was fearful that he would be judged harshly for not putting them to sufficient use. Despite his prolific output, his diaries constitute one long screed against what he perceived to be his indefensible idleness. In setting himself the task of compiling the *Dictionary* he demonstrated just how high the expectations were that he imposed on himself. It also explains the almost narcotic attraction that indolence held for this most conscionable of men. If his bouts of productivity called forth labor that resulted in the *Dictionary*, or the great edition of Shakespeare or the *Lives of the Poets*, it is not difficult to imagine how doing nothing might often have seemed preferable. But there was another driver behind the *Dictionary*.

Most great writers write out of deep personal pain, out of a desire to allay the sorrow of pain. They are wounded in youth and spend their adult lives making writing a means of healing. To find what drove Johnson to undertake the immense labor of compiling a dictionary, we have to go back to the Lichfield of his boyhood, to his unhappy upbringing in the household of a bankrupt bookseller and his aggrieved, termagant wife. From as far back as he could remember, Johnson would never have been able to disentangle the appeal of learning from its association with the failures of his family. If it was in his father's house that he first discovered the books that would feed what he called the "hunger of imagination", it was also in his father's house that he would often have heard his mother berating his father for the folly of trying to make a living out of books. In undertaking his great work, Johnson meant to show that learning could have a good issue after all. The *Dictionary* is splendid proof of both the intensity and the pertinacity of that desire. And we can readily imagine that the reader whom he wanted most to impress was not Lord Chesterfield or Edmund Burke or any of his other learned friends but his mother, Sarah Johnson, who, as he revealed in a letter, counted the days to the publication of the great work and would have seen in its finished folios not only a memorial to her son's prodigious learning but a happy ending to a life radically wretched. She died in 1759 at the age of ninety, four years after the *Dictionary* appeared. It is pleasing to see that Mr. Hitchings has dedicated his book to his parents. I am sure his mother is as proud of his book as Johnson's mother was of his.

A Bright New Look at Edith Sitwell

Edith Sitwell: Avant Garde Poet, English Genius, Richard Greene. Virago. 532 pages.

There are many criteria by which biography can be judged. Does it bring any psychological insight to the portrayal of its subject? Does it place its subject in the context of his contemporaries? Does it have anything of any critical substance to say about the subject's work? Is it well-written? Is it entertaining? Is it animated by that sympathetic fellow-feeling without which biography is too often little more than a kind of prurient gossip? No literary biography of recent years has met all of these exacting criteria with anything like the same élan as Richard Greene's *Edith Sitwell: Avant Garde Poet, English Genius*.

What makes Greene's achievement all the more admirable is that he has found so many new and incisive things to say about a subject that has not been entirely untilled. The superb English biographer Victoria Glendinning wrote a life of the famous sister of Osbert and Sacheverell Sitwell that is still worth reading. Then, again, in her own time Sitwell had several redoubtable admirers: W. B. Yeats, Virginia Woolf, Siegfried Sassoon, Roy Campbell, and W. H. Auden all praised her work. Yet in his new biography of this now unjustly neglected figure, Greene has transformed our view of the poet by looking behind her famous eccentricities and showing us the vulnerable, heroic woman who was capable not only of memorable verse but great kindness, resilience, loyalty, and grace.

Being a poet himself, Greene's animadversions on Sitwell's poetry come with a certain practical authority. In his latest collection, *Boxing the Compass*, he ends with a poetic travelogue of sorts, which includes these striking lines:

> The streets of Georgetown are out of time,
> one ancient house of blue granite on M Street
> was erected before tea and tax

turned colonies into musket-bearing states –
the oldest are stone and then came brick –
houses built at the edge of pavements,
fashionable, then slum, now revived as chic.

In his own work of revival, Greene realizes that Sitwell's reputation has suffered in a critical ethos hostile to her mystery-honoring aesthetics. After noting that many now ignore the work Sitwell did after *Façade* (1920), her collaboration with the composer William Walton, he makes an incisive point: "That evasion happens because we do not yet have the nerve to say that the generation of Philip Larkin imposed as orthodoxy a painfully narrow, indeed incoherent account of where poetry comes from". And this largely as a result of the baleful influence of logical positivism, which "held", as Greene reminds his readers, "that knowledge must be strictly empirical, and that metaphysics and theology are meaningless". Now that an edition of Larkin's complete poetry has been published, it is a good time to reappraise his achievement in this rarely considered light.

As Greene shows, Sitwell refused to comply with the attenuated poetics exemplified by Larkin, insisting instead on "seeing all glory hidden in small forms / The planetary system in the atom, the great suns / Hid in a speck of dusk". Indeed, in a poem she wrote in 1942 entitled "An Old Woman", Sitwell did not hesitate to take on themes that directly contradict the positivists' fashionable nihilism.

> For though the soundless wrinkles fall like snow
> On many a golden cheek, and creeds grow old
> And change, – man's heart, that sun,
> Outlives all terrors shaking the old night:
> The world's huge fevers burn and shine, turn cold,
> Yet the heavenly bodies and young lovers burn and shine,
> The golden lovers walk in the holy fields
> Where the Abraham-bearded sun, the father of all things
> Is shouting of ripeness, and the whole world of dews and
>   splendours are singing
> To the cradles of earth, of men, beasts, harvests, swinging
> In the peace of God's heart. And I, the primeval clay
> That has known earth's grief and harvest's happiness,
> Seeing mankind's dark seed-time, come to bless,
> Forgive and bless all men like the holy light.

The author of these exultant lines, Edith Louisa Sitwell (1887–1964) was born in Scarborough, the oldest of three children of Sir George Reresby Sitwell, 4th baronet, genealogist and antiquary, and his wife, Lady Ida Emily Augusta Denison, daughter of the first earl of Londesborough. Edith's eccentricity, not to mention that of her brothers and parents, may have come from the fact that the Sitwell family included among their ancestors not only kings of France and the English Plantagenets but Robert Bruce and the Macbeths. With this genealogical cocktail raging in the family's blood, it is no wonder that Sir George became enamoured of heraldry and Burke's Peerage. Lady Ida, for her part, became so fond of gambling and drink that she actually landed in prison after involving herself with criminal moneylenders.

Unfortunately, neither parent was very fond of Edith. Her striking looks, which artists as different as C. R. W. Nevinson, Wyndham Lewis, and Cecil Beaton found fascinating, disconcerted them, and they were entirely incapable of entering into her delight in poetry and music. Sitwell was an original and the utter incomprehension that she inspired in her parents, neither of whom was uncultivated, measured something of the boldness of her originality. Even Virginia Woolf, who liked to imagine her own originality peerless, recognized that Edith was different, distinctly different: "I do admire her work", the fastidious Woolf admitted; "& that's what I say of hardly anyone: She has an ear, & not a carpet broom; a satiric vein and some beauty in her."

If Osbert's great multi-volume autobiography showcases the obsessional hobby horses of the Sitwell patriarch, Greene reveals more of the cruelty that he and his extravagant wife visited upon their neglected firstborn. Fans of the autobiography's high comedy will enjoy Greene's own sense of the ridiculous, which is on display on nearly every page of this deeply funny book. After Osbert stood for his father's Scarborough seat as an Asquithian Liberal, for example, a foray into politics for which he had his sister's full personal support, Edith remarked apropos the constituency itself:

> What a strange place – partly a clownish bright-coloured tragic hell, partly a flatness where streets crawl sluggishly, and one drop of rain (no more) drops on one's face half way down the street, and there are no inhabitants, or so it seems, but boys so indistinguishable in their worm-white faces that

> they have to wear coloured caps with initials that one may be known from the other. Osbert didn't "get in". I suppose they found out he was a poet.

Greene's comment on this is characteristically witty: "It can be assumed that on the hustings Edith Sitwell lacked the common touch".

While Greene is sound enough not to overstate the merits of Sitwell's most famous poem, "Still Falls the Rain", which she composed during the Blitz, he does persuasively argue that rhythm is at the heart of the success of most of her best poetry. As Edwin Muir perceptively observed, she was "a cross between Meredith and the Queen of Spades". If there is a careful attention to symbol in her work, there is also an equally careful appreciation of the uses of the incantatory, which the poet must have had confirmed when she prayed.

In addition to being a shrewd critic both of poetry and the psychology of poets, Greene is a deft chronicler of the historical background against which Sitwell lived. He captures the despondent frivolity that followed the Great War, for example, with laconic precision.

> After an evening of pianola music and dancing, one of the party-goers, on his way home, tried to set fire to Nelson's plinth. Going back to Aldershot, Sachie saw drunken women rolled like milk cans along the platform at Waterloo Station and stowed in the guard's van. The reign of peace began the next morning with a hangover and some bruises.

Greene is also good on the precarious life that Sitwell lived in bohemian penury in Bayswater and Montparnasse with Helen Rootham, a failed fellow artist, to whom Sitwell was staunchly loyal and who inspired one of her most eloquent jeremiads. "Invalids, poor things, don't realise how constant their claims on one's time become; they get immersed in a world of their own, and become (through no actual fault of their own) terribly selfish – exerting, quite unconsciously, a kind of moral blackmail". Still, it was the unflagging *caritas* that Sitwell lavished on Helen that prepared her for her conversion to Catholicism. (Helen's brother, Cyril, incidentally, wrote some good music, including a settling for one of Yeats's things and a most moving memorial piece for those killed in the Great War.)

The terrible thing about Greene's biography is that it reveals the extent to which Osbert not only withheld but actually stole portions of his sister's inheritance, a piece of selfishness which only accentuates Edith's own selflessness. When it came to caring for and protecting those she loved, including her brothers, she was irreproachable. Admirers of Osbert's autobiography will find such disclosures of malfeasance sad reading. When I read Marianne Moore referring to Sir George's heir as "valiant Osbert", I could not help but wince.

Despite the unkindness and indeed abuse that she suffered at the hands of family and friends, Sitwell was a warm-hearted, giving, liberal woman whose generosity was of a piece with the celebratory exuberance of her poetry. This quality also comes out in her letters. In one she recommends that a friend look at Michelangelo's drawings in the Uffizi, which she characterizes as "superb with the kind of proud magnificent beauty that my mother had, more than any woman I've ever seen – staring at her image in old age, – equally beautiful in its own way, but with the immortality of the bone, not with the pride of summer". If Lady Ida ever paid her daughter's beauty any comparable mind no record of it survives.

Then, again, Greene vividly captures the sorrow that always threatened to cast out the glee that otherwise animated Sitwell's sense of the richness of life, a sorrow compounded by her long unhappy attachment to the Russian painter Pavel Tchelitchew. "I've been feeling terribly unhappy lately," she admits to one correspondent in the 1930s, "I've seen people behaving in such a dreadful ugly way... And I never can get used to it". By the same token, she was always prepared to take even her gloom and turn it into fodder for her wonderful jokes. "I had such a terrible dream last night," she tells another correspondent; "I dreamt I was in a low shallow grave, that I had to dig with my own nails, and that I couldn't lie down because there were still a few drops of blood left in my heart, and so I wasn't allowed to be dead."

At the end of her life, when excessive tippling and bad health had begun to make her difficult, she still managed to toss off a funny bit of doggerel inspired by the poet from Saint Louis who had left America to become England's literary dictator. After *Old Possum's Book of Practical Cats* appeared, Edith shared this delicious effusion with Graham Greene, who had become infatuated with Sitwell when he was an undergraduate at Balliol:

> I tort a taw a Puddy-Tat a-creeping up on me!
> You did. You taw a Puddy-Tat.
> The Puddy-Tat was me!

In an entry for the old *Dictionary of National Biography*, John Lehmann nicely summed up Sitwell when he remarked how "her capacity for icy, lightning-swift repartee to bores, who were fatally attracted to her, concealed a great sense of fun and also a deep sense of compassion that could immediately be amused by a genuine tale of misfortune". Greene's biography is a tribute to both this sense of fun and this sense of compassion in a subject who here lives anew in all of her sardonic gaiety.

But more than anything else, this new biography is proof that in Richard Greene we have a truly first-rate literary biographer in our midst. Since these talented creatures do not show up on our doorsteps every day, when they do appear we should give them the praise they deserve.

WHAT NEWMAN WOULD HAVE MADE OF VATICAN II

Newman on Vatican II, Ian Ker. Oxford University Press. 167 pages.

IN THE COURSE OF HIS LONG CAREER as priest, poet, historian, philosopher, educator, theologian, novelist and satirist, Blessed John Henry Newman (1801–90) became something of a connoisseur of what he called "the tin-kettle accounts of me which rattle to and fro in the world". When he learned that someone was putting about the rumor that he had lost his mind, he nicely deplored the calumny as a "grave, sleek, imposing lie, which made one smile. People sucked it in greedily and smacked their lips". He was particularly amused by the rumor that a friend had heard in London that "I carried my austerity to such an extent that I would not let my wife wear anything but sad coloured ribbons in her bonnet". In 1850, he wrote his fellow Oratorian Frederick Faber, "The report grows stronger and stronger here, that I am married, and have shut up my wife in a convent". After he converted to Catholicism, he was constantly rumored to be unhappy in his adopted communion and ready to rejoin the Church of England, despite his repeated denials. "Make up my mind to return," he wrote one correspondent, "Why, I could as easily 'make up my mind' to be a Garibaldian or a Siamese twin. Be sure there is as much chance of my turning an Anglican again as of my being the Irish Giant or the King of Clubs."

Since his death, distortions of this fascinating figure have only intensified, though none has been more misleading or more mischievous than the contention that he would have approved of liberal interpretations of the Second Vatican Council. Since such misinterpretations of the Council and indeed of Newman have influenced some of those involved in the recent Synod – Cardinal Kasper, for example, claimed that the radical developments recommended in the first *Relatio* would have met with the approval of the author of *Essay on the Development of Christian Doctrine* (1845) – it is good to have so reliable an authority as Father Ian Ker sorting out what Newman would have truly thought of the Council. The author of the definitive intellectual biography of Newman and several other incisive books about the great convert, Father Ker is the perfect person to address this highly consequential matter and here he does so with acuity and élan. *Newman and Vatican II* is a superb study, which anyone with any interest in Newman or the Council will find richly rewarding.

Father Ker begins his study with an excellent overview of the subtlety of Newman's thought, which so many commentators get wrong, choosing to see him either as a "Tory of Tories" (as Avery Dulles gave out) or a misunderstood liberal (as Eamon Duffy contended). In fact, as Father Ker shows, Newman was never a party man, whether in the political or the religious sense.

Although prepared to support the Tories when they were willing to support Catholic purposes – Newman supported the Earl of Derby's conservative government when it agreed to make Catholic chaplains available to prisoners in English prisons – he was never particularly keen on conservatism *per se*, which he saw as inimical to the necessary integrity of the Church. While he recognized that "The Roman Pontiffs owe their exaltation to the secular power and have a great stake in its stability and prosperity . . . [and] cannot bear anarchy . . . think revolution an evil . . . pray for the peace of the world and the prosperity of all Christian States, and . . . effectively support the cause of order and good government", he also saw that "the Pope never is, and cannot be" conservative in the party sense of the word, for that "means a man who upholds government and society and the existing state of things . . . not because it is good and desirable, because it is established, because it is a benefit to the population, because it is full of promise for the future, – but rather because he himself is well off in consequence of it, and because to take care of number one is his main political principle. It means a man who defends religion, not for religion's sake, but for the sake of its accidents and externals; and in this sense Conservative a Pope can never be, without a simple betrayal of the dispensation committed to him."

With this critical view of conservatism, Newman naturally looked askance at the Ultramontane view of papal infallibility (the issue at the heart of the First Vatican Council in 1870), which he thought untenably extravagant. At the same time, for all his distrust of conservatism, Newman was never less than orthodox, always insistent that the living, organic, perdurable principle of *semper eadem*, which he had learned from his close reading of the Fathers, must always safeguard the authority of the Church's teachings. In a moving passage from *A Letter to the Duke of Norfolk* (1875), he gave eloquent expression to the abiding appeal that this principle had for him, even when he was an Anglican.

> I have one thing more to say on the subject of the "semper eadem". In truth, this fidelity to the ancient Christian system, seen in modern Rome, was the luminous fact which more than any other turned men's minds at Oxford forty years ago to look towards her with reverence, interest, and love. It affected individual minds variously of course; some it even brought on eventually to conversion, others it only restrained from active opposition to her claims; but none of us could read the Fathers, and determine to be their disciples, without feeling that Rome, like a faithful steward, had kept in fulness and in vigour what our own communion had let drop. The Tracts for the Times were founded on a deadly antagonism to what in these last centuries has been called Erastianism or Cæsarism. Their writers considered the Church to be a divine creation, "not of men, neither by man, but by Jesus Christ", the Ark of Salvation, the Oracle of Truth, the Bride of Christ, with a message to all men everywhere, and a claim on their love and obedience; and, in relation to the civil power, the object of that promise of the Jewish prophets ... No Ultramontane (so called) could go beyond those writers in the account which they gave of her from the Prophets, and that high notion is recorded beyond mistake in a thousand passages of their writings.

And as a result of his own fidelity to the ancient Church, Newman had no objections to the eventual definition of infallibility upheld by the First Vatican Council. In fact, he welcomed it, seeing it as a legitimate development of the infallibility that the faithful had virtually accorded the pope for centuries. Moreover, it defined the pope's individual power (his infallibility being limited to *ex cathedra* statements on faith and morals) while strengthening the papacy for the storms ahead in a Europe where, as Newman saw so clearly, "the great apostasia" was proceeding apace.

As for liberalism, Newman might have recognized that there were some aspects of the liberal agenda that were acceptable – for example, he singled out the concept of justice – but he was all his life opposed to what he regarded as the relativism and indeed arrogance implicit in the liberal creed, especially when it sought to dispose of truths of which it could have no proper understanding. After all, in the lives of his own brothers, Newman had seen liberalism degenerate into what he referred to as "the all dissolving, all-corroding skepticism of the intellect", and he was intent on dissuading others from falling prey to a set of political and religious ideas that were antagonistic alike to good governance and true religion. As he wrote in one famous passage, "Liberalism in religion is the doctrine that there is no positive truth in religion, but that one creed is as good as another ... It is inconsistent with any recognition of any religion as true. It teaches that all are to be tolerated, for all are matters of opinion. Revealed religion is not a truth, but a sentiment and a taste, not an objective fact." Here, in addition to anticipating the fallacy of the positivist atheism of Bertrand Russell and Freddy Ayer, Newman anticipated the even more calamitous fallacy of those ecumenists within the Catholic hierarchy who wish to imagine Islam on a par with Catholicism. Of course, for Newman, "We can believe what we choose. We are answerable for what we choose to believe".

Father Ker nicely encapsulates Newman's view of conservatism and liberalism when he observes how: "Having abandoned the attempt as a Tractarian Anglican to construct a *via media* or middle way between Rome and Geneva, Newman found that he had to forge another *via media* as a Catholic between the Ultramontane and liberal wings of the Church. Neither simply conservative nor liberal, he is best described ... as a conservative radical or conservative reformer." A good example of this is the way Newman took issue with both the Ultramontane Cardinal Manning and the liberal Johann Ignaz von Döllinger over the definition of infallibility. As Father Ker is careful to point out, while Newman was "open to development and reform", he was nonetheless unwavering in his recognition that these would always have to be consistent with the tradition of the Church, or what Pope Benedict in his summation of what ought to be the just interpretation of the Second Vatican Council referred to as the "hermeneutic of continuity", rather than the "hermeneutic of discontinuity and rupture".

One does not need to belabor the point to see how pertinent such a distinction is to any sound response to the issues broached by the Synod. In addition to being a most solicitous father of souls, Newman was a prophet, and one of the reasons why Father Ker's book is so welcome is that it addresses issues that are of paramount importance for the future of the Church, a future, which, as Newman foresaw, is proving fraught with grave challenges. In one letter, written to a correspondent in 1877, Newman described the nature of those challenges, which, in light of our own tragic experience, can only confirm the accuracy of his prophecy.

> As to the prospects of the Church, as to which you ask my opinion, you know old men are generally desponding – but my apprehensions are not new, but above 50 years standing. I have all that time thought that a time of widespread infidelity was coming, and through all those years the waters have in fact been rising as a deluge. I look for the time, after my life, when only the tops of the mountains will be seen, like islands in the waste of waters. I speak principally of the Protestant world – but great actions and successes must be achieved by the Catholic leaders, great wisdom as well as courage must be given them from on high, if Holy Church is to be kept safe from the awful calamity, and, though any trial which came upon her would but be temporary, it may be fierce in the extreme while it lasts.

Newman does not make the explicit point here but throughout his Catholic writings he was careful to stress the crucial role that the laity must perform in ensuring that the Church continue faithful to the *depositum fidei*, especially in circumstances where, as in the fourth century, the episcopate proved less than faithful. While Father Ker points out that this is certainly one legitimate reason why Newman can be seen as a formative influence on the Second Vatican Council, he also stresses how Newman's understanding of the faithful laity included the faithful clergy. To make this point, Father Ker quotes from Newman's pivotal essay, "On Consulting the Faithful in Matters of Doctrine" (1859), though even in *The Arians of the Fourth Century* (1832) the Anglican Newman had shown how the laity and clergy preserved the Church from false developments, in which the episcopate connived.

The episcopate, whose action was so prompt and concordant at Nicæa on the rise of Arianism, did not, as a class or order of men, play a good part in the troubles consequent upon the Council; and the laity did. The Catholic people, in the length and breadth of Christendom, were the obstinate champions of Catholic truth, and the bishops were not. Of course there were great and illustrious exceptions; first, Athanasius, Hilary, the Latin Eusebius, and Phœbadius; and after them, Basil, the two Gregories, and Ambrose; there are others, too, who suffered, if they did nothing else, as Eustachio's, Paulus, Paulinus, and Dionysius; and the Egyptian bishops, whose weight was small in the Church in proportion to the great power of their Patriarch. And, on the other hand, as I shall say presently, there were exceptions to the Christian heroism of the laity, especially in some of the great towns. And again, in speaking of the laity, I speak inclusively of their parish-priests (so to call them), at least in many places; but on the whole, taking a wide view of the history, we are obliged to say that the governing body of the Church came short, and the governed were pre-eminent in faith, zeal, courage, and constancy.

Another way that Father Ker shows what might have been Newman's favorable response to Vatican II is by showing how the "Declaration on Religious Freedom" (*Dignitatis Humanae*), the most controversial of the Council's documents, meets the seven notes of legitimate development set out in *Essay on the Development of Christian Doctrine*, a finding which parries the objections of Archbishop Lefebvre and his implacable friends to a document that they clearly misunderstood. Apropos Lefebvre and his theological opposite, Hans Küng, Father Ker makes the insightful observation that "Both Lefebvre and Küng had no doubt as to how the Council was to be understood, and of course paradoxically, like Döllinger and Manning, were in close agreement about its meaning and significance: for both it was a revolutionary event signaling a rupture with the past and tradition". Here, we can see how attentive Father Ker is to the illuminating parallels of history, a quality he shares with Newman, whose reading of history is still not adequately appreciated.

If Father Ker is good at showing how Newman influenced the actual Second Council, he is also good at showing how Newman differed from those who argue for what they claim to be the "spirit of Vatican II". This spirit, as Father Ker rightly shows, is the fabrication of "the liberal ... kind of theologian who justifies dissent from the Church's teachings and believes in a kind of parallel magisterium of the theologians". Since this "parallel magisterium" is often justified by liberal theologians appropriating Newman's understanding of conscience, Father Ker shows how misleading that misappropriation has been. Regarding Newman's celebrated toast to conscience in his *Letter to the Duke of Norfolk*, in which he wrote how, "Certainly, if I am obliged to bring religion into any dinner toasts (which indeed does not seem quite the thing) I shall drink – to the Pope, if you please – still, to Conscience first, and to the Pope afterwards", Father Ker provides the historical context for the statement without which it cannot be understood. In fact, Newman was refuting the contention Gladstone had made in *The Vatican Decrees in Their Bearing on Civil Allegiance* (1875) that "No one can be [Rome's] convert without renouncing his moral and mental freedom and placing his civil loyalty and duty at the mercy of another"; he was not recommending or condoning conscientious dissent from the magisterium on the part of those claiming to be faithful Catholics. Yet, rather than paraphrase Father Ker, one should quote him directly, since he makes his case with characteristic precision.

> Although it is true that Newman did, in accordance with Catholic tradition, hold that conscience is indeed supreme in the sense that it is – to use his own evocative phrase – "the aboriginal Vicar of Christ", with its obvious allusion to the pope who is traditionally called "the Vicar of Christ", this famous toast was never intended by Newman to mean that a Catholic may be led by his conscience to dissent from Church teachings. Of course, he would have agreed with St. Thomas Aquinas that a Catholic may, indeed should, follow an erroneous conscience even if it means leaving the Church. But a believing member of the Church has a conscientious duty to believe the teachings of the Church, not to pick and choose what to believe ...

Moreover, an erroneous conscience might prompt an individual to deviate from Church teachings on, say, abortion, divorce or sodomy, but for Newman such a conscience would have ceased to be a Catholic conscience because it would have been formed without any understanding of the binding truth of the magisterium. For Father Ker, "Newman's theology of the conscience and its relation to the teaching authority of the Church upholds the sovereignty but not the autonomy of the individual conscience". In such elegant discriminations, one can see the command Father Ker has of his subject's finely judicious thinking.

This is one reason why *Newman on Vatican II* is such a vital read, though there is much else about the book to recommend it. Finely researched and wonderfully well-written, it is full of insights that go to the very essence of both the Second Council and Newman. In his penultimate chapter, for example, "Secularization and the New Evangelization", which includes a splendid reading of Newman's neglected novel of conversion, *Callista* (1856), Father Ker shows how Newman both anticipates and exemplifies the genuine spirit of Vatican II by extolling the love of Christ that will always bind the faithful to Him and His Holy Church. Here, Father Ker also presents a portrait of the true Newman, in all his faithful *caritas* and wisdom, which will enlighten liberals and conservatives alike.

Newman's University Redux

The "Making of Men": The Idea and Reality in Newman's University, Paul Shrimpton. Gracewing. 587 pages.

IN THE DEBATE as to what needs to be done to make university education more coherent and more effective, no figure is cited more frequently than John Henry Newman, whose classic study, *The Idea of a University* (1873) tackles questions that still exercise would-be educational reformers today. Some of those questions include whether the governing principle of university education should be utilitarian or non-utilitarian; whether teaching or research should predominate in the hierarchy of university priorities; and what truly constitutes university education. Hitherto, the two most highly regarded books on Newman's treatment of the subject were Fergal McGrath's *Newman's University: Idea and Reality* (1951) and Dwight Culler's *The Imperial Intellect: A Study of Newman's Educational Ideal* (1955). In *The Making of Men*, Dr. Paul Shrimpton of Magdalen College School, Oxford contends that past studies of Newman's educational achievement have suffered from failing to take into account the full scope of Newman's educational endeavors, and he has written his own book to rectify that inadequate appraisal.

Deeply researched and persuasively argued, *The Making of Men* is a major contribution to our understanding of Newman's commitment to university education, which will enliven and refine all future discussions of the subject by encouraging readers to revisit not only Newman's classic text but the practical challenges he addressed, first, as Fellow of Oriel College in Oxford, and, then, as Rector of the Catholic University in Dublin. Accordingly, Dr. Shrimpton draws on Newman's copious correspondence and memoranda, as well as "accounts ledgers, buttery records, punishments books, timetables, rules and regulations, prospectuses, minute books, reports of all types, and a host of other documents", all of which give *The "Making of Men"* an admirable richness.

In addition, the book includes vivid pen portraits of the men who joined Newman in his educational undertakings. Apropos Aubrey de Vere, for example, who was a close associate of Newman in the 1850's when he crossed St. George's Channel 56 times to attend to the fledgling University, Dr. Shrimpton notes how the Anglo-Irish poet and convert found Newman "not an aloof intellectual", but a man of "sweet gravity, simple manners and plain speech". In fact, his "quick sympathy and fierce moods before injustice" reminded de Vere of his countryman, Edmund Burke. In such nicely chosen details, the reader can see why Newman commanded at once the respect and the affection of his colleagues.

The genesis of Newman's interest in education began while he was a student at Trinity College, when Oxford was just emerging from the bibulous torpor about which Gibbon wrote so memorably. "As a gentleman commoner", Gibbon wrote, "I was admitted to the society of the fellows, and fondly expected that some questions of literature would be the amusing and instructive topics of their discourse." Instead, Magdalen's Fellows spoke only of "college business, Tory politics, personal anecdotes, and private scandal", while "their dull and deep potations excused the brisk intemperance of youth". There was no college discipline to speak of and no public exercises or examinations. "At the most precious season of youth", as Gibbon recalled, "whole days and weeks were suffered to elapse without labour or amusement, without advice or account." By the time Newman entered Trinity, the intellectual tone of the university might have improved (thanks, in part, to university-wide reforms implemented by the Dean of Christ Church, Cyril Jackson) but not the tastes of gentlemen commoners. Writing his father, Newman described how he had accompanied fellow undergraduates to their rooms,

> and they drank and drank all the time I was there ... They sat down with the avowed determination of each making himself drunk. I really think, if any one should ask me what qualifications were necessary for Trinity College, I should say there was only one, – Drink, drink, drink.

Once a Fellow at Oriel, Newman set himself against this dissolute ethos by developing the moral and spiritual life of the undergraduates in his charge. Together with his friends, Hurrell Froude and Robert

Wilberforce, he gave his tutoring a deliberate pastoral attentiveness, until the provost, Edward Hawkins demanded that he either stop tutoring along these lines, which he feared would foster favoritism, or leave off tutoring altogether. Newman duly relinquished his tutorial duties, though he remained a redoubtable force in college life and continued to offer spiritual counsel to students and dons alike. One of these, as Dr. Shrimpton shows, was Mark Pattison, who would go on to become Rector of Lincoln College and a lifelong champion of the tutorial solicitude that Newman advocated, even though he eventually abjured his Christian faith. Another was Edward Pusey, the Canon of Christ Church, with whom Newman led the Oxford Movement, who insisted that "It would be a perversion of our institutions to turn the University into a forcing-house for intellect."

Before converting, Newman also sent a series of brilliant letters to *The Times* opposing a reading room sponsored by Sir Robert Peel and Lord Brougham, which would exclude all books of theology from its shelves. Later published as *The Tamworth Reading Room* (1841), the letters attacked the cult of knowledge, which Newman saw as an outcrop of the atheist rationalism of the Enlightenment. That this cult was adopted by the father of Utilitarianism, Jeremy Bentham, did not make it any more palatable. Since the false god of knowledge still stultifies the study of the liberal arts, Newman's objections to it remain compelling.

> People say to me, that it is but a dream to suppose that Christianity should regain the organic power in human society which once it possessed. I cannot help that; I never said it could. I am not a politician; I am proposing no measures, but exposing a fallacy, and resisting a pretence. Let Benthamism reign, if men have no aspirations; but do not ... attempt by philosophy what once was done by religion. The ascendancy of Faith may be impracticable, but the reign of Knowledge is incomprehensible. The problem for statesmen of this age is how to educate the masses, and literature and science cannot give the solution.

In *The Rise and Progress of Universities* (1872), Newman expatiated on what he believed truly constitutes university education. For Newman, "taking human nature as it is, the thirst of knowledge and the opportunity of quenching it" might be "the real life of a great school of philosophy and science" but they "will not be sufficient for its establishment... they will not work to their ultimate end, which is the attainment and propagation of truth, unless surrounded by influences of another sort, which have no pretension indeed to be the essence of a University, but are conservative of that essence". And here Newman commended those influences that foster "faith, chastity and love", not exactly the attributes that will come most readily to mind when one thinks of the current university, or indeed the university with which Newman himself was familiar. Even in his own time, Newman's blueprint for true university education was revolutionary, though now, when the post-modern university has degenerated into gnostic chaos, Newman's prescriptions are perhaps more compelling than they have ever been. No parent chary of his child's truly benefiting from proper university education will doubt the good sense and indeed wisdom of what Newman argues here, when he contends that

> regularity, rule, respect for others, the eye of friends and acquaintances, the absence from temptation, external restraints generally, are of first importance in protecting us against ourselves. When a boy leaves his home, when a peasant leaves his country, his faith and morals are in great danger, both because he is in the world, and also because he is among strangers. The remedy, then, of the perils which a University presents to the student, is to create within it homes... such as those, or better than those, which he has left behind. Small communities must be set up within its precincts, where his better thoughts will find countenance, and his good resolutions support; where his waywardness will be restrained, his heedlessness forewarned, and his prospective deviations anticipated. Here, too, his diligence will be steadily stimulated; he will be kept up to his aim; his progress will be ascertained, and his week's work, like a labourer's, measured. It is not easy for a young man to determine for himself whether he has mastered what he has been taught; a careful catechetical training, and a jealous scrutiny into his power of expressing himself and of turning his knowledge to account, will be necessary, if he is really to profit from the able Professors whom he is attending; and all this he will gain from the College Tutor.

Newman would renew his criticism of the university's misguided faith in knowledge in *The Idea of a University* (1873), which he based on lectures he gave in Dublin in 1852. In one of the lectures, as Dr. Shrimpton shows, Newman took issue with the trifling omniscience that universities had begun to require of their students for "distracting and enfeebling the mind by an unmeaning profusion of subjects" and "implying that a smattering in a dozen branches of study is not shallowness ... but enlargement..." Students were taught not a few things well but many things poorly, with the result that they left their colleges "frivolous, narrow-minded, and resourceless". Indeed, many left "so shallow as not even to know their shallowness".

Yet Newman's refusal to regard knowledge as the end of university education went beyond his contention that the mere accumulation of knowledge left the young uneducated. He also saw the inadequacy of such an end for the moral education of the young.

> Liberal Education makes not the Christian, not the Catholic, but the gentleman. It is well to be a gentlemen, it is well to have a cultivated intellect, a delicate taste, a candid, equitable, dispassionate mind, a noble and courteous bearing in the conduct of life; – these are the connatural qualities of a large knowledge; they are the objects of a University; I am advocating, I shall illustrate and insist upon them; but still, I repeat, they are no guarantee for sanctity or even for conscientiousness, they may attach to the man of the world, to the profligate, to the heartless ... Quarry the granite rock with razors, or moor the vessel with a thread of silk; then may you hope with such keen and delicate instruments as human knowledge and human reason to contend against those giants, the passion and the pride of man.

Against any superficial reliance on knowledge *per se*, Newman extolled what he nicely referred to as "the sovereignty of Truth", convinced that "Error may flourish for a time; but Truth will prevail in the end". Indeed, for Newman, "The only effect of error ultimately is to promote Truth", a reassuring reminder to those who might otherwise despair of the manifold error now entrenched in our current universities, where, as Steven Hayward recently reported in *National Review*, the ascendant "postmodern Left ... openly rejects reason, objectivity and truth as tools of oppression".

Once in charge of the Catholic University, Newman put many of his educational ideas to the test. While respecting the role that research should play in the university, he believed it should be pursued in academies close to but outside the university proper, where teaching should have pride of place. He encouraged his professors and heads of houses to take a pastoral interest in their charges; he made practical recommendations for remedial studies for undergraduates coming to the University unprepared for University work; and he gave students a degree of liberty which shocked the Irish hierarchy. In his Dublin lectures, Newman justified this latitude with a cogency that should appeal to those in our own midst who wish to roll back the salutary freedoms of students.

> If then a University is a direct preparation for this world, let it be what it professes. It is not a Convent; it is not a Seminary; it is a place to fit men of the world for the world. We cannot possibly keep them from plunging into the world, with all its ways and principles and maxims, when their time comes; but we can prepare them against what is inevitable; and it is not the way to learn to swim in troubled waters, never to have gone into them.

The results of Newman's efforts were mixed. By all contemporary accounts, they were nothing as impractical as later critics of Newman's educational views charged. In fact, ironically enough, it was the most practical of the Catholic University's disciplines, the medical school, which enjoyed the most success. Then, again, with regard to Newman's pragmatic approach to principle, Dr. Shrimpton quotes J. H. Pollen, the professor of fine arts at the University and friend of Edward Burne-Jones and John Everett Millais, who confirmed how Newman "encouraged you to put your conclusions into terms; to see what they looked like from various sides; to reconsider, prune or develop them as might be required". In *The Making of Men*, Dr. Shrimpton shows how this is precisely what Newman himself did in trying to make the Catholic University succeed.

The sense of shared purpose that Newman inspired in his professors notwithstanding, the Catholic University failed. Never securing the requisite charter to confer degrees, it never recruited enough students to sustain its enrollments. Then, again, the Irish considered the University too English and the English considered it too

Irish. And Newman never received the support he needed from Archbishop Paul Cullen, who always opposed the considerable role that his rector was prepared to give the laity in the University. However, despite these challenges, the Catholic University that Newman designed and put into practice continues to be the model for all truly Catholic higher education today and *The Idea of a University* remains the best book ever written on university education. Those interested in learning how these two enduring achievements came about will find Dr. Shrimpton's study an enthralling, enlightening read.

Index

Action française 159, 163, 164
Adam, Robert 281
Adams, Henry 352
Addison, Joseph 407
Addison, Paul 260
Alanbrooke, Alan Francis
  Brooke, 1st Viscount of
  Brookeborough 10
Albert, Leon Battista 176
Aldington, Richard 101
Alexander, Michael 217
  on Hopkins, Gerard
    Manley 398–9
  on Jones, David 83–4, 399–400
  *Medievalism: The Middle Ages
    in Modern England* 396–400
Alexandra, Queen of England
  (Alix) 273–8
Alice, Countess of Athlone
  on "arduous profession of
    royals" 139–40
Ambrose, St. 38
American Revolutionary
  War 205–11
  and "elusive loyalists" 209–10
Amis, Kinglsey 58
Arlen, Harold 363, 364
Arnold, Matthew 57, 101, 356
Athanasius, St. 38
Arnold-Baker, Charles
  and *Companion to British
    History* 23, 26–7
  on Aldershot 27
  on Churchill 24–5
  and conversion 25
  on Inner Temple 26
  on Nazis 25–6
  on Philby, Kim 25

Asquith, Herbert Henry, 1st Earl
  of Oxford and Asquith
  and Churchill 1
  and Edward VII 277
Asquith, Margot 369
Attlee, Clement
  on Churchill 1, 8, 256
Auden, Wystan Hugh 58, 60–3,
  201
  on art and religion 63
  on street sellers and
    entertainers 188
  and "The Sea and the
    Mirror" 62–3
Augustine, St. 10, 18–22, 63
  and respect for ordinary
    people 19
  and Newman, Blessed John
    Henry 19
  and Original Sin 20
  on the State 20–1
Austen, Jane 134, 329
Ayer, Sir Alfred Jules 110, 421

Babb, George Fletcher 229
Babeuf, Gracchus 109
Bacon, Sir Francis 145
Bagehot, Walter
  on Sir Robert Peel 29–30
Bainbridge, Beryl 347
  and historical novel 397
Baldovinetti, Alesso 334
Baldwin, Stanley, 1st Earl Baldwin
  of Bewdley
  and Churchill 1, 9
Balfour, Lord Arthur 93
  and Edward VII 277
  on Tenniel, John 99

433

Ball, Frances Teresa 287–8
Balzac, Honoré de 182, 183, 235, 352
Barber, Francis 328–9
Barberi, Dominic 35–6
Barker, Juliet
   on Agincourt 146–51
Barrow, Isaac 408
Barry, Charles
   and Pugin 270–1
   and Palace of
      Westminster 270–1
Batchelor, John 382
Bate, Walter Jackson 326
Beauclerk Topham 322
Beckett, Samuel
   and Fitzgerald, Penelope 345
   and Johnson, Samuel 330, 409
Beerbohm, Max
   and Chesterton, G. K. 57
   on Godwin, Edward 171
   on Irving, Henry 173
Beerbohm Tree, Herbert 169
Bellini, Giovanni
   Portrait of Doge Leonardo Loredan 334–5
Bellini, Jacopo 383
Belloc, Hilaire 11, 53, 57, 279, 298
   on Chesterton's hunger for reality 53
   on Samuel Johnson's prose 407
   "The Prophet Lost on the Hills of Evening" 81–2
Benedict XV, Pope 112–13
   on deification of the State 132
   on nationalism and the Great War 112
Benedict XVI, Pope
   and "hermeneutic of continuity" 421–2
Bennett, Arnold 279
Bentham, Jeremy 57
Beresford, John 285

Bergson, Henri 161
Berlin, Irving 363
   and Porter, Cole 365
   Top Hat 365
Berlin, Isaiah
   on Churchill 1
Bernanos, Georges 158
Bernard, G. W.
   and Henry VIII 339–42
Bernini, Gian Lorenzo 49, 50
Best & Co. 89
Betjeman, John 89, 136
Bible 20, 42, 176, 198, 204, 214, 291, 292, 293, 324, 354
   and Great American Songbook 363–4
   and Victorians 291–5
Binyon, Laurence 380–1
Bismarck, Otto von 99, 112
Blake, William 62, 91
Blavatsky, Helena
   and Yeats, W. B. 56
Blogg, Frances Alice, Chesterton's wife 57, 356
Bloy, Léon
   and influence on Maritain 163
Blunden, Edmund 379
Blunt, Wilfrid Scawen 277
Blyenberch, Abraham 64
Blythe, Ronald
   and Lansbury, George 321
   The Age of Illusion 321
Boer War 8, 276
   and Majuba Hill 29
Bonaparte, Napoleon 100
Bonham-Carter, Violet 11, 256
Borromeo, St. Charles 38
Borromini, Francesco 50
Borrow, George
   and Liebling, Joseph 312
Bosch, Hieronymus 12
Boswell, James 68, 263, 311, 322, 323, 324, 326, 327, 328, 329,

Index

330, 332, 333, 401, 403, 405, 409
Botticelli, Sandro 92, 95, 176
Boyle, the Hon. Robert 193
Bowen, Elizabeth 182, 285
Bowes Lyon, David
Bramante, Donate 49, 335
Brewer, John
   The Pleasures of Imagination 208
Bridges, Robert 152, 214
Brogan, Denis 257
Bronson, Bertrand 403
Brontë, Charlotte 212
Brontës 147
Brookfield, Jane Octavia
   and Thackeray's "uncouth raptures" 194
Brougham, Henry, 1st Baron Brougham and Vaux
   and *The Tamworth Reading Room* 428
Brown, Peter 158
Browne, Sir Thomas 214
   and Johnson's *Dictionary* 404
Browning, Robert 56, 195
Bruce, Robert 414
Brueghel, Pieter the Elder 12
Brummel, Beau 281
Brunel, Isambard Kingdom 280
Brunelleschi 176
Bryce, James 195
Bullock, Alan 257
Burckhardt, Jacob 49, 249, 336
Burden, Wendy 87–90
Burgoyne, John ("Gentleman Johnny") 205, 281
   on American militiamen 208
   and Battle of Saratoga 207, 209
Burke, Edmund 100, 183, 205, 411, 427
   and Johnson, Samuel 322, 328
   on Marie Antoinette 396

   On Conciliation with America 207
   Reflections on the French Revolution 396–7
Burne, Alfred 147
Burne-Jones, Edward 91–5, 400
   and charm 94
   and chivalric kindness 94
   and James, Henry 95
   and Lewis, Wyndham 93
   and Morris, William 92.
   and Ruskin, John 92
   and raconteur 94–5
   and sense of humor 94
   and sense of narrative 95
   on Poynter, Edward, Royal Academician
   on influence of J. H. Newman 91–2
   King Cophetua and the Beggar Maid 94
   Perseus series 93
Burne-Jones, Philip
   on source of his father's art 92–3
Bury, J. B. 249
Butler, Perry 34
Butterfield, Herbert
   and "pleasing sensuousness of moral indignation" 250
   The Whig Interpretation of History 250
Butterfield, William 272
Byron, George Gordon, Lord 212, 279, 382

Caligula, Emperor 338
Camden, William 64
Campbell-Bannerman, Sir Henry
   and Edward VII 277
Canaletto 383
Carpaccio 383
Caporetto, battle of 369, 372–3

Caracalla, Emperor 227, 338
Carlyle, Jane Welsh 279
Carlyle, Thomas 56, 57, 118, 267, 356, 403
　on Victorian Birmingham 91
Carmichael, Hoagy 363, 366
Carnegie, Andrew 224
Carpenter, Humphrey 60
Carson, Edward Henry, Baron 246
Cassell, Sir Ernest 277
Cave, Edward 402
Cecil, Algernon
　and League of Nations 321
Cecil, Lord Edward Christian David Gacoyne 136
Cecil, Lord Robert
　and League of Nations 320–1
Chadwick, Henry
　on St. Augustine 18
Chadwick, Owen 198
Chagall, Marc 158
Chamberlain, Neville 8, 9, 257, 260, 264, 306, 307
　and Munich 264, 306, 307
Chambers, Robert 322
Chandos, Oliver Lyttleton, 1st Viscount Chandos 9
Chapman, R. W. 403
Charlemagne
　and Huguenots 352
　and Salic Law 146
Charles, Earl Cornwallis 205, 207
　and mistreatment of troops 210
　and Battle of Camden 210
　and Clinton, Sir Henry 209
　and Yorktown 210–11
Charles V, Holy Roman Emperor 49
Charles, Prince of Wales 140
Charvet 89
Chatterton, Lady Georgiana 291
Chaucer, Geoffrey 92

Cheever, John 87
Chelsea
　and Blue Plaques of London 279–80
Chesterfield, Philip Dormer Stanhope, 4th Earl of 411
Chesterton, Gilbert Keith 53, 82–3
　and anti-modernism 355–7
　and bonhomie of Fleet Street 56
　and common man 56
　and Father Brown 56
　and Foch, Ferdinand 55
　and intellectuals 56
　and limitation 54
　on "horrible mysticism of money" 1
　on hagiography 35
　on holiness 36
　on marriage 54–5
　on "oil of the Pharisees" 43
　and Pound, Ezra 56
　on shallows and depths 55–6
　"Lepanto" 84
　"The Song against Grocers" 83
　Manalive 54
　Orthodoxy 57, 357
　St. Francis of Assisi 57
　St. Thomas Aquinas 57
　The Everlasting Man 57
　The Man Who Was Thursday 56
　The Napoleon of Notting Hill 56
　The Thing 357
　The Victorian Age in Literature 57, 356
　Where All Roads Lead 54
Christie, Agatha 129
Chrysostom, St. John 38
Churchill, Clementine 5, 6, 10
Churchill, Jennie 274
Churchill, John, 1st Duke of Marlborough 5

Index

Churchill, Randolph (father of Winston Churchill) 2
  and religion 2
  and Ulster Protestantism 2
Churchill, Randolph (son of Winston Churchill) 8
Churchill, Winston Spencer 1–11
  and appeasement 254
  and Catholicism 2, 3, 4, 6–7
  and Chamberlain, Neville 8–9
  and Christianity 3
  and Christian civilization 10–11
  and Churchill, Randolph (son) 8
  and Churchill, Randolph (father) 8
  and egoism 10
  and Edward VII 277
  and English Civil War 2
  and fondness for brandy 24–5
  and fondness for smoking cigars 6
  and Gibbon, Edward 4
  and gold standard 1
  and Harrow 8
  and historians 9–10
  and House of Commons 2, 8
  and Jews 8
  and laws against Popery 2
  and magnanimity 9
  and military history 1
  and Mosley, Diana and Oswald 8
  and Navy 1
  and nominal Christianity 5
  and oratory 8–9
  and Pearl Harbor 9
  and poor 4, 5
  and Protestantism 3
  and Ranke's *History of the Popes* 7
  and religion 2–3, 4, 5, 6
  and Sandhurst 3, 8
  and sympathy for those in distress 7
  and totalitarian evil 1, 10
  and unemployment insurance 1
  and war 7
  as author and historian 256–61
  on "non-God religions, Nazism and Communism" 114
  Frontiers and Wars 257–8
  History of the English Speaking Peoples (1956–8) 2, 257, 258, 260, 262, 265, 266
  Lord Randolph Churchill 8
  My Early Life: A Roving Commission 4
  The Second World War 6
Cicero 129
Clark, Jonathan 326
Clark, Kenneth
  and National Gallery 306–10
  on Catholic Church 50–1
  on Counter-Reformation 76
  on Davies, Martin 309
  on Hess, Myra 310
  on Leonardo 177
  on postwar European civilization 310
  on Ruskin's prose style 386
  Civilization (1969) 51
Clarke, Samuel 408
Clemenceau, Georges 162, 318–19
Clement VII, Pope 51
Clinton, Sir Henry 205
  and Yorktown 211
  and Lord Cornwallis 209
  and Siege of Charleston 210
Clive, Robert, 1st Baron Clive 253, 281
Cloetta, Yvonne 121
Clovis 352
Cobbett, William 57
  and Pugin 271
  Rural Rides 271

Cockerell, Sir Charles 270
Cole, Heather 190, 196
Cole, Henry 195
Coleridge, Samuel Taylor 147, 201, 403
Collingwood, Robin George
  on Fascism 131
  on "fashionable scientific fraud" 132–3
  on history 131
  on Prussianism 131
  on Rugby School 128–9
  on tendentiousness in historians 130
  An Essay on Philosophical Method 130
  Autobiography 128
  The Idea of History 129
  The Principles of Art 130
Colville, Sir John Rupert "Jock" 7–8, 258
Compton-Burnett, Ivy 172
Comte, Auguste 110
Congress of Vienna 319
Conlon, D. J. 58
Connolly, Cyril 126
Conquest, Robert 84
Constantine, Emperor 49
Coolidge, Calvin 225
Cooper, Diana 145
Cooper, Sir Alfred Duff, 1st Viscount Norwich 256, 264, 265
Courtauld, George 352
Coward, Nöel 136
Cowley, Abraham 64
Crashaw, Richard 77–8
Cripps, Stafford 279
Crispi, Francesco 107
Cromwell, Oliver 258, 259
Cromwell, Thomas
  and dissolution of monasteries 251
  and *malleus monarchorum* 340
Cullen, Cardinal Paul 287
Curry, Anne 147
Curzon, George Nathaniel, Marquis Curzon of Kedleston 6

Dalrymple, Theodore
  Life at the Bottom: the Worldview that Makes the Underclass 132
Dance, George 280
Dante 106, 338
Daudet, Alphonse 217
David, Elizabeth 89
Davie, Donald 84
Davidson, Harold, Rector of Stiffkey 6
Dawson, Christopher
  on "encroachments of state power" 111–12
Deaken, William 251
Deborah Vivien Cavendish, Duchess of Devonshire
  on Elizabeth the Queen Mother 140
Defoe, Daniel
  and Liebling, Joseph 312
  Robinson Crusoe 281, 357
De Maria, Robert
  and Johnson, Samuel 326, 402
Demosthenes 129
Descartes, René 161, 177
Desmoulins, Elizabeth
  and Johnson, Samuel 328
De Valera, Eamon
  and Irish neutrality 285–6
Dickens, Charles 57, 96, 97, 282
  "Night Walks" 282
  David Copperfield 54
  Nicholas Nickleby 282
  Oliver Twist 282
  Pickwick Papers 282

Disraeli, Benjamin 98, 99, 281
  and biography and history 267
  Contarini Fleming 267
Dissolution of the
  Monasteries 341–2
Dixon, Richard Watson 216
Dodgson, Charles ("Lewis
  Carroll") 96–100
  and wine cellar of Christ
    Church 99
Dodsley, Robert
  and Johnson's *Dictionary* 401
Donaldson, Frances 142
  and fox hunting 361–2
Donne, John 75–7
  on the appeal of suicide 76
Doyle, Richard "Dicky" 98
Dublin 214, 284–90
Dürer, Albrecht
  and Renaissance
    portraiture 338
Dreyfus Affair 159, 162
Drummond, William 64, 65
  and Shakespeare 68
Dryden, John 64, 98, 101
  on Donne 76
Duffy, Eamon
  Stripping of the Altars 340
Dunsany, Edward John Moreton
  Drax Plunkett 18th Baron
  and the immortal Jorkens 182

Eden, Emily 212
Edict of Nantes 351, 352
Edward III, King of England 146,
  147
Edward VI 336
Edward VII, King of England 13,
  273–8
  and Albert Edward, Prince of
    Wales 273–5
  and Alexandra 274
  and biographers 274
  and distaste for
    xenophobia 276
  and flare for diplomacy 276
  and Dublin 13
  and Elizabeth II 275
  and *Entente Cordiale* 276
  and George V 276
  and Great War 276
  and Joyce, James 13
  and ministers 277
  and obligations of
    constitutional monarchy 277
  and philanthropy 276–7
  and appeal for contemporaries
    275, 276, 277–8
Edwardians 137, 172
Elgar, Edward 134
Eliot, George 195, 279
  and Fitzgerald, Penelope 345
Eliot, Henry Ware
  on marriage 105–6
Eliot, Thomas Stearns 58, 101–6,
  201, 225, 409
  and Arnold, Matthew 392
  and McKim, Mead and
    White 227
  and *The Criterion* 104
  and religion 393, 395
  and Woolf, Virginia 105
  on Chesteron, G. K. 355, 400
  on fallacies of romantic art 392
  on Jonson, Ben 67–8
  "Ash Wednesday" 106
  "Marina" 393
  "Virgil and the Christian
    World" 399
  After Strange Gods 392
  Four Quartets 106
  The Waste Land 106, 218, 392,
    395
Elizabeth, the Queen Mother
  and abdication crisis 137
  and Battle of Britain 138

and Black Watch 136–7
and "bogus upheavals" 140
and charm 134, 137, 140
and childhood in Italian
　villas 135
and delight in food 135–6
and education of children in
　Christian principals 138
and George VI 138–9
and Great War 136–7
and literary friends 136
and *louche* ancestry 135
and munificence 139
and Sitwell, Edith 139
and unflagging diligence 140
on Churchill, Winston 139
Elizabeth II, Queen of
　England 134, 135, 138, 139, 140
Ellington, Edward Fitzgerald
　("Duke") 363, 367–8
Elton, Sir Geoffrey Rudolph 249,
　250
Erasmus, Desiderius 338, 339
Eton College 135, 274, 320, 344
Evans, F. M. 98
Everest, Elizabeth Anne,
　"Woom" 8
Ewart, William 280
Eyck, Jan van 334

Faber, Frederick 418
Faulkner, William 87
Feast of St. Mark 335
Feiling, Keith 257
Fichte, Johann Gottlieb 109
Figes, Orlando
　The People's Tragedy 107
Fisher, Lord John ("Jackie") 369
Fitzgerald, Francis Scott 87, 329
Fitzgerald, Penelope 91, 343–8
　and historical novel 397
　and human failure 347–8
　The Beginning of Spring 346–7

Fitzgibbon, John, 1st Earl of
　Clare 299
Foch, Ferdinand 55
Forbes Robertson, Johnston
Ford, Ford Madox 252, 315
Foster, Stephen 363
Fourier, Charles 110
Fox, Charles James 100
Foxe, John
　Foxe's Book of Martyrs 292
Francis de Sales, St. 127
Francis I, King of France
　and Leonardo 177
Francis II, King of France 351
Frank, Semyon Ludovich 114
Franklin, Benjamin
　and "barbarity and cruelty" of
　British in American
　War of Independence 206, 208
French Revolution 57, 108, 109,
　268
Freud, Sigmund 62
Froude, James Anthony
　and Henry VIII 339
　and Huguenots 349–50
Froude, Richard Hurrell 37
　and pastoral nature of tutorial
　charge 427–8
　and sanctity 38
Fry, Elizabeth
　and teetotalism 293

Galileo 51
Galsworthy, John 280
Gandhi, Mahatma 280
Garibaldi, Giuseppe 109
Garrick, David 322, 328
Garrigou-Lagrange, Reginald
　on blasphemy of
　impenitence 124
　on mysteries of iniquity 122
Gaucort, Raul de 148
Gauricus, Pomponius 338

Index

Gautier, Théophile 217
Gaulle, Charles de 165
Gay, John 284
George III, King of England 100, 135, 253, 326
  and American War of Independence 205, 206
George V, King of England
  and his father, Edward VII 276
George VI, King of England 134, 136
Germain, Lord George
  and American Revolutionary War 205
Germany and Germans
  and *Kulturkampf* and German Catholic Centre party 112–13
  and spoils of Nazis 25–6
  and Troeltsch, Ernst 110
Gershwin, George 363, 367–8
Ghirlandaio, Domenico 334
  and *Portrait of a Lady* 337
Gibbon, Edward 4, 5, 131, 205, 207, 249, 259, 307, 318, 427
  and formation as historian 207
  and Lord North's debating skills 207
Gielgud, John
  and Guiness, Alec 297
Gilbert, William Schwenck 280
Gilson, Etienne 57, 152
  on Maritain, Jacques 166–7
Giorgione 234, 383
Girouard, Mark
  Sweetness & Light: The Queen Anne Movement 230
Goldsmith, Oliver 322, 328
Gomme, Laurence 280
Gladstone, William Ewart 28–34, 98, 280
  and Bagehot, Walter 29–30
  and Irving, Henry 171
  and liberalism 31–2
  and Macaulay, Lord 28
  and sin 34
  and Tractarianism 33
  and Vatican Decrees 111
Glover, Dorothy 121
Goethe, Johann Wolfgang von 24
Gordon, Lyndall 103
Gore-Booth, Countess Constance 183
Gossaert, Jan
  An Elderly Couple 337
Gothic 272, 396–400
Grasse, François-Joseph Paul, comte de
  and the Chesapeake 209
Grattan, Henry 284, 285
  and speech on Act of Union 289–90
Graves, Robert 257, 379–80
Gray, Effie
  on Ruskin in Venice 384
Great Exhibition 185, 195, 271, 272
Gregory, St. 38, 154
Greene, Donald 403
Green, John Richard
  on Henry V 146
  on Henry VIII 339
Greene, Graham 238–44
  and literature and faith 242–3
  and Newman, John Henry 125, 242–3
  and mundanity of evil 25
  and "revolt against married domesticity" 241
  and Waugh, Evelyn 124, 242
  and "workshop criticism" 126
  on Chesterton, G. K. 126
  on Maugham, Somerset 126–7
  on Rolfe, Frederick 126
  "A Visit to Morin" 118–19
  A Burnt-Out Case 242
  A Sort of Life 120, 238

Brighton Rock 119, 122, 240
The End of the Affair 123–4, 240
The Heart of the Matter 119, 123, 240
The Honorary Consul 242
The Human Factor 242
The Man Within 240
The Power and the Glory 120, 125, 240
The Stamboul Train 240
The Third Man 240
Greene, General Nathaniel
  and amateur soldiers of America 208, 210
Greene, Vivien (nee Dayrell-Browning) 120–1
Grosjean, Marie Louise, Chesterton's mother 55
Gross John 58
Guest, Ivor 3
Guinness, Alec 296–300
  and Catholic Tradition 298
  and conversion 296, 298
  and failure 299
  and fondness for Catholic authors 298
  and Francis de Sales 299
  and grace 297, 299
  and illegitimacy 298
  and Julian of Norwich 298
  and mother 296–7
  and Neame, Ronald 300
  and personal characteristics 299–300
  and struggles to live the devout life 299
Blessings in Disguise 296
My Name Escapes Me 298
The Card 300
The Horse's Mouth 300
Tunes of Glory 300
Guinness, Desmond
  and Irish Georgian Society 289
Guinness, Merula 300
Gurney, Ivor 376–7

Habington, William 78–80
Haigh, Christopher
  English Reformations 340
Haigh-Wood, Maurice 103
Haigh-Wood, Vivien 101
Halifax, Edward Frederick Lindsey Wood, 1st Earl of 262
Hall, Edward
  on Henry V 146
Hallam, Henry 3, 250
Handel, George Frideric 214
Harding, Warren G. 225
Hardy, Thomas 378
Harris, Sir Arthur Travers, "Bomber Harris" 7
Harriss, Gerald
  on Battle of Agincourt 150–1
Harrow School 8, 350
Hart, Lorenz 366
Hastings, Max 260
Hastings, Selina 121, 142
Haughey, Charles 182
Hausmann, George Eugéne 227
Hawkins, Edward 428
Hawthorne, Nathaniel 329
Hayward, Steven
  on postmodern university 430
Hazlitt, William 403
  and Liebling, Joseph 312
  on Henry V 146
Heaney, Seamus
  on Auden 60
Hegel, Georg Wilhelm Friedrich 24
Hemingway, Ernest 87
Henry V, King of England 146–51
  and Catholic faith 146–7
  and reasons for invading France 147

Index 443

and siege of Harfleur 148–9
and Battle of Agincourt 149–51
and Fleet prison 148
Henry VIII, King of England 322
Hess, Myra 310
Hewison, John
  on Ruskin and Venice 382–6
Hibbert, Christopher 147
Hill, Christopher 254, 258
Hill, Geoffrey
  and Coleridge, S. T. 221
  and critical writings 217–22
  on Arnold, Matthew 219–20
  on Burton, Robert 220–1
  on Eliot, T. S. 218–19
  on Hopkins, G. M. 221–2
  on Swift, Jonathan 220
  on Vaughan, Henry 220
  "Lachrimae" 82
Hilton, Tim 382
Himmelfarb, Gertrude 187–8, 189, 255
Hitchings, Henry
  and Samuel Johnson 326, 401–11
Hitler, Adolf 8, 10, 30, 62, 115, 259, 260, 262, 264, 306, 307, 315, 319, 321
  and Craig, Gordon 172
  and Elizabeth, Queen 134
  and Pope Pius XII 115–17
Hobbes, Thomas 259
  and Johnson's refusal to cite in his *Dictionary* 408
Hobsbawn, Eric 254
Hodge, Alan 257
Holbein, Hans 334, 338
Holland, Henry 281
Holroyd, Michael 168–74
Hopkins, Gerard Manley 72–4, 86
  and correspondence 212–16
  and "fine delight that fathers thought" 157
  and Society of Jesus 216
  and literary criticism 214
  and Our Lady 74–5
  and philology 213
  and poetry 213
  and St. Ignatius of Loyola 216
  on alms 152
  on character 215
  on conversion 212
  on Doughty's *Arabia Deserta* 214
  on fame 215–6
  on music 213–4
  on respect for failure 215
  "The Leaden Echo and the Golden Echo" 215
  "The Windhover" 398
  "The Wreck of the Deutschland" 215–16
Homer 129
Hooker, Richard 410
Hoover, Herbert 225
Horace 64
Howard, Deborah
  on Ruskin's view of the Gothic in Venice 385
Howard, Michael 249
Howe, Admiral Richard, Lord
  and American Revolutionary War 205
Howe, General Sir William
  and American Revolutionary War 205
  and Battle of Long-Island 207–8
Hughes, Ted 136
Huguenots 349–54
  and Blessed Virgin 352
  and diaspora from France 351
  and emigration into England 353
  and iconoclasm 352–3

Hume, David
    and American Revolutionary
        War 207–8
Hunt, Leigh 279
Huxley, Thomas 57
    and Bible 291, 293–4
Hyde, Douglas 16

Ibsen, Henrik 168
Ireland and the Irish 6, 179–83
Industrial Revolution 271, 358
Irish Republican Army (IRA) 14, 287
Irving, Henry 168–74
Islam 11, 62, 108, 421

Jacob, E. F.
    on Henry V 146, 147
Jackson, Cyril 427
Jacob, Sir Ian 7
James, Henry 60, 195, 230
    and Henry Irving 174
    and New York 233, 236
    on Burne-Jones, Edward 95
    on "critical sense" 217
    on St. Peter's Basilica and
        Roman Catholicism 51–2
    on Ruskin and Venice 382
    Italian Hours (1909) 51–2
    The Portrait of a Lady
        (1882) 106
    The Sacred Fount (1901) 102–3
Jennings, Elizabeth 84–5
Jerome, Jenny (Winston
    Churchill's mother) 2
John, Augustus 173, 279
John Lobb 89
Johnson, Philip 89

Johnson, Samuel 201
    and American Revolutionary
        War 207
    and "decent provision for the
        poor" 1, 327
    and "chief glory of every
        people" 375
    and holy fear 324, 329
    and letters 212
    and Mellon, Andrew 223–6
    and mother 411
    and spiritual writings 322–5
    on biography 296, 300
    on charity 324–5
    on Church of Rome
    on confession 324
    on duties of life 118–19
    on forgiveness 325
    on Inquisition 324
    on "light to the repositories of
        science" 410
    on purgatory 323
    The Adventurer 327
    The Idler 327
    *A Journey of the Western Isles of
        Scotland* 327, 333
    Lives of the English Poets 223
    The Rambler 325, 327, 331, 403, 406
    Rasselas 226, 327
    Taxation No Tyranny 207
Jonson, Ben 64–70
    and conversion 66
    and tradition 67
    on poverty 65
    on power of money 66
    "An Execration upon
        Vulcan" 69
    "Epistle Mendicant" 65
    "Epistle to Elizabeth, Countess
        of Rutland" 66
    "To Heaven" 67
    Discoveries 65

Sejanus 66, 67
Staple of News 66
The Masque of Queens 67
Volpone 66, 67
Jones, David 380, 397, 399, 400
  "Religion and the Muses" 83–4
Joplin, Scott 363
Jowett, Benjamin
  on conversions to
    Catholicism 213
Joyce, James 12–14, 58, 235
  and British passport 12–13
  and Dublin 284–5
  and Edward VII 13
  and Jonson, Ben 67
  and O'Brien, Flann 12–14
  and *Robinson Crusoe* 281
  and Roman Catholicism 71–2
  and Sloane, John 235
  and *The Dalkey Archive* 15–16
  and Trevor, William 388
  on Gladstone 29
  "Ivy Day in the Committee
    Room" 13
  Dubliners 284
  Finnegans Wake 72
  Ulysses 71–2
Joyce, Stanislaus 71–2
  on *Ulysses* 71–2
Julius II, Pope 49, 50, 335–6

Kant, Immanuel 128, 161
Kavanagh, P. J. 58
Keats, John 212, 279, 397–8
  and Richardson, Sir Ralph 398
  "La Belle Dame sans
    Merci" 397–8
Keble, John 155
Keegan, John
  on Italian army in Great
    War 372
Keen, Maurice 151
Kendall, Tom
  *Modern English War
    Poetry* 378
  *Poetry of the First World
    War* 375–81
Kenner, Hugh
Keppel, Alice 274
Ker, Ian 158, 197–200
  on *Callista* 425
  on Chesterton, G. K. 53–9
  on Newman, J. H., and Vatican
    II 418–25
  on Bible 198
Kermode, Frank 201
Kershaw, Ian
  and Hitler, Adolf 321
Keynes, John Maynard
  and Treaty of Versailles 319
Kierkegaard, Søren 62
Kipling, Rudyard 60
  on death of Edward Burne-
    Jones 95
Klieforth, Alfred W.
  on meeting with Pacelli 116
Knox, Ronald 6, 145, 216
Knowles, Dom David 6, 252
  and England during the English
    Reformation 341
Koterski, Father Joseph
  and More, St. Thomas 341
Küng, Hans 423

Laforge, Jules 103
Lamb, Charles 279
Landor, Walter Savage 82
Langtry, Lillie 274, 279
Lansbury, George 321
Lardner, Ring 87
Larkin, James 288
Larkin, Philip 84
  and Sitwell, Edith 413
Lawrence, David Herbert 62
Le Carré, John 259
League of Cambrai 334–5

Lecky, William Edward
  Hartpole 267
Lee, J. J.
  and Irish neutrality 285–6
Lefebvre, Marcel 423
Leonardo da Vinci 175–8
  and Borgia, Cesare 177
  and Florence 176
  and Milan 176–7
  and Sforza, Ludovico 176–7
Leo the Great, St. 38
Leslie, Shane
  on Churchill's *Lord Randolph Churchill* 8
Lewis, Clive Staples
  on Donne 76
Lewis, Wyndham 101
Leybourne, George ("Champagne Charlie") 281
Liddon, Henry Parry 212
Liebling, Joseph 89
  and literary influences 312
  and Ross, Harold
  on liberation of France 317
  on World War II 311–17
  "Paddy of the RAF" 313
  "Westbound Tanker" 313
  "Channel Crossing" 313
  "Mollie" 313, 316–17
  Between Meals: An Appetite for Paris 313–14
  Normandy Revisited 312
  The Road Back to Paris 312
Lomazzo, Gian Paolo
  and *passioni dell' animo* 338
Lorenzetti, Ambrogio 95
Lloyd, Marie 281
Lloyd George, David
  and Churchill, Winston 1
  and finance bill 277
  and oratory 277
  and Treaty of Versailles 318–20
Lotto, Lorenzo 334

Louis IX, St
  and Huguenots 352
Lowell, Robert 152, 316
Luther, Martin 49, 161
Lutyens, Mary 382
Lyell, Charles 294–5

Macaulay, Thomas Babington, 1st Baron Macaulay 259, 403
  and Boswell, James 267
  and Churchill, Winston 3
  and Gibbon, Edward 234
  and Johnson, Samuel 403
  and Ranke's *History of the Popes* 7
  on Catholicism 7
  on Gladstone, W. E. 28–9
  on Johnson, Samuel 402
  on walking 234
  on war 252
Machiavelli, Nicolò
  The Prince 177
MacIntyre, Alasdair 30
Mackesy, Piers
  The War for America 205
McKim, Mead and White 227–32
  and Eliot, T. S. 229
  and James, Henry 230–1
  and Mencken, H. L. 230–1
  Boston Public Library 232
  Metropolitan Club 227
  Metropolitan Museum 227
  Municipal Building 227
  Percy Rivington Pyne House 231
  Pennsylvania Station 227
  Robert Goelet House 230
  University Club 227
  Villard Houses 227
  Washington Square Arch 227
  Watts-Sherman House 230
McQuaid, Archbishop John Charles 285

Maderno, Carlo 49
Maitland, F. W. 250
  on Stubbs, William 397
Malory, Sir Thomas 92
Mandeville, Bernard
  The Fable of the Bees 408
Manning, Henry Edward
  and 22 Carlisle Place 283
  and "deification of the civil power" 110
Mare, Walter de la 344
Marlborough House 277
Maritain, Jacques 83, 158–67
  on anti-Semitism 164
  on marriage 160
  Trois Reformateurs 161–2
Maritain, Raïssa 160–1
Marx, Karl 62, 107
Marxism 108
Mary, Blessed Virgin, Mother of Jesus Christ 154–5
Mary I, Tudor, Queen of England 64
Matthew, Colin 29
Matthew, St. 38
Maugham, Somerset 283
Mauriac, Francois 158
Maurras, Charles 164
Mayhew, Henry 97, 184–9
  London Labour and the London Poor (1851) 82, 184–9
Medievalism 396–400
Mellon, Andrew 223–6
  and contempt for Catholic Irish 225
  and Wall Street Crash (1929) 225–6
Memling, Hans 334
Mencken, Henry Louis 230, 231
  "On Suicide" 90
Meredith, George 415
Metternich, Prince Clemens Lothar Wenzel 319

Michelangelo 49, 50, 176, 336
  "The Last Judgment" 51
Middendorf, John H.
  "Johnson on Wealth and Commerce" 409
Mill, John Stuart 57
Millais, Sir John 195
  and Huguenots 354
Milton, John 74, 84, 215, 322, 333, 399, 410
  and defense of *sola scriptura* Christianity 292
Mitford, Nancy 124, 283
Mommsen, Theodor 24
Monro, Harold 345
Moran, D. P.
  and Georgian era in Dublin 289
Mordaunt, Lady Harriett 275
Mordaunt, Sir Charles 275
Mor, Antonis 336
  and portrait of Mary Tudor 336–7
More, St. Thomas 322, 340–1
Morley, John 29
Morris, William 91, 272
Mosley, Diana 8, 289
Mosley, Oswald 8
Muir, Edwin
  on Sitwell, Edith 415
Murphy, William Martin 288
Murray, Archbishop Daniel 287
Murray, Elisabeth
  Caught in the Web of Words 405
Murray, John Middleton 101
Mussolini, Benito 8

Namier, Sir Lewis 249, 252–5
  1848: The Revolution of the Intellectuals 254
  England in the Age of the American Revolution 253

The Structure of Politics at the Accession of George III 253
Nash, John 268, 271
National Gallery (London)
  during World War II 306–10
National Gallery (Washington)
  and Mellon, Andrew 224
Neame, Ronald
  on Guinness, Alec 300
Nelson, Horatio, Viscount Nelson 281
Neri, St. Philip 38
Nero, Emperor 49, 110
Newman, Blessed John Henry 35–48, 158, 356
  and gravestone: *Ex umbria et imaginibus in veritatem* 53
  and Huguenots 354
  and King of Clubs 418
  and liberalism 421
  and sanctity 35–48
  and subtlety of thought 419
  and Vatican I 111
  and Vatican II 418–25
  on apostasy of England 80–1
  on Anglo-Catholicism 32
  on Bible 292
  on "faith, chastity and love" in college setting 429
  on literature 85
  on pastoral responsibilities of college tutor 429
  on "sovereignty of Truth" 430
  on "tin-kettle accounts" of himself 418
  "Nature and Grace", (1849) 44
  "Religion a Weariness to the Natural Man" (1828) 43
  "The Glories of Mary for the Sake of her Son" (1849) 47–8
  "The Second Spring" (1852) 81
  "The Weapons of Saints" (1837) 37–8
  "Truth Hidden When Not Sought After" (1830) 43
  "Unreal Words" (1839) 44
  A Letter to Duke of Norfolk 420
  Idea of a University 322, 426–32
  Meditations and Devotions 46
  Rise and Progress of Universities 408–29
Nicene Creed 153
Nicholl, Charles
  on Leonardo 175–8
Nietzsche, Friedrich Wilhelm 56, 356
Nightingale, Florence 213
North, Lord (Frederick) 205
  and conduct of Revolutionary War 206–7
  and management of war debt 206
  and "unalterable suavity" in debate 207
Norton, Charles Eliot 195
Norwich, Lord John Julius 146
Nuttall, A. D.
  and narcissism of ahistorical critics 333

Oath of Supremacy 336
O'Brien, Flann 12–17
  At-Swim-Two-Birds (1939) 13–15
  The Dalkey Archive (1964) 12, 15–16
  The Poor Mouth (1941) 16
  The Third Policeman (1940) 12, 15, 16
O'Brien, Kate
  on Dublin's "Four Hundred" 181
O'Casey, Sean 12
O'Connell, Daniel 285
O'Connor, Flannery
  on Catholic dogma and the novelist 71–2

Index 449

Oddie, William 58, 355–8
Oliphant, Mrs. Margaret 195
  and Fitzgerald, Penelope 345
Olivier, Laurence 149
  and Osborne, John 305
O'Rourke, P. J. 89
Orwell, George 126
  on Auden 60
  on Catholicism and the novel 71
  The Road to Wigan Pier 186–7
Osborne, John 301–5
  Look Back in Anger 301, 303
  The Entertainer 301, 305
O'Shaughnessy, Andrew Jackson
  The Men Who Lost America 205–11
Ottoman Empire 1
Owen, Wilfrid 375
Oxford Movement 37, 91, 428

Pacelli, Eugenio Maria Giuseppe Giovanni (later Pope Pius XII)
  and *Mit Brennender Sorge* (1937) 115–16
Palladio 384, 385
Palmerston, Henry John Temple, 3rd Viscount 281
Pankhurst, Sylvia 279
Parmigiano
  Portrait of a Collector 337–8
Parnell, Charles Stewart 13, 183
Pater, Walter 215
Patey, Douglas Lane
  Evelyn Waugh: A Critical Biography 141
Pater, Walter 4, 215
Pattison, Mark 428
Paul III, Pope 50
Paul, VI, Pope
  and Greene, Graham 243
Paul, St. 38
Peel, Sir Robert 29, 428
Péguy, Charles 119, 158

Pemble, John 382
Percy, Thomas 396
Perroy, Édouard 148
Perugino 176
Peruzzi, Baldassare 49
Philip IV, "the Fair" 352
Pisanello, Antonio 334
Pitt, William, 1st Earl of Chatham 259
  and Bailey's *Dictionary* 404
Pius IX, Pope
  and liberalism 111
  Syllabus of Errors 111
Pius XII, Pope
  and Hitler 116–17
Plautus 64
Plumb, Sir John Harold 257, 259
Pocock, J. G. A.
  on British and the American War of Independence 205
Poe, Edgar Allen 87
Ponsonby, Frederick ("Fritz") 278
Pontormo, Jacopo da 334
Pope, Alexander 284
Porta, Giacomo della 49, 50
Pound, Ezra 68, 101
Powell, Enoch 118
Powell, L. F. 403
Poynter, Edward 94
Prior, Matthew 213
Pritchett, V. S. 58
  on Greene, Graham 122
  on "the privilege of the storyteller" 388
Pugin, August Welby Northmore 267–72, 396
  and Barry, Charles 270–1
  and Catholic faith 270
  and contented family man 269
  and *Contrasts* 273
  and conversion 269–70
  and creative understanding of the past 272

and Gothic 267–8
and how principles of Gothic helped him transcend limitations of Neo-Gothic. 268
and inadequate freedom to develop his full genius 271
and lifelong passion for antiquities
and Nash, John 268, 271
and Ruskin 272
and vituperation of Smirke and Cockerell 270
Big Ben 273
The Grange 269
House of Lord 268
Palace of Westminster 268
Peer's Lobby 273
St. Augustine's 267
St. Chad's 267
St. Giles 267
Punch 98
Purcell, Thomas 213
Pusey, Edward 212, 428
and biblical scholarship 292–3

Raffles, Sir Thomas 263
Raine, Craig 203
on Eliot, T. S. 391–5
Ramsden, John 9
Raphael 49, 334, 336
Portrait of Pope Julius II 335
Ranke, Leopold van 7, 249
Read, Herbert 101
Reade, Winwood 3
The Martyrdom of Man (1872) 3
Reynolds, Joshua 328
Rickwood, Edgell 378–9
Ritchardson, Henry Hobson 228
Ritchie, Anne Thackeray 195–6
Roberts, Andrew
and "non-working class" 188
and Churchill at Harvard 266
A History of the English Speaking Peoples Since 1900, 260, 262–6
The Holy Fox: The Life of Lord Halifax 401–2
Robertson, Graham
on Burne-Jones, Edward 94–5
Rochambeau, Jean-Baptiste, comte de
and Battle of Yorktown 211
Rochester, John 340
Rodney, Sir George
and American Revolutionary War 205, 209
Roosevelt, Franklin Delano 225–6
Roosevelt, Theodore
and "milk-and-water righteousness" 30
Rose, Kenneth
The Later Cecils 320
Rosebery, Archibald, Earl of 277
Rossetti, Dante Gabriel 92
Rothschild, Nathaniel (Natty) 278–9
Rouault, Georges 158
Rousseau, Jean Jacques 110, 161
Ruskin, John 57, 74, 97, 98, 128, 356, 382–6, 396
and influence on Edward Burne-Jones 92
and influence on Penelope Fitzgerald 345–6
and Bible 291, 294–5
and Venice 382–6
on Gothic 272
on Pugin, A. W. N. 272
on *Punch* 98
on St. Mark's 386
on San Giorgio Maggiore 385
on Turner 97
Modern Painters 384

Index 451

Praeterita 383
Stones of Venice 92, 272, 382, 384, 385, 386
Russell, Bertrand 421
Russell, Lady Christabel (nee Hulme Hart) 245–8
Russell, Geoffrey, 4th Baron Ampthill 245–8
Russell, George William ("AE") 288
Russell, John Hugo, 3rd Baron Ampthill 245–8
Russell, Lord John 98
Russell, William 183

Sade, Marquis de 110
Sage, Lorna 87
Saint-Beuve, Charles Augustin 217
Saint-Simon, Claude Henri de Rouvroy, Comte de 110
St. Aubyn, Giles
"Hypocrisy only flourishes where standards are high" 274
St. Peter's Basilica 49–52
Salisbury, Lord Robert 277
Sandwich, John Montague, 4th Earl of
and American Revolutionary War 205
Sassoon, Siegfried
and Graves, Robert 379–80
"A Prayer in Old Age" 85
Memoirs of a Fox-Hunting Man 361
The Weald of Youth 377–8
Satie, Erik 158
Saud, Ibn, King of Saudi Arabia
and Churchill, W. S. 6
Savigny, Friedrich Karl von 24
Sayres, Dorothy 129
Scarisbrick, John Joseph, MBE, vii

on Henry VIII 341
Schopenhauer, Arthur 161, 356
Scott, Gilbert 272
Scott, Robert Falcon 280
Scott, Sir Walter 396
Scruton, Roger
and fox hunting 362
Seeley, Sir John Robert
and British Empire 252–3
The Expansion of England 252
Sephardic Jews 351
Shakespeare, William 68, 98, 149
and Eliot, T. S. 102
A Midsummer Night's Dream 204
Coriolanus 202
Cymbeline 169
Hamlet 168, 177, 202
Henry V 149
Julius Caesar 201, 202
King Lear 202
Love's Labours Lost 203
Macbeth 169, 334
Much Ado About Nothing 169, 203
Richard II 204
Richard III 102
Romeo and Juliet 169
The Merchant of Venice 169, 171
The Tempest 63, 202
The Winter's Tale 170
Twelfth Night 169
Titus Andronicus 142
Shaw, Artie 302
Shaw, Bernard 12, 56, 57, 173, 183
on Craig, Gordon 172
on Dublin slums 288–9
on Irish immigrants to United States 288–9
on Irving, Henry 170
on Terry, Ellen and Henry Irving 168, 172, 183, 219
Shaw, Norman 230

Sheed, Wilfrid 58
  and Great American
    Songbook 363–8
Shelden, Michael
  and misreadings of Graham
    Greene 125–6
Shelley, Percy Bysshe 61, 279
Sheridan, Richard Brinsley 281
Short, John Francis
  and Bunny Berigan's "I Can't
    Get Started" 367
Shrimpton, Paul
  *The "Making of Men": The Idea
    and Reality of Newman's
    University* 426–32
Simon, Sir John 247
Sitwell, Edith 412–17
  and Larkin, Philip 413
Sitwell, Sir George Raresby, 4th
    Baronet 414
  and delight in *Burke's
    Peerage* 414
Sitwell, Lady Ida
  and criminal moneylenders 414
  and "proud magnificent
    beauty" 416
Sitwell, Osbert
  and autobiography 414
  and malversation 415–6
Sitwell, Sachaverell 412
Sitwells 136
Sixtus V, Pope 50
Skeat, Walter 213
Slater, Ann Pasternak 103
Smirke, Robert 270
Smith, Frederick Edwin, 1st Lord
    of Birkenhead 6, 246
Smith, Sydney
  and Huguenots 354
  on Americans 263
  on Boulogne 212
Smith-Stanley, 14th Earl of
    Derby 419

Soames, Mary (Winston
    Churchill's daughter) 11
Sokolov, Raymond
  *Wayward Reporter: The Life of
    A. J Liebling* 313
Southern, R. W. 151
Southwell, Robert 75
Spanish Civil War 62
Spurgeon, Charles Haddon 293
Stafford, Jean
  and Liebling, Joseph 315–6
Stalin, Joseph 30, 258
Stephen, James Fitzjames 37
Stephen, Leslie 37
Sterne, Laurence 13, 211
Stevens, Wallace 84
Stoker, Bram 171
Stone, Norman 373–4
Strachan, Hew
  and Treaty of Versailles 321
Strachey, Lytton 173
Strathmore and Kinghorne,
    Claude George Bowes
    Lyon 14th Earl of 134–5
Street, George 272
Stubbs, William 250, 397
Sturgis, Russell 229
Surtees, Robert Smith 96, 118
  and John Jorrocks 360
Sutherland, Lucy 253
Swift, Jonathan 56, 212
  and Dublin 284, 285
  and philology 406
Swinburne, Algernon
  on Jonson, Ben 67–8
Swinburne, Richard 52–7

Taine, Hippolyte Adolphe 217
Talleyrand-Périgord, Charles
    Maurice de, Prince of
    Benevento 113
Tate, Allen 158
Taylor, A. J. P. 24, 254

Index 453

Taylor, Charles 30
Tenniel, John 96–100
  and Gillray, James 99–100
  and Mayhew, Henry 187
Tennyson, Lord Alfred 171, 195,
  377, 394, 397, 398
  "The Lotos-Eaters" 398
Terence 64
Terry, Ellen 168–74
Thackeray, William
  Makepeace 96, 190–6
  and Bearded Lady of
    Kentucky 193–4
  The Roundabout Papers 193–4
  Vanity Fair 192–3
Thadden, Elizabeth von
  and resistance to Nazi evil 26
Thomas, Aquinas St. 57
Thomas, Keith 40
Thomism 161–2, 164
Thompson, Edward Palmer 254
Thompson, Francis 81
Thorndyke, Dame Sybil 279
Thrale, Hester 326
Thurber, James 87
Titian 334, 383
Tocqueville, Alexis de 107
Tolkien, J. R. R 344
Treaty of Versailles 26, 253, 318,
  321, 373
Treece, Henry 344
Trevelyan, George Macaulay 250,
  259
Trevor, William 387–90
  and Pritchett, V. S. 388
  Cheating at Canasta 387
Troeltsch, Ernst 110
Trollope, Anthony 96
Trollope, Father George 120
Trotsky, Leon
  and social engineering 107
Turner, Joseph Mallard
  Willliam 98, 236, 383

Ruskin on Turner 97
Twain, Mark 280

Urban III, Pope 51

Vanderbilt, Cornelius 87
Vasari, Gorgio 51, 177
  on Raphael's Portrait of Pope
    Julius II 335
Vatican 49, 186
  and the Great War 115
Vatican Councils
  First 34, 111, 419, 420, 424
  Second 418–25
  "Spirit of Vatican II" 424
Vaughan, Robert 64
Venice 382–6
Verdun 371
Vere, Aubrey de 427
Verney, Richard 19th Baron
  Willoughby de Broke 358–60
  and *Hunting the Fox* 358–60
Verocchio, Andrea
  and Leonardo 176
  Tobias and the Angel 176
Veronese, Paolo 383
Vichy 165–6
Victoria, Queen of England 57,
  97, 99, 136, 212, 269, 272, 273,
  275, 277, 292, 309
Victorians 57, 58, 91, 93, 100, 121,
  141, 152, 189, 192, 241, 252, 255,
  257, 267, 272, 195, 274, 291, 292,
  294, 295, 339, 356, 397, 403
Virgil 64, 129
Vittorio Veneto, battle of 373

Waller, Edmund 68
Walpole, Horace 205, 212, 396
Walston, Lady Catherine 121, 122,
  242
Ward, Mrs. Humphry
  Robert Elsmere 34

Wars of Religion 351
Warwick, Frances (Daisy),
    Countess of 274
    and adultery 275
Watts, G. F.
    and portrait of Matthew
        Arnold 58
Waugh, Alec 142–3
Waugh, Alexander 87
Waugh, Alexander, "the
    Brute," 142
Waugh, Arthur 142
    and Dickens, Charles 144
    on Eliot, T. S. 391
Waugh, Auberon 145
Waugh, Evelyn 121, 300
    and baiting of Arthur
        Waugh 143–5
    on Auden, W. H. 60
    on Leigh, Vivien 142
    on Churchill, W. S. 10
    "What I Think of My
        Elders" 143–4
    Brideshead Revisited 134
    Decline and Fall 144
    A Handful of Dust 144, 247
    A Little Learning 391
    *The Ordeal of Gilbert
        Pinfold* 142
    Put Out More Flags 316
    Rossetti 143
    Vile Bodies 144
Wellesley, Richard Colley
    Wellesley, 1st Marquis 183
Wellington, Arthur Wellesley, 1st
    Duke of 262
Wells, Herbert George 3, 57
    and *Outline of History* (1920) 3
Well, Joseph 232
Whig Interpretation of
    History 250
Whitman, Walt 215, 234, 235, 355
    and "ever returning spring" 237

Wilberforce Robert
    and pastoral character of
        tutorial charge 428
Wilde, Oscar 171, 246
    "De Profundis" 215
Wilenski, R. H.
    on *King Cophetua and the
        Beggar Maid* 94
Williams, Charles
    The Descent of the Dove
        (1939) 62
Wilson, Charles, 1st Baron
    Moran 6–7
Wilson, Edmund 233
Wilson, Woodrow
    and Gladstone and Fourteen
        Points 30
    and Treaty of Versailles 318–21
Wisden's Cricketing Almanac 142
Wiseman, Carinal Nicholas 98
Wodehouse, Sir Plum
    Grenville 283
Woodward, Llewelyn 251
    and anti-Christian bias 251–2
Woolf, Virginia 37
    and Johnson, Samuel 329
    on "Alice books" 96–7
    on Eliot, T. S. 105
    on Gibbon, Edward 318
    on Sitwell, Edith 414
Wordsworth, William 70, 147,
    394
Wraxall, Nathaniel 205
Wyatt, James
    White's Club 229–30

Yeats, John Butler
    and Sloan, Dolly 236
    and Sloan, John 234–5
    on Hopkins, Gerard Manley 216
Yeats, William Butler 84, 179, 183,
    216, 288, 289, 412
    and Auden, W. H. 62

    and Chesterton, G. K. 56
    and contempt for the Catholic
      Irish 56
    and Jonson, Ben 65, 68
    and Rootham, Cyril 415
    and Sitwell, Edith 412
    on Catholic Church 72
Young, George Malcolm
    and fondness for Gibbon and
      Macaulay 259
    on battle of Agincourt 150
    Portrait of an Age 257

Zambaco, Maria 95
Zeldin, Theodore
    on Dreyfus Affair 162

www.ingramcontent.com/pod-product-compliance
Lightning Source LLC
Chambersburg PA
CBHW030330240426
43661CB00052B/1588